IFRS, Fair Value and Corporate Governance

The Impact on Budgets, Balance Sheets and Management Accounts

Dimitris N. Chorafas

AMSTERDAM • BOSTON • HEIDELBERG • LONDON • NEW YORK • OXFORD
PARIS • SAN DIEGO • SAN FRANCISCO • SINGAPORE • SYDNEY • TOKYO
CIMA Publishing is an imprint of Elsevier

ELSEVIER

CIMA Publishing is an imprint of Elsevier
Linacre House, Jordan Hill, Oxford OX2 8DP
30 Corporate Drive, Suite 400, Burlington, MA 01803

First edition 2006

British Library Cataloguing in Publication Data
A catalogue record for this book is available from the British Library

Library of Congress Cataloguing in Publication Data
A catalog record for this title is available from the Library of Congress

ISBN–13: 978-0-7506-6895-8
ISBN–10: 0-7506-6895-4

For information on all CIMA Publishing publications
visit our website at http://www.cimapublishing.com

Printed and bound in Great Britain

06 07 08 09 10   10 9 8 7 6 5 4 3 2 1

To accounting standards setters and regulators who are tasked with keeping the financial ship afloat

> For *is* and *is not* come together;
> *Hard* and *easy* are complementary;
> *Long* and *short* are relative;
> *High* and *low* comparative;
> *Pitch* and *sound* make harmony;
> *Before* and *after* are a sequence.
>
> Laotse (600 BC)

Contents

ix

Preface

Since 2005 companies admitted to trading on a regulated market within the European Union are required to produce their consolidated financial statements in accordance with International Financial Reporting Standards (IFRS). Because the new rules involve a cultural change, to help companies tune their systems and procedures in developing comparative information for their balance sheet, profit and loss statement, and cash flow, IFRS-compliant balance sheet information has been required since as early as 2003.

The changeover from the mosaic of different heterogeneous national accounting standards to the International Financial Reporting Standards has not been easy. For many companies, and their management, IFRS and most particularly the concept of fair value in IAS 39, has amounted to a phase shift – which must happen not only at headquarters but also at all business units to achieve compliant reporting.

Modern business with its race to global markets, has been running for some years beyond the development of realistically enforceable laws, regulations and rules. The basic issue in this continually widening gap between the speed of innovation and technology on one hand, and the speed with which accounting standards and regulatory controls are developed on the other, might be breached by IFRS and its fair value option.

Written for board members, CEOs, CFOs, treasurers, accountants, auditors, analysts, consultants, standards setters and regulators, this text presents the reader not only with an overview of the new accounting standards but also with:

- How they can best be implemented, and
- What sort of benefits companies can derive from their usage.

The process of meeting IFRS requirements presents both opportunities and challenges to all types of enterprises. As many companies have found out, abandoning the classical accruals accounting for marking to market their transactions and portfolio positions has not been easy – and the timetable is tight. The conversion process has affected several functions within the organization, including balance sheets, P&L statements, risk management, information systems and management accounting.

The book divides into four parts. Part 1 has five chapters, starting with the broader perspective of accounting requirements posed by intensifying business competition, then examining the way standards boards work, particularly the International Accounting Standards Board (IASB); what IFRS is and is not, including its effect on corporate finance; the objectives as well as the controversy surrounding IAS 39.

Fair value is one of the keywords of the new accounting standard. It is also a pervasive subject, and one that can have significant impact, particularly in connection to financial reporting, as the reader will see in this text. The first brief encounter the reader has with fair value is in Chapter 1, but its definition comes in Chapter 3, in connection to the dynamics of IFRS; and is further enlarged in Chapter 4, because of its emphasis in IAS 39.

It has been a deliberate choice not to limit the discussion on fair value in one chapter but rather to spread it throughout the book. Though there is a risk of being repetitive, multiple treatment provides a better assurance that the reader will gain a good understanding of this important subject.

For instance, Chapter 10 discusses fair value in connection to valuing the entity's assets; Chapter 12 introduces fair value concepts into forward-looking statements; fair value enters into Chapter 15 because its theme is virtual balance sheets; and in Chapter 16, given the impact stress testing has on both fair value and the computation of relative risk.

The Basel Committee has addressed two areas of supervisory guidance closely connected to IAS 39. One is best defined by the issue of what constitutes a sound risk management practice, and associated exposure control under the fair value principle. The other is the broader domain of how a bank's use of fair value might affect supervisory assessment of the institution's:

- Regulatory capital, and
- Risk management system.

Because the introduction of IFRS into the mainstream of company accounting requires considerable effort, the better managed companies have seen the need of instituting an IFRS conversion project, run through clear objectives, formalized structure, time and cost constraints, design reviews, and neat definition of deliverables. Companies whose management is worth its salt have also sought strategic project guidance to assure alignment of IFRS conversion with business goals, through a *task force* composed of senior company executives.

IFRS project management and the task force's mission are the two themes of Part 2. Both chapters in this section of the book are based on real-life experiences. As such, they can help guide the hand of managers who want not only to convert to IFRS but also to capitalize on money spent on this process to better their corporate governance. A similar objective has been sought by top-tier firms in connection to the Year 2000 (Y2K) project in the mid- to late-1990s.

Placing the accountability for IFRS conversion at top level of the organization has significantly helped in terms of timetables, costs, and compliance to new accounting norms. Knowledge that the board, CEO, and the executive vice-presidents are behind the project has been instrumental in its acceptance, as well as in establishing internal and external communications. Also in establishing appropriate IFRS training programmes through the firm.

Part 3 concerns itself with important applications, which can significantly benefit from IFRS conversion. A prerequisite for benefiting from a new, more sophisticated accounting system is to properly study differences in accounting procedures and in financial reporting, assess systems impact, develop and implement a testing plan, and make sure the new rules seep down the organization.

The five chapters of Part 3 address themselves to an equal number of issues fairly vital to successful governance of an enterprise: Management accounting, budgeting and financial planning at large, ways and means for valuing assets, business ethics and reliable financial disclosure, and forward-looking statements, are the main themes of this part of the book.

It is worth noting in this connection that norms and rules behind these issues preoccupy not only accounting standard setters but also bank supervisors. Originally established to monitor implementation of core principles of Basel II for effective banking supervision, the Committee's Core Principles Liaison Group (CPLG), which includes banking supervisors from 16 non-Group of Ten countries, has expanded its work to matters relating to, and affecting, accounting and auditing.

In the junction of IASB's and Basel Committee's work is the problem of proper guidance. In business terms, benevolent guidance of senior management in terms of decisions and actions is the process of generating and applying norms, rules and regulations to guide the hand of executives and professionals towards a path of success in assigned mission. This is also the aim of advisory activity to senior management, from strategic planning to unqualified audits.

Along this same frame of reference, Part 4 includes five case studies detailed in an equal number of chapters. They include the balance sheet and its use as a management tool; importance of economic capital, and the fact it finds itself at both sides of the balance sheet; developing practices of real-time balance sheet at an acceptable accuracy; how sophisticated accounting solutions help in stress testing and in risk management; and a comprehensive definition of the role of the audit committee.

The book has many case studies based on actual experiences. This puts one in mind of a remark of Abraham Lincoln: 'You cannot build a reputation on what you are going to do.' But also of another well-known remark of the famous US president: 'If you never try, you will never succeed.' The aim of this book is to prompt companies and individuals to try to succeed.

My debts go to a long list of knowledgeable people and their organizations, who contributed to the research which led to this text. Without their contributions this book the reader has on hand would not have been possible. I am also indebted to several senior executives for constructive criticism during the preparation of the manuscript.

*   *   *   *   *

Let me take this opportunity to thank Mike Cash for suggesting this project, Elaine Leek for the editing work, and Melissa Read for the production effort. To Eva-Maria Binder goes the credit for compiling the research results, typing the text, and making the camera-ready artwork.

Dimitris N. Chorafas

Selected Abbreviations

BAC	Banking Advisory Committee of the EU
BCBS	Basel Committee on Banking Supervision
CPA	certified public accountant
CESR	Committee of European Securities Regulators
FVA	fair value accounting
FASB	Financial Accounting Standards Board
FIN	Financial Accounting Standards Board Interpretations
FSAP	Financial Services Action Plan
IAMIS	internal accounting management information system
IAS	International Accounting Standard
IASB	International Accounting Standards Board
IASC	International Accounting Standards Committee
IAIS	International Association of Insurance Supervisors
IFAC	International Federation of Accountants
IFRS	International Financial Reporting Standards
IOSCO	International Organization of Securities Commissions
PIOB	Public Interest Oversight Board
POB	Public Oversight Board
SEC	Securities and Exchange Commission
US GAAP	US Generally Accepted Accounting Principles

Part 1

Business Competition,
Standards Boards and
Corporate Accounting

New Rules of Competition and Accounting Standards

1. Introduction

The rules of competition have changed tremendously since the end of World War II. The new rules which established themselves over six decades, and most particularly during the past 10 years, require senior managers to be proactive, and periodically reinvent their company and its products. The alternative is going into oblivion. To stay alive, the CEO and board members must steadily ask themselves:

- What's important to their customers, and
- Where their company can make new money, within regulatory and compliance guidelines.

To create the next profit zones in a globalized and highly competitive market economy where innovation and technology hold the high ground, every entity must appreciate that both itself and its competitors benefit from the six freedoms: to *enter* the market, engage in *competition*, *set* prices, make *profits*, *survive* or *fail*, and *exit* the market.

Promoted by a market economy, these freedoms bring with them responsibilities. Among the most important are: good governance; accuracy of financial accounts; sound budgeting; management accounting as a decision tool; cost/effectiveness; market sensitivity; customer orientation; rapid research, development, and implementation (R, D&I); time to market; cash flow management; profitability; and social duties. A dynamic market economy rests on four pillars:

1. A *legal system* supportive of individual and corporate accountability.

A corrupt legal system and a malfunctioning law enforcement industry are the antithesis of what this bullet point states, yet today they are the hallmark of many countries. This is one of the major risks assumed with globalization. Moreover, soft laws (that is laws permitting all sorts of accounting and financial manipulation), as well as lack of appropriate laws, destroy the market economy.

2. A dependable and modern *accounting system* which makes it possible to accurately reflect individual transactions and financial status.

Parochial, incompatible accounting rules and unclear compliance guidelines do not answer the requirements of a globalized economy. To operate successfully, the free market must provide a level playing field; without it, all kinds of swindles from 'creative accounting' statements to favouritism and malfeasance, have a hey-day.

The design of a modern accounting system has been the goal of the International Accounting Standards Board (IASB) (see Chapter 2). Implemented from 1 January 2005, the product is the International Financial Reporting Standards (IFRS, see Chapter 3). An integral part of IFRS is International Accounting Standard 39 (IAS 39) and the concept of *fair value* associated with it (see Chapters 4 and 5 on fair value, and in Chapter 12 a case study on estimating fair value in real estate).

As this text will explain, IFRS is a phase shift in management thinking, as far as general accounting, the valuing of balance sheet positions, and financial reporting are concerned; and also on the use of financial accounting for management accounting reasons (management accounting is discussed in Chapter 8, the balance sheet and income statement in Chapter 13).

3. Thorough revamped *regulatory rules* and *supervisory procedures*, to make sure that every person and every entity appreciates the limits within which it has to operate.

Applicable from 1 January 2006,[1] in the banking industry this is the aim of the new Capital Adequacy Framework (Basel II), promoted by the Banking Committee on Banking Supervision (BCBS). A problem faced by Basel II is that too much freedom has been left to each jurisdiction in regard to implementation, while some big economies like China and India have given notice they will not adopt the new rules. As far as these countries' own interests are concerned, they are making a major mistake in doing so.

The reason why countries who do not adopt Basel II for all of their banks are heading in the wrong direction, is that they live under the illusion that through protectionism they can hide the huge risks their banks have taken. A similar statement is valid about refusing to adopt transparent accounting rules, which reflect today's market value rather than old costs, which are usually totally disconnected from current reality.

4. A large amount of market sensitivity, along with a culture of *ethics* and of personal responsibility for what *is done* and what *is not done* while it should have been done.

Ethics is virtue and, as Socrates said, virtue is knowledge which cannot be taught. Virtue has a great deal to do with a person's, a company's and country's culture. Ethical standards need upgrading, as the horde of chief executives and finance directors brought to trial demonstrates (more on this below in section 6).

Moreover, the modern enterprise needs to listen carefully to its customers, paying close attention to what they want and do not want. Business conditions and products in demand are changing rapidly – which eventually alters the rules of the game for any company. Whether it likes it or not, every firm is exposed to the shifting behaviour of its customers.

Finally, shareholder activism makes its own contribution to better management, shaping up the lethargic governance of companies, helping to dismantle the comfortable 'old boy' network, and pressing for a plan of action. For instance, in May 2005 foreign investors forced the resignation of Werner Seifert as chief executive of Deutsche Börse, and engineered a reshuffle of the exchange group's supervisory board.

2. The financial industry's raw materials

According to expert opinion, of all industries in the globalized market economy the one poised for rapid growth in the next 15 years is financial services. Some estimates suggest that, by 2020, the financial industry will account for almost 10% of global gross domestic product (GDP). Though this may be an exaggerated figure, it is nevertheless an indicator of shift taking place in the relative weight of industry sectors.

The growth of the economy, at large, will not be even around the globe. One study done in 2005 expects that the financial industry in China, Russia, India and Brazil will grow more than twice as fast as that in the rest of the world. By contrast, countries in Latin America and in Africa will not see any significant increase in the weight and importance of their financial sector. Overall, in countries where the financial industry progresses rapidly, private banking is expected to be one of the winners.[2] Other industry segments poised for growth are pension funds, mutual funds, and health insurance. Experts also bet on the growth of retail banking, while wholesale banking will most likely move slower, and lending may achieve growth rates of just 2% per year.

Another of the predictions currently made on the future of banking and of financial services at large is that consumers will become more sophisticated and discriminating about where they put their money. Savvy savers and investors will also ask for documentary evidence on risk and return, including comprehensive reliable accounts. This will increase the importance placed on accounting standards (see section 3). In all likelihood:

- Tomorrow's financial services industry will not be a scaled-up version of today's,
- But will rather take on a new pattern characterized by greater competitiveness, innovation, and *accountability*.

In the background of the growth projected for the banking industry is the explosion of financial assets. Financial assets and financial liabilities are traded in the exchanges or over the counter (OTC). The latter are *bilateral agreements* guaranteeing one party's contractual right to receive (or obligation to pay), matched by the other party's corresponding obligation to pay (or right to receive). This duality is at the root of practically all transactions.

Recording transactions and their value is one of accounting's functions. However, not all instruments can be unequivocally classified into financial assets and financial liabilities. For instance, contingent rights and contingent obligations meet the definition of assets and financial liabilities even though they are not always recognized in statements. What makes the difference is:

- The accounting standards, and
- Regulatory rules being adopted.

A most precious commodity among all financial assets is cash. *Cash* is a raw material of the financial industry which acts as medium of exchange. It is, therefore, the basis on which all transactions are measured and recognized in financial statements. A deposit of cash with a bank, or other institution, represents the contractual right of depositors to obtain cash, or use some other instrument against their credit balance.

Closely associated with the concept of financial assets is the *time value* of money. Two notions underpin the calculation of actuarial *present value* (see Chapter 7). Money today is worth more than the same amount time hence; and the difference is made up by the rent of money, or interest. The concept of time value finds its roots in the fact that people:

- Prefer present money to future money, and
- Choose present goods over future goods.

Even if they have no immediate need for money for reasons of consumption or investment, people and companies appreciate that money can be moved into the future earning an interest. Such interest, however, may not be commensurate with *risks* being assumed. Like the price of any commodity, the price of money varies, with:

- Supply and demand
- Credit rating of the borrower
- Legal restrictions and customs
- Prevailing market factors, and
- Length of time for which money is lent.

The concept of *interest* is steadily evolving and this evolution must be reflected in accounting standards. What a person, or a company, gains with the capital which it manages must compensate *credit risk(s)*, *market risk(s)*, *liquidity risk(s)* and other risks being assumed. It should also leave a residual profit that represents the productivity of capital.

The whole theory of capitalism is based on the fact that capital used in business and industry is *productive*. Capital can (or, at least, should) be employed to earn more capital at a rate higher than the cost of borrowing. This is increasingly achieved by *leveraging* one's resources. But leveraging involves a mare's nest of risks.[3]

The value of assets and liabilities, as well as risk and return, must be reflected in the books a person or entity keeps, by applying the rules of accounting – which brings up, once more, the need for *reliable and universal accounting rules and standards*. This is the aim of IFRS by the International Accounting Standards Board and other accounting standards like the United States Generally Accepted Accounting Principles (GAAP) (see section 3).

One of the controversial rules of IFRS concerns its treatment of gains and losses with *derivative financial instruments*. Derivatives have changed both the size of leveraging and the span of time characterizing commercial banking. Economists used to contrast the *span of time* inherent in a life insurance policy or an employee retirement plan, with the shorter time period of commercial banking. But the life cycle of securitized products and other instruments embedded in a retirement plan may be 30 years. This has also revolutionized classical rules of commercial banking.

- In some countries, France and Italy being examples, commercial banks can only lend short term.
- With derivative financial instruments the timeframes in commercial banking have been lengthened *de facto*.

9

For example, securitized mortgages, which run over 20 or 30 years, have become fairly popular. This has significantly increased exposure because nobody can foretell what the interest rates will be two or three decades down the line – and accounting standards should be able to track the change in market value.

Unlike cash, and other more classical assets or liabilities, derivative instruments defy actuarial studies because the latter were not made for superleveraging, and trades closely resemble financial gambles. As an article in *Business Week* had it, returns from gambling through financial instruments supply 30% of all US company profits, up from 21% in the mid-1990s – and such 'profits' don't come only from the financial industry but also from manufacturers and retailers.

For instance, at Deere, the farm-equipment company, financial deals produce nearly 25% of the company's earnings.[4] And while General Motors is having trouble selling cars, its ditech.com mortgage business is very profitable. GM's financing operations earned $2.9 billion in 2004, while the auto-making operations lost money.

There is a major risk that this wholesale substitution of a *physical economy* by a *virtual economy* can lead to a casino society. Sound accounting standards should reflect this change. Moreover, a major problem with finance dominating the corporate landscape is that any threat to financial earnings has a magnified impact on economic stability, and by 2005 several threats were gathering.

3. The crucial issue of global accounting standards

The effort towards a more widely applicable accounting standards got a boost in October 1998, when the Group of Seven (G7) finance ministers and central bank governors called on the International Accounting Standards Committee (IASC), predecessor to IASB, to make further improvements to its accounting standard. In return, they promised to promote its national use within their jurisdictions.

Both the Basel Committee on Banking Supervision and the International Organization of Securities Commissions (IOSCO) have assessed the original draft of an International Accounting Standard (IAS), each from its own particular perspective. The BCBS thought that IAS has been generally suitable for prudential supervisory purposes, although it felt that two of its standards, IAS 30 and IAS 39, required further comment.

IOSCO accepted the IAS accounting rules, and in May 2000 it recommended that its member organizations generally allow the use of IAS in their jurisdictions, as a criterion for gaining access to their national stock exchanges. However, the question about homogeneity between IAS (now IFRS) and US GAAP remained open for some time. Eventually the need for rapprochement between accounting rules led to a closer collaboration between IASB, the United States Financial Accounting Standards Board (FASB), and the Securities and Exchange Commission (SEC).

SEC's co-involvement is welcome for two reasons. First, it is the overarching US government agency for FASB. Second, one of the main purposes of accounting standards is investor and creditor protection. It is wise that the rules governing this process do not vary from one jurisdiction to the next, even if specific ways and means to implement investor protection might differ.

- National standards enshrine codified accounting legislation, all the way to penalties imposed for breaking the rules.
- By contrast, international accounting standards contain no universally applicable, legally protected regulations, unless their rules are voted by parliaments.

The members of the EU intend to do just this with IFRS. Its rules will be endorsed EU-wide by means of a special legislative procedure known as comitology. In procedural terms, the European Commission presents its proposal to endorse (or reject) IFRS to the Accounting Regulatory Committee (ARC), a body consisting of representatives of member states and chaired by the Commission.

- *If* the ARC accepts the Commission's endorsement proposal,
- *Then*, the Commission prepares the legal framework for applying the new accounting principles in the EU.

There is also the European Financial Reporting Advisory Group (EFRAG), a technical committee consisting of experts from the member states, to advise the Commission on the introduction of IFRS. EFRAG has a Technical Expert Group (TEG). Another player is the Subcommittee on Accounting and Auditing of the EU's Banking Advisory Committee (BAC), which consults the Commission in all issues regarding banking and banking supervision.

Underlying the co-involvement of all these different committees is the fact that the creation of a single European financial market means that accounting practices have to be harmonized more extensively than has been achieved thus far by means of the EU's different accounting directives. In this sense, IFRS is an appropriate instrument for achieving that goal.

Until the advent of IFRS, the accounting standard with the most widespread international appeal has been the US GAAP, developed by the FASB. The application of US GAAP is mandatory for:

- All American companies, and
- All foreign companies wishing to be listed on a US stock exchange.

For internationally operating credit institutions and other industrial companies, some jurisdictions have permitted that they make a choice in financial reporting between their national accounting standards, and US GAAP. An example of a country which has allowed that choice is France. Basically, that permission concerns companies which are listed in the United States and therefore have to use US GAAP in their reporting in the United States.

In late 2005, European regulators tentatively concluded that some entities that use accounting rules developed in the United States, Canada, and Japan should be required to provide additional information to investors if they want their securities to continue trading in Europe. This is contained in a recent report by a working group of the Committee of European Securities Regulators (CESR) which states that:

- Accounting standards in the aforementioned three countries are close enough to international standards to not require complete restatements,
- But, at the same time, there are several areas where investors need information that may not be available in those countries.

The most important area where CESR called for additional disclosures regards Japanese rules on mergers, and on consolidating the operations of subsidiaries. In such cases, CESR said, Japanese companies should be required to disclose how both their:

- Balance sheet and
- Earnings statement

would be different if the international accounting standards were used. CESR also stated that additional calculations of earnings might be needed by some companies, regarding the use of special purpose vehicles (SPVs) that are not consolidated. Twisting the rules to avoid consolidation is one of the elements which played a role in the Enron scandal.

While standards cannot be expected to be failproof and foolproof at the same time, the way to bet is that rigorous accounting rules and greater transparency reduce the likelihood of fraud. This is of course a relative statement, not an absolute one. The frauds of Enron, Adelphia Communications, WorldCom, and so many others (see section 6), have happened under US GAAP, which is one of the best and toughest standards.

Contrary to US GAAP, which applies in America and is not an internationally recognized accounting standard, at the present time IFRS has been adopted across many borders, an example being the countries of the European Union (EU); but it is not a global accounting standard. The use of internationally uniform and appropriately rigorous accounting standards can clearly be instrumental in:

- Enhancing transparency in enterprise finances, and
- Promoting the stability of the financial system as a whole.

The first step in achieving these goals is to properly reflect the right value of assets and liabilities, and help in determining profits in an accurate and unambiguous manner. Going beyond investors, this is protecting creditors, and it also assists in preserving capital. Basically, the rules of accounting standards vary according to the principle which is applied. A main dichotomy is between:

- The accrual principle reflecting historical cost, and
- Marking to market, which provides an estimate of current *fair value*.

The essence of the accrual concept is that income arises from *operating events*, and only from such events. The sale of a product is one such event, with two operations in the background. A sale of the product for $1000 is an *increase* in the owner's equity; but taking such product from the inventory, where it had been marked $600 because of accrued costs, is a decrease in the owner's equity.

- An increase in equity is a *revenue*
- A decrease in equity is an *expense*.

If the expense exceeds the revenue, *then* the owner suffers a *loss*; but the owner realizes a *profit* in the opposite case. *Income* is associated with changes in the owner's equity, and such changes are conditioned by what has *accrued* in the books – the $600 in the inventoried position of the product being sold being an example.

Marking to market is a different ball game. In this case, what counts is not the accrued cost of the product but its fair value under current market conditions. This is the value a willing buyer would pay a willing vendor, under other than fire sale conditions. (A complete discussion on fair value *vs* accruals is presented in Chapter 4, in connection to IAS 39.)

One of the main differences between accounting standards regards the options being provided. Several national accounting standards, the German being an example, have allowed for options under commercial law. By contrast, US GAAP contains no explicit options, and with IFRS options are limited.

US GAAP lacks explicit options mainly because of the plurality of its individual provisions and density of specific regulations. Experts say US GAAP is a case-based system rather than a code-based system, reflecting the fact that US law is based on case law. Moreover US GAAP is characterized by fluidity, its rules being constantly amended or supplemented. This may be difficult to match through accounting standards where many interests necessarily converge.

4. The prudential principle of financial statements and marking to market

My professors at the Graduate School of Business Administration, UCLA, taught their students that the majority of accountants believe they exist to give a true and fair picture of a company's performance during a given period of time. This conforms to the seminal work by Luca Paciolo[5] and goes beyond the more limited view of accounting, which is to account for transactions – a reason why accountants are often called 'bean counters'.

Paciolo, who was a Franciscan monk and mathematician, did not invent accounting. Rather, as Euclid had done with geometry, in the late fifteenth century he compiled work on the art of keeping accounts, and in 1494 he published *Summa da Arithmetica Geometria Proportioni e Proportionalita*, which became the bible of accounting. (More on the seminal work of Paciolo in Chapter 2, section 3.)

The broader view of accounting which we are taking today is justified by the fact that what is really being recorded is the economic and financial life of an enterprise, which is ever-changing. Even if one wanted to stick to the more limited view and narrower role, the question 'Which transaction is recorded? Simple or complex?' would need to be answered.[6]

- Simple transactions begin and end on specific dates, a process which coincides nicely with the concept of historical cost – hence accruals.
- By contrast, complex transactions, like those involving compound financial instruments, do not fall into this simplistic pattern – and, beyond that, they have a dynamic price behaviour.

A frequently encountered form of a compound financial instrument is that of a debt product with an embedded conversion option (embedded derivatives are discussed in Chapter 5), for instance, a bond convertible into ordinary shares of the issuer. The sophistication of such instruments goes beyond the confines of parochial accounting systems. IFRS requires the issuer of such a financial product to present separately on the balance sheet the:

- Liability component, and
- Equity component.

On initial recognition, fair value of the liability component is the present value of the contractually determined stream of future cash flows. These must be discounted at rate of interest applied at the time of transaction by the market to substantially similar cash flows. (The algorithm for discounting is presented in Chapter 12.) The fair value of the option comprises:

- Its time value, and
- Its intrinsic value (if any).

IFRS requires that on conversion of a convertible instrument at maturity, the reporting company derecognizes the liability component, and recognizes it as equity. The challenge is that complex instruments, like the example which has just been given, continue multiplying; making the daily practice of accounting more coordinated. These are cases a simple accounting system finds difficult to handle.

Accounting, for instance, for stock options or pro-forma accounts, requires the use of more advanced tools than first in/first out (FIFO) or last in/first out (LIFO) concepts, both based on historical costs. Today's complex transactions, innovative financial instruments, and products subject to dynamic pricing cannot be handled through such approaches. If they do, this will end in accounting numbers that are simply meaningless.

This does not mean that the new accounting rules characterizing IFRS (and US GAAP) are beyond reproach. Critics of fair value mechanisms, and of accounting procedures that go with them, say that 'the supposed superiority of market value over historic cost is riddled with problems'. For instance:

- Which market?
- Which value?
- At which time?

Theoretically, such critics have a point. Practically, these are arguments for the birds for the simple reason that the company's assets find themselves in the market not on Cloud 9, and market value is king. Marking to market has, of course, a downside – except that this not the one the critics say. The problem most frequently present with derivative financial instruments traded over the counter (OTC) is that they do not have an active market. They are practically priced only twice:

- When they are sold, and
- When they come to maturity.

In between, they have to be priced through models and, sometimes, marking to model is like marking to myth. That is why US GAAP has introduced the concept of *management intent*. Figure 1.1 shows that along with effectiveness of execu-

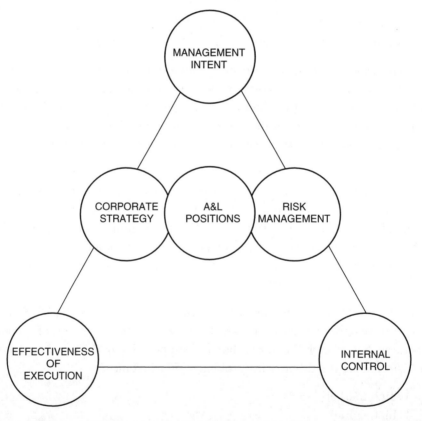

Figure 1.1 Management's intent is a dominant force in valuing the company's inventoried assets and liabilities (A&L) positions

tion and internal control, this concept is one of the pillars in governance. Under certain conditions, US GAAP allows use of historical value:

- *If* management intends to keep the instrument to maturity. In this case, it can be accounted for through accruals.
- *If*, however, management earmarks this instrument for trading, then it must be marked to market in financial reporting.

This is the accounting rule set by Statement of Financial Accounting Standards 133 (SFAS 133) by the Financial Accounting Standards Board. Other rules look into balance sheet reporting practices, and they aim to provide equal treatment, in spite of the fact that modern business has a growing number of products and transactions which defy uniform rules. For instance, to serve the aim of a level ground, IFRS requires financial disclosure of carrying amounts of each item in the following list:

- Financial assets, at fair value through profit or loss
- Held-to-maturity investments
- Loans and receivables
- Available-for-sale financial assets
- Financial liabilities at fair value through profit or loss
- Financial liabilities measured at amortized cost.

An entity which has designated a financial liability at fair value through profit or loss must disclose the amount of change in fair value that is not attributable to changes in a benchmark interest rate; also, the difference between its carrying amount and the amount the firm would be contractually required to pay at maturity to the holder of the obligation.

Under the rules of IFRS, the practice of minimum disclosure is acceptable if the laws of a jurisdiction permit it, *and* if basic accounting principles characterizing a prudential and rigorous financial reporting policy are observed. (More on minimum and maximum disclosures in Chapters 3 and 4.) Policies and practices recording economic reality must:

- Reflect assets and liabilities, financial position and profitability in an accurate manner
- Account for all balance-sheet events under the principle of materiality, and
- Observe the going-concern principle in all aspects of financial reporting.

Both accuracy and precision are necessary in income recognition. IFRS also provides for qualitative exposures describing management's objectives, policies, and processes for managing the enterprise as a whole, and its risks. Other qualitative disclosures aim to contribute information about the extent to which the entity is exposed, based on its internal control.

Qualitative information also includes the entity's objectives, policies, and processes for managing its capital, as well as data about observing capital targets set by regulators all the way to consequences of non-compliance. Quite often, qualitative information contributes a useful insight into how a company views and manages its risks. In many cases, qualitative information has more predictive value than quantitative data, because it gives insight into the entity's ability to:

- React to adverse situations, and
- Adapt to changes in risk patterns, managing ongoing developments in the external environment.

The inputs described in the above paragraphs magnify the information contained in financial statements. While classically in financial reporting qualitative disclosures were done in footnotes which nearly nobody read, with IFRS they are upgraded to constitute integral and vital parts of financial statements. Such disclosures involve important information that complements and explains the quantitative information.

5. Managing the differences in accounting standards: a case study

Differences in accounting standards hit a globalized economy in four ways: they make it difficult to compare results in one country or region with those in another; make it impossible to establish a level playing field for all companies; lead to confusion and significantly more work for compliance reasons; and complicate the task of regulators who need to solve the home–host problem in prudential supervision.[7]

The subject of this section is that of the challenges presented because of the first and second of these problems. For this case study, based on a 2004 experience, assume that Bank Alpha is an international financial institution of European origin with extensive operations in the United States. As a US company listed on the New York Stock Exchange (NYSE), Bank Alpha is confronted with significant differences which arise in its accounts between US GAAP and rules regarding financial statements in its home country.

- The bank must make a detailed reconciliation of home country and host country reporting on shareholders' equity and net profit, editing figures to fit US GAAP rules.
- At the same time, financial statements under home country rules are prepared in order to meet local regulatory requirements, and in compliance with national banking law.

Some of the differences between accounting systems turn on their head practices the credit institution has classically followed. For instance, in contrast to commercial balance sheet required in Bank Alpha's home country, a financial statement drawn up according to US GAAP does not serve to prudently measure distributable profit. Moreover, based on home country commercial code, the accounting system prevents:

- Income from being reported before gains have actually been realized, or
- The risk of losses has been either averted or properly measured.

Let's now introduce another variable. In contrast to the accounting norms based on commercial law, financial statements drawn up according to IFRS are geared mainly towards providing information considered relevant for investors. As such, like US GAAP, they are designed to give a true and fair view of the entity's:

- Assets
- Liabilities
- Profitability, and
- Overall financial situation.

While this is indeed serving investor interests and provides for creditor protection, those accountants of Bank Alpha who were not exposed to US GAAP found it to be an alien culture to them. It is, they said to the CEO, a different sort of reporting not necessarily focused on recognition and measurement rules for purposes other than transparency.

Another argument advanced by the bank's home country accountants has been that with investor-oriented financial statements, a true and fair view of an entity's actual financial situation requires a more extensive application of market valuation. A direct after-effect has been that of abandoning the bank's historical cost as a *value ceiling*, which home country accountants held in esteem.

The CEO of Bank Alpha answered this argument by saying that while the principle of market valuation is not contained in the commercial law of most

European countries, it has become the guiding concept of modern finance, as well as a notion underpinning globalization. The CEO added that under his watch the credit institution has become a global bank and from his viewpoint:

- Either the commercial law will have to change, or
- It will become irrelevant within the globalized economy to which his country is a major exporter.

The CEO also impressed upon his accountants the need to be flexible and adaptable to the new rules, underlining the fact that in a short timeframe they would have to apply IFRS, which while different from US GAAP, follows similar guidelines.

Prudently, the CEO required a simulation study involving the old and new accounting systems. For comparative purposes, Bank Alpha's financial figures have been restated for the past two years, to conform to the presentation to be used in the near future. This made evident changes in method of presentation, including the reclassification of:

- Money market paper issued as *debt*, and
- Money market paper held as *trading portfolio* assets.

A particularly important test was that of a merger which intervened in the preceding years, recorded under the *pooling of interests* method of accounting. Under this method, a single uniform set of accounting policies was adopted and applied retrospectively for the restatement of comparative information. Integrating the operations of the two predecessor banks, included a good deal of:

- Streamlining activities
- Consolidating banking premises, and
- Eliminating duplicate information technology infrastructure.

It has been a board decision that the introduction of IFRS provides an excellent opportunity to reduce the differences characterizing systems and procedures of the merged banks, by establishing institution-wide accounting policies that are in accordance with the new rules. Nevertheless, even after the effort to base the integrative work on the common accounting standard, there were still issues that required the application of judgment, and the making of estimates in preparing the financial statement.

Many of the judgments made in applying new accounting principles depended on an assumption, which management believed to be correct, that the bank must maintain sufficient liquidity to hold positions or investments until a particular trading strategy matures. This meant that the institution did not need to realize positions at unfavourable prices in order to fund immediate cash requirements.

A blue ribbon task force was set up to cope with this problem, in view of the fact that increasingly regulatory authorities want to see a clear definition of hypotheses made by reporting entities that affect accounting practices. Along this reference, for example, IFRS requires that a reporting entity discloses all significant accounting policies and practices – including the general principles and method for applying them to transactions, events, and conditions arising in its business. In the case of financial instruments, such disclosure includes criteria for:

- Identifying financial assets as available for sale, and
- Designating, on initial recognition, financial assets or financial liabilities at fair value through profit and loss.

In the case of Bank Alpha, both bullet points identify an experience which it had already had with financial reporting under US GAAP. This was a totally different experience from the one followed over a long stretch of time under the home country's accounting system, briefly described in the preceding paragraphs.

Other different practices in disclosure concerned whether purchases and sales for financial assets are accounted for at trade date or at settlement date; when an allowance is used to reduce the carrying amount of impaired financial assets; criteria for determining when the carrying amount of impaired financial assets is directly reduced; whether an impairment loss has occurred; amounts charged to the allowance account against the carrying amount of impaired financial assets; and also, the policy for determining when loans are no longer past due.

In its different host country operations, Bank Alpha also found that differences between jurisdictions exist in regard to regulatory rules impacting other aspects of financial reporting. A practical example is that of allowances and provisions for credit losses. Commercial banks typically have an extensive loans portfolio exposed to credit risk.

- These loans are initially recorded at cost, that is the net amount of proceeds lent.
- Then, they are held at amortized cost, reduced for credit reserves. With this, differences between jurisdictions become apparent.

There is also the general principle that results of all credit-related activities would be adversely affected by any deterioration in the state of the economy, or economies in which an institution operates, because of the impact economic conditions have on creditworthiness. Global economic and political conditions can also impact on operating results and financial position by affecting:

- The demand for banking products and services, and
- The credit quality of new borrowers and counterparties.

Similarly, any continued prolonged weakness in international securities markets impacts upon a bank's business revenues through its effect on its clients' investment activity and the value of their invested assets. A downturn, for example, would reduce revenues from wealth management business. As far as the management of Bank Alpha is concerned, the bank's policies in this regard apply world-wide. But the law of the land varies by country of operations, and this has implications in terms of financial reporting.

6. Taking liberties with accounting standards and business rules

Management malpractice has several origins, and comes in many forms, but the market, and prosecutors, are no more lenient with old and new creative accounting gimmicks than in the past (see Chapter 11 on creative accounting). Moreover, the company's senior management is not the only stakeholder characterized by unfair practices. Other parties are:

- Labour unions asking for more and more benefits, when they should know the company cannot afford them.
- Shareholders pressing for increasingly profitable figures, faster capital appreciation, and fatter dividends.
- The government itself, whose craven failure to prosecute wrong-doers has been at the origin of a boom in scams.

While the wave of scandals led to more business failures, bankruptcies and near-bankruptcies are nothing new. Over the years they have been the way to prune from the market system its weakest nodes and links. What is relatively new is the massive number of scams which hit the industry and the economy as a whole when:

- Business ethics are set aside
- The rules of competition are purposely violated
- Accounting standards are manipulated, lack focus, reflect only past realities, are uneven, or are altogether unreliable.

Beyond regulatory compliance, financial institutions and all other entities must be on the alert to avoid involvement in different scandals. Misdeeds are being revealed with increasing frequency.[8] Major corporate scandals which happened or came to light in the early years of the 21st century have also cost the banks plenty of money because they involved legal risk.

Enron, the seventh largest American company at its time, theoretically focusing on energy trading but practically it was a hedge fund, went bust in December 2001. Two months earlier, in October 2001, Enron had declared a $1 billion write-off on bad investments and a $1.2 billion reduction in equity capital. In the aftermath, US authorities launched an inquiry into Enron. In November 2001 Enron restated its financial statements for the period 1997–2001 to account for nearly $600 million in losses which had been concealed in complex financial transactions – and Standard & Poor's downgraded Enron's debt to junk bond status.

The year 2002 had plenty of bankruptcies, many of them involving scandals: Adelphia Communications, Global Crossing and WorldCom, to name a few. WorldCom was the world's largest provider of internet and e-commerce services. In June 2002, the company admitted to having significantly manipulated its accounts, especially by wrongly declaring costs as capital expenses. In the period from 2001 alone, $3.8 billion of alleged profits should have been stated as losses instead. In July 2002, WorldCom filed for the largest bankruptcy in US history.

In 2003 came the Parmalat scam. This was theoretically a multinational food and dairy company based in Italy. Practically, it has been a hedge fund with a dairy line on the side.[9] The public downfall came in November 2003, when Parmalat failed to repay a 150 million euro ($187.5 million) bond despite apparently large amounts of cash and liquid assets on its balance sheet. A month later, Bank of America stated that a document purporting to show a large account of a Parmalat subsidiary at Bank of America had been forged. As a result, a 3.95 billion euro ($4.94 billion) black hole emerged in Parmalat's accounts.

On 27 December 2003 Parmalat was declared insolvent. A month thereafter, in January 2004, Parmalat's new administration admitted that the company's level of debt was over 14 billion euro ($17.5 billion), almost eight times more than previously stated. This has been the largest bankruptcy ever. Prosecutors are still working on the Parmalat case. Both international and Italian banks which financed the dairy firm have already been tangled in legal fights. Also, the court rejected the request of Calisto Tanzi, Parmalat's ex-CEO, to be spared legal proceedings. Tanzi joined the line of other chief executives on their way to trial for malfeasance.

Mid-January 2005, Bernie Ebbers, the former WorldCom chief executive officer, went on trial on fraud charges. The trial of Ken Lay and Jeff Skilling, Enron's former chairman and former chief executive, also came up in 2005. Neither are these the only ex-CEO legal travails. Richard Scrushy, former chief executive of HealthSouth, is also in court for alleged accounting fraud.

Quite interesting is the case of Dennis Kozlowski, former Tyco CEO, as well as Marc Swartz, his former CFO. Their first trial ended without conviction, but the second trial began in January 2005 in New York State Supreme Court. That first trial, which lasted more than six months, was terminated in controversy centring on one elderly woman juror who received a threatening call and letter. Originally indicted in 2002, Kozlowski and Swartz faced charges of:

- Allegedly stealing about $170 million in unauthorized bonuses, and
- Allegedly gaining $430 million on share deals benefiting from an inflated stock price after lying to investors.

Another CEO who failed to appreciate one of the basic rules of business in the 21st century – that directors, auditors, and lawyers are more powerful than ever – is Maurice R. 'Hank' Greenberg, former chief executive of America International Group (AIG). Yet, this is a shift in corporate life which has fundamentally altered relations between CEOs and the professionals they depend on.

Some of these professionals, who in the years following World War II largely worked as advisors, have been assuming new power. Directors, for instance, were always supposed to work for shareholders, not for the CEO, though many were members of rubber stamp boards and only a few exercised their power as watchdogs in moments of genuine crisis.

This started changing in the early 1990s with the revolt of IBM's board against its CEO. A dozen years later the boards toppled Fannie Mae CEO Franklin D. Raines, Boeing CEO Harry C. Stonecipher, New York Stock Exchange CEO Richard A. Grasso, Walt Disney CEO Michael D. Eisner, and Hewlett-Packard CEO Carleton S. Fiorina, among several others. Similarly, in March 2005, accounting problems led independent directors at Delphi Corp, to force out the chief financial officer.

Dozens of similar cases are playing out in office towers across the United States. The reason for defiance among directors is that watchdogs are finally facing genuine liability for their failure to act. For instance, board members at Enron and WorldCom are paying off fraud claims from their own pockets.

Whole companies may disappear in a scandal, as the case of Arthur Andersen documents. This led to an earthquake among certified public accountants (CPAs). The US Big Five in the accounting world became the Big Four after prosecutors effectively put Arthur Andersen out of business for its role in the Enron scandal.

Suddenly, board members became much more prudent and proactive. At Delphi, tipped off by an SEC inquiry, the audit committee hired investigators to probe accounting problems. The CFO had to quit after the board lost confidence in him. Thereafter the company had been restating its financial accounts.

At Electronic Data Systems (EDS), KPMG, the CPA, demanded more documents to determine how big a write-down to take on troubled assets, delaying quarterly earnings release. KPMG got its way. In the aftermath, EDS took a $375 million charge. At Countrywide, the new auditor declared some loan sales improperly booked over a technical issue. Despite the CEO's objections, the company:

- Had to restate results, and
- It also pledged to tighten internal controls.

Acting on a tip, Echostar directors ordered an investigation of company financial controls, discovered problems, and obliged the CEO to discipline an executive and clean-up the accounting.[10] What practically all of these cases have in common is that fiddling around with accounting is no longer as acceptable as it used to be.

Beyond the opportunity for fraud of Enron, WorldCom, and Parmalat dimensions, weak accounting standards and unreliable financial reporting help in creating major and sustained asset price bubbles. Historical evidence suggests that high stock returns and inordinate capital gains on residential property trading induce an increasing number of investors to enter the market in the belief that the price of these assets will continue to rise.

- Traders bid up prices for a while, and
- The visible capital gains this generates initially confirms expectations that huge profits are within every investor's reach.

In the aftermath, asset prices become fragile, sensitive to news, and subject to bubbles. As the stock market hecatomb of 2000 documents, bubbles blur the information content of asset prices, making accounting evidence and the content of financial reports irrelevant. By so doing, they destroy investors' ability to act on a factual and documented basis – and thus kill the goose which might lay the golden egg.

Notes

1   D.N. Chorafas, *Economic Capital Allocation with Basel II. Cost and Benefit Analysis*, Butterworth-Heinemann, Oxford and Boston, 2004.

2   D.N. Chorafas, *Wealth Management: Private Banking, Investment Decisions and Structured Financial Products*, Butterworth-Heinemann, Oxford and Boston, 2006.

3   D.N. Chorafas *Integrated Risk Management*, Lafferty/VRL Publishing, London, 2005.

4   *Business Week*, 28 March 2005.

5   D.N. Chorafas, *Financial Models and Simulation*, Macmillan, London, 1995.

6   D.N. Chorafas, *Transaction Management*, Macmillan, London, 1998.

7   D.N. Chorafas, *After Basel II. Assuring Compliance and Smoothing the Rough Edges*, Lafferty/VRL Publishing, London, 2005.

8   D.N. Chorafas, *Management Risk. The Bottleneck Is at the Top of the Bottle*, Macmillan/Palgrave, London, 2004.

9   D.N. Chorafas, *The Management of Equity Investments*, Butterworth-Heinemann, Oxford, 2005.

10   *Business Week*, 25 April 2005.

The International
Accounting Standards Board
and Corporate Governance

1. Introduction

The history of the International Accounting Standards Board (IASB) goes back to 1973, when the International Accounting Standards Committee (IASC) was created. IASC has been a private-sector entity whose members included professional accounting bodies and private firms from several countries. Its original objective was to provide technical support to developing countries in their efforts to establish appropriate accounting standards but, over the years, this aim was enlarged.

Featuring part-time board representatives from around the world, mainly industry specialists, accountants, and financial analysts, the way IASC worked was, up to a point, similar in terms of role and operations to the US Financial Accounting Standards Board (FASB). In 1999, the International Accounting Standards Committee issued an accounting standard that required the use of fair values for certain financial products, in particular:

- Derivative instruments, and
- Debt and equity securities held for trading or available for sale.

More precisely, International Accounting Standard 39 (IAS 39, see Chapter 4 and Chapter 5) distinguishes between four categories of financial assets: held for trading, held-to-maturity investments, loans and receivables originated by the firm, and available-for-sale assets, including issues that do not belong to any of the previous three classes.

As it will be recalled, that same year (1999) FASB published Statement of Financial Accounting Standards 133 (SFAS 133), which promoted a similar approach to fair value accounting, specifically in connection to derivatives held for trading. By contrast, those held to maturity continued to be reported through accruals, the difference being made by *management intent* (see Chapter 1).

In 2000, IASC underwent major restructuring, and the International Accounting Standards Board was created in 2001. IASB adopted the International Accounting Standards (IAS) prepared so far by IASC. The output of its work has been the new standard of accounting and financial reporting known as the *International Financial Reporting Standards* (IFRS, see Chapter 3).

IFRS as a whole, and most particularly IAS 39, were to have a particularly important impact on financial firms, including banks and other institutions. IAS 39 has been heavily criticized and considered prematurely finalized. Such criticism is light-hearted. As General George Patton said: 'One does not plan and then try to make the circumstances fit those plans. One tries to make plans fit the circumstances. I think the difference between success and failure in high command depends on the ability, or lack of it, to do just that.'

This is precisely why IASB, IFRS, and AIS 39 are so closely connected to good corporate governance. It is also the reason why the present chapter addresses itself, at the same time, to issues regarding IASB standards and governance effectiveness.

Modern standards are not monolithic. They are adaptable to changing markets, conditions, and factors underpinning them. In December 2000, an integrated and harmonized standard to use *fair value accounting* (FVA) for all financial instruments, including loans and deposits – regardless of the intention with which they are held – was put forward by the Joint Working Group of Standards Setters (JWG), in which the IASB and national accounting standards setters are represented.

This proposal for full FVA, which could apply to trading book as well as banking book instruments, was received with scepticism by the banking industry as well as parts of the supervisory community.[1] One of the criticisms has been that an across-the-board FVA implementation will, more or less, do away with the distinction between banking book and trading book, which was established in the late 1980s.

The main argument against the FVA proposal, however, is that there would be increased volatility in financial statements. Another issue of concern was based on the inadequate development of credit risk models and that valuation methods for non-marketable instruments would be used to derive fair values (see section 7 on the need for a model culture).

Ultimately, the move towards a more extensive use of fair value progressed even if this generalized FVA standard was not adopted. In August 2001, IASB announced that it would undertake a project to amend IAS 39. In 2002, an Exposure Draft, including a proposal to give firms the irrevocable option to apply FVA to any financial instrument *if* the firm chose to do so when entering the transaction, was published and comments were invited. A further exposure draft on macro-hedging was issued in August 2003 for public consultation.

In December 2003, IASB released the revised versions of its IAS 32 and IAS 39 standards (see Chapter 4), which came after extensive consultation. Further amendments to IAS 39 were issued early in 2004 and in July 2005 – though effective implementation of IFRS started in January of that same year.

2. Service to industry by the International Accounting Standards Board

Formed in 2000/2001, and appealing to the private sector, IASB has no capital and its budget depends on its contributions. It is the responsibility of the Board of Trustees to ensure that these contributions keep coming, enabling the organization to perform its duties and face its accounting responsibilities in an able manner. IASB's contribution is underlined by the fact that a globalized market needs to have:

- Generally applicable accounting and financial standards, and
- Most particularly, standards established by an independent body.

A globalized market can work effectively *if* it has available standards which are universally accepted, correctly applied, and properly enforced. Universality of accounting standards helps in creating a level playing field. It also permits cross-comparisons and this sets the stage for more sophisticated economic and financial analysis, with greater coverage and market impact.

Precisely for this reason, IASB cooperates with many national and international organizations in developing its accounting standards. It works closely with the Financial Accounting Standards Board (FASB) in the United States; the International Organization of Securities Commissions (IOSCO), which represents securities regulators; the International Association of Insurance Supervisors (IAIS), and other national and international accounting standards bodies as well as regulatory authorities.

At the same time, readers should appreciate that updating, upgrading, and changing accounting standards is no kid's game. Goals have to be set, designs have to be created, some compromises have to be made, intensive training of managers and accountants should take place, and a project with responsibility for the new standards implementation must be set up (see Chapter 6). It should also be appreciated that, like a critical review by rating agencies, a change in accounting standards could bring:

- A company's assumed risks, and
- Potential losses into the open.

The fact that hidden risks and losses may become *transparent* is a *positive* not a negative contribution of a new accounting standard. The losses were there but hidden, maybe because with the old standard management knew how to cook the books. Or, alternatively, because the old accounting standard was not fine grained enough to capture all types of risks.

Good governance (see section 7) is always characterized by *the need to know*, because by knowing management can change its way of doing business when this is wrong. Sam Walton, one of the most successful businessmen of the post-World War II years, described in the following manner the way his mind worked: 'When I decide that I am wrong, I am ready to move to something else'; he also described Wal-Mart's greatest strength as its management's ability to turn on a dime.

A project, process, department, business unit, or executive in charge of it, may prove unable to deliver what was planned and promised, and as Walton aptly remarked on another occasion: 'One should never underwrite somebody else's inefficiencies.' This dictum fits neatly with the ineffectiveness of an accounting system which, after more than 500 years of steady service, is starting to show its age (see section 3).

For this reason, we should all feel indebted to the International Accounting Standards Board, whose objective is promoting more efficient accounting standards, thereby benefiting all industry sectors and the handling of financial issues at large. Notice, however, that IASB develops these standards but cannot impose them. In the European Union, it is the European Commission which must see to it that IFRS is applied in the 25 member states. Other countries which have decided to implement IFRS are Australia, New Zealand, South Africa, and more.

Corporate implementation of IFRS aside, one of the main challenges that lie ahead is to assure compatibility with American accounting and financial reporting standards. To this end, IASB is working closely with the US Financial Accounting Standards Board. Experts from the two entities work together in London, and IASB also collaborates with the Securities and Exchange Commission, to which FASB reports – without this meaning that IFRS and US GAAP are presently compatible.

How long will it take until IAS and GAAP are in full synchronism? Today, nobody can answer this question. The most likely reply is 'rather a long time'. But *if* this query is rephrased to something less ambitious, for instance: 'How long will it take until international companies have a fairly similar accounting and financial reporting structure?', *then* the answer might be by 2010.

Global companies participating in this research expressed the opinion that a process of accounting reconciliation between different standards makes sense.

There is an absolute need for common standards, not only in connection to differences prevailing between IFRS and US GAAP, but also in regard to the broader issue of incompatibilities and gaps characterizing national accounting standards that remain in effect in those countries which have not adopted IFRS.

This is the global companies' viewpoint. Among other reasons, compatibility of standards simplifies their accounting and it provides a fair basis for better governance (see section 7). Both regulators and standards setters are aware of these facts. In our meeting in late January 2005, Kevin Stevenson, Technical Director of IASB, suggested that current differences between US GAAP and IFRS may be classified into three groups:

- *Small ones* that prevail in the short term and are likely to be resolved in the not too distant future
- *Major standards projects*, where one of the standards bodies has made headway, or has already developed sound rules.
- *Major issues requiring a new project,* where no standards body currently has an answer. An example is accounting standards for leasing.

The third bullet point here brings into perspective the very significant role research, development, and implementation (R, D&I) plays in modern enterprise, including in the accounting functions. The R, D&I budget is a measure of a company's, an industry's, and an economy's commitment to staying in business. Therefore, it is a prime indicator of survivability – and it is often valued in this manner.

There are many other challenges associated to standards setting, particularly in the case of a global accounting standard intended to replace national accounting standards of those jurisdictions subscribing to it. Not the least is the need for a forward-looking standards design which can effectively help vital daily governance operations such as risk control:

- In uncovering hidden or latent risks which are there, and
- In providing effective documentation of results obtained through corporate-wide risk management functions.

This second bullet point is in effect materializing because statements of risk disclosure, for instance, in connection to credit risk, are within the perspective of financial reporting standards within IFRS. This is a positive development. The relationship which exists between IFRS, hedge accounting, and risk management is discussed in Chapter 5.

3. The seminal work of Luca Paciolo: a flashback

There is no doubt that Luca Paciolo,[2] the father of what is today known as *accounting*, was a brilliant person. He was a Franciscan monk of the order of 'Minor Observants', but he was also an analytically oriented mathematician and friend of Leonardo da Vinci,[3] another genius of the late 15th century. Da Vinci and Paciolo were part of a circle of intellectuals who explored *frontiers of knowledge*, particularly at the edges of what was then high technology. As Da Vinci's biographer has it: 'We know that he participated to the work of Fra Luca Pacciolo … in the search of "divine proportion" and "the golden cut".'[4] (Both are mathematical concepts and have nothing to do with precious metals or the Almighty.)

In the 15th and 16th centuries, the renaissance centres of Europe were characterized by the spirit of science expressed by Nicholas of Cusa, the founder of modern experimental science. Luca Paciolo, Leonardo da Vinci and many other known mathematicians and scientists of the 15th century were disciples of Cusa. The work of Paciolo was essentially like that of Euclid in the 3rd century BC. Euclid of Alexandria, the ancient Greek geometer, did not discover geometry – a science developed in Egypt thousands of years before him for reasons of taxation of large landlords. What Euclid has done is to assemble together all the then available laws and rules of geometry,

- Making out of them a complete coherent and non-contradictory system, and
- Developing the first known consolidation of geometry based on the principle that through two points can be drawn only one straight line (other geometries have been developed during the past two centuries which do not observe this principle).

Like Euclid, Luca Paciolo was widely travelled and a very versatile personality. He taught mathematical sciences in many Italian cities as well as abroad, prior to producing in 1494 (with a second edition in 1521) his most notable work, *Summa de Arithmetica Geometria Proportioni et Proportionalita*, the title reflecting the work Paciolo did with da Vinci on divine proportion and the golden cut.

One chapter of this book, entitled 'Tractatus de computis et scripturis' is wholly dedicated to *accounting*. Rules aside, Paciolo also gave advice on sound accounting practice. Not only the *general ledger* and balance sheet find their origin in his work, he also contributed the vital concept of the *accounting period* when he wrote that: 'Books should be closed every year, particularly in a partnership, because frequent accounting makes for long friendship.'[5]

Paciolo himself describes double entry accounting as being of Venetian origin. Other authors today disagree, having found evidence that the Genovese were using double entry in the 13th century. (There has always been contention between Venetians and Genovese about who was first in discovering something.[6]) But while, either way, double entry accounting was already in use in his time, Paciolo was the first to:

- Structure the double entry approach in a mathematically meaningful sense, and
- Suggest the different books in which original evidence, through vouchers, should be posted.

Historically, the concept behind double-entry accounting seems to have originated about a century and a half prior to the publication of Paciolo's book. Other references regarding non-structured double entry accounts have been found in Florence, dating from 1395. However, evidence of practical applications is more recent, with the most ancient *journal* being that of Andrea Bargarigo, who operated in Genoa in 1430.

Though Paciolo structured rather than invented double entry accounting, the journal, and other important accounting books, he has nevertheless made a great contribution because his structuring provided a higher level of reliability in financial statements (see also section 4). The 15th century bookkeeping process as pictured by Paciolo was concerned with:

- Debtor/creditor accounts
- Receipts and disbursements, and
- Recording changes in proprietorship, though the latter to a lesser extent.

The careful reader will not fail to notice that this is precisely what fair value accounting, and therefore IFRS, aims to do today. The basis of Luca Paciolo's financial reporting was to mathematically match recorded cost against recorded income of a given time period (usually a calendar year).

- This could be seen as equivalent to today's income statement and cash flow analysis, and
- Paciolo's method contrasted to that of the early 12th century where recording was limited to historical data (principally used for cost control).

Here is another interesting reference. Jewellery, according to Paciolo, should be priced at *current quotations* – which practically means our *marking to market*.[7]

And in case of doubt, Paciolo recommended that prices should be higher rather than lower. German and French writers of the late 15th century dwell upon the pricing of inventories at *true* value, as suggested by the master.

All business operations, from the simplest to the most complex, have benefited from Luca Paciolo's mathematical formalization – and, therefore, normalization – of double entry. He may be seen, so to speak, as a one-man IASB and FASB at the same time.

Moreover, the normalization Paciolo provided made possible other advances in business operations and financial settlements. *Delivery versus payment*, one of the currently avant-garde ways of handling securities transactions, would have been impossible without the ability to simultaneously:

- Debit cash, and
- Credit securities

in two different accounts – or vice versa. This is what Figure 2.1 shows by exhibiting, as an example, double entry through electronic bookkeeping into the accounts of Client A and Client B. This approach involves a simultaneous operation into four books all of which are databased.

4. Journal, general ledger, and contractual rights

The example Figure 2.1 has presented is a modernization, through information technology, of an existing infrastructural procedure, on which rests the whole tradition of practical accounting. It is always rewarding to look at a system's beginnings because it allows one to learn a good deal about its foundations. In his writings, Luca Paciolo suggests that three accounting books should be kept:

- The memorial
- The journal, and
- The general ledger.

The *memorial* is a type of first entry and voucher on which must be transcribed all accounting operations 'day-per-day and hour-per-hour', that is, in a chronological order. In the memorial are registered, as well, all the entries which represent operations without classification into debits and credits. (Both the practice and the name *memorial* remain today. For instance, they are part of the law in the Grand Duchy of Luxembourg.)

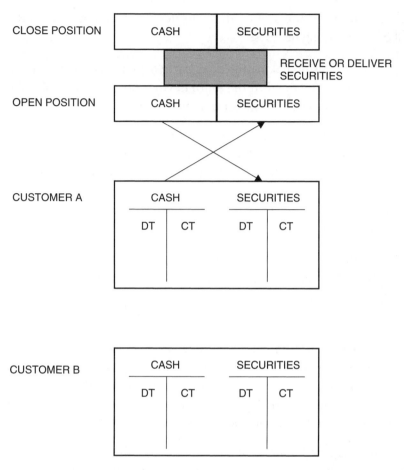

Figure 2.1   Delivery *vs* payment means that we do the operation simultaneously on four books which are databased

In the *journal*, the operations described in the memorial are entered in separate credit and debit accounts with indication of foreign currency operations. The cities Paciolo had visited in his research on accounting had different currencies in which they traded with one another. In the old master's tradition, which continued till the end of the 17th century, neither balances nor reports were made in the journal. Its goal was:

- An organized, meticulous transcription of all transactions
- A chronological record showing the names of accounts to be credited or debited

- A register of amounts of credits and debits providing useful information about transacting business.

Posting is the process of making the changes to the balances of accounts, according to instructions contained in the journal. No account balance should ever be changed, except on the basis of a journal entry.

It is in the *general ledger* that each entry which was made in the journal will be divided with precision in credit and debit columns with balances on each page and appropriate reports to the continuation of the account. The ledger is a device for *reclassifying* and *summarizing* by accounts information originally listed in chronological order in the journal. Paciolo seems to have been the first to define that the total of *credits* and of *debits* should correspond.

- The methodology he established includes the definition of the need of keeping subsidiary books, such as books for inventories.
- This methodology also specifies that all books should be validated by the merchants' corporation, in the city where the enterprise resides.

Therefore, it seems that, among other contributions, Paciolo was among the first to recognize the importance of verification – therefore, of regulatory action – and to write about it. Both the principles characterizing accounting, and the directive concerning the need for verification, amount to a giant step towards financial reform, much bigger than what IFRS is proposing.

The fact that, since its normalization in 1494, the function of accounting includes the posting, accumulation, and communication of financial data concerning economic activities, is nothing less than transparency in accounts. The data are typically expressed in monetary units while, as a process, accounting is concerned with the translation of financial transactions into business records:

- Collecting information about transactional operations of different types
- Recording such data in a homogeneous and dependable manner, and
- Transmitting financial results to interested persons, in a comprehensive way.

In terms of their dynamics, accounting reports aim to meet the need for objective reporting. This involves different presentation services which may serve a great number of purposes, but each one rests on a mathematical infrastructure. The genius behind Paciolo's work is that the underlying concept is so *flexible* that it can be used in many other applications than general accounting, for instance in contracting a bill of materials (BOM) which must be updated by:

- Product
- Due date, and
- Manufacturer.

Whether we talk of money, financial instruments, engineering products or any other goods, proper accounting procedures permit us to tally valuables entrusted to custodians, and also to compare results against the stewardship expected of them. The reader should never forget that *financial accounting* has the function, indeed the primary objective, of providing information to parties outside the company: investors, creditors, regulators, the taxman. Hence,

- To show the disposition of properties given over for prudential but productive management, and
- To permit to measure value, worth, and ownership – with argument giving way to evidence provided by *reliably accounting* for something (see section 5).

Words like 'reliable' and 'useful' always connote some purpose for which the figures are to be used. Many of the problems accountants face in this regard are textbook type, but others are not. In the latter case the whole profession of accounting is concerned with the recognition of a new problem, and its impact, as well as with finding ways towards its solution – a job increasingly falling upon the shoulders of standards boards.

A practical example of a notion that does not seem to have existed in Paciolo's time, but today confronts IASB, is *contractual rights* and *contractual obligations* to receive, deliver or exchange financial instruments. These are themselves financial instruments meeting the corresponding definition (see also Chapter 3) because they ultimately lead to:

- Receipt or payment of cash, or
- Acquisition or issue of an equity.

A novelty of our time, promoted through derivatives, is that the exercise of contractual right or satisfaction of contractual obligation may be absolute, or contingent on the occurrence of a future event.

Assets or liabilities that are not contractual, like income taxes, are created in the wake of statutory requirements imposed by governments. These are *not* financial assets or liabilities. By consequence, *deferred tax allowances* (DTAs) are not financial assets, even if they are reported as such by some banks while supervisory authorities look the other way – and they are written in the entity's books in violation of accounting principles.[8]

Neither are prepaid expenses and other items for which the future economic benefit is the receipt of goods or services, rather than the right to receive cash or another financial asset. Also, items like deferred revenue and (most) warranty obligations are *not* financial liabilities because the outflow of economic benefits associated with them:

- Is not a contractual obligation to pay cash or another financial asset.
- Rather, it is some sort of delivery of goods and services.

Post-mortem additions to a carefully crafted system are tricky things, particularly so when conflicts of interest try to accommodate the unaccommodatable (an example being the DTAs). System design does not work that way, and this is another reason why AISB's redesign of accounting should be most welcome.

In conclusion, as a mathematician Luca Paciolo essentially did far more than normalize the journal and the general ledger. Neither notion was totally new. Available evidence indicates that a sort of general ledger was kept in Sienna as far back as in 1255, and by the mid-15th century a similar concept seems to have been used by merchants and credit institutions all over North Italy, in Genoa, Milan and Venice. But,

- Neither of these followed standard layouts, and
- Neither was based on firm principles with rules that can have universal impact.

Able solutions to both problems have been Luca Paciolo's contribution. Finally, it is interesting to note that the first systematic approach to mercantile accounting is to be found in a book on practical mathematics. Paciolo also seems to have structured teller procedures, but his most important legacy still is the mathematical theory which explains the mechanism of double entry and its importance in keeping under control both transactions and the economic results of management.

5. Higher level of reliability in financial reporting

Since 1494 and the contribution of Luca Paciolo, accounting is concerned with a higher level of reliability in financial record-keeping and reporting, starting with the journal of transactions. Accounting, however, is only one of the pillars on which a dependable reporting system rests. There exists no universal methodology which integrates the other pillars like management ethics and risk control. But it is possible to learn from engineering, stretching the concept of *reliability* into the business domain. For instance,

- *If* we measure financing staying power at 0.9997 level of confidence as equal to AA credit rating by Standard & Poor's,[9]
- *Then* we would require a fully dependable financial reporting system able of providing evidence which confirms that level, not any other level down the grading line.

This concept can be extended to the whole banking industry in a given market. Reliability theory teaches that for a system with 100 parts connected in series, even if each has *99%* mean reliability, the overall reliability will be no better than *40%*. The notions to keep in mind are that there is a much bigger number of banks in any important market, and a 99% level of confidence is all that is required when reporting to regulators about their derivatives exposure.

A contrary view of what is written in the preceding paragraphs would be that financial markets do not work *as if* they were engineering systems, and therefore the rules underpinning reliability engineering do not apply. If such a statement were made, it will be very weak – and this is for two reasons:

- Rocket scientists working in the banking industry, have been extensively using the Weibull distribution in risk management.[10]

The tool they employ in financial studies is precisely the same Weibull distribution which has been used, with considerable success, for reliability engineering studies since the early 1950s.[11]

- Colossal amounts of money in bilateral derivatives contracts, traded over the counter (OTC), interconnect major financial institutions among themselves in a way closely resembling an engineering system with black boxes arranged in tandem.

Starting with the premise that proper study on this interdependence, and its impact on systemic risk, is not yet done (though it should be done without delay), one can in no way refute the argument about the use of reliability engineering in the study of systemic risk. Moreover, in science, we are much more confident when we reject a hypothesis than when we accept it:

- When we *reject* a hypothesis, we do so because there is *evidence* it should be rejected (which is not the case of using the Weibull distribution in the financial industry).
- When we *accept* a hypothesis, what we practically say is that there is no evidence for rejecting it – until a 'nasty' new fact shows up to destroy a whole theory, not just a hypothesis.

This discussion fits nicely within the IFRS (and Basel II) perspective because, as explained in the Introduction, the key objective of the new accounting rules is to provide a realistic basis for valuing transactions and positions inventoried in the entity's portfolio. In fact, professional associations are actively searching for an accounting base that will permit interactive frames of reference for risk management to be represented in crisp terms like the two interlinked cases shown in Figure 2.2.

The study of the long leg of a credit risk distribution, as the one shown in Figure 2.3, has a good deal to do with stress testing and risk management. In both cases, the background is provided by accounting data and statistics – and both must be reliable.

As we saw in Chapter 1, accounting, auditing, and risk control correlate. It is not just banks which must look most carefully into their capital adequacy. All entities should be adequately capitalized, beyond the minimum regulators require, and they should provide capital adequacy information to:

- Their shareholders
- Supervisory authorities, and
- Financial market at large.[12]

Information on an entity's capital adequacy as well as capital allocation requires a robust, unbiased, and forward-looking accounting system. This also helps in terms of market discipline – which is an issue underpinning arguments between standards setters and banking supervisors. Many banks think they have a valid risk management function in place and a better perspective than the standards body about 'what is needed'. This is, of course, the old argument about self-regulation, which has been shattered with:

- The 1929–32 Great Depression, and
- The September 1998 bankruptcy of LTCM, the Rolls-Royce of the hedge funds, which nearly tore the world's financial fabric to pieces.

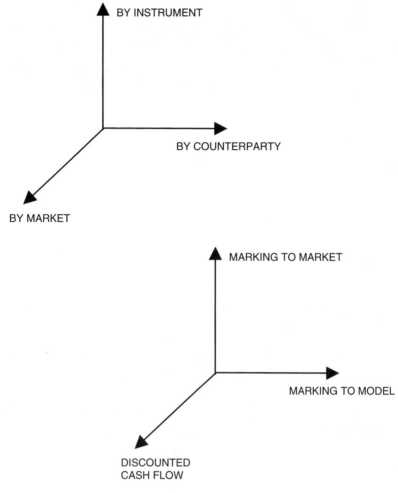

Figure 2.2   Interactive frames of reference for total risk management which require forward-looking accounting standards

As a conclusion to this section, it is wise to borrow a page from the July 2004 Exposure Draft of IFRS. It states that the objective is to require entities to provide disclosures in their financial statements that enable users to evaluate the significance of financial instruments for the firm's financial position and performance; nature and extent of risks arising from financial instruments to which the entity was exposed during the period and at reporting date; and adequacy of capital. This statement kills two birds with one well-aimed stone:

- It complements, at accounting side, requirements already outlined by Basel II, and

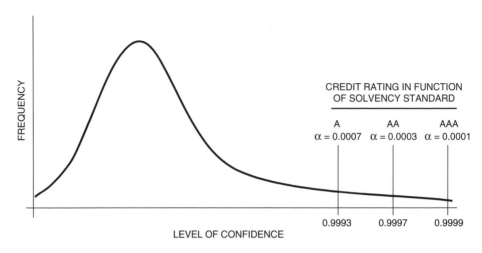

Figure 2.3   Major risk management components are an exercise in reliability

- It provides the company's management with a brief description of what is required for an effective tool for first-class governance.

Figure 2.4 presents in a nutshell the sense of the second bullet point. Reliable financial reporting is at the core of many subsystems with vital management accounting information (see Chapter 8). As an example, Figure 2.4 shows a dozen of them which, taken together, provide corporate management with leading edge technology – *if*, and only if, accounting information on which their interactive reports are based is absolutely reliable (see also in section 7 the discussion on the U-curve).

6.   Obsolete standards become counterproductive

In the 1960s I was invited for a meeting by the then president of Allgemene Bank Nederland (ABN). Prior to lunch, he showed me around the building, then said that it was 50 years old, but still functional. 'I am now planning a new headquarters,' the president added, 'and if I am going to be as successful as my predecessor was, it should serve my bank well, for at least the next fifty years.'

Part of our discussion, as well as the reason for my having been invited, was the information technology (IT) supports which should be embedded into the projected headquarters of a global bank to keep it functional for at least five decades. By the

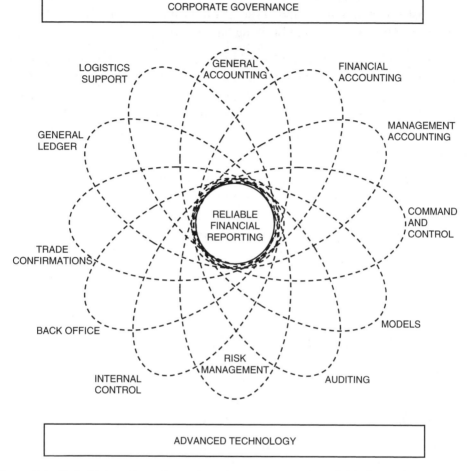

Figure 2.4 Typical interactions of complex subsystems, targeting reliable financial reporting

1960s, IT was already a force in banking, and clear-eyed management wanted to take full account of state-of-the-art solutions, as well as of future developments.

At the time, both ABN and AMRO, Holland's two big banks which were then two separate and competitor credit institutions, were ahead of the curve in information technology. The same was true of Citibank. In fact, some years later in the late 1970s, Walter Wriston, Citibank's CEO, said that banking was *information in motion* – an excellent label. I bring up these two cases for two reasons:

- When we want the solution we are designing to live on, we must plan its life cycle at the drafting stage – not post-mortem, and

- Today, integrating high technology requirements into *any* standard is a 'must'; but at the same time the standard itself must be advanced. Anything short of that, and we are not doing our job properly.

As we will see in Chapters 4 and 5 (and in section 8), one of the most highly disputed issues of IFRS is IAS 39, the standard that covers marking to market financial instruments. This happens because people do not like to change their habits and, at the same time, they are afraid of the unknown. Yet, IAS 39 is not just an alternative to accruals, it is a standard designed for our epoch, though it still needs to be analysed in its full multi-dimensional impact in:

- Judging company performance and assumed risk
- Satisfying regulatory and supervisory demands, and
- Stimulating business growth by providing a means to measure risk and return regarding products and customers.

The concept targeted by the first bullet point is the fair valuation issue and its importance in corporate governance. Valuing at market price is, no doubt, a challenging concept and further work is indeed necessary to achieve transparency, consistency, and comparability in fair value accounting, as well as to:

- Gain a better understanding about what the direct and indirect consequences of implementing this not-so-radical concept are.
- Continue developing fair value methods, beyond the current rudimentary and open to manipulations accounting standards, by learning through real-life applications.

After all, what are our options? The obsolete book value? This is an approach that obliges senior management to run a company in a highly competitive and fast-changing business environment by looking through the rearview mirror. It is pretty clear to see that the pre-2005 accounting standards are no good.

Those who take the contrary view say that there are too many rules associated with the new standards. The answer is that there is no such thing as freedom without laws and rules, but neither are laws and rules written without a precise objective. The precise objective of IFRS is to provide a level playing field where:

- Deals being made are written in clear accounting terms, and
- Assets held in inventory are priced in a way commensurate with the market economy's values.

The price attached to each position must represent current value – not an obsolete or irrelevant reference which, among other ills, provides the means to game the system. Responsible entrepreneurs, of which there are millions, do not look for short-term maximization of profits through creative accounting, but pursue a long-term objective, coherent with the reason why they are in business.

Nobody should doubt there will be winners and losers with the new accounting standards, as with any new system. It is widely expected that IAS 39's greatest impact will be on banks and insurers (see section 8), but this is not necessarily true because the new standards will apply to *all* companies that:

- Do hedging, or
- Deal in derivative financial instruments.

Marking to market evidently affects all entities that use derivatives as part of their business. Therefore, all companies must carefully study the impact of International Financial Reporting Standards (IFRS) on their balance sheet and income statement. 'All' means plenty, because IFRS affects more than 7000-plus listed European companies and their financial reports which should:

- Provide reliable information about their financial position and performance, and
- Help a wide range of users in making better-focused economic decisions, without book value ambiguities.

As is to be expected, there are changes from past practices. Chapter 3 will explain why profits will be affected by new numbers, such as stock option expenses and dynamic valuation of financial instruments. The IFRS statement will also have to accommodate charges for stock options. Moreover, numbers traditionally regarded as exceptional, like restructuring costs, or gains and losses on trading assets, will increasingly be seen as part of operating performance.

These changes are evolutionary, and they are necessary to reflect the switches which have taken, and continue to take place in the global business environment. Another rather significant impact on the profit and loss statement will come from fair value estimates of items in assets and liabilities. Derivatives are a case in point. They have often been used for blurring the distinction between:

- Operating performance, and
- Changes to the balance sheet.

The experience of American companies with marking to market, in the 1999 aftermath of Statement of Financial Accounting Standards 133, is that fair valuing the entity's assets and liabilities is not easy – but it is doable. As mental compensation for the added difficulty, at least in the first years, everybody should bear in mind that fair value of A&L is much more relevant than historical cost – and it is part of good governance.

A valid approach to business decisions always draws on market views of a company's value, based on forecasts of future cash flows. True enough, unlike historic cost, there is a question mark over the dependability of fair value measurements. A particular challenge is when there is no active market for many of the assets and liabilities. Models are used, but valuation models have to be carefully scrutinized because assumptions are usually subjective. As for the argument that hedge accounting makes company profits more volatile, just remember that:

- IAS 39 does *not make* the P&L 'more volatile'.
- What it does is to make *transparent* its volatility.

It is up to the management of the company to see to it that its income is not volatile, as it is up to the entity's board to accustom itself on how to handle changes like accounting for goodwill. Let's face it – like historical costs, goodwill amortization has been an accounting function, and it is time it came to an end.

7. Core variables in corporate governance

It is beyond doubt that the value of any accounting standard is in direct proportion to its service of, and support for, core variables and their impact on a company's staying power, as well as on the economy as a whole. According to ECB, the top five core variables are:[13]

- Earning ratio
- Solvency ratio
- Leverage
- Firm size, and
- Age of firm.

Earning should be seen relative to total assets. Higher profits are not only good for shareholders. They are sought after because they imply a lower likelihood of financial distress. The *solvency ratio* is computed as shareholder funds relative to total assets. This provides information on the ability of a firm to generate satisfactory earnings in past years. The past, however, is not a predictor of the future; that is why we need forward-looking statements (see Chapter 10).

Leverage is debt over total assets. A high level of leverage implies instability in ownership of funds. Another negative is that when companies get into difficulties it is not easy to service and repay their loans, bonds, and other financial obligations – no matter what different eggheads may say about debt being preferable to equity.[14]

Thinking by analogy, the ECB study characterizes *firm size* as the *logarithm of total assets*, with the additional characteristics that older firms tend to be larger than newer firms. Based on the effect of firm size, ECB advances the hypothesis that:

- An optimal firm size does not exist, hence there is a trade-off between being relatively small and being relatively large.

The ECB suggests that this would indicate that the effect of firm size on the probability of experiencing financial distress is nearly U-shaped because small firms have a higher probability of falling into financial difficulties as they are not as resistant to the shocks they might encounter. On the other hand, larger firms also have a high probability of falling into distress, if:

- They are inflexible
- Have serious management problems, or
- Lose contact with the market, as IBM did in the 1980s.

ECB's U-curve is a very interesting concept and it finds its counterpart in reliability engineering (see section 5). As Figure 2.5 shows, teething troubles and baby failures are encountered at an early stage.[15] But towards the end of useful life there are worn-out failures:

- Man-made products wear out, as one knows from one's car, oven, or refrigerator; also from failures with space shuttles.
- The management of companies also wears out, after the innovators and promoters are gone. When the fat cats take over, all they care for is their own survival, not the company's, as witnessed by the fat options they lavishly distribute to themselves.[16]

According to that same study, the fifth core variable is the *age of the firm*. Other things being equal, age helps in survival. With all due respect, this is pure theory. Of the 100 largest US firms quoted on the New York Stock Exchange in 1910, almost a century ago, only *one* is still in the top-100 list: General Electric. The others dropped out, and the majority disappeared.

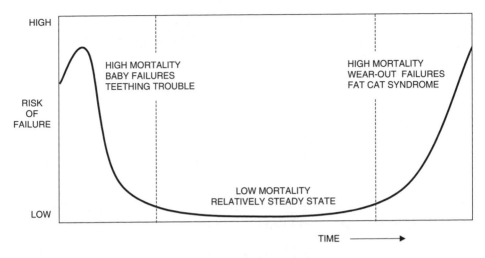

Figure 2.5   All systems, all products, and all entities go through a U-curve transition in mortality

The way theorists have it, firms learn about their 'efficiency' as they operate in the industry. In practice, firms create inefficiencies as they operate. Look at General Motors. Also according to theory, firms know the average level of market profitability, but they do not know their own potential. In practice, they know neither.

This blue sky has its counterpart in another theory that the probability of financial distress decreases along with an increase in firm size. General Motors, Ford, Fiat, not to mention Enron, WorldCom and Parmalat suggest precisely the opposite. But creating silly theories like the Modigliani–Miller 'debt is good for you' hypothesis can win you a Nobel prize – hence it serves a purpose, albeit a personal one.

Leaving aside then the fifth core value, and concentrating on the first four, we can see that IFRS contributes to providing corporate governance with a compass much more reliable than that given by the old method of accruals. This is self-evident with earnings, solvency, and leverage. Regarding size, I would only make the remark that:

- A crucial factor entering firm size should be its capitalization, which is a way of marking to market its assets
- But at the same time, very slow and very rapid increase in capitalization, as in the case of Enron, Global Crossing, WorldCom, and others, suggests that the company is moving up the right leg of the U-curve in Figure 2.5, because of a rapidly developing fat cat syndrome.

The list of core values in corporate governance can be improved by the addition of another bullet point: *top management accountability*. The Basel Committee on

Banking Supervision says that much when, in its supervisory guidance on the use of the fair value option, it states that: 'The Committee acknowledges that the responsibility for financial reporting also may rest with the board of directors and that the responsibility may vary by jurisdiction. Accordingly, "senior management" here refers to the parties that are responsible for financial reporting in any given jurisdiction.'[17]

In the summary of the recommended 17 best policies and methods regarding governance, control, price verification, and audit practices for enhancing public confidence in public reporting, the Basel Committee further notes that a clear and delineated governance structure should exist, including provision for:

- Appropriate segregation of duties, and
- Documented procedures for escalation of issues and exceptions to the board of directors or the audit committee. (The role of the audit committee is discussed in Chapter 17.)

Another point made in the same document is that a senior management grouping should have responsibility for the governance and oversight of control and valuation policies and procedures. This group should report the results of its work directly to the board of directors or the audit committee. Moreover,

- Initial responsibility for the determination of fair value should reside with the risk-taking business, and
- Ultimate responsibility for determining the fair values incorporated into financial statements must be outside the risk-taking functions.

In short, it is the Basel Committee's thesis that senior management should assure there are adequate human resources, with appropriate experience, training, and reward to guarantee that internal control, risk management, and independent price verification functions are performed to the highest standards. This is a matter not only of corporate accountability but also, and most particularly, of personal accountability. In a way, it is on a par with reliable financial reporting, as we will see in Chapter 11 in connection to the US Sarbanes–Oxley Act.

8. Accounting standards and corporate governance: a case study in insurance

The Geneva Association, which is a well-known research and development laboratory as well as advanced training centre of the global insurance industry, provides an example on the need for the sort of studies I suggest. The Association has discussed the International Financial Reporting Standards and their effects on insurance, reinsurance, financial services and the wider economy at its 30th General Assembly meeting of June 2003. Its members have been working intensively on the subject of accounting standards because, in their opinion, the then existing accounting systems were not as efficient as they should be.[18]

As is to be expected, when professionals engage in discussion with a far-reaching after-effect, this leads to the identification of important issues that require further research attention. An interesting point made during the 30th General Assembly was that, in the past, the most common reaction from an economist, when faced with technical accounting problems, has been indifference. More recently, however,

- The issue of accounting and its standards shot up on the list of top priorities in the insurance and financial services industry, and
- The economic implications of IFRS accounting rules have been seen as both important and challenging, with possibly enormous impact on the industry.

To better appreciate the interest expressed by the insurance and reinsurance sector of the economy, it should be recalled that in 1997 the former International Accounting Standard Committee had started to work on an international standard for insurance contracts. In May 2002, IASB decided to continue that work, splitting it in two phases:

- *Insurance Phase 1*, as an interim step for developing a standard, and
- *Insurance Phase 2*, for tentative development of a *fair value* model for assets and liabilities arising from an insurance contract.

Phase 1 was committed to introducing a fair valuation of assets (under IAS 39) while liabilities valuation remained based on local standards, none of which today reflects fair value. The Association believes that this mixed approach does not allow for risk matching across asset and liability values, nor for consistency. On the other hand, one should remember that the famous A/L *acid test* for forecasting a company's *default point* (DP) is based precisely on that dual standard:

- Assets at market value
- Liabilities at book value.

The point some insurers make is that valuation of assets and liabilities should reflect the specific, long-term nature of the insurance business. They also note that application of fair value measurements, envisaged in Phase 2, will affect the nature of the products that are sold, particularly so in life insurance, probably because of introducing short-term volatility in an industry that has generally a very long-term view – and business models which reflect this longer-term approach.

Clearly enough, there exist two different viewpoints. If we were in the immediate post-World War II years, or even in the 1980s, the aforementioned argument would have been correct. But not today because, since the 1990s, insurance companies have considerably increased their risk appetite. First by loading themselves with equities (particularly British insurers) and getting hurt when the bubble burst. Then, after year 2000, by:

- Getting active in derivatives games and tricks like *prepays*,[19] and
- Going into credit derivatives in a big way as protection sellers – a highly risky short-term horizon which contradicts the longer-term perspective and is *not* their business.

Nobody said that the introduction of a full fair value accounting system – which is modern and dynamic – might not have some unwanted consequences. Quite likely it will lead to an increase in the cost of capital for the industry, thereby repositioning insurance and reinsurance capacities. Given the fact that insurance companies are long-term investors will also have an impact on equity markets and their volatility, making more evident the result of market slump as portfolios are marked to market.

The good news is that the fair value accounting model will produce financial statements which are much more effective at distinguishing good company performance from bad. This is a major 'plus', assisting in good governance and outweighing likely (but not certain), bad news.

Insurers generally say that they support the objective of developing high quality international accounting standards, that can improve financial reporting worldwide. At the same time, however, they express concern about whether the insurance contracts project of IASB, currently under study, will result in the required high quality accounting standards for insurance.

Some insurance experts seem to question an 'experimental approach with unforeseeable consequences'. This is not a rational reaction. As we will see in Chapter 15, experimentation is a basic ingredient of modern management. Behind this worry lies another one: that, in the current business environment, a fundamental change in accounting standards for a large industry, like insurance, may affect:

- Whole national economies, and
- Global investment and commerce.

There is a contradiction here. On one hand, insurers and re-insurers want the new accounting standards by IASB to go *far enough* and *deep enough* in solving current and future problems of accounting insufficiency. And on the other, they are afraid that *if* they do go far enough and deep enough, they will upset the industry and 'whole national economies'.

It is not easy to reconcile these two positions, but it is reasonable to expect that once past the resistance to the novelty of IFRS, and most particularly IAS 39, the senior management of most companies (and of whole industry sectors) will appreciate the assistance on decision support they are getting from the new accounting rules.

In fact, this is already happening. The insurers' rather negative position is changing, as reflected in an article by Dr Joachim Kölschbach, in the Geneva Association's monthly bulletin of June 2005.[20] In the January 2005 meeting of the Association, Kölschbach says, IASB reviewed the project plan for Phase 2 and decided to take a fresh look at financial reporting by insurers, including:

- The aim of close interaction with the FASB, and
- Support for IASB/FASB convergence.

According to Kölschbach, IASB has tentatively decided that claims liabilities should be discounted, and they should include a provision for risk and uncertainty. This is subject to the general requirement on *materiality*. Stand-ready obligations will be measured either at the unearned portion of premiums received, potentially less acquisition cost; or prospectively as future obligations, including discounting and risk provisions. Issues currently under discussion include:

- Revenue recognition
- Performance reporting
- Financial instruments, and
- Revisions to IAS 39 clauses for insurance firms.

An Insurance Working Group (IWG) set up by IASB in 2004, as support to the handling of technical questions in both non-life and life insurance topics, worked on some of 14 issues identified by the International Accounting Standards Board. Four models discussed by IWG are:

- Lock in
- Amortized cost
- Current entry value, and
- Current exit value.

The preferred models seem to be those including discounting of insurance liabilities and provisions for risk. There seem to be strong arguments for *discounting*, but concerns were raised over the uncertainty of estimating claim liabilities, and of adding a series of discounting assumptions.

In connection to *gain or loss on initial recognition*, some IASB members reportedly favoured a loss to be recognized at inception since that shows the true economic position. This is opposed by the insurance industry because, in its opinion, accounting would not reflect economic reality when the contract, which was intended to be profitable, would be shown as making a loss at inception. (A similar issue exists in banking in connection to recognizing new loans in the banking book.)

What the reader should appreciate from these 2005 references concerning the insurance industry's position is that the altogether negative view of IFRS by the industry has considerably evolved during the past couple of years. Though several issues are still in discussion, the benefits provided by the new accounting rules are being recognized in terms of the contribution they make to corporate governance. (The planned timetable foresees a discussion paper by early 2006, an exposure draft after mid-2007, and a final standard by mid-2008.)

Notes

1 ECB, *Monthly Bulletin*, 2004.
2 The name is variously spelled Paciolo, Pacciolo, Paccioli by different authors.
3 Or de Vinci, depending on the author.
4 Marcel Brion, *Leonar De Vinci*, tome premier, Le Livre Club du Libraire, Paris [year not noted].
5 Robert N. Anthony, *Management Accounting*, Irwin, Homewood, IL, 1956.
6 This is suggested from evidence which exists in the archives of the state of Genoa dating from 1340, and of Venice dating from 1406–34.
7 Morton Backer (ed.), *Handbook of Modern Accounting Theory*, Prentice Hall, New York, 1955.
8 D.N. Chorafas, *After Basel II: Assuring Compliance and Smoothing the Rough Edges*, Lafferty/VRL Publishing, London, 2005.
9 D.N. Chorafas, *Economic Capital Allocation with Basel II: Cost and Benefit Analysis*, Butterworth–Heinemann, London and Boston, 2004.
10 D.N. Chorafas, *How to Understand and Use Mathematics for Derivatives, Volume 2 – Advanced Modelling Methods*, Euromoney Books, London, 1995.
11 D.N. Chorafas, *Statistical Processes and Reliability Engineering*, D. Van Nostrand Co., Princeton, NJ, 1960.
12 D.N. Chorafas, *Economic Capital Allocation with Basel II: Cost and Benefit Analysis*, Butterworth–Heinemann, London and Boston, 2004.

13 ECB, Financial Stability Review, Frankfurt, June 2005.

14 D.N. Chorafas, *The Management of Equity Investments*, Butterworth-Heinemann, London, 2005.

15 D.N. Chorafas, *Statistical Processes and Reliability Engineering*, D. Van Nostrand Co., Princeton, NJ, 1960.

16 D.N. Chorafas, *Management Risk: The Bottleneck Is at the Top of the Bottle*, Macmillan/Palgrave, London, 2004.

17 Basel Committee on Banking Supervision, 'Supervisory Guidance on the Use of Fair Value Option under IFRS', Consultative Document, BIS, July 2005, Basel.

18 Geneva Association, *Insurance Economics*, No. 48, 2003.

19 D.N. Chorafas, *Corporate Accountability, with Case Studies in Finance*, Macmillan/Palgrave, London, 2004.

20 Geneva Association, *Progress*, No. 41, June 2005.

Dynamics of International Financial Reporting Standards

1. Introduction

Disclosures about risks associated with financial instruments are useful to all stakeholders: regulators, investors, the entities themselves, and the general public. Banks are supervised for their deposit-taking, securities deals, and portfolio positions, among other issues. With innovation in the financial industry in high gear, it has become very difficult to satisfactorily differentiate an entity active in derivative instruments (see Chapter 5) from a speculator holding a portfolio of risky assets. Uncertainty is omnipresent for a number of reasons:

- From the way liquidity and solvency are managed
- To a timely evaluation of exposure and proactive control of assumed risks.

As Chapters 1 and 2 brought to the reader's attention, plenty of users of financial statements want to have reliable information about exposure(s) arising from different financial instruments, including, but not limited to, credit risk, market risk, and operational risk. Investors, correspondent banks and regulators also need to know the ability of entities they are dealing with to identify, measure, monitor, and control the different risks they take.

All this enters into disclosure standards, along with the fact that clear and consistent requirements should apply to all entities. This way the market operates on a level playing field, and users receive comparable information about risks they incur. We can summarize under seven points what is new in corporate accounting with IFRS, and at the same time which are the new standards' pillars. These are (in alphabetical order):

- *Derivatives*: The company's balance sheet must show the current market value of all derivative instruments which it contains; there is no more hide and seek. Derivatives can be recorded on both sides of the balance sheet (see Chapter 14).
- *Fair value:* This will, in all likelihood, be the most significant impact of IFRS. Fair value of assets and liabilities that have not been traded will become a culture, uncertainty over its measurement when no ready market exists for certain issues notwithstanding.

The valuing of the company's assets at market price is part and parcel of the quantitative evaluation and disclosure. *Fair value* is not just 'any' market price, but one agreed upon by a willing buyer and a willing seller under other than fire sales conditions. (This definition comes from the Financial Accounting Standards Board.)

- *Goodwill*: Companies can no longer amortize goodwill from acquisitions. Instead, they must conduct an annual impairment review, taking a charge if the asset's value falls.
- *Intangible assets*: Management must both disclose and quantify the value of assets like patents, software, customer lists, trademarks, research and development projects. These can no longer be lumped into goodwill.
- *Reduction of exceptions*: A number traditionally seen as exceptional, as for example restructuring costs or gains and losses on trading assets, will increasingly be regarded as part of the firm's operating performance. The mixing of company assets and pension assets is no longer permitted.
- *Pensions*: Companies need to account on their profit and loss statement of the year for the full impact of pension liabilities, as well as for pension assets.
- *Stock options*: Management can no longer bury the cost of stock-based compensation as footnotes to financial accounts. The company must show full value of all options granted to executives and employees.

The first two bullets partly overlap, because not only will derivatives be measured at fair value and included on the balance sheet, but also all dealing and most investment securities held by banks will be measured at fair value. Moreover, banks are expected largely to consolidate special purpose vehicles (SPVs), which have been often used to hide risks. In short, financial institutions will need to:

- Review their hedging strategies and SPV policies, and
- Make changes to their current solutions for keeping exposure non-transparent, or definitely become transparent.

In the opinion of the European Central Bank, the new standards may also change banks' behaviour, especially their risk management practices, because they could cause concern over risk-taking if the impact on the accounts becomes less clear. Reserves for credit losses will be affected by the introduction of a new provisioning methodology, while the fund for general banking reserves will be reclassified as equity.[1]

These and other changes in financial reporting, as for example the recognition of actuarial losses on pension obligations, may result in a decrease in equity and the reclassification of certain capital instruments from equity to liabilities. The new accounting culture will clearly have profound effects on the balance sheets and P&L statements of the 7000 listed European companies which switched their books to IFRS. How fast will the new rules sip down the investment community? Some experts reckon that:

- It will take up to two years before analysts and investors fully come to grips with what the changes mean.
- But in the end analysts and investors will have a much better understanding of a firm's financials, because IFRS forces companies to disclose more information than ever before.

IFRS rules will also unveil items that many European companies either buried as footnotes in their financial reports or simply did not reveal at all. The aforementioned derivative financial instruments and pension liabilities are examples. Still the most important underpinning of IFRS's dynamics is the switch from historical cost accounting to fair value accounting.

2. Positive and negative opinions on IFRS

Along with US Generally Accepted Accounting Principles (GAAP), IFRS is emerging as a sound basis for international financial reporting. As already stated, the European Union has made IFRS obligatory for financial reporting by listed companies in its member states, replacing the current parochial national accounting standards. A total of 90 countries around the world will either permit or require the use of the new accounting standard. Among them are Australia and Switzerland, who have decided to implement IFRS,[2] while other countries like Japan and China announced their intention to move in the same direction.

As is always the case when different interests exist, and several lobbies, there has been some criticism of the IFRS rules while they were shaping up and thereafter (see the case study in Chapter 2). For instance, mid-2003, some French banks repeatedly signalled their opposition to the principle of reporting on derivatives at their fair value. And there have been, as well, plenty of arguments regarding the hedge accounting regime (see Chapter 5).

Because of the uncertainty prevailing in the early years of this century around conversion to the new accounting system, several experts implored businesses to get 'in at the beginning' of the implementation of the International Accounting Standard (now IFRS). Also, in collaboration with IASB's standard setters, to seek a valid application methodology. (A case study on IFRS project management is presented in Chapter 6.)

In September 2004, Jon Symonds, chief financial officer at AstraZeneca, the pharmaceutical company, and chairman of the 100 group of directors, gave his full support to the IFRS project, but criticized political ambiguities undermining its creditability. 'It is a sad event when we see the politicization of accounting,' Symonds said, referring to derivative financial instruments.[3]

Symonds believes the decision by the European Commission to only give partial endorsement to IAS 39 forgoes the chance to gain a 'better understanding of volatility' as opposed to the present situation where it is ignored 'in the profit and loss'. And he called on business leaders for a concerted effort to make the market aware of what IFRS will mean to:

- Their accounts, and
- Their company.

Many central banks have been supportive of the work accomplished by IASB. In mid-2000 the Deutsche Bundesbank stated, in its monthly report, that: 'IAS 39 ultimately represents the first concrete reflection of efforts undertaken by the IASB to advance the use of fair value accounting for financial instruments. The original all-embracing concept of full fair value accounting had encountered open criticism and reservations. The more specific provisions in IAS 39 were then developed as an interim solution, albeit without any set expiry date.'[4]

Some parties also expressed concern about the potential IFRS impact on credit risk. In late 2004, Moody's Investors Service published a Special Comment which addressed this issue. Several factors could potentially impact the credit rating of an individual issuer converting to IFRS, Moody's suggested.[5]

Issues singled out by Moody's include disclosure of risks or financial characteristics not previously evident from the reporting under local/national accounting standards; market perceptions changing to the detriment of the issuer, restrictive banking or other covenants being breached when the numbers are restated. Moody's also mentioned adverse regulator behaviour in response to the new financial metrics as well as changes in behaviour of issuers in regard to:

- Managing risk
- Remunerating staff, or
- Designing and selling particular types of financial instruments.

According to prevailing expert opinion prior to the introduction of IFRS, the new rules were going to have a substantial impact not just on accounting but also on the way business is conducted. Pessimists spoke of 'great implications' for a number of business segments, and of major implementation costs because of aligning reporting systems. Others expressed concerns that the IFRS implementation will mean different philosophies at each side of the balance sheet:

- Assets being reported at fair value
- While liabilities of long duration remain at nominal value, computed through the accruals method.

We have briefly spoken of this A/L criterion in Chapter 2. The asset side of a bank's balance sheet typically consists of cash holdings, but also financial assets, trading assets, loans and receivables, investments in property, and goodwill. Financial assets must be measured at fair value. Assets are created by the bank providing money, goods or services directly to the debtor like originated loans and collection of receivables. These are:

- Initially recognized at cost
- But subsequently measured at amortized cost to impairment.

Critics said that by marking to market their assets, while using the accruals method for their liabilities, companies may face a substantial mismatch between these two classes. While the majority of assets will be measured at fair value, the accounting basis for liabilities will remain amortized cost under accounting requirements that may vary by jurisdiction. (Indeed, part of the phase shift with the new standard is that the balance sheet will no more balance the way it used to. See Chapter 13.)

The pros answered that these points presented no real problems, and that the way to bet is market prices will in all likelihood reserve surprises. For instance, a change in interest rates will lead to volatility in the value of assets even if liabilities remain at nominal value. Adjustments will therefore be necessary through the P&L account. The truth however is that companies have an option in responding to the potential mismatches. Take insurance firms as an example.

To align the duration of assets and liabilities, insurers may value a substantial part of their bond portfolio as held-to-maturity. The challenge is that the held-to-maturity hypothesis will not be sustained if the insurer needs to sell financial assets classified as held-to-maturity at an early stage. In this case, the company:

- Needs to reclassify all held-to-maturity assets as available-for-sale, and
- It would not be allowed to classify any financial assets as held-to-maturity for the following two years.

This can be carried further into other instruments held in the asset side of the balance sheet, affected by the fair value methodology. A dynamic accounting system ensures that companies will have to adjust their books in response to changes in stock market prices, credit default probabilities and other factors.

One unwanted consequence may be that companies become keen users of financial hedges. On the other hand, because IFRS requires all firms to price and describe separately the features of the hedges in place, the efficiency of such hedges will be scrutinized more closely. Some experts suggest that investment management companies will have to develop new financial products to respond to these challenges. We shall see.

According to the opinion of other experts, the new accounting framework will have further reaching consequences for the financial industry, when considered together with major regulatory changes embedded in Basel II,[6] and a renewed focus on corporate governance. The reason is that the new accounting framework:

- Helps to improve investors' understanding of the dynamics of modern business
- But might also entail higher volatility of earnings and, in consequence, of equity prices.

For their part, financial analysis generally welcomed the move to IFRS because they believe that the introduction of the new standards will increase management's sensitivity to assumed exposure. They also looked very positively at greater disclosure requirements. Investors, too, hope that IFRS dynamics will improve their understanding of numbers reported by industrial and financial companies, while at the same time revealing some of the nature of underlying assumptions. Similar comments also characterize the reaction of credit rating agencies.

3. Disclosure about capital and fair value

It comes as no surprise that IFRS rules reflect the International Accounting Standards Board's belief that information about capital is useful for all companies. This is evidenced by the fact that several entities now set internal capital requirements, and industry norms have been established for certain industries like banking and insurance.

The Basel Committee on Banking Supervision has upped regulatory capital requirements, linking them to the exposure assumed by the institution. The 1996

Market Risk Amendment obliged banks to account for market risk, over and above the 8% capital ratio for credit risk implied by the 1988 Capital Accord (Basel I).[7] Since its draft status of 1999, Basel II has introduced the:

- Process of internal ratings-based (IRB) calculation of capital requirements, and
- Associated notion of risk-based pricing.[8]

All this has had an effect. As ECB statistics show, banks are willingly increasing their capital reserves. The trend in Figure 3.1 is most welcome. For its part, the Insurance Advisory Steering Committee (IASC) has proposed, in its draft statement of principles, that capital disclosure requirements should be introduced for insurers. Solvency II, a new capital accord for insurers, is in the making. Other branches of industry seem to be moving in a similar way.

All this evidence had an impact on IASB when it concluded that the information about capital should be disclosed by all entities. Also that such disclosure should be set in the context of a discussion of the firm's objectives, policies, and processes for managing capital. As Walter Wriston once said, information about capital is just as vital as capital itself.

A company may manage capital in a number of ways, and it may be subject to many different capital requirements. An example provided by IASB is that of a

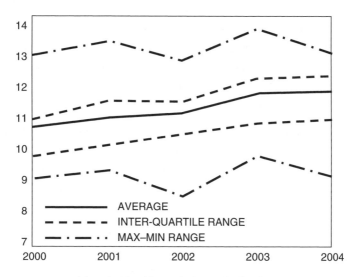

Figure 3.1   Four-year trend (2000–2004) in capital ratio by big banks in Euroland (*Source:* European Central Bank, Financial Stability Review, June 2005)

conglomerate which includes entities that undertake both insurance and banking activities, operating in different geographic regions.

- An aggregate disclosure of capital requirements, and of how capital is managed, must provide comprehensible information.
- If this is not achieved, then the financial statement distorts its user's understanding of the entity's capital resources, and of its financial staying power.

In that case, IFRS states, the company must disclose information on its capital base separately. Some companies have objected to that clause, yet it is only normal that every entity shall disclose information that enables users of its financial statements to evaluate its capital as well as the adequacy of such capital. This must be done in no uncertain terms, and the way to do it is through fair value (more on this later).

IFRS specifies that every company shall also disclose qualitative information about its objectives, policies and processes for managing capital. Such information must include, but not be limited to, a description of what top management regards as capital, its status, and its adequacy in relation to the firm's assumed obligations. Also:

- How is it meeting its objectives for managing capital?
- When is it subject to externally imposed capital requirements?
- What is the nature of these requirements?
- How are these requirements incorporated into the management of capital?

Another qualitative input is the consequences of non-compliance *if* and when the entity has not complied with capital targets set by externally imposed capital requirements (usually by regulators) to which it is subject. It would be superfluous to underline that this mainly qualitative information should be accompanied by quantitative data about capital targets set by management, including how well these targets are met.

IFRS rules on fair value require that for each class of financial assets and liabilities, a firm must disclose its worth in a way that permits it to be compared with the corresponding carrying amount in its balance sheet. For financial instruments such as short-term trade receivables and payables, when the carrying amount is a reasonable approximation of fair value, no other disclosure of value is required.

Fair value is volatile, and *volatility* in fair value is primarily, but not exclusively, due to *market risk*. For instance, currency exchange risk arises on financial instruments that are denominated in a currency other than the functional currency of the entity. Other examples of fluctuation in fair value are commodity price risk and equity price risk. As with death and taxes, no firm and no investor can escape from volatility.

Volatility has always been embedded in the company's assets. All IASB asks for is to disclose its after-effect. IFRS requires that in disclosing fair value, a company must group financial assets and liabilities into classes. It can offset them only to the extent that their related carrying amounts are offset in the balance sheet. Moreover, an entity has to disclose in its financial statement:

- Method and assumptions applied in determining fair values of financial assets and financial liabilities, and
- Hypotheses which have been used, such as estimated prepayment rates, rates of projected credit losses, interest or discount rates, and so on.

Behind these requirements lies the need for every entity to disclose information that enables the stakeholders, who are using its financial statements, to evaluate the nature and extent of risks arising from financial instruments to which the firm has been, and continues being, exposed:

- During the period, and
- At reporting date of the financial statement.

And has already been brought to the reader's attention, this quantitative presentation should be enhanced through qualitative disclosures for each risk arising from financial instruments. For instance, how this exposure arose; which methods are used to measure the risk; which are the policies and processes for managing the risk; and whether there are any changes in the above references, from the previous reporting period.

As an example, it is not enough that in the *trading portfolio* assets and liabilities are recorded at fair value from time to time, without exact periodicity. As the reader will recall from Chapter 2, Luca Paciolo said the same thing in 1494. Fair value must be calculated at each balance sheet date, with changes recorded as trading income in the P&L statement or, correspondingly, as a trading loss. Key judgements affecting this accounting policy relate to how the bank determines fair value for each item in assets and liabilities. As cannot be repeated too often:

- Where liquid markets exist, fair value is based on quoted market prices.
- For complex or illiquid financial instruments, however, banks have to use projections, estimates, and models to determine fair value – a good approach being discounted cash flow.

There are, as well, judgmental factors such as the need for credit adjustments, liquidity adjustments, and other valuation adjustments affecting the reported fair value of different assets and liabilities in the portfolio. Because of these judgmental factors, and risks embedded into assumptions being made, senior management must make sure that:

- Hypotheses and estimates being used are reasonable, and
- They are supportable in the prevailing market environment.

In conclusion, qualification is a necessary supplement of quantification, and both qualification and quantification are often based on hypotheses. The range of assumptions being made, estimates being used, and number of different products covered mean that it is not always possible to meaningfully quantify the impact of different market factors – both present and projected. Senior management should, however, always control that assumptions and estimates being made are reasonable and supportable by the market.

4. IFRS requirements for maximum and minimum risk disclosure

In connection to *maximum credit risk disclosure*, IFRS requires reporting the amount that best represents a company's maximum exposure to credit risk. For a financial asset, this amount is typically the gross carrying amount, net of any offset in accordance with IFRS rules, and of any impairment losses recognized in line with rules outlined in IAS 39. Activities that give rise to credit risk, and associated maximum exposure to credit risk include, but are not limited to:

- Granting loans and receivables to customers
- Placing deposits with other entities
- Entering into derivatives contracts, such as foreign exchange instruments and interest rate swaps
- Dealing in credit derivatives, and so on.

When the resulting asset is measured at fair value, the maximum exposure to credit risk will equal the carrying amount in the entity's financial report. Amounts disclosed in *maturity analysis* are contractual undiscounted cash flows. Examples are different financial obligations, prices specified in forward agreements to purchase financial assets, streams of floating rate swaps, and the like.

There is a counterpart of minimum disclosures based on one of the assumptions underpinning IFRS: that because companies view and manage risk in different ways, standard financial disclosures reflecting how an entity manages risks are unlikely to be comparable between different firms. Indeed, some disclosures might even convey little or no information about the risks the entity has assumed.

To overcome the limitations outlined in the preceding paragraph, IASB has specified *minimum disclosure* requirements concerning risk exposures, able to provide a common benchmark for financial statements. The aim is to have statements understandable by users when they are comparing assumed risk across different entities. Three groups of exposure are targeted by minimum disclosures:

- Credit risk
- Market risk, and
- Operational risk.

For instance, in connection to credit risk the company should disclose the fair value of collateral pledged as security, and other credit enhancements. Another vital piece of information to be reported regards credit quality of assets that are neither past due nor impaired. This approach:

- Gives a good insight into the credit risk of assets, and
- Helps users of financial statements appreciate whether such assets are more or less likely to become impaired in the future.

IFRS requires separate disclosure of financial assets that are past due to impairment, a move designed to provide users with information about financial assets with the greater credit risk. Also required is an analysis of the age of financial assets that are past due as at reporting date, but not yet impaired.

Useful information called for by the new accounting rules concerns, as well, the status of collateral and other credit enhancements which have been obtained. Apart from the insight this provides in terms of expected risk, such references are useful because they reveal important data about:

- The frequency of leaning activities, and
- The entity's ability to obtain and dispose of collateral obtained.

In connection to market risk, IFRS calls for disclosure of a sensitivity analysis for each type of exposure associated with market variables. Sensitivity analysis should take place for all types of market risk, and it should be done in a way that is easy to calculate and understand. This type of information can be most helpful not only to third parties but also to the company's own management:

- As a compass for its decisions, and
- As an indicator of how the entity manages its market risk(s).

Among market risks to which a financial company may be exposed are: *residual value risk*, as in the case of writing residual value guarantees, and *prepayment risk*. For instance, a bank having fixed rate prepayable loan assets may find that as interest rates decrease, loan prepayments increase because borrowers refinance their debt at a lower rate of interest. This has happened massively in the United States in the early years of the 21st century, because of rock-bottom interest rates.

IASB acknowledged that a simple sensitivity analysis that shows a change in one variable has limitations, such as failure to reveal nonlinearities in sensitivities, or disclose the effects of interdependencies between variables. For this reason IFRS requires additional disclosure when the sensitivity analysis is unrepresentative of risk inherent in a financial instrument.

While IASB is doing a good job in establishing modern, sound, and fair international accounting standards, some of the authorities who should see to it that it is fully implemented and complied with take a hand in watering down IFRS implementation and its impact. This is typically done through amendments to the draft of the IFRS discussion paper which came into effect following political pressures. As an example, the initial statement that:

> *This Standard contains requirements for the presentation of financial instruments and identifies the information that should be disclosed about them.*

has been replaced by:

> *The objective of this Standard is to establish principles for presenting financial instruments as liabilities or equity and for offsetting financial assets and financial liabilities.*

The new version has, however, retained the original definition that the new international accounting standard applies to the classification of:

- Financial instruments, from the perspective of the issuer of financial assets, financial liabilities and equity instruments

- Interest, dividends, losses, and gains related to business activities
- Circumstances in which financial assets and financial liabilities should be offset.

Some entities, particularly in the banking industry, have criticized IASB for not following the Basel II standard in expected loss (EL) which is Basel II's IRB approaches for corporate, sovereign, and bank exposures, as well as for retail exposures. This is the cost components of a loan covered by provisioning in financial statements.

IFRS, however, does not address itself only to the banking industry, and moreover the exposure algorithm continues to evolve. Originally, the amount of EL was calculated as the product of:

- Probability to default (PD)
- Loss given default (LGD)
- Exposure at default (EAD).

But after the Basel Committee's Madrid meeting of October 2003, this EL equation went out of the window, precisely at the insistence of these same commercial banks which said that they accounted anyway for EL through classical provisioning. Since then, the equation has been modified for stress testing, and is used in computing unexpected losses (UL):

$$UL = SPD \bullet SLGD \bullet SEAD$$

where, respectively, SPD, SLGD, SEAD, stand for stress PD, stress LGD, and stress EAD. Given this change, IASB could not have used the EL formula even if it wanted to. And it did not need to use it either, since IASB is an independent standards body. Beyond this, it is not a good idea to interlink standards formulas, because this leads to a very inflexible system.

Incurred loss under IAS 39 is covered through provisions that are based on objective and evident observations. For financial assets that are valued at amortized cost, like loans and receivables, as well as for held-to-maturity financial instruments, the provision requirement for defaultable instruments is computed as the difference between:

- The asset's carrying amount, and
- Present value of estimated cash flows discounted at the financial asset's original effective interest rate.

Financial assets in the available-for-sale category are measured at fair value, as the difference between historical cost and current fair value, resulting in a shift from capital into the profit and loss account. In the IFRS accounting system, defaults are calculated across the residual maturity of the loan portfolio, with an assessment of potential default threat based primarily on objective observations at time of valuation.

5. The greater transparency provided by IFRS

IFRS promotes transparency, practically at par with US GAAP, but greater than any of its predecessor national accounting systems. 'Sunshine is the best disinfectant,' said Dr Louis Brandeis, US Supreme Court Justice. 'Sunshine' means transparency and transparency can give investors a much better understanding of risk and return which characterizes their financial assets. Some experts expect that this will help to lower the risk premium, reducing the cost of equity capital. Other experts, however, disagree as to the end result.

- One of the opinions I heard in my research is that there will be a positive impact on the cost of capital only if the additional volatility is already priced in by investors.
- Another opinion made reference to a prognostication of positive impact *if*, and only if, investors think they have greater insight into the business whose equity they purchase.
- Still others, however, say there will be no impact on the cost of capital if the additional volatility is already priced in by investors. Differences in opinions is what makes the market.

On the other hand, three contradictory opinions do not lead to a conclusion. Where most experts agree is that the introduction of the new IFRS rules will certainly *raise* risk awareness and sensitivity. As a result, management will need to promote a stronger risk culture inside the firm, as well as an awareness amongst shareholders, employees, clients and other stakeholders that risk has its price.

In my opinion, increased transparency will see to it that companies will face growing pressure to produce more detailed risk reports, which are comprehensive as well as comprehensible to their readers. These analytical risk reports should be both quantitative and qualitative, including:

- Cash flow sensitivity, and
- Analyses of risk concentration.

For instance, there should be increased focus on credit risk exposure in the aftermath of more stringent impairment rules. This is altogether positive, particularly at a time when creative accounting practices, restatements of earnings, revelations of accounting fraud, and other corporate scandals have undermined public confidence in financial reporting.

Greater transparency is not only welcomed by investors, but also by rating agencies, equity analysts, and regulators, who want accounting standards to reflect more accurately the economic and financial nature of the business. Only those who have something to hide resist transparency. But those who resist transparency are the few trying to misguide the many.

As far as corporate governance is concerned, transparency in financial statement and a properly functioning internal control correlate. IFRS specifies that an entity's internal organizational and management structure, as well as its system of internal financial reporting to the board of directors and chief executive officer, will normally be the basis for:

- Identifying the predominant source and nature of risks, and
- Pin-pointing differing rates of return facing the entity in its current operations.

The board, CEO, and executive vice-presidents need properly functioning internal control channels.[9] They may also be assisted by on-line datamining and knowledge artifacts instrumental in determining which type of risk gets out of established control limits, and where this happens. The impact of these factors on the entity's financial reporting content and structure is self-evident.

A good example where the internal control reporting structure finds fruitful application is *liquidity risk*. Beyond credit risk and market risk, IFRS require disclosure of maturity analysis for financial liabilities, that show the remaining earliest contractual maturity, and therefore case outflow. Such information targets the risk that the entity:

- Will encounter difficulty in meeting commitments associated with financial liabilities, and
- Will likely be confronted with liquidity problems that might turn into insolvency.

Liquidity risk arises because the entity could be required to pay its liabilities on their earliest contractual maturity date. *If* it has failed to properly match cash inflows and outflows, it may have to employ fire brigade approaches. Because, however, a contractual maturity analysis does not necessarily reveal the *expected maturity* of outstanding liabilities, IFRS requires a description of how the liquidity risk portrayed by *contractual maturity* analysis is managed. Such a description should include disclosure of factors like:

- Expected maturity dates of liabilities, and
- Assets held by the company to mitigate liquidity risk.

IFRS further calls for the company to describe *how* it manages liquidity risk inherent in maturity analysis of financial liabilities. This is an example of the quantitative and qualitative aspects of financial reporting, of which we spoke in preceding sections.

Under IFRS rules, liquidity risk is essentially a *mismatch risk* to be studied through contractual maturity analysis for financial liabilities. The new accounting discipline allows an entity to use its judgment to determine an appropriate number of *time bands*. For instance, not later than one month, or not later than one year. Such time bands must, however, be realistic, reflecting the case(s) where an entity has to pay a due amount or to receive a payment.

Another important but rather obscure issue addressed by IFRS is *synthetic instruments*. On this subject bankers cannot quite agree on a unique definition. According to the International Accounting Standards Board, a *synthetic instrument* is a financial instrument acquired and held to emulate the characteristics of another instrument. Such is the case of a floating rate long-term debt combined with an interest rate swap that involves:

- Receiving floating payments, and
- Making fixed payments synthesizing a fixed rate long-term debt.

But in the research I did for a book on 'wealth management',[10] commercial and investment bankers gave me different definitions of synthetic instruments, and some were at a loss to find one because of too many new terms coming up at the same time.

Following the IASB definition, IFRS specifies that each of the individual financial products that together constitute a synthetic instrument represents a contractual right or obligation with its own terms and conditions. The complexity arises from the fact that though part of an integrative product marketed and inventoried in its own right:

- Each individual part may be transferred or settled separately, and
- Each is exposed to risks that may differ from the risks to which other financial instruments in the same lot are exposed.

Therefore, when one of the financial products entering into a synthetic instrument is an asset, while another is a liability, these two are *not* offset. As a result, they should be presented on an entity's balance sheet on a net basis, unless they meet specific criteria outlined by the international accounting standard, which might permit offsetting.

Moreover, according to the rules of IFRS, financial disclosure of concentrations of risk should include a description of the shared characteristic that identifies each concentration. Examples are industry distribution of a portfolio of loans, and geographic distribution of counterparties to trading, loans or other deals. Such counterparties may comprise individual countries, groups of countries or regions within countries – or, alternatively, physical or legal entities.

Notice as well that when quantitative information at the reporting date is unrepresentative of the entity's exposure to risk during the period, IFRS requires further information to be provided such as highest, lowest, and average amount of exposure. An example given by IASB is that if a company has a large exposure to a particular currency but at year-end unwinds the position, it can disclose a graph that shows the exposures at various times during the period in reference, including the highest, lowest, and average exposures.

6. Regulators, more stringent accounting standards, and early aftermath of IFRS

In a letter published on 21 April 2002, the Financial Services Authority (FSA) has turned up the heat on companies regarding implementation of international accounting standards. The aim of this letter was to encourage issuers to disclose all relevant information as soon as the impact of the change to IFRS on their 2004 financial statements could be quantified in a sufficiently reliable manner.

What essentially the regulator told chief executives of listed companies is that when they have compiled price-sensitive data about the effect of the new accounting rules, this information must be disclosed without delay. Notice that at the time IFRS rules were still in the making, though some already had a workable form. The objective of FSA's letter was to avoid companies:

- Sitting on potentially significant information, and
- Worrying that such information could unnerve investors and send their share prices tumbling.

From their perspective, one reason companies are uneasy with greater transparency is that they have no experience with its aftermath. Another reason is that they would not know in advance what the IFRS would give in terms of profits and losses reported to the market, compared to the old parochial accounting standards. (See the case study with Vodafone at end of this section.)

Particularly worrisome to some companies has been IFRS treatment of derivatives, pensions, and stock options. Many CEOs felt that by changing the rules of the national accounting standards they have been following for many years, IFRS is transforming earnings and balance sheets, as well as revealing previously undisclosed figures banks and other companies kept close to their chest.

For their part, regulators are right to be worried about the limited visibility available through previous accounting standards, and the way companies used them for financial reporting. In early October 2003, FSA had written to almost 300 banks and building societies in the UK after uncovering a series of failures in the way they managed their Treasury operations.

The Financial Services Authority had conducted a review of more than 25 unnamed banks and building societies, and seems to have been disappointed because it found 'at least one material failing' in the systems and controls of 'most firms' it had visited. In a letter to all chief executives of credit institutions in the UK, FSA said 'firms are still failing to address, effectively, some fairly basic issues' in spite of 'numerous, well-publicized examples of material losses arising from inadequate controls within Treasury operations'.

Among other occurrences, for example, has been the case of rogue traders who exploited weak controls and lax scrutiny in Treasury operations to conceal fraud. When internal controls are wanting, and accounting standards are not of the highest sensitivity, such practices tend to multiply. Therefore, a good deal of FSA's attention focused on whether systems, procedures, and controls banks put in place are robust enough to:

- Monitor
- Identify, and
- Manage risks arising in Treasury operations.

As the regulator saw it, the results of its study highlighted a number of concerns including the way banks separate their front office activities from back office operations. Sound management ensures the two are kept at arm's length, because the latter controls the former; but this is not what a large number of banks are doing.

Here is, as a case study, what took place at a bank required by European Union regulations to change its financial reporting to International Financial Reporting Standards. In early 2005, the firm published fourth quarter and full year 2004 results under local accounting standards. But at the same time, the bank started communicating on the impact of IFRS, and also revised shareholders' equity under 'light' IFRS – 'light' means excluding IAS 32 and IAS 39 (see Chapters 4 and 5).

Not long thereafter, still in the second quarter of 2005, the bank published its first quarter 2005 results and revised shareholders' equity under 'full' IFRS (including IAS 32 and IAS 39). A simulation of 'full' IFRS with the previously prevailing national accounting principles has shown where the most impact from first-time adoption of IFRS can be anticipated:

- From a balance sheet standpoint, the main changes came from consolidating the securitization-related special purpose vehicles (SPVs), but with no impact on equity.
- The bank fully recognized in equity the unamortized actuarial losses on its defined benefit plans.
- The bank reclassified its fund for general risks, already included in its Tier 1 regulatory capital base. Therefore, Tier 1 equity did not benefit from the same mitigation effect as shareholders' equity.
- The bank had to record additional specific provisions for individually significant loans, owing to the requirements of IAS 39 to apply net present value discounting when calculating provisions for loan losses. (In some cases, this might substantially decrease equity.)
- The bank revalued its 'available-for-sale' debt securities to their fair value, which translated into a minor decrease in shareholder equity from recognized unrealized capital gains and losses.

- From a P&L viewpoint, the flow of specific provisions was higher than under past accounting standards. This was, however, accompanied by recognition of higher income on non-performing loans.

What these and similar changes can mean to the bottomline can be exemplified through an example on Vodafone, in connection to IFRS. For the year to March 2006, Vodafone will issue results which, for the first time, exclude amortization of goodwill. Such amortization has produced swings of up to £15 billion between the pre- and post-goodwill figures.

For instance, in 2002 a £13.4 billion amortization charge, plus £5.4 billion of exceptionals, ended in producing a £15.6 billion loss, even though the company's operating profit that year was £7 billion. This loss was considered the biggest ever in the UK industry. Instead of amortization, IFRS requires companies to write down goodwill if it fails an annual impairment test.

On the other hand, according to one major international bank, under IFRS Vodafone's operating profit is likely to fall about 5% because of new rules on consolidation of its overseas assets. A particularly large impact on the income statement will come from the fact that Vodafone's Italian operations cannot be integrated, as has hitherto been the practice.

Incidentally, this is a good example on how biased the 'free market' can be, because of local interests. Vodafone controls 76% of Vodafone Italia, and because Italians are heavy mobile users it derives 10–11% of its revenue from it. But under IFRS,

- It will not be able to consolidate Vodafone Italia, because of the 'golden share' held by the Italian government.
- Vodafone Italia has to be reported as a financial asset subject to marking to market.

At the end of the day, Vodafone did all right, as in January 2005 it turned a $10 billion loss for 2004 into a $17 billion net profit by applying the new rules of International Financial Reporting Standards to its balance sheet. Under IFRS, Holland's Akzo Nobel saw its 2004 net income rise by $115 million.

Along a similar line of financial reporting, Germany's Bertelsmann wrote off $813 million in 2003 for such items as its depreciation of TV rights. The write-off in 2004 has been zero, a change which helped boost the company's net profit nearly fivefold, to $1.6 billion.

But IFRS increased the costs of other companies. The fact that it requires to expense stock options, chopped $743 million from GlaxoSmithKline's 2004 earnings. Other firms have been forced to disclose the full extent of their pension plan deficit, wiping billions off their balance sheet.

What about the effect of these changes on the stock market? Of European companies that have restated their 2004 earnings under IFRS, none has seen a dramatic shift in its share price. One of the basic reasons is that company valuations are largely based on cash flow, and that practically remains the same under IFRS as it was under the national accounting standards system.

Notes

1 European Central Bank, Financial Stability Review, June 2005.
2 In Switzerland, listed companies generally will be required to report either under US GAAP or IFRS from 2005.
3 *The Accountant*, October 2004.
4 Deutsche Bundesbank, Monthly Report, June 2002.
5 Moody's, Special Report, October 2004.
6 D.N. Chorafas, *Economic Capital Allocation with Basel II: Cost and Benefit Analysis*, Butterworth-Heinemann, Oxford and Boston, 2004.
7 D.N. Chorafas, *The 1996 Market Risk Amendment. Understanding the Marking-to-Model and Value-at-Risk*, McGraw-Hill, Burr Ridge, IL, 1998.
8 D.N. Chorafas, *Economic Capital Allocation with Basel II: Cost and Benefit Analysis*, Butterworth-Heinemann, Oxford and Boston, 2004.
9 D.N. Chorafas, *Implementing and Auditing the Internal Control System*, Macmillan, London, 2001.
10 D.N. Chorafas, *Wealth Management: Private Banking, Investment Decisions and Structured Financial Products*, Butterworth-Heinemann, Oxford and Boston, 2006.

The Controversy over IAS 39

1. Introduction

Most of the clauses contained in the International Accounting Standard (IAS), a predecessor title to IFRS, might have been agreed upon more or less easily if it were not for two of the new accounting system's pillars: IAS 32 and IAS 39, which cover financial instruments, especially derivatives. Both, and most particularly IAS 39, became the object of heated dispute which, for some time, threatened to wreck the chance of getting a single set of accounting standards at global scale.

IAS 39 includes provisions for impairment of financial assets on recognition of financial contracts; rules for valuation of financial assets, particularly the use of *fair value*; and requirements for instrument-specific tracking of hedge effectiveness (see Chapter 5). All these standards are a direct reflection of the nature of transactions taking place in the modern economy.

In a nutshell, *IAS 32* provides rules for reliable disclosure and presentation of financial instruments. When IAS 32 and IAS 39 were revised in 2003, disclosures about financial instruments that had been in old IAS 39 were moved to IAS 32. By consequence, IAS 32 now includes practically all financial instruments' disclosure requirements.

Reportedly, as a result of intensive lobbying by banks and insurers, the European Commission threatened to reject IAS 32 and IAS 39 if a number of changes were not made to soften the rules. Politics was the name of the game, engineered by covert interests which either because of blindness as to what has to be done in terms of reliable financial reporting (see Chapter 2), or for reasons of huge conflict of interest, fail to see:

- The growing financial complexity of risk, and
- Urgent need to control it, starting with more detailed disclosures and greater transparency than in the past.

Transparency and accuracy in financial reporting is the job of the standards setter. Subsequently, after appropriate rules are put in place, they become instruments in the hands of the regulator, whose job is to assure that laws, norms, and rules are observed, and that risk remains within prudential limits.

Ironically, the objections mounted against IAS 32 and IAS 39, in particular regarding fair value, were hurting some of the same people who worked through politicians to get these standards dropped. Listing in New York Stock Exchange, the world's largest capital market, is an example. The Securities and Exchange Commission was contemplating letting European firms listed in America use international accounting standards rules, instead of American ones.

- But this had no chance of taking place in the absence of reliable and robust treatment of financial instruments, and
- Without fair value clauses, the Financial Accounting Standards Board, which sets accounting rules in the United States would most likely give up trying to converge its standards with those of IASB.

The great merit of IAS 39 is that it sets forth requirements for determining reliable fair values which apply to all portfolio positions. The following quotation explains the way the Basel Committee looks at this issue:

> *A key issue underlying fair values in general is whether they can be obtained directly from observable prices or through a robust valuation technique. Even with observable prices, care needs to be taken to ensure that the market in question is reasonably liquid and that the observable prices are representative of actual trades. The issues surrounding valuation models warrant further consideration.*[1]

It would be difficult to phrase in more comprehensive terms the merits and demerits of fair value accounting. In Basel's opinion some cases, like derivation of interest rate yield curves for major currencies with deep markets, do not raise significant issues of reliability. But serious reliability concerns arise:

- Where there are not established valuation techniques with a clear and rigorous basis, or
- Where one or more important inputs to valuation are not observable, even indirectly, from liquid markets.

The regulators of the Group of Ten countries have a good grasp of this problem, since modelling is integral (and important) part of Basel II. Basel's concerns pertain to the valuation of illiquid instruments, an issue especially relevant to the fair value process. This is everybody's concern. But also everybody appreciates that the crumbling structure of historical cost has lost whatever respect it had left because of:

- Derivatives, and
- High leverage.

The foregoing equation helps in appreciating that fundamental to the dispute on IAS 32 and IAS 39 has been a question of how to value financial assets and liabilities. As the preceding chapters explained, the fact that the accruals method values them at original cost makes little sense today now that financial markets are huge, fairly liquid, dynamic, and *highly leveraged*. Moreover, capitalizing on the fact that hedge funds are pooled vehicles of speculation, subject to no regulatory action, one can do anything one wants with macro-creative accounting. Indeed, many banks escape supervisory control of their financial status by:

- Lending to
- Trading with, and
- Being closely associated to hedge funds.

This is one more reason, and a major one, why controlling the bank's exposure by marking their portfolio to market is nearly the only way regulators have to peep into what hedge funds are doing and guesstimate how far they may be from blowing the world's financial fabric to pieces (more on this in Chapter 5).

Of course, it is not only hedge funds who speculate. Banks and insurance companies are especially heavy users of over-the-counter derivatives. Even pension funds are getting addicted to them. To value these highly leveraged and risky instruments at their original cost is totally meaningless, because the exposure they carry is huge and it can change within the day. Therefore, IASB correctly wanted to:

- Put derivatives and other financial instruments on the balance sheet at their fair value, and
- Assure they are reported in a way that accounts are transparent, accurate, and comprehensible.

Many European banks and insurers, especially French ones, object to this. They (wrongly) argued fair value accounting is artificial and misleading, because it ties day-to-day volatility in markets to their long-term businesses (which is a total misrepresentation of facts). They also said that for those financial instruments which are not traded on liquid markets, values are unreliable (which is true).

IASB stuck to its guns, insisting that injecting more fair value into accounts is much the best course. It also said that investors should decide for themselves what constitutes excessive volatility. 'If banks don't want to disclose these fair values, they should not turn to the public markets for money,' said Jeannot Blanchet, an analyst at Morgan Stanley.[2] Blanchet is right. One can add that *if* a bank does not want to be subject to high volatility, *then* it should not speculate.

2. Financial instruments defined according to IAS 39 and IAS 32

The International Financial Reporting Standards, most particularly IAS 32 and IAS 39, define a *financial instrument* as a contract giving rise to a financial asset (or equity) and a financial liability (or equity) of another entity. This is fairly similar to the definition by FASB – and, therefore, US GAAP. A *financial asset* is:

- Cash
- Demand and time deposit
- Commercial paper
- Equity of another entity
- A contractual right, and more.

This 'more' is accounts, notes, loans, receivables and payables, leases, rights and obligations with insurance risk under insurance contracts, employers' rights and obligations under pension contracts, and so on. Debt and equity securities are financial instruments from the perspectives of both the holder and the issuer, including investments in subsidiaries and joint ventures.

Asset-backed securities, such as collateralized mortgage obligations (CMOs), repurchase agreements, and securitized packages of receivables are also assets. The same is true of a long list of derivatives, including options, rights, warrants, futures, forward, and swaps, provided that they have a positive value (they are in the money) and not a negative value (they are out of the money) for the holder. *If* they have a negative value, *then* they are financial liabilities. A *financial liability* is:

- A contractual obligation to deliver cash or other financial asset to another entity
- A contract that will, or may, be settled in the entity's own equity instruments, or
- An obligation to exchange financial assets or financial liabilities with another entity, under conditions that are potentially unfavourable to the holder.

Under IFRS, some of what is currently shareholder funds will be classified as liabilities. For instance, if a bond pays no cash but compensates its holder in shares, it will belong to the liabilities column. This changes significantly the method of meeting T-1 regulatory capital requirements. Like SFAS 133 in the United States, IAS 39 expands the use of fair value for measuring and reporting on assets, liabilities, and derivative instruments. It provides for limited use of hedge accounting (see Chapter 5), but sets criteria for:

- Recognition, and
- Derecognition.

The definitions just given come beyond IAS 32, which requires compound instruments such as embedded derivatives to be split into their components and accounted for accordingly (see Chapter 3).

Most of the examples given in the preceding paragraphs represent *contractual rights* and *contractual obligation*. By definition, a contractual right (obligation) is the legally supported right (obligation) to receive (pay) cash or another financial asset from another entity; or, to exchange financial assets or financial liabilities with another entity under conditions that are:

- Potentially favourable to the holder, in the case of right, and
- Potentially unfavourable to the holder, in the case of obligation.

A contractual right may also be a contract that will, or may, be settled in the entity's own equity instruments. It is a non-derivative for which the entity is, or may be, obliged to receive a variable number of the entity's own equity. *If* it is a derivative *then* this contractual right will, or may, be settled by means other than by the exchange of a fixed amount of cash, or another financial asset, for a fixed number of the entity's own equity instruments.

An important part of the new accounting standards, specifically of IAS 39, is the classification of financial assets which guides management's hand in reporting on financial assets and liabilities. Critical is the classification of an instrument as a liability or as equity. IAS 39 requires financial assets to be classified in one of four categories:

- Financial assets at fair value, through profit or loss
- Available-for-sale financial assets
- Loans and receivables, and
- Investments held to maturity.

Among themselves, these four classes help to determine how a particular financial asset is recognized and measured in financial statements that are made public, and are used by investors in their decisions. As previous chapters have brought to the reader's attention, homogeneity in definitions, and in account classifications, helps in creating a level field for all players.

Financial assets at fair value, through profit or loss, has two groups: (i) designated and (ii) held for trading. *Designated* includes any financial asset specified on initial recognition to be measured at fair value, with fair value changes reflected in profit or loss (more on this in section 3). The *held for trading* class includes all derivatives, except those designated hedging instruments. It also includes financial assets:

- Acquired or held for the purpose of selling in the short term, or
- For which there is a recent pattern of short-term profit taking.

Available-for-sale financial assets (AFS) are any non-derivative financial assets designated on initial recognition as being available for sale. *Loans and receivables* are non-derivative financial assets originated or acquired with fixed or determinable payments, that are neither quoted in an active market, nor held for trading except in case of securitization. (More on AFS financial assets in section 4.)

The *held-to-maturity* investments, that do not meet the definition of loans and receivables, are non-derivative financial instruments with fixed or determinable payments that an entity intends, and is able, to hold to maturity. Held-to-maturity is an a priori management decision. Its nature is well-defined in SFAS 133 by the Financial Accounting Standards Board as *management intent* (see also Chapter 1).

Several experts say that, in many aspects, IAS 39 is close to US financial reporting rules on financial instruments. In particular, they point to the fact that financial assets are to be classified into categories, some of which require fair value measurement. As has been explained in Chapter 3, there is nothing really negative about this – while there are several positive points. But there is a major 'plus' in the likelihood that IFRS and US GAAP might be converging. Nevertheless, as should be expected, the outlook of the different industries varies. According to the Geneva Association, in jurisdictions where insurance liabilities are measured at amortized cost, IAS 39 will cause asset and liability mismatches and imbalances that affect the financial results of insurers. This is an argument that is worth paying attention to, but it is *not* a reason for leaving IAS 39 aside. (See also the case study on insurance in Chapter 2.)

In its brief review of the seminal work by Luca Paciolo, Chapter 2 made the point that the advent of balance sheets has been a most important novelty in the accounting profession. But as Chapters 13 and 14 will document, because of rapid innovation in financial instruments, balance sheet do not balance anymore. Trying to show they are balanced is a deformation of financial reporting, generally inherent in today's balance sheets. All that IAS 39 does is to bring this inconsistency into the open. Always remember the dictum of US Supreme Court Judge Louis Brandeis, 'Sunshine is the best disinfectant'.

3. Recognition and derecognition of assets and liabilities

In terms of initial recognition of a financial asset or a financial liability, IAS 39 requires that this is done when, and only when, the entity becomes a party to contractual provision of the instrument. With this, the company becomes subject to provisions in respect of regular handling of a commodity. The rules specify that:

- All financial assets and liabilities must be recognized on the balance sheet, and this includes all derivatives.
- A financial asset is recognized (or derecognized), following purchase (or sale) using either trade date or settlement date accounting.

Two groups of financial liabilities are recognized by IAS 39. The first (which has been introduced in section 2, in its incarnation as 'assets') is a group of liabilities to be recognized at fair value through profit and loss; the second includes financial liabilities measured at amortized cost using the effective interest method. Like financial assets, financial liabilities at fair value through profit or loss have two subclasses:

- Designated, and
- Held for trading.

A financial liability is *designated* by the entity as a liability at fair value through profit or loss, upon initial recognition. An example of financial liability characterized as held for trading are securities borrowed in the short term, which have to be returned. As we have already seen, according to IAS 39 initially financial assets and liabilities should be measured at fair value, including transactions costs.

If a market for a financial instrument is not active, an entity must establish fair value of its recognized instruments, by using valuation techniques employing a maximum of direct market inputs. *If* there is no active market to provide an input, or the range of reasonable fair value estimates is significant, *then* the entity should measure the instrument at cost less impairment.

A financial asset is *impaired*, and impairment losses are incurred, only *if* there is objective evidence, as a result of one or more events that occurred after the initial recognition of the asset. In this case, the amount of the loss is measured as the difference between the asset's carrying amount and the present value of estimated cash flows discounted at the financial asset's original effective interest rate.

The basic premise in IAS 39 for *derecognition* of a financial asset is to determine whether the subject under consideration for derecognition is an asset in its entirety, with specifically identified cash flows, or a fully proportionate share of specifically identified cash flows from a financial asset. Once the issue of derecognition has been determined, an assessment is made as to whether the asset has been transferred. If so, it must be judged whether the transfer of that asset is eligible for derecognition.

An asset is transferred if either the entity has transferred the contractual rights to receive the cash flows, or it has retained the contractual rights to receive the cash flows from the asset but has assumed a contractual obligation to pass those cash flows on. This is specified, in IAS 39, as an arrangement that meets the conditions that the company:

- Is obliged to remit those cash flows without material delay to their lawful owner,
- But has no obligation to pay amounts to the eventual recipient, unless it collects equivalent amounts on the original asset, and
- Is prohibited from selling or pledging the original asset, other than as security to the eventual recipient.

Next to determining that the asset has been transferred, the entity must establish whether or not it has transferred substantially all of the risks and rewards resulting from ownership of the asset. *If* it has neither retained nor transferred all of the risks and rewards associated to that asset, *then* the entity must assess whether it has relinquished control of the asset or not.

- *If* the entity does not control the asset, *then* derecognition is appropriate.
- But, if the entity has retained control of the asset, *then* it must continue to recognize it to the extent to which it has a continuing involvement in the asset.

Similarly, a financial liability should be removed from the balance sheet when, and only when, it is extinguished. This means when the obligation specified in the contract is discharged, cancelled, or has expired. If so, gains and losses from the extinguishment of the original financial liability must be recognized in the profit and loss statement.

Where there has been an exchange between an existing borrower and lender of debt instruments with substantially different terms, or important modification of terms of an existing financial liability, this transaction must be accounted for as:

- An extinguishment of the original financial liability, and
- Recognition of a new financial liability.

Notice that, with only a few exceptions, IAS 39 applies to all types of financial instruments. Among the exceptions are interests in subsidiaries, associates, and joint ventures (accounted for under IAS 27, IAS 28, or IAS 31). However, exceptions are void *if* there is a derivative instrument present, on an interest in a subsidiary, associate, or joint venture.

Among the exceptions are: employers' rights and obligations under employee benefit plans (to which applies IAS 39); financial instruments that meet the definition of own equity (under IAS 32); contracts requiring payment based on climatic, geological, or other physical variables, again except in the case where derivatives are embedded in such contracts; contracts for contingent consideration in a business combination; rights and obligations under insurance contracts, except if insurance (or reinsurance) contracts involve the transfer of:

- Financial risks, and
- Embedded derivatives (see Chapter 5).

Within the scope of IAS 39, financial guarantees provide for payments to be made in response to changes in a specified variable such as price, rate, or index, and derivative financial instruments. Those guarantees are not derivatives, and therefore are excluded from IAS 39, *if* they provide for specified payments to be made to reimburse the holder for a loss it incurs because a specified debtor fails to make payment when due.

The rules of IAS 39 ensure that such excluded guarantees must be initially recognized at fair value and subsequently at the higher of the amount determined under IAS 37 and the amount initially recognized under IAS 39 minus amounts amortized as revenue. No doubt, plenty of learning will be necessary to fine-tune these rules and iron out problems associated to their implementation. Not everything with an impact on good governance can be engineered in advance; much must evolve through practice.

4. Assets available for sale under IAS 39: results of a simulation

A crucial issue with accounting under IAS 39 is the recognition of fair value in categories such as *available-for-sale* financial assets, defined in section 2. The corresponding changes in balance sheet values must be posted directly to a separate equity item which, as a revaluation reserve, can be equated to unrealized reserves and therefore as additional capital available for prudential reasons.

By contrast, if the alternative accounting option is taken of posting such changes to the profit and loss account, the change in the value of the asset flows directly into retained profits, considered to be core capital. Given this bifurcation, experts suggest that supervisors must find appropriate methods of:

- Treating the different outcomes of such valuations, and
- Making possible comparison to other components of the various classes of regulatory capital.

To appreciate the depth of this argument, it is necessary to recall that banks classify some of their financial assets, including investments not held for trading purposes, as available for sale. This classification is based on management's determination that these assets are not held for the purpose of generating short-term trading gains. For instance, in connection to compliance to IAS 39 they elect to record changes in fair value of available-for-sale assets in a separate component of *shareholders' equity* rather than in income.

- *If* they made a different election, *then* any changes in fair value of unrealized gains or losses would be reflected in the income statement, also
- *If* they reclassify them as trading assets, *then* changes in fair value would have to be reflected in income rather than shareholders' equity.

Provided the supervisory authority in the jurisdiction in which a credit institution is based allows it, classifying private equity investments as financial investments available for sale, and carrying them on the balance sheet at fair value (with changes in value being recorded directly in equity), presents certain advantages. Correspondingly, unrealized losses which are determined to be permanent are recorded in the income statement as impairment charges.

Notice that because quoted market prices are generally unavailable for many of these instruments, fair value is determined by applying valuation techniques which require assumptions and estimates. The reader should appreciate that different assumptions and estimates lead to different valuation results – which is the weak point of marking to market when there is no direct market for the instrument.

As has been already stated in Chapter 3, and the reader will see repeated in several places in this book, fair value is no financial penicillin. It is only the better method currently available. Critics are right when they say that the determination of when a decline in fair value below cost is permanent is judgmental by nature, and therefore profit and loss is affected by differences in this judgmental process. Where they are wrong is that they forget P&L under historical costing is *pure fiction.*

Up to a point, the downside is that unlike fair value accounting for marketable financial instruments, there are considerable problems involved in calculating the fair value of loans and other instruments for which no active and liquid market presently exists. This is mitigated by the ongoing securitization of all sorts of loans. In other than securitization cases, and inferences based on them, individual modelling and marking to model:

- Is based on assumptions that have to be made,
- These assumptions offer a considerable amount of discretionary choice, and
- There may as well be unavailability of dependable data, and algorithmic insufficiency.

All three reasons can seriously impair the reliability of fair value estimates. (The culture of modelling is discussed in Chapter 7.) Critics also add that full fair value accounting might lead to a greater volatility of results, which could affect the stability of the financial system (*as if* gambling in derivatives does not impair it!), and may trigger a change in banks' behaviour as they:

- Might be prompted to shorten the length of time during which interest rates and capital are locked in, and
- Do other nasty, but undefined, things which may have (equally undefined) negative long-term effects.

A coin, these critics should know, has two faces and both must be examined to judge if it is genuine or fake. Banks cannot argue against modelling fair value when they use, very extensively, models for market risk and (more recently) for credit risk. In fact, some mathematically illiterate credit institutions have used value at risk (VAR) to model credit risk – as $VAR_{99.95}$ – which is one of the most ridiculous things to have happened so far in the 21st century in the banking industry.[3]

Instead of irrational criticism, what banks can do, and should do, is to use simulation to study their position and properly balance their assets and liabilities in order to reduce volatility in their unrealized gains and losses. The same is true of insurance companies. Here is the result of a simulation of implementation of IAS 39 by a major credit institution.

- The opening balance of Unrealized Gains/Losses on available-for-sale investments was a net gain of $1 billion, net of taxes.

The gain was due to unrealized marked to market gains on financial investments classified as available for sale. These were principally attributable to private equity investments, but also included other financial instruments held by the institution.

- The opening balance of changes in fair value of Derivative Instruments designated as cash flows hedges, was a net loss of $250 million, also net of taxes.

This was due to unrealized marked to market losses on derivatives designated as cash flow hedges. Such losses were previously recorded in the balance sheet as part of deferred losses. As far as this ahead-of-the-curve financial institution is concerned, all movements within the aforementioned categories are now recorded, each year, in the statement of changes in equity.

Take leasing as an example. IAS 39 applies to lease receivables and payables only in limited respect; yet it could have an important impact. It applies to lease receivables with regard to derecognition and impairment provisions; and to lease payables in respect of the derecognition provisions. But IAS 39 also applies to derivatives embedded in leases – and that can be a source of big differences.

A simulation done by another big bank has shown that the most significant impact of IAS 39 would have been on its leasing portfolio of $1.3 trillion carried off-balance sheet – an amount roughly equal to the gross domestic product (GDP) of Spain. The lesson to retain from these references is that:

- Well-managed banks use technology to reposition themselves
- They don't spent their time lobbying and staying behind.

In conclusion, the world is changing, as this $1.3 trillion in leases shows. It is better to be proactive than reactive. Therefore, entities should do their homework using the new standards to define what is wanted and unwanted exposure along the curve shown in Figure 4.1. Banks, insurers, and other institutions

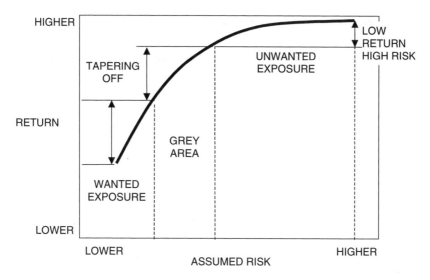

Figure 4.1   Risk and return are correlated nonlinearly. Investors must appreciate the shape of the risk and return curve

which are stonewalling rather than proactive risk being forgotten in the dust of financial history.

5.   The challenge of fair value and the IAS 39 controversy

As we have seen since Chapter 1, *fair value*, which is one of the keywords reflected in the title of this book, is a pervasive subject, and a fairly controversial one particularly in connection to financial reporting. The first encounter the reader of this book had with the definition of fair value was in Chapter 3 on the dynamics of IFRS (as defined by FASB). The term has also been extensively used in section 3 of this present chapter.

It has been a deliberate choice not to limit the discussion of fair value to one chapter, but to spread it throughout the book. At the risk of being repetitive, this provides a better assurance that the reader will gain a full appreciation of this important subject because fair value benefits and challenges are treated in closer relations to the problems that arise. In this sense:

- Chapter 10 discusses fair value in connection to valuing the entity's assets
- Chapter 12 introduces fair value concepts into forward-looking statements

- Fair value enters into Chapter 15 because its theme is virtual balance sheets, and
- In Chapter 16, fair value is examined in terms of impact on stress testing and the computation of relative risk.

The careful reader will recall that SFAS 133, by FASB, was the first to put stress on fair value financial reporting. IAS 39 came right after and the resistance which it encountered encapsulates much of the debate in the accounting profession over what worth to ascribe to the items in a company's inventoried positions. Chapter 1 mentioned FIFO, LIFO, and weighted average, as methods widely used for valuing inventories of physical goods at original cost. These were developed for physical inventories; they are not good for financial instruments.

As we saw in section 3, today in Europe many banks are disputing whether fair value accounting gives a really more meaningful insight into their economic performance, and their assumed risks, than historical measures. Chapter 2 has mentioned that many insurers have a similar critical position. Both bankers and insurers, however, fail to offer a better alternative, by all likelihood because they do not know what to suggest.

While American banks are accustomed to fair value accounting, because Statement of Financial Accounting Standard 133 is already 5 years old, and they have got accustomed to it, many EU banks and financial services companies are complaining about the introduction of market values for their business. As we have already seen, a fairly superficial argument by IAS 39 opponents is that it would lead to volatility in income statements, which:

- Will reflect its exposure to the oscillating derivatives markets
- But would not necessarily capture the 'underlying economic performance' of the company.

This argument is near-sighted, because it forgets that volatility is embedded into the banks' books because of the financial instruments which they contain, and most particularly the ever-growing amount of risky derivatives products (see Chapter 5). As a suggestion, a more sophisticated approach to fair value, but one that is alien to the way of thinking of most people, would be based on *possibility theory*. Probability theory, in which most students are trained today, is a special and relatively limited case of possibility theory and its fuzzy engineering applications.[4]

A simple example of fuzzy sets is how long it takes to drive from Monte Carlo to Lucerne through the Gotthard tunnel. On the average it may take 6 hours (the fair value), but it is equally likely that it would take 5 h 45 min or 6 h 15 min. As Figure 4.2 shows, it is less likely, but still possible, that it takes 5 h 15 min (if traffic is light and weather conditions are good), or 6 h 45 min (if traffic is heavy and weather conditions are bad).

Let's turn this example into buying and selling financial instruments, or any other product. The product may have a ticket value, a willing buyer is likely to negotiate the price asked by a willing seller – unless the willing buyer cannot imagine life without the product or service he or she wants to acquire. Notice that variations to fair price are fuzzy sets, depending on how the negotiation goes.

- Such variations are not margin of error.
- They are a negotiating margin, inherent in any fair value.

Contrary to the flexibility and relative accuracy of the possibilistic model we have just been discussing, because of its emphasis on historical costs, which in most cases have become irrelevant, accruals accounting masks the true performance of a company – whether it is prosperous or in trouble. It is not historical costs but market valuations of a company's assets and liabilities which can be

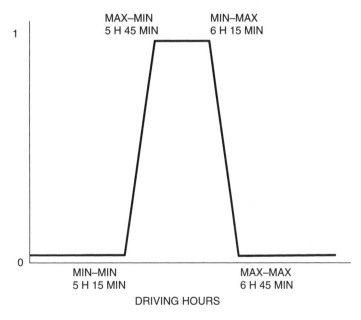

Figure 4.2 A possibility theory distribution: timeplan for driving from Monte Carlo to Lucerne over Gotthard

revealing to investors and regulators, though they could make entities with a deteriorating financial position show up their frail status.

Transparency never harmed anybody, if that body had nothing to hide. *If* many companies and (curiously enough) some heads of EU governments are uncomfortable with the way IAS 39 makes bad hedges transparent, it is because they have things to keep out of public view. By (correctly) obliging them to show the value of instruments they use, IFRS renders every stakeholder a great service. Politicians, however, have very short-term priorities, and the European Commission tried to brokerage a bad compromise by:

- Removing the requirement for companies to mark to market instruments used in hedging, and
- Deleting parts of the fair value option, to placate those who have good reasons (of hide and seek) to oppose it.

Experts say it is unclear how this EU version will work in practice. But most worrying for many in the accounting profession, as well as among regulators, is the precedent set by political interference in what should be an independent standard setting process. I had a professor at UCLA who taught his students that *if* you let a company choose its accounting system, *then* it can prove anything it likes.

Accounting standard and risk management rules should not be subject to *lobbying*. Political lust and greed is totally opposite to rationality. For instance, insurers are urging the IASB not to restrict the use of the fair value option too much. They say the IAS 39, post-EU interference, would make the fair value option difficult for them to apply. In essence, IASB is trying to strike a balance between:

- Allowing practical use of fair value, and
- Meeting the concerns of insurance firms who keep their hedges (read: speculations) close to their chest.

It is indeed most interesting to notice that while some politicians, who do not necessarily understand much about accounting and fair value, declared themselves against IAS 39, European insurers have called on the International Accounting Standards Board to preserve it. In mid-January 2004, the Comité Européen des Assurances (CEA), which represents national associations of insurers in 32 European countries, criticized proposals to limit the fair value option.

The CEA wants the European Commission to enlarge the fair value option it has endorsed, with a workable alternative that would allow insurers to measure both financial assets and liabilities at fair value. On the other side of the fence one finds the European Union's internal market Commissioner; and other politicians. The Commissioner warned whoever would listen that the drawing up of standards was 'not just a technical exercise', adding: 'There is a question: What is the political accountability in this area?'[5]

A nice, simple, and accurate answer to this query is that *if* at the end of the 15th century Tuscany's politicians had interfered with the work of Luca Paciolo, we would not have had for more than 500 years a sound and functioning accounting system.[6] It is the great wave of new, complex, and risky financial instruments which now makes mandatory the revision of the 1494 rules:

- This must be done in a sound and rigorous manner,
- Without the politicians making a mess out of it.

This case of political interference with accounting standards setting is serious – not only because European Commissioners are not elected officials, which makes a mockery of democracy. A statement once made by Rufus Choate, the great American lawyer, fits well situations like this: 'I should guess, from his bearings, that he is wondering whether God made him, or he made God!'[7]

It is, precisely, part of political accountability to explain the reasons of IAS 39 to companies that suddenly find that marking to market derivative instruments ends in major swings on corporate profitability. Behind the swings lies the fact that they have overloaded themselves with toxic waste. IAS 39 is only the messenger; and it is bad policy to shoot the messenger:

- Because derivatives are leveraged instruments, measuring fair value in the short term makes profit and loss results volatile.
- Since this is something the market dislikes, even if the P&L swing is positive, companies should be prudent to avoid derivatives overleveraging.

Indeed, the very positive result from implementation of IAS 39 is that it brings the hazardous use of derivatives instruments, by many firms, to light. Some Italian industrial groups, not only Parmalat and its likes but also bureaucratic entities, provide an example of the aftermath of going bust for the sake of 'good-looking profit figures'.

When in 2004 PriceWaterhouseCoopers replaced Ernst & Young as the certified public accountant of Poste Italiane, Italy's state-controlled post monopoly, it implemented IAS 39 on its statements for the last four years. This demonstrated that Poste Italiane had incurred a 104 million euro derivatives loss, mainly due to exotic swaps the bureaucrats had entered into in 2000.

- Most were quanto dollar swaps, a combination of interest and foreign exchange rates, and
- This is a derivative instrument well beyond the bureaucrats' skills or understanding of what they were doing.

When in December 1995 California's Orange County went bust, after having leveraged its $7.5 billion to $21.5 billion through collateralized mortgage obligations (CMOs) and other derivatives, the County's Treasurer and his associates were prosecuted. They stated something similar to their colleagues at Poste Italiane in their defence: that they did not understand the instruments. *If* one does not understand what one is doing, *then* better to go home (or to prison); one should not take other people's money to the edge.

6.   The March and July 2005 Draft of IAS 39

While the clauses of IAS 39 have been applied in financial statements since January 2005, this was done in the understanding they were still tentative. Negotiations were going on with the objective of finalizing them, and these negotiations were not easy because of widely varying viewpoints among stakeholders.

Mid-March 2005 it was reported that international accounting standards setters could endorse a revised version of the IAS 39 rule on financial instruments, after it won widespread support at a public meeting on 16 March. This rule proposes giving companies the discretion to show liabilities as well as assets at market value in accounts (what insurance companies asked for) – a choice that can have huge impact on:

- Earnings
- Balance sheets
- Credit ratings, and
- The ability to compare one balance sheet to another.

As stated in section 5, the European Commission objected to the original IAS 39 rules, and carved out parts from the international accounting standards which have been enforced in the European Union in 2005. The March 2005 version of IAS 39 threw the spotlight back on the Commission, as well as on the question of whether part of the carved-out clauses could or should be reinstated.

The final decision is a political one, and this is unfortunate because it means the balance would tilt to the position of the player who has more political clout. As it will be recalled, at the heart of the Commission's objection to the original IAS 39 rules is that marking to market assets and taking at book value liabilities creates an accounting mismatch because historic cost is not matched to market value.

If this is really the European Commission's thesis it is a self-defeating one, because its argument simply acknowledges that market prices, hence fair value, are better than historical costs. Presumably, under the pressure of covert interests, the EU Commission was publicly supporting exactly the reverse, failing to take the proverbial long, hard look.

For their part, regulators have been worried that companies could use fair value accounting to manipulate earnings – which is nothing new, because through creative accounting companies manipulate earnings anyway, EBITDA being an example.[8] In spite of this concern, however, European regulators appeared to back the new version of IAS 39, though representatives from Australia expressed concern that earnings would not be comparable if some companies used fair values and others chose not to.[9]

The Australians are right. There is much to say about the ills of cherry picking, as we will see in Chapter 10. For instance, *if* Vodafone was allowed to cherry pick (see the case study on Vodafone's IFRS results at the end of Chapter 3), then it would surely retain the pre-IFRS consolidation in financial reporting while there is no doubt it would choose to benefit from the new rules regarding goodwill.

Different financial institutions will be affected in different ways by compliant IAS 39 reporting, depending on the type and amount of their exposure. For instance, Deutsche Bank let it be known that it has 500 billion euro off-balancing for its most important customers, a large amount of which may have to be brought on balance sheet.

The aftermath of IAS 39 as a result of special exposure characterizing the banking sector, led the Basel Committee to take a good look at the new accounting standards. The July 2005 Basel document, mentioned in the Introduction, states that the purpose of the IAS 39 *fair value option* was to simplify its application which imposes a mixed-attribute measurement model on financial instruments because under IAS 39,

- Some financial assets and liabilities must be measured at fair value, and
- Other assets and liabilities must be measured under the method of amortized cost.

Basel's supervisory guidance brings the banks' attention to the fact that the mixed-attribute model of IAS 39 'requires derivatives to be recognized on the balance sheet as either assets or liabilities at their fair value, regardless of whether a hedged item is held at fair value.'

Many experts agree that the fact changes in fair value of derivatives are recorded directly in profit and loss is a sound principle. The July 2005 document by Basel impresses on bank management that in applying the fair value option to illiquid instruments credit institutions should employ a more rigorous valuation process than the one typically used for liquid instruments.

The Basel Committee on Banking Supervision is right to be concerned about the fine print, because starting in the go-go 1990s, banks have cornered themselves into trading book positions with no active reference market. As the histogram in Figure 4.3 shows, interest rate derivatives have the highest frequency closely followed by credit derivatives (mainly a 21st century huge market) and equity derivatives. How a highly paid (and skilled) top management in commercial

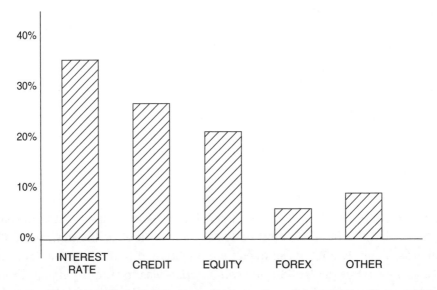

Figure 4.3   Classes of trading book positions with no active reference market (*Source:* Statistics by Basel Committee on Banking Supervision)

banks, investment banks, and insurance companies committed that sort of blunder is a mystery.

This blunder, however, does not mean that regulators and accounting standards setters could, or should, close their eyes to such ineptitude – and the Mount Everest of risk it has piled up. Even guarantees given by one derivatives gambler to another are rather meaningless because:

- Protection buyer, and
- Protection seller have exposure to nearly the same big risks.

AIS 39 includes rules for *financial guarantees* that provide for payments to be made in response to changes in a specified variable such as price, rate, or index. These are derivatives within the scope of the new rules, but guarantees are not derivatives, and therefore are excluded from IAS 39 *only* if they provide for specified payments, for instance, payments to be made to reimburse holders for a loss they incur because a specified debtor fails to make payment when due. IAS 39 states that such 'excluded' guarantees:

- Must be initially recognized at fair value, and
- Subsequently recognized at the higher of two alternatives.

By contrast, loan commitments are outside the scope of IAS 39 if they cannot be settled net in cash or another financial instrument; they are not designated as financial liabilities at fair value through profit or loss; and the credit institution does not have a past practice of selling the loans that resulted from the commitment shortly after origination. This will drop from the exclusion clause if the bank securitizes its loans – a fast-growing practice.

By contrast, contracts to buy or sell financial items and non-financial items are within the scope of IAS 39. Financial items are always under AIS 39. Non-financial items interest AIS 39 if they can be settled net in cash or another financial asset and some other conditions.

Notes

1 Basel Committee, 'Supervisory Guidance on the Use of the Fair Value Option by Banks under IFRS' (Consultative Document), BIS, July 2005, Basel.
2 *The Economist*, 6 March 2004.
3 D.N. Chorafas, *Economic Capital Allocation with Basel II: Cost and Benefit Analysis*, Butterworth-Heinemann, Oxford and Boston, 2004.
4 D.N. Chorafas, *Chaos Theory in the Financial Markets*, Probus, Chicago, 1994.

5   *The Financial Times*, 17 January 2005.
6   For evident reasons, a somewhat less nice answer would be that 'political accountability' is an unknown quantity.
7   Claude M. Fuess, *Rufus Choate, the Wizard of the Law*, Minton, Bald & Co, New York, 1928.
8   D.N. Chorafas, *Management Risk. The Bottleneck Is at the Top of the Bottle*, Macmillan/Palgrave, London, 2004.
9   *The Financial Times*, 17 March 2005.

IAS 39 and the Recognition
of Derivatives Risk

1. Introduction

The Basel Committee has addressed two areas of supervisory guidance closely connected to IAS 39. The one is best defined by the issue of what constitutes sound risk management, and associated exposure control processes, under the fair value principle. The other is the broader domain of how a bank's use of fair value might affect supervisory assessment of the institution's:

- Regulatory capital, and
- Risk management system.[1]

This is an area which lies at the junction of responsibility of IASB and BCBS, and it concerns all financial instruments. The International Accounting Standards Board defines a *financial instrument* as a contract that gives rise to a financial asset of one entity and a financial liability, or equity, of another entity. Examples of financial instruments are cash, demand and time deposits, commercial paper, leases, accounts, notes, loans receivable and payable, rights and obligations with insurance risk under insurance contracts, employers' rights and obligations under pension contracts, debt and equity securities, asset back securities, and derivatives.

IASB defines a *derivative* as a financial instrument whose value changes in response to a change in the price of an *underlying* such as an interest rate, commodity, security, or index. A derivative typically requires no initial investment, or one that is smaller than would be needed for a contract with similar response to changes in market factors. Moreover, the derivatives contract is settled at a future date.

This is a more generic definition than the earlier one which first came in the 1980s and looked at derivatives as instruments with characteristics such as exchange-traded futures and over the counter (OTC) forwards, options, caps and floors, interest rate swaps (IRS), and forward rate agreements (FRAs). Over the years, the range of derivative products has grown, and it continues growing; hence, the need for generic definition.

Embedded derivatives are one of the issues of interest in the present chapter. Some contracts that themselves are not financial instruments may have financial instruments embedded in them. This is the case of a contract to purchase a commodity at a fixed price for delivery at a future date. Such a contract has embedded in it a derivative that is indexed to the price of the commodity, which is essentially a derivative feature within a contract that is not a financial derivative. IAS 39 requires that under certain conditions an embedded derivative is separated from its host contract and treated as a derivative instrument.

Derivative financial instruments are typically illiquid, and many are simply gambles on some future value which is absolutely impossible to predict at present. Such is the case of 30-year interest rate swaps. Many of these instruments are based on rough guesstimates and wishful thinking, and turn out to be a sort of *financial toxic waste* in the portfolio of the company which traded them.

Because the large majority of derivative products (some 75–80% of them) are traded outside of official exchanges, in the form of bilateral deals between two counterparties, nobody really knows the actual dimension of toxic waste in the banks' trading books – including the financial institutions who own them. Banks aside, a substantial amount of derivatives betting is done by *hedge funds*, which are not subject to any kind of regulation or supervision. According to the Bank for International Settlements (BIS),

- In early 2005 the outstanding volume of over the counter derivatives alone amounted to $248 trillion, while the annual turnover of exchange-traded derivatives is close to $900 trillion.
- If so, because exchange-traded derivatives account for about 22% of the total, the total of annually traded derivatives stands at more than $4 *quatrillion*, with some $3.2 quatrillion OTC.

This is akin to a financial hydrogen bomb with the power to blow the world's financial fabric to pieces many times over. Therefore, IASB is absolutely right to want all sorts of derivatives priced at fair value. That's the only way to learn which entity is bankrupt because of its derivatives exposure; indeed, when the value of inventoried derivatives is opaque, companies may be bankrupt without even knowing it.

This is not the first time accounting standards bodies have required that derivatives are fair value priced. In 1999, in the United States, FASB had issued SFAS 133 'Accounting for Derivatives Instruments and Hedging Activities' which is currently part of US GAAP. All American companies today are reporting in accordance with SFAS 133, and its corresponding amendments under SFAS 138. SFAS 133 requires measurement of all derivative financial instruments, including those embedded in other contracts, at fair value.[2] Also, to recognize them in the consolidated balance sheet as:

- An asset
- Or a liability, depending on rights or obligations under the applicable derivative contract.

For derivatives designated as fair value hedges (see section 3), the changes in fair value of both the derivative instrument and the hedge item are recorded in other income (expense), net. For derivatives designated as cash flow hedges, the effective portions of changes in the fair value of the derivative are reported in other comprehensive income (OCI), and subsequently reported in other income (expense), net when the hedged item affects other income (expense), net.

Under US GAAP, changes in the fair value of derivatives not designated as hedging instruments and ineffective portions of hedges are recognized in other income (expense), net in the period incurred. There is absolutely no reason why European and Asian companies should be given a blank cheque to bring the global financial system to bankruptcy by gambling with derivative instruments whose value is unknown.

2. AIS 39's approach to hedges made through derivatives

The regulators are tasked with keeping the financial ship afloat. IAS 39 is a good example of carefully written rules commensurate with the risks being assumed today by all sorts of companies, and most particularly by financial institutions. At root, it is a strong accounting standard related to truly hedging portfolio risk, and this is the reason why it is resented by some institutions.

Well-managed companies do appreciate that they need a strong accounting standard rather than a weak one, because the latter can lead them into trouble. Therefore, to a rather significant degree, underlying the arguments advanced against IAS 39 lies the fact that banks have different degrees of:

- Appreciation of their exposure, and
- Sophistication in their risk management solutions.

IAS 39 is not the only component part of IFRS to represent a well-crafted set of accounting rules fitting our epoch. Another example of a higher level of stewardship connected to accounting standards is provided by IAS 32 (see Chapter 4). IAS 32 states that *if* an instrument includes both debt and equity characteristics, *then* these must be separated in accounting into:

- Debt, and
- Equity.

As an example, convertible bonds must be separated into debt and equity parts. If the convertible bond is redeemable, then it is debt. If it is perpetual, it is equity. Underlying this accounting rule is the bifurcation associated with financial instruments depending on intent. The pattern can be seen in Figure 5.1.

A similar approach to careful distinction between items that look alike but are not the same prevails under AIS 39. Derivatives such as options, futures, forwards, interest rate swaps and currency swaps are products meeting the definition of a financial instrument. However, FRS rules specify that a purchased call option, or other similar contract acquired by an entity that gives it the right to *reacquire* a fixed number of its own *equity*, is not a financial asset of the entity.

Reacquisition along the lines described in the preceding paragraph may take place in exchange for delivering a fixed amount of cash, or another financial asset. The reason for the aforementioned distinction lies in the fact that any consideration paid for such a contract is deducted from equity.

Because today's financial instruments are complex, if a light approach is taken in handling them, these will lead to confusion. To provide the proper basis, IFRS rules state that derivative financial instruments create *rights* and *obligations* that have the effect of transferring between counterparties one or more of the financial risks.

- These risks are inherent in an underlying primary financial instrument, and
- For that reason they qualify as risk elements in financial instruments, in IFRS reporting.

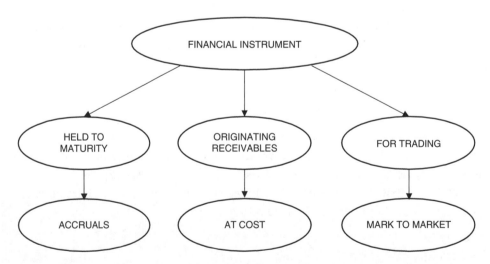

Figure 5.1   Different accounting rules address the way in which a financial instrument is handled

This is consistent with the fact that IAS 39 defines a derivative as a financial instrument whose value changes in response to the change in the underlying, but more so because of leverage. Leveraging comes from the fact:

- A derivatives transaction requires either no initial investment, or a small investment, and
- The derivatives contract is typically settled at a future date.

Sophisticated approaches to accounting are necessary because, in principle, all derivative contracts with a counterparty may be designated as hedging instruments (except for some written options). By contrast, an external non-derivative financial asset, or liability, may not be designated as a hedging instrument except as a hedge of foreign currency risk.

In the general case, specific cash flows inherent in a derivative cannot be designated in a hedge relationship while, according to IAS 39, other cash flows are excluded. But *intrinsic value* and *time value* of an option contract may be separated, with only the intrinsic value being designated as a hedge.

In their normal course of business, companies do different types of *hedges* to protect themselves from market moves – at least theoretically so. Hence the need for *hedge accounting*, which is examined in section 3. Some of these hedges are for interest rate risk management. An example is fair value hedges through interest rate swap agreements to:

- Control exposure to interest rate movements, and
- Achieve a mix of floating and fixed-rate debt, while trying to minimize liquidity risk.

Interest rate swaps designated as fair value hedges effectively convert fixed-rate debt to floating rate, by receiving fixed rate amounts in exchange for floating rate interest payments over the life of the agreement. This is done without an exchange of the underlying principal amount. That sort of hedge may be addressing the firm's current risk but the reader should appreciate that the hedge itself involves risk, and this could affect profit and loss. IAS 39 specifies that:

- The gain or loss from the change in fair value of the hedging instrument is recognized immediately in profit or loss, and
- The carrying amount of the hedged item is adjusted for the corresponding gain or loss with respect to hedged risk, which is also recognized immediately in net P&L.

Alternatively, the company may enter into cash flow hedges through interest rate swap agreements. These aim to reduce the impact of interest rate movements on future interest expense, by converting a portion of its floating-rate debt to a fixed-rate. But there is risk behind a cash flow hedge:

- Attributable to a particular exposure associated with a recognized asset or liability, and
- Likely to affect profit and loss at some future period specified by the contract.

With IAS 39, the portion of the gain or loss on the hedging instrument that is determined to be an effective hedge is recognized directly in equity and recycled to the income statement when the hedged cash transaction affects profit or loss. But if the hedged cash flow(s) result(s) in recognition of a non-financial asset or liability, the entity can choose to adjust the basis of the asset or liability for the amount deferred in equity.

A company may also have foreign exchange hedges. These can be part of its currency exchange risk management programme, on reducing transaction exposure in connection to consolidated cash flow. A transaction exposure may result from payments made to, and received from, overseas companies and, as such, it could be material to the consolidated financial position.

Alternatively, there may be a hedge of a net investment in foreign operation or some other commitment in foreign currency, to be accounted for as a fair value hedge or cash flow hedge. IAS 39 provides clear rules for fair value hedge accounting for portfolio hedges (macro-hedging).

Practically all of the examples we have seen in this section on legitimate hedging activities, and their instruments, may involve considerable risk, even if such positions are taken for exposure management reasons. Therefore, the marking to market fair value option specified by IAS 39 must be applied to any derivative financial instrument. If my understanding is correct,

- Central bankers and regulators want to strengthen this definition, making this information transparent for market discipline reasons.
- By contrast, commercial bankers do not want the new rule, even if it is to their interest to know their exposure, in order to be in charge of it.

A very useful feature of IAS 39 is that it provides a procedural hierarchy on how to determine fair value. Marking to model is a possibility, but as Warren Buffett states, sometimes marking to model becomes synonymous to marking to myth. A sound rule is that when one cannot see a price in the active market, one must be very reasonable – indeed, quite conservative in fair value estimates. This is most important with IAS 39 because:

- It specifies that all derivatives must be marked to market, and
- It provides accounting rules for hedging all the way to treatment of core deposits (demand deposit accounts, DDAs).

Another major improvement of IAS over past and parochial accounting standards is that the latter have been principally concerned with registering historical numbers – not real economic and financial decisions which affect the company's future. For a long time, the emphasis on past cost has been an accepted accounting practice, but in a market characterized by globalization, deregulation, innovation, and rapid technological development reliance on past numbers can be self-destructive.

3. The art of hedge accounting

In principle, but only in principle, hedging aims to reduce the risk on a *hedged* instrument by combining it with a *hedging* instrument. In reality there are risks inherent in both hedged and hedging instruments depending, to a large extent, on the way the market turns. The hedging instrument may be an option, forward, future or swap.

- Theoretically, through hedging, value changes in one instrument are offset by value changes in the other instrument.
- Practically, this is never the case, because the behaviour of the hedged and hedging instruments is quite often *asymmetric*.

Moreover, if different accounting valuation methods are used for the different instruments, for instance historical cost and accruals for the hedged item and marking to market for the hedging, this will result in volatility in the profit and loss account. Hence the use of a specific accounting treatment, known as *hedge accounting*.

The process of hedge accounting is fairly sophisticated and one must pay attention to it. For this reason project management for IFRS conversion, in Chapter 6, singles out hedge accounting as a major sub-project. The Introduction made reference to hedge accounting under IAS 39, saying that it provides two key methods companies can choose from:

- 1. *Fair value hedges*, which aim at controlling exposure(s) to changes in fair value of a recognized asset or liability.

Under IAS 39, fair value hedging is permitted only for micro-hedges.

- 2. *Cash flow hedges*, for which evidence must be furnished of a sufficient volume of variable future cash flows for the hedging relationship.

There exist specific circumstances under which cash flow hedges, whose objective is that of controlling exposure to variability in future cash flows from the hedged item, may not be the best way (more on this later).

As should be expected, for both methods IAS 39 requires a high degree of effectiveness as well as comprehensive formal documentation of the hedging relationship. Hedge accounting is permitted, if specific conditions prevail, and the process focuses on the hedging relationship which should be expected to be:

- Effective in achieving offsetting changes in fair value or cash flows attributable to hedged risk, and
- Formally designated and documented, including the company's risk management objective(s) and strategy for undertaking the hedge.

In terms of its mechanics, hedge accounting works in two ways. It either defers the recognition of losses, or brings forward the recognition of gains in the profit and loss statement. In this manner, gain or loss from the hedged instrument is recognized at the same time as the offsetting gain or loss from the hedging instrument.

According to many experts, full fair value accounting does away with hedge accounting practice. But others think that hedge accounting has a role to play in the modern firm. To avoid situations where hedging relationships are identified ex post to deliberately massage profits and losses, the International Accounting Standards Board laid down a number of specific requirements to qualify for hedge accounting. The most important are:

- A hedging relationship is clearly identified and documented at inception
- Such relationships must be conceived in an effective manner, and
- The after-effect of the hedge must be highly probable, if this is a forecasted transaction.

The message conveyed by these three bullets points is that a hedge can only qualify for hedge accounting if it passes *identification, effectiveness and after-effect tests*. For instance, in terms of effectiveness changes in the value of the hedged and the hedging instruments should almost fully offset each other at designation. That is:

- Relatively easy to do when planning a hedge
- But very difficult to realize at the end, where it really counts.

Asymmetries between hedged and hedging instruments can turn the hedge on its head. In addition, according to IAS 39, actual results realized over the life of the hedge must remain within a narrow margin in order for it to continue to be considered effective. This is a precondition for hedge accounting. Benefits from hedge accounting can be achieved if and when countervailing changes in value cancel each other in terms of amount. This will depend greatly on:

- The quality of the hedge
- The way in which it is implemented, and
- Market(s) behavior, which is beyond the control of the entity making the hedge.

Moreover, it is important to notice that not all instruments qualify for hedge accounting. IAS 39 clearly states that a hedge item can be a single recognized asset or liability, firm commitment, highly likely forecast transactions, or net investment in a foreign operation. A hedge might also be a group of assets, liabilities under the same conditions outlined in the preceding sentence – or a held-to-maturity investment for foreign currency or credit risk, but not for interest risk or prepayment risk.

Also qualifying for a hedge is a portion of cash flows of a financial asset or financial liability at fair value; or a non-financial item for hedging foreign currency risk as well as a macro-hedge. Hedging may also concern a portion of the portfolio of financial assets, or financial liabilities, that share the risk being hedged. These are the items to be most carefully studied for hedge accounting in an IFRS implementation project, like the one discussed in Chapter 6.

IAS 39 does not permit strategies based on hedging entire portfolios, and this is for a good reason. Such strategies could easily degenerate into king-size gambles. Additionally, under IFRS only hedging transactions with third parties are eligible for recognition. Internal contracts within a company or group do not qualify for hedge accounting.

Even with these constraints, hedge accounting is important to banks because it permits them to defer putting gains and losses on derivatives through their income statements. The problem, however, is that many 'hedges' through derivatives are nothing more than risky gambles. Regulators are aware of this; that is why many countries already have in place, since the late 1990s, legislation requiring banks to report on recognized but not yet realized gains and losses.

- The United States did so through the Statement of Financial Accounting Standards 133.
- The UK through the Statement of Recognized Gains and Losses (STRGL).

- Switzerland, by obliging banks to report 'other assets' and 'other liabilities', which is essentially recognized gains and losses from derivatives contracts.

It is also appropriate to take notice that IAS 39 provides rules for *discontinuation* of hedge accounting. Hedge accounting must be discontinued if the hedging instrument expires or is sold, terminated, or exercised; the hedge no longer meets the outlined hedge accounting criteria.

For cash flow hedges, hedge accounting must be discontinued *if* the projected transaction is no longer expected to occur; or the company revokes the hedge's designation. Also, there is no sense in doing hedge accounting when the item to be hedged is one that would normally not be recorded at fair value, because the rules allow that it is held at cost less impairment.

Keeping all these issues in mind, one can make the statement that IAS 39 *hedge accounting* permits a company to mitigate some risks *if* it succeeds in being fully compliant with specified hedge criteria. The better managed banks chose to apply hedge accounting whenever they meet these criteria, so that their financial statements clearly reflect the economic hedge effect obtained from the use of hedging instruments which should normally be accounted for at fair value.

Differences and discrepancies between fair values of hedged and hedging instruments will affect P&L even if, over the whole life of the instrument, they might be expected to balance out. Therefore, senior management should appreciate that applying hedge accounting means that changes in fair values of designated hedging instruments do affect reported profit and loss in a given period. This can happen not only to the extent that a hedge is ineffective, but also because of market reasons.

4. Being prudent with embedded derivatives

The notion underpinning *embedded derivatives* has been explained in the Introduction. According to IAS 39 rules, they must be accounted for at fair value with changes in fair value recorded in the income statement. There are, however, some minor exceptions. For example, for the insurance industry, Phase I (see Chapter 2) exempts derivatives from measurement at fair value:

- *If* the derivative itself is regarded as an insurance contract, or
- *If* it is closely related to the host insurance contract.

Some people, and in fact whole industries, like exceptions. By majority, however, exceptions are borderline cases, and decisions concerning them may be erroneous. In this specific case, exceptions are difficult to define because an embedded derivative is a feature within a contract, while cash flows associated with that feature may behave in a way similar to a standalone derivative.

Not only in banking but also in insurance and other financial industry sectors, contracts that do not entirely meet the definition of a derivative instrument may contain embedded derivatives in implicit terms. These affect some or all of the cash flows required by the contract. Such hybrid instruments are used because:

- They could double the investor's initial rate of return,
- But they also involve increased risks for both counterparties.

An example is a contract to purchase a commodity at fixed price for delivery at a future date, which has embedded in it a derivative that is indexed to the price of the commodity. According to IAS 39, that derivative even if not standalone, must be accounted for at fair value on the balance sheet, with changes recognized in profit and loss.

IAS 39 further requires that an embedded derivative be separated from its host contract and accounted for as a derivative when (i) economic risks and (ii) characteristics of the embedded derivative are not closely related to those of the host contract. Or a separate instrument with the same terms as the embedded derivative would meet the definition of a derivative,

- *If* an embedded derivative is separated,
- *Then* the host contract is accounted for under the appropriate standard.

Examples of embedded derivatives which are not closely related to their hosts, and therefore must be separately accounted for, are commodity indexed interest or principal payments in host debt contracts; equity conversion options in debt convertible to ordinary shares from the perspective of the holder; leveraged inflation adjustments to lease payments and commodity indexed interest or principal payments; in host debt contracts, and more.

An interesting case is currency derivatives in purchase or sale contracts for non-financial instruments where the foreign currency is not that of either counterparty to the contract, and is not the currency in which the related good or service is routinely denominated in commercial transactions. Or, it is not the currency commonly used in such contracts in the environment in which the relevant transaction takes place.

IAS 39 rules specify that separation of the derivatives part must take place; a separate instrument with the same terms as the embedded derivative would meet the definition of a derivative; and the economic risks and characteristics of the embedded derivative are not closely related to those of the host contract.

- *If* IAS 39 requires that an embedded derivative be separated from its host contract, but the company is unable to treat the embedded derivative separately,
- *Then* the entire combined contract must be handled as a financial asset or financial liability held for trading.

It is only normal that new accounting standards reflect on, and indeed facilitate, the handling of embedded derivatives and other issues with hybrid characteristics and with prerequisites which, so far, have not been of a commonly encountered nature. As such, the contribution IAS 39 makes is significant. It is part of the rule that rigorous accounting standards should address domains such as:

- Compliance
- Financial responsibility
- Interpretation of facts and numbers
- Role of auditors, and
- Role of regulators.

The need for compliance to rules and regulations is too evident to be discussed in this book. In connection to the second bullet point, it is advisable to recall that board directors, and most particularly the CEO and CFO, are personally responsible for the content of their company's financial statement. As the 2002 Sarbanes–Oxley Act explicitly states (see Chapter 11), CEOs and CFOs cannot wash their hands of this accountability.

Precisely because the threshold of personal accountability has been significantly upped, American companies are now hiring experts in scrutinizing the contents of financial statements, including classes of objects that usually got a lower degree of attention from accountants as well as internal and external auditors. This change is for the better.

5. IAS 39 as an agent of risk management

No gambler ever hankered for the feverish delight of the gaming table as much as some banks are doing today in trading among themselves, and with hedge funds, novel, obscure, and highly risky derivative financial instruments. Only fair value accounting can lift the veil of secrecy surrounding derivatives gains and losses.

IAS 39 and other vital parts of IFRS target the accounting side of the art and science of risk management. To appreciate that point one should recall there are two sides in the equation of capital and enterprise: the cost of capital, and its exposure to potential loss because of misjudging risk and return. The cost of capital is set by the market; the risk to which capital is confronted is defined by the amount of exposure being assumed.

- A greater volatility indicates higher but also more uncertain return, with its counterpart being the likelihood of higher losses.
- Uncertainty plays an important role in addressing the risk involved in business transactions. With derivatives, risks are generally shifted toward the more uncertain future.

IFRS would not have been worth its salt if it did not contain the needed accounting tools and methods for mapping uncertainty and risk embedded in inventoried portfolio positions. 'The growth and complexity of off-balance-sheet activities and the nature of credit, price and settlement risk they entail, should give us all cause of concern,' said Gerald Corrigan, former president of the New York Federal Reserve.

Other well-known financial experts expressed similar opinions. C. Feldberg, also of the New York Fed, was to suggest that 'Sophisticated trading strategies and complex instruments, by their nature, require robust risk management and controls.' The way I look at IAS 39, it is as a tool aiming to answer Corrigan's and Feldberg's concerns. In a compliance sense, good accounting standards provide the necessary initiative for tracking assumed exposure, by putting a price tag on it.

Problems must be identified when they are still small before becoming a torrent; and damage control must be exercised nearly in real time. Looking at risks 'later on' is too late. As Alexander Lamfalussy, former general manager of the Bank for International Settlements and of the European Monetary Institute (today European Central Bank), once said: 'There might never be a problem. But – and it is a big but – if there were, it would be a very big problem.' This will be the time when the gaming table is overturned.

The world's financial system, which serves everybody – not just the banking industry and the hedge funds – cannot afford taking that sort of mega-risk.

Moreover, the result of deregulation is that governments move away from the position of lender of last resort, and companies now need to capitalize to protect themselves and their clients. One of the results of deregulation is that risk is transferred to the private sector.

- The cost of managing risk(s) is thereby moved to the individual firm, and
- Each entity must compete for funds required to finance future growth, as well as to protect itself from exposure(s) taken in the past.

As Eskil Ullberg has it, 'This situation creates an interesting "battle" for capital in the financial markets. Different instruments may be needed to separate these in different risks and invite investors with the right risk appetite, in order to create an efficient financing mechanism.' The size of the risk appetite should be quantified, and IAS 39 helps in doing so.

With reference to the insurance industry, Ullberg poses the question: 'How can we strike a balance here that both protects the policyholders and meets the needs to free up capital needed for economic growth, without introducing any additional systemic risks in the financial system at the same time?' And he responded to his query in seven words: 'The answer may be in the market.'[3]

This is precisely where IAS 39 is of assistance. It helps (indeed, it prompts) companies to assess the market – and then to report to the market by means of reliable financial statements. This is a two-way process, while at the same time market values give the company's own management a snapshot on risk and return.

Of course, the accounting rules IAS 39, and IFRS at large, while necessary are not enough. To succeed in managing their risks in an effective way and at acceptable cost, new knowledge-enriched mechanisms need to be developed. The real-time balance sheet presented in Chapter 15 is an example.

Even rudimentary tools, like value-at-risk (VAR), may be of assistance as alarm mechanisms.[4] Figure 5.2, from the 2004 Annual Report of the Bank for International Settlements (BIS), presents to the reader a dramatic picture: In less than 3 years the value at risk exposure of major investment banks has doubled – and the lion's share of it is in instruments involving interest rate risk.

Every bank must examine its interest rate risk figures in significant detail, because credit institutions could be affected by changes in interest rates in several ways. In their banking books, they may be exposed to fixed rate loans, and in their trading book to IRSs, FRAs, and other instruments.

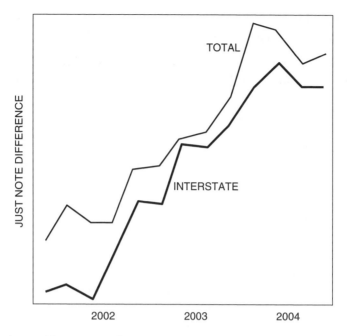

Figure 5.2   Value at risk exposure of major investment banks in the 2002–2004 timeframe (*Source:* Bank for International Settlements, Annual Report 2004, Basel)

Mismatch, or repricing risk, is the risk that banks' interest expenses will increase by more than interest receivables when interest rates change. Its origin lies in the maturity mismatches between assets and liabilities. To better appreciate the deeper meaning of this exponentially growing type of exposure, it is proper to bring to the reader's attention that even in ordinary daily practice, many balance sheets are left exposed to interest rate risk, because:

- Changes in short-term and long-term interest rates happen all the time, and
- These translate into a change in net present value (NPV) of their liabilities, which is a most challenging issue.

In order to lessen the impact of interest rate risk, assets backing the liabilities should be chosen so that they broadly match the duration and convexity of these liabilities.[5] This is, however, an 'ideal' solution; therefore, one which is easier said than done. The principle is known; the challenge is to execute it.

The market does not necessarily offer all possibilities one might wish to have in doing the 'ideal' balancing. At least not every day. For instance, in Euroland there are few bonds available with maturities beyond 10 years, making difficult the elimination of balance sheet interest rate sensitivities. One way is to turn to equities, often with a dual objective:

- Trying to emulate assets for long-term hedge of liabilities, and
- Attempting to increase the yields on the investment portfolio.

Killing two birds with one well-aimed stone happens sometimes in children's stories, but not in real business life. Some entities react to their growing balance sheet mismatches by seeking higher returns in the credit *derivatives* market, which is a different gamble. In the aftermath, their portfolio becomes more risky, and

- When equity markets tumble, as had happened in 2000,
- The losses on equity holdings strain the company's solvency, and its reserves are eroded.

Financial institutions who would like to avoid, or at least prognosticate, adverse effects on their balance sheet, must monitor their exposure to interest rate changes very carefully, doing so at least daily and running stress tests which include the after-effect of changes in interest rates. IAS 39 provides the raw material for such tests (see also Chapter 16).

For instance, a common stress test is to assess the impact on the balance sheet of an upturn in long-term interest rates of the magnitude seen in 1994, when yields on US 10-year bonds increased from 5.8% in January to 8.1% in November – or 230 basis points. Credit institutions may also be exposed to *valuation risk* on their investment and trading portfolio, as well as to the risk of an adverse impact of interest rate changes on the:

- Credit quality and ability of customers to service debt
- The evolution of demand for credit
- Basis risk, which arises from imperfect correlation in the adjustment of rates earned and paid on different instruments with otherwise similar repricing characteristics, and
- Optionality, such as prepayment, within the banking book, or in connection to off-balance-sheet items.

Measuring *valuation risk* in the banking book requires detailed information on remaining maturities as well as purchasing prices. It is also necessary to assess valuation risks in fixed income trading portfolios. Both types of information are rather scarce at the present, but the fact of compliance to accounting standards by IAS 39 is an added stimulus for senior managers to require that their immediate assistants provide better and better results of the type discussed in this section.

6. IAS 39 and alternative investments: a case study

Of the three major risks addressed by the new Basel Committee Capital Adequacy Framework (Basel II), *credit risk* is associated to the counterparty's ability or willingness to face up to its contractual obligations; *market risk* is due to volatility in interest rates, exchange rates, equity prices, and other variables; *operational risk* is involved in financial transactions and/or the management of assets, including fraud, execution risk, legal risk, and technology risk.

Exposure is also a function of the *type of loss* that is covered; for instance life, fire, and accident insurance. And there are also other risks to account for, some of which fall at the junction of the above mentioned classes. An example is *pricing risk*, a hybrid of market risk and operational risk. What all these risks have in common is that:

- A certain event is probable, but *not* certain
- Risk is the cost of this uncertainty, and *return* is the reward provided to whomsoever faces it in an able manner.

Risk and return are related because there is no significant gain without the ability to overcome adversity. In the general case, the doors of risk and of return are adjacent and identical. Therefore, the first step in overcoming adversity is identifying fundamental risk factors, and establishing metrics and determining linkages. This is precisely what IAS 39 requires that companies do for their financial reporting.

But which companies? The answer is companies quoted in public exchanges where their equities are traded: tapping the capital market for funds (equity or debt); being regulated, and being under steady supervision. Regulatory authorities have the mission to keep publicly quoted companies under close watch, and modern risk-sensitive accounting standards are the cornerstone in this edifice.

But there are also financial companies that are not regulated. Some of them are small, and their failure would not do much damage to the global financial system, though it would hurt their clients. Others are big, indeed very big, because they balloon their capital through inordinate leveraging. The name all of them share in common is *hedge funds* – and they are not regulated (more on hedge funds and the regulatory loophole in section 7).

Leaving aside the fact that many banks, particularly investment banks, have become giant hedge funds, what interests us in this section is that the application of IAS 39 should be a 'must' not only by publicly quoted entities but by all companies – a statement that can be extended all the way to private investors. A case study helps in explaining the reason for this statement.

Wealthy investors with no expertise in risk management account for a good deal of the money that runs, and gets lost, into hedge funds coffers. The rest comes from banks, insurance companies, and even pension funds – who gamble with the savers' and pensioners' nest egg. In early June 2005, the Merrill Lynch/Cap Gemini World Wealth Report stated that 8.3 million people around the globe have more than $1 million each and try to find a home for it.

Again according to Merrill Lynch, the average wealthy person has 34% of his or her assets in equities, 27% in fixed income, 12% in cash, 13% in property and *14% in 'alternative investments'*,[6] like hedge funds and private equity. This gives a measure of the cash flow hedge funds get from private individuals – which they can superleverage through borrowing and trading games.

Since year 2000 private bankers have tried to sell their clients the idea that 20% of the wealth should be in alternative investments. How does that money fare? Table 5.1 presents a real-life case study on how investors are cheated by their bankers through alternative investments. The bait on the hook is 'capital protected'. These two words mean that the investor will get his money back at maturity of the issue, which typically is in 5, 6 or 7 years. During that period:

- The investor gets no interest whatsoever, and even at the low 3% one can do with investment-grade corporate bonds in the early 21st century, over 6 years this represents a compound loss of about 20% in earnings, and
- The investor also carries a good deal of credit risk, because if in these 6 years the bank providing capital protection goes bust, which can happen, there is no more capital protection to talk about and the invested capital goes up in smoke.

As in the case of permanent paradise after death, the investor is of course told to wait till the end of the 6-year period for the 'profits'. And like in the case of an after-life garden of Eden, this is silly. The best test is marking to market at the end of the first year to find out if the alternative investments are indeed a 'good deal' or a cheat.

This is precisely what IAS 39 means when it stipulates that companies should mark to market their assets, for financial reporting purposes. And that is what I did with three alternative investments, as a test. As Table 5.1 shows, I bought from a very well-known global bank three of the many structured financial products

Table 5.1 Cheating investors through popularized derivatives. A case study

	Market Values				Alternative Investments			
'Alternative Investment'	Start value at beginning of term	Current value (12.7.05)	Difference in points	Difference in %	When bought	On 12.7.05	Investor gain/loss	Final difference to investor disfavour
'CPU SMI' Zurich Stock Exchange	5693	6323	Up 630	+11.1%	100	101–102	1%	−10.1%
'Certificate Plus Nikkei' Tokyo Stock Exchange	11 488	11 623	Up 135	+1.0%	100	96–97	−4%	−5%

The 10% Bonus Coupon Note has no index for direct comparison. The bank who sold the 'alternative investment' says that over the elapsed year its overall performance was 6.80%. What investors got was 1.37% – a difference of 5.43% to their disfavour.

they tried to sell me over the years. This credit institution, like practically all of its competitors, has hundreds of different structured derivatives in its inventory for sale to investors. Of those I chose:

- One bet on the Zurich stock exchange
- Another bet on the Tokyo stock exchange, and
- A third one on a basket of 20 American, European and Japanese stocks.

The 'Bet on SMI', a structured derivative product,[7] was sold by the bank as an 'interesting *defensive* alternative' to direct investment in the Swiss equity market. The 'how it works' documentation said that the investor participates at maturity 100% in the overall performance, which corresponds to the development of the Swiss Market Index (SMI), with a cap at 4.00% per year. This means that the 100% participation is a lie, because if the SMI rises 11% in a year, the investor in the derivative instrument will only get 4%.

The bet on Nikkei 225, also a structured derivative, was advertised and sold as an 'interesting alternative' to a direct investment in the underlying Japanese index. The catch was the *knock-out*. This meant that *if* the Nikkei at least once reaches a specified knock-out level during the instrument's entire lifespan, *then* the investor will not get a minimum repayment as his or her asset would then be fully exposed to any decline in the index. So much for capital protection, even excluding credit risk.

In fact, as the reader can see in Figure 5.3, in the 1999–2004 timeframe the Nikkei 225 nearly hit the knock-out level, which would have meant that the house (in this case the bank issuing the alternative investment) would have collected a good part of the investors' money laid on the table. It should also be noticed that an investor in these supposedly 'PLUS' derivative instruments has no claims to any dividends distributed by the companies represented in the Swiss Market Index (SMI) or in the Japanese Nikkei 225.

This evidently makes a mockery of the claim about an 'interesting defensive alternative'. Moreover, the daily price of these instruments was fixed by the same bank selling them, without access to an open market and in the absence of supervisory control – leaving the way open to all sorts of conflicts of interest. Under these conditions the 'opportunity' offered to the investor was between:

- Losing small, and
- Losing out the big way.

The third alternative investment has been a 10% Bonus Coupon Note. All considered, this was a better deal. Apart from the fact that the capital protection of

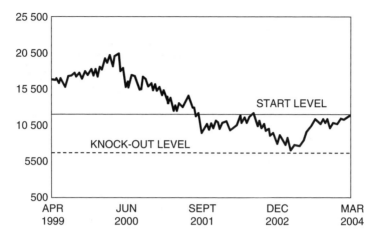

Figure 5.3   Nikkei 225 index performance in the 1999–2004 timeframe

100% at maturity was not constrained by a knock-out clause, it did offer partic-ipation in each single stock, up to a performance of 10% (quite superior to 4%). It also paid a minimal bonus coupon every year. In this case too, however, the interim price of the derivative security:

- Was not established by the open market
- It was set by the bank which had sold the security, and which was evi-dently interested in bringing water to its own mill.

As it can be attested from Table 5.1, a little over a year down the line all three bets did well, though Tokyo only slightly so. The SMI index rose an impressive 11.1%, but investors were cheated of their profits. Instead of gaining *at least* the advertised cap of 4%, all they got was 1% in the buyback price – established by the vendor bank itself. Figure 5.4 shows how much of investors' capital gains went up in smoke.

The Nikkei 225 did not perform so well, with the index gaining just 1%. But this was not true for the investor. As the reader can see in Table 5.1, investors *lost* 5%, namely the 1% they should have gained and 4% on drawing down the price of the instrument. From an investor's viewpoint, the case of the 10% bonds coupon was only slightly better (see Table 5.1). How can that happen? There are two reasons for it:

- 1. Since the design stage, the structured derivative instrument sold to the investor is loaded in the bank's favour.

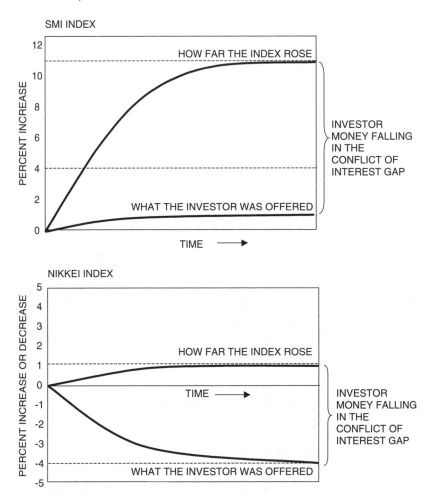

Figure 5.4 How investors in 'interesting defensive alternatives' have lost their reward

This means that the investor does not really stand a chance. The prospectus is so murky in its writing that even an expert cannot decipher what it says. Prior to buying, I asked for information, asking for word of honour that the SMI and Nikkei derivative instrument emulated the corresponding index – and got it. When the end-of-year test showed that this was not at all the case, the bank's words changed to: 'We didn't mean that ...'.

- 2. The bank who sold the 'alternative investments' made the market, there-fore it could decide whatever it wanted in terms of pricing, since nobody controls it – at least not until now.

Yet, the home country of this bank has adopted IFRS and IAS 39. Therefore, all instruments in its portfolio, and posted prices, should have been marked to market. Here is another important reason why marking-to-market is vital, and IAS 39 should be welcome as a rule. The problem is not that entities cannot price to market, but that in their pricing they have got one short leg and one long leg.

7. Closing the loophole of hedge funds

Alternative investments, the cases which have been discussed in section 6, are essentially structured derivatives deals, with leveraging and plenty of risk. Many are designed by hedge funds and marketed by banks to their clients. However, the name *hedge fund* is a misnomer, because what they really do is to speculate. There are also companies which are hedge funds but masquerade under a different label.

The bankrupt Enron was a hedge fund with a gas pipeline on the side.[8] Italy's also bankrupt Parmalat was a hedge fund under cover of dairy products.[9] In both cases, the window dressing was regulated, the huge gambles which took place in the background (carefully hidden from public eyes and supervisory scrutiny) were not. In neither case was the real size of the hedge fund side known, even in approximate figures of recognized gains and losses. Under these conditions the practice of leverage can take very large dimensions.

The leverage of hedge funds is typically a medium two-digit number; 50 is not unheard of. But there are exceptions. Before it crashed in September 1998, Long Term Capital Management (LTCM), also known as the Rolls-Royce of the hedge funds featuring a couple of Nobel prize winners, had an exposure of $1.4 trillion with a capital of $4 billion; this means a leverage of 350 or 35 000%.[10]

LTCM's exposure is an extreme event, but even when some hedge funds say that their leverage is 'only' 10 or 15 times their capital, they usually fail to account for the fact they are mostly running on bought money and that their derivatives trades significantly add to the leverage factor. Neither is LTCM the only hedge fund which went down the tubes. This happens quite often, particularly in the aftermath of financial events which make the speculators' bets unravel.

For instance, a major financial event came on 5 May 2005, when Standard & Poor's downgraded to junk $453 billion in outstanding debt of General Motors and Ford Motor Corporation. On Wall Street, some analysts said that General Motors crisis is:

- A national disaster for Corporate America, and
- It could actually detonate the world financial-monetary system because too many leveraged funds are overexposed to GM's and Ford's debt.

In the aftermath of this unprecedented downgrade, stock markets and bond markets suffered massive losses, particularly so after traders pointed to evidence of severe problems at several large hedge funds, as direct consequence of GM's and Ford's woes. The hedge funds mentioned in this respect included GLG Partners, Bailey Coates, Cromwell Fund, Marin Capital, Highbridge Capital, Sovereign Capital, and Asam Capital Management.

London-based GLG Partners had $13 billion under management, and it was listed as the largest hedge fund in Europe, and second largest in the world. On 10 May 2005, GLG issued a statement that 'All the funds are fine and we have no concern.' The market however was sceptical, and the same was true of the hedge fund's investors.

Also London-based Bailey Coates Cromwell Fund, established in July 2003, had $1.3 billion in capital plus another $2 billion in bank credits. Euro-Hedge, a private entity that tracks European hedge funds, suggested that by early June 2005 the capital of Bailey Coates imploded to $635 million. On 20 June management announced the fund's immediate liquidation.

California-based Marin Capital Fund was set up in 1999, raising $1.7 billion in capital. Its specialty was credit derivatives, a risky business.[11] The hedge fund made big bets with GM debt, lost out with the S&P downgrading, and mid-June 2005 management decided to liquidate the fund. (This is by no means the only gambler who bet on GM debt and lost.)

As was stated at a financial conference, Highbridge Capital wrote a letter to investors on 10 May 2005 noting: 'It is our understanding that recent volatility in the structured credit markets is apparently related to the unwinding of an unprofitable collateralized debt obligation (CDO) tranche correlation by one or more parties. ...' CDOs relieve banks of some of their credit risk by transferring it to entities who buy them – like insurance companies, pension funds, and hedge funds.

A year earlier, in 2004, Highbridge was bought by JP MorganChase. It is therefore part of a bigger group, as well as proof that commercial and investment banks own unregulated hedge funds. Sovereign Capital, a British hedge fund, is closely linked to Lazard Brothers. This fund is heavily involved in East Asian markets, and news of the possibility of its collapse caused panic among Asian bankers and investors.

These are no rare exceptions. According to Merrill Lynch, about 17 percent of Deutsche Bank's clients in its debt sales and trading business are hedge funds. When the bank was named as one of the victims of the GM/Ford fall-out, the bank's chief financial officer claimed that his institution's exposure is fully collateralized. However, according to its own 2004 Annual Report, Deutsche Bank at 2004 end held derivatives positions, mostly interest rate derivatives, of a nominal volume of *$21.5 trillion*. In terms of real money, under stress market conditions, this is double the GDP of the Germany economy.[12]

Aman Capital Management, which has been based in Singapore, has reportedly lost most of its investors' money. Established in 2003 by UBS and Salomon Brothers derivatives traders, Aman aimed to be the flagship hedge fund of South-East Asia. By the end of March 2005, however, Aman's capital had shrank to $242 million, and the hedge fund subsequently suffered new large derivatives losses, leading to a late June 2005 announcement that:

- The hedge fund is no longer trading, and
- Management will distribute whatever is left of the capital to investors.

Because what they do not have in capital they make it up in loans, particularly from the banking industry, one of the main issues that worries many experts, as well as the regulators, is the *pyramiding of borrowing*. Hedge funds borrow to bet on the market.

- Funds of funds, which through banks commercialize the hedge funds products to retail customers, also borrow and hold leveraged positions.
- Individuals who buy alternative investments borrow to invest in funds of funds; they are the ultimate suckers.

All this amounts to highly geared bets whose outcome is technical, obscure, and subject to the whim of markets. Critics are rightly concerned by the fact that, moreover, the hedge funds' and funds of funds' fee structure encourages their managers to borrow aggressively. Such fees are often calculated on the basis of all the 'managed' money: equity plus debt. As a result,

- More borrowing means more pay, and
- This is an enormous conflict of interest.

'It is a house of cards,' says one London fund of funds manager. 'Each level of debt amplifies the rest – and that is hard to manage.'[13] Regulators who tried their hand in bringing some sense of risk control into the runaway hedge fund industry got fired by the politicians instead of being thanked for their efforts.

A recent case is that of William Donaldson, founder of Donaldson Lufkin Jenrette the investment bank (he sold it some years ago to Crédit Suisse for $11.8 billion, a high price), former president of the New York Stock Exchange (NYSE), and until recently chairman of the Securities and Exchange Commission (SEC), the American regulator. At a 1 June 2005 press conference, announcing his early resignation, Donaldson made it clear:

- He was forced to leave SEC, and
- The primary issue of contention was his effort to regulate hedge funds.[14]

In Europe, as in the United States, the regulation of hedge funds is a political issue which goes nowhere, because of strong headwinds blowing from embedded interests. On 13 June 2005, Gerhard Schröder, the German Chancellor, gave a keynote address at an economic policy congress of his Social Democratic Party (SPD). In this he said that governments are obliged to protect the freedom and the stakes that have been achieved through regulations. What Schröder essentially targeted was the:

- Short-term engagement of some hedge funds in Germany
- Criteria under which they operate, and interests they serve.

Schröder said that the government wants stable financial markets, and that is why it needs transparency of hedge funds' wheeling and dealing. This has essentially been a call about internationally unified minimum standards for hedge funds, as well as measures for the improvement of transparency on the oil markets (another big gambling field of hedge funds). But after these fireworks nothing has happened, and the destruction of the global economy continues unabated.

Notes

1 Basel Committee on Banking Supervision, 'Supervisory Guidance on the Use of Fair Value Options under IFRS', Consultative Document BIS, July 2005, Basel.
2 With the exception of those held to maturity according to *management intent* (see Chapter 1).
3 Eskil Ullberg, 'A Risk Management Approach to the Cost of Capital – Great Challenges for Business, Insurance and Regulators', Geneva Association, *Progress*, No. 41, June 2005.

4   D.N. Chorafas, *The 1996 Market Risk Amendment: Understanding the Marking-to-Model and Value-at-Risk*, McGraw-Hill, Burr Ridge, IL, 1998.

5   D.N. Chorafas, *The Management of Bond Investments and Trading of Debt*, Butterworth-Heinemann, London, 2005.

6   D.N. Chorafas, *Alternative Investments and the Mismanagement of Risk*, Macmillan/Palgrave, London, 2003.

7   D.N. Chorafas, *Wealth Management: Private Banking, Investment Decisions and Structured Financial Products*, Butterworth-Heinemann, London and Boston, 2006.

8   D.N. Chorafas, *Corporate Accountability, with Case Studies in Finance*, Macmillan/Palgrave, London, 2004.

9   D.N. Chorafas, *The Management of Equity Investments*, Butterworth-Heinemann, London, 2005.

10 D.N. Chorafas, *Managing Risk in the New Economy*, New York Institute of Finance, New York, 2001.

11 D.N. Chorafas, *Credit Derivatives and the Management of Risk*, New York Institute of Finance, New York, 2000.

12 *EIR*, 27 May 2005.

13 *The Economist*, 12 June 2004.

14 *EIR*, 17 June 2005.

Part 2

Implementing IFRS

Project Management for Implementation of IFRS

1.   Introduction

The study, and adoption, of new standards, like IFRS, which present a phase-shift from long-established thinking, policies, and procedures, calls for a most significant intellectual effort. This is true with nearly all modern business practices, from globalization to technology, which require that more intellectual effort is organized around the problem to be solved, rather than at the side of traditional functions such as production, marketing, lending or administration.

The implementation of IFRS calls for a well-organized project with budget, timetable, quality of deliverables, and follow-up. From planning to execution, this effort requires *project management* principles, including the making of design reviews. This is the subject of the present chapter, which aims to present the reader with:

- Critical issues confronting an important project
- Specific references to the application of IFRS, and
- Approaches to a successful implementation process and its control.

Starting with the fundamentals, the first crucial question concerning any important problem is: 'What's the problem?' With IFRS, the salient problem is the phase shift from accounting methods based on accruals, which have become almost a second nature, to new accounting principles with which most accountants have no experience. Fair value is an example.

Once this issue of change of standards is overcome, the next salient problem comes up: 'What's the aimed at solution to the problem?' The answer is more realistic pricing of assets and liabilities, given that a fast-changing, globalized, dynamic market economy has made book value nearly irrelevant.

Still another crucial query is: 'Which are the most important factors entering into this problem?' The critical factors are not one or two, but several. The foremost is conceptual change, precisely because of the phase shift to which reference has been made. The next is intensive training in the new accounting principles, followed by the rules of project management which will define:

- Resources to be committed
- Timetables to be respected
- Costs to be incurred, and
- Results to be expected from the implementation.

All this is written in the understanding that IFRS will impact many areas of the company's business beyond the accounting and finance operations, but at the same time there will be opportunities presented by IFRS. To capitalize on these opportunities, it is important to identify the key differences, between old and new systems, make an accounting policies review, see where methods might have common elements, and change reporting approaches including consolidation processes and IT support.

Sure enough, there will be changes to the way management information is presented, regarding both form and content (see Chapter 8). Other changes will affect internal communications for employees and board members, as well as external communications for stakeholders and other users of financial statements. All this should be an integral part of project management for IFRS.

Most certainly, crucial company functions like internal and external audit, risk management, and the internal control system will be affected. The way to bet is that IFRS will have short- and long-term impact on the way profit and loss is calculated, the balance sheet's content, and damage control activities. In short, it will affect:

- Control systems
- Compliance tests
- Liaison with regulatory authorities.

In turn, all this will have an after-effect on human resources, from recruitment of staff with IFRS experience, to the revision of performance incentives. And information systems, too, will need changes from functional specifications to business usage requirements. Some people look at all these references as 'problems', but in reality they are opportunities.

2. Prerequisites for a successful IFRS project

Every project comes in stages of progress and costs representing human and other resources. Projects of whatever kind, particularly the larger and more complex, can only be completed to any degree of satisfaction *if* they are directed and controlled with specific goals in mind. This is true of both the:

- Technical content constituting the project's work, and
- Ways in which all specialist fields are brought together to produce a satisfactory result.

Every project needs to be coordinated, starting with its goals, and adequacy of resources put in motion to reach these goals. On one side of the project's balance sheet are benefit(s) from its execution; on the other are possible disadvantages compared to the current method. Both need to be brought in perspective.

For a multinational company, one of the major opportunities for the institution of a project connected to IFRS rules of accounting and reporting is that there will be, more or less, one single financial reporting regulation facilitating greater access to the markets. Therefore, other things being equal, there will be a lower cost of capital. Common standards should also facilitate improved communications with analysts, investors, regulators, and other users of financial statements.

In regard to the IFRS project itself, advantages from a well-planned and controlled management effort include the fact that the conversion process will be condensed into a short, more intensive timeframe, with better control over cost and quality. The disadvantage is that there may be a certain rush to fulfil requirements. A prerequisite to proper project management, however, is not only to assess the scope of the conversion, but to appreciate that:

- For large or complex organizations, this will be a major project
- A comprehensive evaluation of its financial impact must be made, and
- The longer the project lasts the more difficult and expensive it is likely to become, while the chances of success are lessened.

As most, if not all, of the decisions taken in advancing a project involve cost, the institution must study which sort of manageable timetable and what kind of leadership can achieve the best value for money. This relatively better method must be aimed at the analysis of:

- Implementation decisions, and
- Actions that have cost consequences.

Therefore, time, quality, and cost forecasts must be valid and accurate; it must be possible to cost alternatives so that the best one is chosen; and there must be consistency within the base of deliverables. There should be cost categories with a relationship to each successive stage of the project and of the functionality which it delivers.

In terms of aftermath, senior management should be aware that the introduction of IFRS will change the reported results and financial position of the company, with the effect that the perception of stakeholders, and of the market, is likely to be affected. Moreover, conversion to IFRS will most likely have repercussions for each jurisdiction the company operates, depending on how each current accounting standard differs from IFRS and its rules. Quite likely, the greater these differences are, the more they will add to:

- Costs, and
- Human resources.

On the other hand, failure to comply with the new accounting rules and regulations will probably result in qualified audit reports, potentially leading to reduced shareholder confidence, poorer market perception, a lower share value, and maybe penalties applied by supervisory authorities. In short, there is really no option to implementing IFRS in the most successful manner possible.

The fact that there is no option to the method of implementing IFRS resembles the case of the Year 2000 problems (Y2K) of the late 1990s. Then, as now, poorly managed institutions tried to do patchwork, like windowing. By contrast, well-managed entities saw the Y2K compliance process as appropriate time to re-engineer:

- Information technology systems
- Internal management reporting, and
- Internal and external performance measures.

Both IFRS and Y2K represented an excellent opportunity to assure that financial information is obtained in the most effective way, and that any dark areas at the edges of the company's financial reporting system – whether for procedural or IT reasons – are cleared out, and their input/output is restructured.

These advantages of course will not come of their own free will, which brings us back to discussion of the issue of project management, and its prerequisites: planning the conversion project, studying the budgeting of costs, establishing timetables, elaborating personal responsibilities, analysing the impact of changes on accounting results and financial position, and determining how the implementation strategy may become most cost-effective.

Project management should work hard in identifying any resource constraints, providing appropriate liaison with Finance, IT, Risk Management, Human Resources and other departments which must contribute to, or are affected by IFRS. Steady communication of project progress, both internally and externally to the market, is also a 'must'.

Another crucial requirement is that of regularly reviewing progress, including the assurance that the project is on time and to budget (more on this in section 5, when we discuss about design reviews). There is a clear need to maintain a continuity of progress data. This is a requirement which marks all projects that are worth the money spent on them.

Long years of experience in project management have taught me that the best approach is to proactively identify problems, assure they are visible to all stakeholders (secrecy never pays), and show that they can be resolved quickly and effectively. Successful project managers plan for an integrated team approach, with:

- Well thought-out project structure
- Clearly defined individual roles and responsibilities.

A rapid implementation timetable requires detailed planning of milestones showing the status of the project and highlighting any possible roadblocks. Another helpful tactic is the ability to identify and document degree of involvement in changing accounting procedures. Preferably, this should be done in a structured way which can be best described in discrete steps:

- Identification of each step's functionality and consistence
- 'Then' and 'now' differences and similarities
- Analysis of the range and scope of what is necessary to meet defined functionality
- Synthesis of discrete tasks, and evaluation of resources necessary to complete those tasks
- Evaluation of feedback of project experience, to carry the work further on.

These are the general guidelines. It goes without saying that the chosen project management solution should be tailored to meet the institution's specific requirements. Generalizations are hopeless. There will be many factors to be considered when assessing project management requirements for IFRS conversion, depending on the size and the company, its goals and project objectives, skills available to do the job, and history of management ability to deliver:

- On budget, and
- On time.

Quality of project deliverables relates to functional requirements that must find satisfactory answers. Quality characterizing previous projects can be a guide for corrective action. Another very important consideration is whether the IFRS project has full support of the CEO and of the board, as well as whether other members of senior management understand, appreciate, and support IFRS requirements and objectives.

3. The role of project management

Beyond clear objectives, timetables, and budgets and quality of deliverables to be respected, project management must assure that human and technical resources are available, at necessary quantity and skill, to implement the IFRS directives. One of the conditions is that the project leader obtains corporate-wide commitment in terms of participation to the project. Another 'must' is the ability to monitor results of the activities relating to the implementation of IFRS, as well as to:

- Assure that critical issues are thoughtfully analysed
- Both leadership and guidance are on hand, commensurate with personal responsibility, and
- Interdisciplinary issues, which require a corporate rather than departmental focus, are resolved in a timely manner.

In this connection, a great deal can be learned from other projects, particularly those connected to new information technology. Interdisciplinary coordination by senior management is often done through a *task force* whose role is resolving strategic and tactical issues (see Chapter 7).

In connection to information technology projects, this task force has often been known as a 'steering committee' – a title I prefer not to use. Its mission has typically been that of providing direction and of elaborating policies which result in the resolution of strategic and tactical technology issues. Also, of obtaining corporate-wide commitment to IT policies and solutions.

Figure 6.1 translates this task force framework into an IFRS-oriented process, adapted to rapid implementation. The IFRS project team will need to structure this block diagram in a way that takes into account the unique situation of the institution for which it works, by assessing objectives, analysing needs, assuring resource availability, and making sure the proper linkages are provided for interdependencies. Apart from the main functional goals, it is also necessary to consider the need for specialists in areas such as:

- Taxation
- Pensions
- Derivatives, and so on.

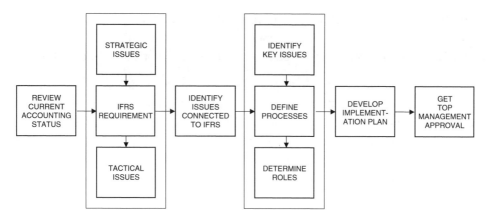

Figure 6.1 Work plan up to approval from top management

Another important element to successful project management is required involvement from various business departments like legal, internal audit, risk management, human resources, investor relations, subsidiaries, business units and, most evidently, information technology. Outsourcing part of the work to be done should also be considered if it proves to be necessary.

It should be evident to the reader that because so many departments and specialists need to be involved, prior to starting the IFRS project everyone should be clear about his or her role, what others are responsible for, and how everybody is to work together to achieve project objectives. This should be done within the realm of integrating personal role and responsibilities, for full-scale IFRS project management.

Moreover, while typically many companies are at ease with this definition of the task force's role, the less clear-sighted may require further explaining, particularly in regard to:

- Individual contributions, and
- The establishment of priorities.

Both permit the task force to focus on the resources needed for interdisciplinary coordination, and also help to guide the project manager's hand. With IFRS, this is of prime importance, because it is an interdisciplinary project *par excellence*. Priorities and resource-level needs/allocations fall within the responsibility of the task force for review and approval and within project control for execution. The project manager must establish:

- Which part of the IFRS project impacts more than one department
- Which will probably have corporate-wide impact, and
- How friction that might develop down the line can be pre-empted at the start.

Good project management is also necessary to complete the conversion process within time and budget. What is needed is an integrated team of specialists able to assure that resource needs are met, and that each department, as well as each individual within the company, develops IFRS knowledge and expertise through the IFRS project. In terms of management proper, there are different scenarios to choose from, but all tend to involve:

- The CEO
- Director of finance
- Director of accounting
- Director of internal auditing
- Director of information technology
- Director of personnel and training
- Several accounting and finance employees
- Several system programmers, analysts, and communications specialists.

Members of the board also need to contribute, taking the time to understand the change from the company's current accounting policies, impact of IFRS on financial statements, restructuring of management information (see Chapter 8), and communication links to stakeholders and the authorities. The project manager must present in a comprehensive manner to the board, the CEO and senior executives:

- The IFRS conversion project phases, and
- The support necessary to attain the project milestone plan.

The better policy is to visually demonstrate *what* must be done, *by whom* or *what* team, and *when*. Also what will be the timing of deliverables. A project plan reflecting agreed roles and responsibilities should identify measurable milestones and interdependencies. At any point in time the plan must show:

- A clear picture of the project status, and
- How it is performing against the original goals.

The project manager should also highlight problem areas, steps taken to resolve them, and what more may be needed in terms of top management approval. For every worthwhile project, it is vital that a strong consensus is reached that project management must have the latitude to pursue relevant issues with a strong, open-minded independence. The task force should be given:

- The authority to pursue any and all IFRS issues which fall within its charter, and
- The ability to resolve, by bringing to terms, the different issues independently of departmental or other vested interests.

Both points are critical to the ongoing credibility of the IFRS project. The reader should also take notice that, other things being equal, management support will be more forthcoming *if* progress review meetings are well organized with clear purpose (see section 5 on design reviews). Also, if agendas are distributed to focus the meetings, and minutes are taken to capture the:

- Key issues being raised, and
- Decisions that are reached.

A well-managed project ensures that there are always status reports, with updates on goals reached and procedural changes, if any, being made. Also very helpful are issue resolution memos, action logs, and task force checklists. The project should maintain a complete history of:

- What has happened, and
- What did not happen that should have happened.

This must be accessible to all project team members and to management. A thorough record of past events is most helpful, as well, for new project team members and their orientation. Therefore, the project journal should be organized in a way that is easy to understand; being databased, it is simple to access and to mine.

Other databased information must include project team contact list, team structure roles and responsibilities, milestone plans, issues logs, project status reports, and IFRS technical information. Issue memos, meeting agendas, and minutes are other important elements of a memory facility. These requirements may sound 'obvious', yet the number of cases in which they are not met is depressing.

4. Milestone planning for IFRS

Every project needs to be established on a firm basis – and that means elaborating a plan beyond setting goals, identifying problems and resolving the most pressing issues. Project management should, from the outset, track all matters needing attention, resources needed to concentrate on them, as well as type and frequency of controls. This means making transparent the status of all issues, maintaining a history of *what* they were, *how* they have been approached, and *how* they have been resolved.

- Management and technical issues need to be openly discussed in search of a solution
- After a solution is found, the issues that were in question must be closed so that implementation begins.

As with every project a crucial query is: '*Where* to start?' The approach widely followed, and one which sounds reasonable enough, is 'at the beginning'. As far as project planning is concerned, that's wrong! A much better method for project *planning* is to start at the end – the final deliverables, the goal we want to reach. This approach has been developed by Jean Monnet, former banker and father of the European Union. What Monnet did was to divide project *planning* from project *execution*. As shown in Figure 6.2:

- Planning should start at the final milestone, and move milestone-by-milestone towards the beginning.
- Execution, by contrast, follows the normal path from beginning to end of the project, again milestone-by-milestone.

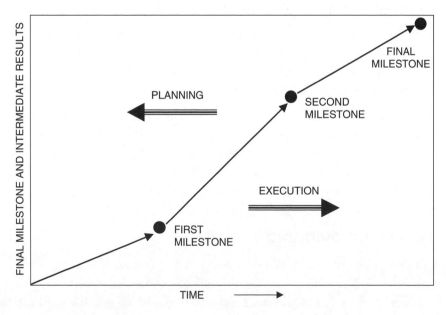

Figure 6.2   Backwards simulation of a plan designed to meet specific objectives

This is essentially a backwards simulation of goals, resources, costs, time schedules, and quality of deliverables. Since project management is confronted with so many challenges, it should definitely benefit from proper *methodology*. That is why I suggest the Monnet method. Whether the IFRS implementation is done fully in-house or it is partly outsourced, the best way to plan is to start, not at the beginning, but at the end of it.

The backwards simulation of an execution plan is designed to meet not only budgetary requirements but also human factors, which are dominating the successful completion of projects. Emphasis is placed on end results. Behind this inverse walkthrough, which starts at the projected end of the project, lies the fact that very often project managers do not put on the table all the necessary resources, including those to be kept as reserves. The backwards walk-through will make evident whether:

- The project's scope has been ill-defined
- The project lacks people with appropriate skills
- The chosen technology is substandard
- The project's progress is managed poorly
- Managers ignore best practices and lessons learned
- Users are resistant to change, and
- Top management sponsorship is lost from sight.

Mid-way fire brigade approaches do not help. Fred Brooks has been the *Project 360* coordinator and right hand of Thomas Watson Jr, IBM's CEO in the 1960s. In his excellent book *The Mythical Man-Month*, Brooks conveys an important message which can be summed up in a short sentence: 'Nine women will not make a baby in one month.'

Starting the planning process at the last milestone is a technical methodology which helps to assure that the company's accounting system will be converted to IFRS in a disciplined, consistent, and comprehensive manner. It is also a procedure that allows high-level impact assessment of differences between current accounting and IFRS, including disclosure requirements. A key advantage of such 'end results' assessment is that in the execution phase it will act as an initial project scoping step because of having identified the major accounting areas that will be impacted. Such a focus can be of significant assistance to IFRS accounts conversion, because it permits a better understanding of the changes necessary in accounting policies and procedures.

Talking from the viewpoint of personal experience with a good number of big projects, the backward simulation method has demonstrated that moving in this way corrects many of the ills that may otherwise exist in a crucial changeover, because it:

- Obliges people to think in terms of intermediate goals and resources needed to meet them, and
- Makes it mandatory to conduct design reviews at pre-identified milestones, after the project starts and goes forward (more on this in section 5).

Also at planning stage, both senior management and project management need to consider the IFRS options, and then agree and approve new policies that will be adopted. The role of the task force (see Chapter 7) cannot be emphasized in better terms. It is important to recognize that, in addition to deciding what these new accounting policies will be, the company should evaluate the present accounting policies to determine whether the current approach should be:

- Simply modified, or
- Thoroughly revamped.

By means of an integrative plan for IFRS implementation, Figure 6.3 brings all of the notions presented in the preceding paragraphs into perspective. First it identifies eight channels which will be co-involved in the IFRS effort. While four of them have to do with accounting and auditing (including hedge accounting), the scope of the other four ranges from business requirements to risk management.

Each of these eight channels is an integral part of IFRS implementation – as a contributor to it, or because of being affected by it. Also, each of these channels has lots of preliminary work to do. Completion of this preliminary work should be followed by the first major design review which:

- Approves, rejects, or asks for changes.
- In short, if it approves, it puts the project on its tracks.

After all eight channels concerned with the design review (see section 5), as well as top management, have approved the development project and agreed on IFRS accounting policies and practices up to that point, the required work by channel, in terms of conversion work, starts. All issues of interdependencies such as impact on other financial areas, systems solutions, subsidiary reporting, and so on, should be squarely faced.

Throughout the project, many issues will need to be identified and resolved. Training is the cornerstone, and the same is true of the design of IFRS financial statements to be produced after conversion. This should be made a priori, to assure all necessary information will be reported in compliance with IFRS. A

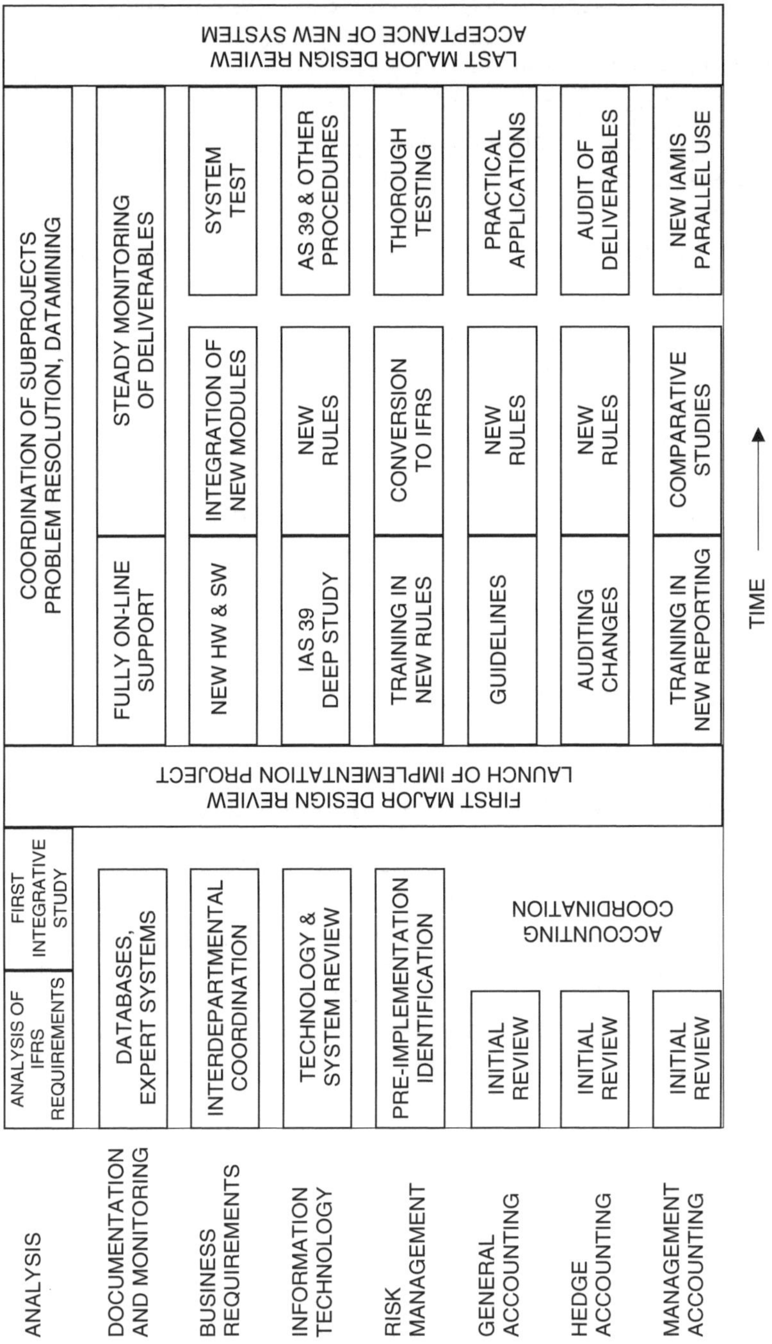

Workstream	Pre-launch phase	Post-launch		
ANALYSIS	ANALYSIS OF IFRS REQUIREMENTS · FIRST INTEGRATIVE STUDY	COORDINATION OF SUBPROJECTS, PROBLEM RESOLUTION, DATAMINING		
DOCUMENTATION AND MONITORING	DATABASES, EXPERT SYSTEMS	FULLY ON-LINE SUPPORT	STEADY MONITORING OF DELIVERABLES	
BUSINESS REQUIREMENTS	INTERDEPARTMENTAL COORDINATION	NEW HW & SW	INTEGRATION OF NEW MODULES	SYSTEM TEST
INFORMATION TECHNOLOGY	TECHNOLOGY & SYSTEM REVIEW	IAS 39 DEEP STUDY	NEW RULES	AS 39 & OTHER PROCEDURES
RISK MANAGEMENT	PRE-IMPLEMENTATION IDENTIFICATION	TRAINING IN NEW RULES	CONVERSION TO IFRS	THOROUGH TESTING
GENERAL ACCOUNTING	INITIAL REVIEW	GUIDELINES	NEW RULES	PRACTICAL APPLICATIONS
HEDGE ACCOUNTING	INITIAL REVIEW	AUDITING CHANGES	NEW RULES	AUDIT OF DELIVERABLES
MANAGEMENT ACCOUNTING	INITIAL REVIEW	TRAINING IN NEW REPORTING	COMPARATIVE STUDIES	NEW IAMIS PARALLEL USE

ACCOUNTING COORDINATION (spanning GENERAL ACCOUNTING, HEDGE ACCOUNTING and MANAGEMENT ACCOUNTING in the pre-launch phase)

FIRST MAJOR DESIGN REVIEW — LAUNCH OF IMPLEMENTATION PROJECT

LAST MAJOR DESIGN REVIEW — ACCEPTANCE OF NEW SYSTEM

TIME →

Figure 6.3 Project management planning for IFRS implementation

---

Box 6.1   A brief description of 14 steps in IFRS conversion

1.   IFRS checklist completed
2.   Examination of IAS 32 and IAS 39 issues
3.   IFRS impact assessment and scoping
4.   Understanding of differences with current accounting
5.   Hedge accounting requirements
6.   Determination of IFRS policies and procedures to be adopted
7.   Steps in conversion and interdependencies identified
8.   Links to risk management
9.   Information technology work completed
10. Tax consequences evaluated
11. IFRS numbers and disclosures produced
12. Work connected to auditing completed
13. Work connected to internal control completed
14. IFRS compliant financial statements produced

---

brief description of IFRS conversion steps is shown in Box 6.1. All the issues that arise should be identified and resolved in a timely and definite manner.

5.   Design reviews for better project management

Every well-managed project is subject to steady control. Section 4 presented to the reader a methodology for IFRS project planning, including the Monnet methodology, and 14 basic steps in IFRS conversion. Management planning and control is a fully integrated activity.

- Planning without control is daydreaming, and
- Control cannot be exercised without fundamental planning principles.

In spite of this, a challenge I often encountered in my professional work is that many companies lack the regular *progress review* culture, and they do not appreciate what it takes to maintain a state-of-the-art verification environment. As projects in the financial industry, like IFRS, continue to increase in complexity,

- Verification requires technological, financial, *and* management skills, and
- Therefore, policies, ways and means to face the challenges posed by verification must be developed and implemented.

A sound policy in reaching this goal is the institution of frequent *design reviews*. The mission of a design review is to control the project schedule, cost, functionality, and quality during the development cycle. The schedule is all-important because time-to-implementation is a crucial factor in product and process design; but, as we have already seen, the other factors, too, are crucial.

The project manager's overview of the project he or she leads is, in principle, complex. Design reviews taking place at milestones make sure that supervision becomes *focused*, hence easier. But this must be a continuous process toward a defined objective.

Absence of an effective, comprehensive, and continuous management control results in discontinuities and loss of data which should be available for project vision. This is true of all the stages of development through which all projects transit:

- Inception
- Analysis
- Synthesis
- Implementation
- Testing.

All five are terms that have broad relevance to a project's progress, even if different industries use their own names for these stages. Moreover, the way to bet is that each stage will have different needs for data control than the next. Personalization of data needs is seldom met by traditional, slow-moving, uncritical stage-related procedures which are in common usage.

For instance, as far as costs are concerned, available cost data needed to make correct design decisions are usually only total cost. There are no details and no data readily adjustable to the changed parameters of the project. That's poor management. Cost must be a major theme in design reviews, whether the project is made in-house or is partly outsourced (see also section 6).

Take quality criteria as another example. Some companies operate in a vacuum when they are verifying quality because they have not made it an explicit target in management control. Therefore, it is not subject to thorough and complete verification. When this happens, the project review process is wanting.

Still another 'must' is the control of timetables by milestone, and within each milestone targets regarding advancement towards the deliverables. While practically all projects establish timetables, the simplest being a Gantt chart invented 90 years ago, few really track progress against the planned time schedule – nor do they take corrective action to control slippages. As a result, there is plenty of delay in project completion. Moreover:

- Very few projects are able to control timetables, quality and cost at the same time.
- Yet, these factors work in synergy, and all three are most crucial to *all projects* at *all times*. Hence, they should be religiously observed.

In connection to IFRS, or any other project, companies should also specialize in design review of know-how. Automation or no automation, creative work is still done by people. Complex projects require people who have a variety of experiences and knowledge of multiple design and verification issues. Therefore, not only should a financial institution undertake design reviews but also:

- Devote years to developing a sound planning methodology and control tools to drive its projects, and
- Bring a high level of expertise to the technical- and cost-auditing of projects, as well as possess the necessary wider range of domain expertise.

Let me add that as far as this process of design review is concerned, the necessary know-how and methodology can either be developed in-house or bought from consultancies. However, whether design reviews are done with in-house skill or are partly outsourced, senior management should have a design review culture and appropriate approach to control. An example on a methodology which I learned in the early 1960s at General Electric, and which I have been using since then very successfully, is given in Figure 6.4. It calls for:

- Major design reviews at 25%, 50%, 80%, and 90% of a project's timetable
- These are milestones which roughly correspond to 10%, 25%, 50%, and 75% of the project's cost.

In between the major design reviews should be verifications, or minor design reviews, preferably done weekly. 'Every project has a risk factor associated to it,' suggested a Royal Bank of Canada senior executive at a conference: 'If it is late or of low quality, the decision is to kill it. Design reviews are made every two weeks, evaluating both *projects* and *project managers*.' Weekly is a better frequency than bi-weekly. The policy which I follow is that:

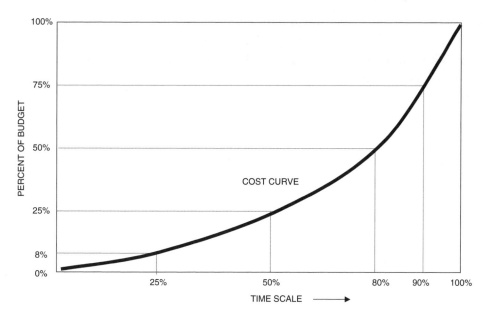

Figure 6.4   The need for design reviews is present in any project, and should be followed by corrective action

- The major design review can kill a project, if need be.
- The objective of the minor design review is to solve problems, redirect the effort, and do away with conflict – but it can also lead to an extraordinary major design review.

It is not easy to kill an ongoing project. Major banks I have been associated with as consultant to the board have objected with the argument that having invested so much money, time, and effort in a project they want to be allowed to finish it. It takes the patience of a saint to demonstrate that a project that started wrongly, or features slippages:

- Is *not* going to finish as planned
- Budget overruns and time delays will be a 'sure' thing, and
- The quality of deliverables will be substandard, far below what was originally projected.

The question then is: Is it better to lose all that time and money and fall behind – or kill the project and, if it is vital like IFRS, start anew with a better project manager and much closer senior management supervision? I believe the answer is self-evident.

Killing a project is one of the difficult but necessary decisions to be taken by the task force, provided its members participate in the major design review in forming their opinion. Or, the decision may be taken by an expert design reviewer who has audited the project and has full CEO support in the decision to throw the project in the waste basket.

These are two alternatives. Provided that the design review principles outlined in the foregoing paragraphs are observed, there are good reasons to adopt a policy of outsourcing this top level project control. The value of critical verification done by outsourcing lies in:

- The quality of personnel of the insourcer
- The independence of opinion that person can presumably provide, and
- The speed at which critical criteria can be verified, helping the entity achieve quicker time-to-implementation and other positive results.

A basic requirement, however, is that the insourcer should be a senior person, knowledgeable in design reviews – and that the outsourcer's top brass participates at the front line of each design review. This will give added authority to the review, while the outsourcer's management will learn from the insourcer's verification expertise. This is also important because there are some tough decisions which the insourcer cannot take on his or her own.

In conclusion, design reviews are a 'must'. In several cases their outsourcing provides expertise and focus on verification tasks and, therefore, produces better results. This means faster time to implementation and a greater emphasis on costs and quality. Design reviews are a complex issue which requires an experienced team of professionals committed to the verification function. But make no mistake about it: the final responsibility for results rests with the top management of the institution, not with third parties.

6. Paying attention to cost control

The three key variables controlled by design reviews are: timetables, quality/functionality being delivered, and cost. All must be measured both in absolute values and in relative performance against standards established at start of the project (see section 4). Costs matter, and cutting costs is in no way synonymous to cutting corners. This means that for its IFRS project the entity must have:

- A disciplined and tailored approach to working, but flexible enough so that it can be modified to needs as they develop, and

- A properly studied system of cost control including standard costs, so that there are no overruns of the project's budget, while quality standards are upheld.

Although at most entities in many cases cost performance relies heavily on the history of cost performance of similar projects, a satisfactory methodology can change that by establishing a new approach to evaluate projects entirely objectively. Evaluation of cost versus deliverables should never be omitted at any project stage, or design review.

In the majority of cases, becoming cost-effective in what one is doing requires a new departure. It also calls for achieving the earliest possible feedback of cost data. Steady test of cost *vs* deliverables helps to:

- Enlighten decisions, while the project is progressing, and
- Avoids proceeding from one stage to the next in ignorance of the real cost effects of work already done.

An IFRS project can be defined in terms corresponding to its activities. Subsequently, tests have to be done so as to arrive at estimates with an accuracy proportional to the depth of analysis. A different way of looking at this work is that there must be a *cost model* allowing the project manager and his or her assistants to learn as the project advances, thereby improving the cost accuracy.

The board and CEO must appreciate that the answer to the query: 'How much will the IFRS implementation cost?' cannot be linear. Much depends on the organization, skill, and technology employed in the IFRS project, as well as on top management's determination to get commendable results.

An important reason for ensuring that cost data has up-to-the-minute validity is that decisions taken in the earliest project stages have the greatest cost consequences. Such early decisions must be illuminated by the best possible information on costs. The relevance of project stages to cost data is one of key issues underlying the design reviews discussed in section 5. Costs must be associated to every stage of the IFRS project, expressed at different levels:

- At high level, in reference to a summary plan
- More detailed, in connection to a milestone plan
- Very detailed, when costing is associated to task checklists.

Every step in IFRS implementation, as well as every technical or management process, has a cost associated to it. Other component parts of the project, from status reports to organization, planning and control chores, information system solutions, and so on, also have associated costs. The same is true of training, accounts conversion, impact assessment, tax planning for IFRS disclosures and more.

Particular attention must be paid to the cost of outsourcing part of the IFRS project deliverables, *if* a decision is taken to do so. In the general case, to bring costs down, companies tend to outsource some of their duties, but outsourcing may present surprises in timetables, quality of deliverables, and cost. Hence the queries:

- Under which conditions should outsourcing take place?
- How far can outsourcing work be kept under control?
- How well can an outsourcing agreement compete with in-house solutions?

A factual and documented answer to these queries requires gaining a broader perspective of what could, could not or should not be outsourced. It is short-sighted to examine this issue only from the narrower angle of 'costs' – if for no other reason than because cost savings may be an illusion. The goods and services we require must be considered from the broader viewpoint of procurement:

- No matter where they may come from
- No matter where they may be sold
- For whatever purpose these transactions take place
- At any cost level considered to be acceptable.

From the user's point of view the quality of IFRS accounting they will obtain is influenced by several factors: its on-line accessibility, operational relevance, applicability and validity to their job. It is more or less immaterial to the user if the part of the deliverables he or she needs has been made in-house or has been outsourced. What is material is:

- The quality of project results, and
- The cost of the service being rendered.

This is particularly true if the user is going to pay for the new IFRS services from their own budget, as should be the case. And because cost is a material issue to the company anyway, the control of costs is one of the tasks of the IFRS project manager. A basic management principle, however, is that it is only possible to control costs if the use of resources is subject to the project manager's choices and decisions.

For reasons outlined in the preceding paragraphs, whether we talk of board, CEO, or project management level, easy-going ways of managing costs are ineffective due to a lack of clear goals, and absence of continuity in cost control. Moreover, in addition to the following principle of cost control there is the issue of:

- Quality of available cost data, and
- Interaction of cost with performance.

With these concepts in mind, senior management must appreciate that the design of a project should definitely incorporate a costing and control component by project activity and milestone. Decisions in this regard frequently require that a balance is struck between the desired standard of technical performance and allowable cost.

People responsible for costing and cost control must also keep in mind that there are a number of ways in which the validity of quality of cost data can vary, each way affecting the exercise of cost control. Requirements of high-quality data can be phrased, briefly, in three bullet points:

- Relevant and applicable to the project in which it is used
- Readily accessible to those making decisions that have cost consequences
- Related to each project stage, to provide continuity of cost basis throughout each stage, and for the whole project.

It is also advisable to keep in perspective that if the breakdown of project details is not taken far enough, parcels of work that appear separately in the database will be too large and too general to be useful in formulating budgets or in appraising future cost options. On the other hand, if the hierarchy of costs extends too far into too many levels of subdivision, the parcels of work to which cost data refer may become too small and the number of them too great.

Several researchers on cost planning and cost control have shown that the accuracy of cost allocations tends to deteriorate exponentially with the number of categories over which costs are allocated. Therefore, the project's component parts should be subdivided only to the point at which it can be said that the work is clearly defined in a comprehensive and comprehensible way.

This essentially means that a balance must be struck which provides the right quantity and quality of cost data to an appropriate degree of detail. Quite often the use of non-comprehensive numbers and of excessive detail is the refuge of the unable who has been asked by the unwilling to do the unnecessary.

An IFRS Task Force Case Study. Top Management Responsibility

1. Introduction

No major project, IFRS or any other, can succeed without full understanding, appreciation, and support by top management. As we have seen on repeated occasions, IFRS is not just an accounting and procedural issue, it is a cultural issue affecting the whole organization. Therefore, a high level *task force* should be established to:

- Develop the new accounting strategies that support the company's business needs, and
- Father the IFRS project, all the way from planning and control, and assurance of deliverables.

Chapter 6 has mentioned that the term *task force* was deliberately chosen to avoid the appellation 'steering committee', which got itself a bad name with information technology projects in the 1960s and 1970s. Also, a task force has wider duties than the steering committee, because of being a direct contributor to the functionality, performance, and success of the project under its authority.

Composed of senior executives (see section 2), the task force should assure that the firm's new accounting culture, as well as associated systems and procedures jointly developed and implemented by all departments, are able to sustain and improve the entity's business strategy.

This requirement can be best accomplished through a comprehensive plan in which all units participate. Interdepartmental collaboration in the IFRS project can assure effective and responsive utilization of concepts and tools. This should be clearly outlined when the task force is established.

- Its mission is to identify and analyse all IFRS issues with strategic importance to the company, and
- Its role must be to help in resolving issues of authority and responsibility, formulating policies/directives that guide the project's studies and actions.

For this reason, task force membership should include department heads or higher level executives overseeing critical functions, and it must be chaired by an executive vice-president of the corporation. Small membership comprised of innovative, respected, and knowledgeable people is necessary to allow the task force to resolve strategic and tactical issues effectively.

From my experience from similar projects, I can suggest that the most active department heads, who are not afraid of change, are the appropriate task force members, given their institution-wide perspective. The choice of a chairperson known to deliver at high quality, on time and on budget, is necessary to give the task force credibility. As a body, and individually, each task force member should utilize effective meetings and communications procedures. He or she must be provided with staff support to operate successfully.

- Strict agenda and meeting procedures are needed to assure effective use of membership efforts, and to retain their participation.
- Company-wide effective communications regarding the IFRS project are vital to disseminating task force information without use of the company's grapevine.

Staff and financial resources are necessary to support task force activities, including oversight of the IFRS project under its authority, as outlined in Chapter 6. After the project is finished, the task force owes the company one more duty: to set up, using the best elements who participated in the IFRS project, a research and development (R&D) operation focusing on further evolution of accounting standards and adaptation to this evolution (more on this in section 2).

Speaking from past experience, seven steps are necessary to initiate task force activities and continue them in a successful way to completion. First, a review with executive management of task force duties, to receive their concurrent endorsement of this initiative's purpose, charter, and membership – as well as budget, timetable and quality of deliverables of the project the task force will monitor.

Second, after executive management concurrence, the definition of time to be spent by task force members to allow them to prepare for their participation, as well as to make sure everybody understands his or her responsibilities. The third step is entity-wide announcement of the task force's charter and its mission to assure everybody in the firm understands not only its role but also the role of the IFRS project.

Fourth, the membership of the IFRS task force will require *accounting education*, if each member is to analyse the issues confronting it effectively. All members do not need to be accountants, but a brief accounting education program is important and should be initiated as quickly as possible – preferably prior to the first meeting.

The fifth step concerns the critical role to be played by the *first* task force meeting, since this will set the tone for future meetings and project efforts. At this first meeting an unambiguous definition should be made of the corrective action subsequent meetings will, in all likelihood, need to take.

Training task force members should include not only the dynamics of IFRS, outlined in Chapters 2 and 3, but also some of the mechanics, the rationale behind IAS 39, and importance of fair value accounting. Just as important is training on the impact of IFRS conversion. This is necessary because task force members will be expected to do:

- IFRS impact assessment
- Evaluation of conversion work, and
- Confirmation of IFRS policies and procedures.

The sixth step is that of task force participation in the design reviews, whose need, role, and function has been defined in Chapter 6. The seventh step concerns preparation for the task force's last meeting. Its effectiveness is important to assure the light in which the task force's efforts will be seen. Its success must be fully demonstrated on the strength of deliverables it has produced.

Finally, apart of having been at the receiving end of a training effort, task force members must look into the development of a wider IFRS training strategy within headquarters and business units, including workshops and seminars. They would also have to authorize an IFRS communications strategy, including the communications roll-out. Individual companies may choose to add to these duties, tax planning under IFRS being an example of the added baggage the task force has to take on board.

2. The Task Force's chairperson, membership, and work schedule

Choice of the right chairperson is necessary to give the task force credibility and an unbiased perspective. This person must not only be respected by other members of the organization, and open to innovative ideas, but also a facilitator able to steer the IFRS project through straits and headwinds.

Regarding qualifications, the same goes for the IFRS task force's membership. With regard to number of members, in my experience a high single-digit number is best. Three to five people are not representative enough as a group; and more than ten soon become a small parliament. At the same time, for the task force's role to be effective, several pitfalls should be avoided. For example:

- The chairperson must guide but not dominate the meetings, and
- The meetings should not be 'played' to gain favours from 'this' or 'that' corporate officer.

The services of a good secretary are critical to the success of the task force. His or her duties must include setting up meetings, establishing agendas, writing the minutes, assuring staff work completion, documenting task force results, and more.

The chairperson must see to it that all task force members feel free to speak their mind. This is the only way to provide a corporate-wide perspective, and an excellent blend of business knowledge and clout. On the other hand, the chairperson and task force members must be free to check how well the IFRS project manager performs his or her duties.

- This can be done effectively through regular, and frequent person-to-person meetings
- It is unwise to lose time waiting for the more sparsely timed design reviews, where critiques made about the project have a wider echo.

Moreover, members of the task force can take the initiative to organize IFRS information meetings, aimed at widening the cross-section of participants and spurring innovative and creative thinking. This policy assures a wider-ranging view of corporate functions, and gives the task force clout to make decisions and pursue roll-out and change-over issues.

The approach outlined in this section evidently requires time from busy executives. Hence the need that the task force is run efficiently. Furthermore, persons with experience in IFRS changeover suggest that an objective outsider's viewpoint would benefit the project.

- A knowledgeable third party can bring applications know-how the company lacks, and
- An independently minded person can help task force members to ensure the project operates effectively.

Also, the IFRS task force members should have the right, on a periodic basis, to bring a designated manager or professional of their department to attend the meetings – though only the task force members should be allowed to vote in the course of such meetings. This policy:

- Permits managers with detailed understanding of specific issues to express opinions relevant to their area of expertise, and
- Spreads accountability and responsibility for task force activities and IFRS project progress wider within the organization.

Considering the importance of the IFRS task force to the company, the chief executive officer should review and make known his approval of the most important decisions. Moreover, the members should be appointed by the chief executive with the board's consent, while the secretary is chosen and appointed by the chairperson.

In order to get the best possible results, the task force should utilize effective meeting and communications procedures and, as already mentioned, be provided with staff support to operate successfully. Strict agenda and meeting procedures are needed to assure effective use of membership time and effort, as well as to retain participation.

- It is advisable that the agenda is limited to only those items/issues that *truly* qualify for task force deliberation.

Such items are of different kinds: for example, issues relating to the company's accounting culture as well as policies, and what can be termed technically strategic issues. Another class is issues with sufficient impact on financial reporting to require senior management involvement and approval.

- Prior to each meeting, the items to be discussed should be separated into information-only and action items/issues.

Information-only items are those that provide members of the task force with insight and knowledge. As such, they should be limited to those that are meaningful. *Action items* are those for task force decision. For them, the advice is that every attempt should be made to come to a resolution during the meeting.

- Each task force member should have the right to introduce and present agenda items.

Full participation by all members of the task force in structuring the agenda provides the mechanism for major issues to be brought forward from persons with the salt of the earth. It also assures active, ongoing participation and interest of the other members, who might otherwise feel that the meeting is not worth their time.

It is also most important that the agenda is finalized well ahead of the meeting. For instance, two weeks prior to a monthly meeting. This will give members time to come prepared for the discussion. The agenda should include items proposed by task force members, but it should be finalized by the chairperson and circulated by the secretary.

Experience with important projects teaches that any research and analysis on agenda issues should be completed and circulated to members at the same time as the agenda, or shortly thereafter. This ensures that task force members are prepared to discuss issues – not just listen to 'show and tell' presentations. It also allows members to discuss issues with their assistants prior to meetings.

It is my experience that the analysis and research provided to task force members should be done on a competent staff work basis and it should be complete. Patchy jobs done while running to the airport to catch a plane are not admissible. If this analysis includes contradictory opinions, it may have to be reviewed by the secretary to ensure it meets fair presentation criteria. The criteria to characterize all analysis and research efforts include:

- Comprehensive issue definition
- Sound background, both business and technical
- Description of alternatives for resolution
- Definition of factors with which to evaluate alternatives
- Cost/benefit and risk evaluation analysis for each alternative, and
- Definition of decisions which the task force is being asked to make.

Effective presentation of research and analysis results ensures better use of membership time, and enhances the odds that they continue to participate actively. Moreover, the chairperson should consider holding the task force meetings offsite, especially when the agenda requires a full day to complete. This avoids distractions and helps in creating an atmosphere that facilitates open discussion on the different issues, and better decisions.

Finally, it is important to bring to the reader's attention that innovation in accounting standards is not going to end with the current versions of IFRS, IAS 32, IAS 39, and the other component of the new standards. Therefore, as mentioned in the Introduction, after the IFRS project is successfully completed, it is wise to keep a nucleus research and development laboratory, oriented to accounting issues and standards evolution. Chapters 1 and 2 have already explained why the research effort is indivisible from the mainstream of activities of the modern enterprise.

3. The impact of communication and of case studies

Effective communication is always vital to obtaining and disseminating criteria, decisions, progress, and results of a project. This is evidently true of IFRS: from guidelines established by top management, to status reports and the deliverables. Communication of task force policies and directions help to guide everybody's efforts, and it is generally viewed as a key ingredient of success. Therefore, a key role of the task force is to:

- Keep all levels of management informed about IFRS issues, and
- Guide operational decision-making close to the realities being confronted, thereafter appropriately informing all stakeholders.

One of the major problems I have found with projects as significant, from an organizational perspective, as the implementation of IFRS is that quite often the needed business and technology guidance is missing. To close this gap, the task force should employ a variety of methods, including:

- Periodic presentations to all department heads, on business/technology issues, by the chairperson and secretary on task force activities and IFRS project progress.
- Department head presentations and discussion sessions with their management teams, on this same wavelength.
- Mailing meeting summaries on task force activities and IFRS project programs to all department heads, and offering more detailed descriptions, as required.

Other effective strategies are use of normal information memos for progress update, videotape interviews and education sessions on vital issues for distribution throughout the organization, and ad hoc managers and professionals meetings as the need arises. In my experience, the best way to inform in these management and professional meetings is through case studies.

For example, an interesting case study is that of IFRS implementation in a small credit institution, which included IFRS impact assessment as part of a company's preparation for the 2005 deadline. In a specific case I have in mind, the project team consisted of a small group of people, including financial and accounting specialists who assisted in conducting impact assessment. The subprojects were outsourced to a consultancy:

- Training the entity's specialists in IFRS
- Help in setting up hedge accounting procedures, and
- Controlling financial statement conversion according to IFRS standards.

In the general case, very interesting case studies can be developed by visiting firms that are ahead of the curve in IFRS implementation, learning from them both good news and bad news – like adverse reactions, bottlenecks, inconsistencies, cultural problems, and cases of obstructionism. In a case study, bad news is more important than good news.

Prior to taking a more sophisticated example, which looks into the IFRS conversion project of a multinational conglomerate with many subsidiaries around the globe, it is advisable to clear up some terms. The Basel Committee defines financial conglomerates as entities conducting within one financial institution or group at least two of the three traditionally distinct activities of banking, securities, and insurance. But BCBS also notes that this general definition could lead to different legal definitions depending on jurisdiction.

For example, a new EU Directive on financial conglomerates requires the presence of insurance to qualify a conglomerate, since the capital regulation for banks and securities firms is already laid down under a single framework by the second Capital Adequacy Directive (CAD 2). By contrast, in the United States the notion of financial conglomerates, adopted by the Gramm–Leach–Bliley Act of 1999, is that of a financial holding company which can but is not bound to offer the full range of financial services.

In the case of the entity which is the subject of the present case study, all aforementioned three lines of business were present. The IFRS project was organized at corporate level and involved a steering committee with representatives from the three main divisions. Many other people were involved, including:

- Project manager
- Sub-project managers (by country)
- Lots of company personnel, and
- Some 30 consultants (too many).

At headquarters the project manager had overall responsibility, with IFRS conversion teams established through a matrix organization at country and main division level, supported by their local accountants and auditors. This matrix organization did not work particularly well.

Milestones in this project have been IFRS, and most particularly IAS 39 impact assessment at both corporate and subsidiary level; revision of accounting policies and procedures; extensive personnel training; consolidation procedures;

tests for IFRS compliance; and roll-out of headquarters and subsidiary reporting packages. The project required:

- Plenty of technical advice
- A new accounting policies and procedures manual
- New software for financial reporting at headquarters and subsidiaries
- The resolution of logistical problems throughout the IFRS project, among other issues.

Particularly challenging has been IAS 39 conversion, as the conglomerate was required to produce IAS 39-compliant accounts for two recent acquisitions, in host countries. Adoption of IAS 39 called for significant systems changes in both new entities. It also had business impact; particularly affected was the risk management system.

One of the political hurdles in this project was establishment of the steering committee, obtaining consensus for its membership throughout the conglomerate, and elaborating the nature of staff support necessary to research and analyse the complex issues to which reference has been made, on a global scale of operations. Political conflicts were (and usually are) particularly taxing.

With the CEO taking a hands-off attitude, several steering committee members pointed out that given their regular job they do not have time to research different IFRS implementation issues in depth. But they also pointed out that thorough complete analysis is vital to reaching appropriate decisions. Given the nature of cross-country operations, the CEO decided to establish by country issue-oriented sub-committees responsible for specific subjects such as:

- Project management structure, milestone plan, communication processes
- Consolidation of risk management, in order to develop a new corporate-wide system for control of exposure, and
- Fair value studies and IAS 39 review involving about 300 topics, from strategic considerations to implementation and documentation.

The policy chosen by the board and CEO was that the sub-committees should give priority to strategic issues, and develop recommendations for the steering committee. The chairperson of each sub-committee was responsible for accessing needed in-house and external resources. However, as far as consultancies were concerned, their confirmation required compliance with the firm's normal approval and procurement processes – a fairly lengthy process.

While further details cannot be revealed, from what has been stated so far the inference is that this has been a costly, slow, and not so successful project. But as has been already emphasized, when it comes to case studies bad news is better than good news – because it points out to the reader the steps and approaches which should be avoided.

4. Assuring compliance to IFRS standards

Compliance, the dictionary says, is the act of submission, yielding, or acting in accord. It is a process which, in order to be effective, must be set as a policy and start being implemented at the organization's top level. Compliance best operates in a corporate culture that emphasizes standards of ethics and integrity, as well as paying attention to rules and regulations. The best compliance policy is that the board of directors, CEO, and senior management lead by example.

For any practical purpose, compliance is an act of management. The same is true of lack of compliance. Failure to consider the impact of management actions, in terms of observance of rules and regulations, on the firm's shareholders, bondholders, customers, employees, the general public, and the markets, can result in reputational risk as well as in *compliance risk* – which is the risk of:

- Legal, and/or
- Regulatory sanctions.

The aftermath can be material financial loss, as well as business loss. Because of the wider damage which can be created, all the way to business risk, compliance is not just the responsibility of a specialist compliance staff working for the company. Everybody in the organization must perform his or her part of a corporate *compliance function*.

An integral part of the mission of the task force on IFRS implementation (see sections 2 and 3) is to instill at all levels of the organization the compliance principle. This is equally true of accounting standards, financial reporting models and practices, and regulatory capital requirements – where such requirements exist, as is the case in the banking industry.

On the other hand, rules and regulations to which companies are subject, and to which they should be compliant, must not be contradictory. For instance, during

2003 and 2004 the Basel Committee's accounting-related activities focused on resolving differences of view on the International Accounting Standards Boards' *fair value* option. Agreement was reached in early 2005, and IASB has now approved and issued a final standard which addresses BCBS' essential concerns.

Basel has also taken an active interest in the IASB's project to enhance financial instrument disclosures. Financial reporting transparency will include greatly enhanced disclosures of financial risks, as well as exposure risk related to management practices. This is broadly similar to the principles and requirements under Pillar 3 of Basel II.[1] In this manner, credit institutions cannot say that there has been a bifurcation in rules to which they must comply.

Also for the reason of creating a homogeneous group of rules and regulations to which banks must comply, the Basel committee has been actively engaged in the developments associated to the Public Interest Oversight Board (PIOB). Its mission is to act as regulator of the accounting and auditing profession, as well as to oversee global standard-setting activities undertaken by the International Federation of Accountants (IFAC).

Moreover, in response to a rapidly growing need for guidance in the domain of compliance, in April 2005 the Basel Committee published a guidance paper on principles and practices for compliance, within the regulated banking environment. Its focal points are those of:

- Maintaining an effective compliance function, and
- Adopting structures, procedures, and controls appropriate to the entity and its risk appetite.

Because the responsibility for compliance starts at the vertex of the organization, whether we talk of new accounting rules, transparent financial reporting, or maintenance of capital adequacy, the entity's board of directors is the first party responsible for overseeing the management of compliance risk. The board should also approve the bank's compliance policy, and establish a permanent and effective compliance function.

In terms of IFRS implementation and compliance to its directives, the board should regularly assess whether the company is effectively managing its compliance risk, and what kind of corrective action has been taken in case of non-compliance by a department or subsidiary. Moreover, the day-to-day oversight of compliance function should be independent from operational management. This concept of independence involves four related elements:

- The compliance function should have a formal status within the organization.
- There should be a compliance officer with overall responsibility for coordinating the control of compliance risk.
- Compliance function staff must have access to the information and personnel necessary to carry out its duties, and
- The head of compliance, and his or her staff, should not be placed in a position where there is possible a conflict of interest between compliance responsibilities and any other duties.

The message the reader should retain is how much is down to personal accountability in assuring compliance, and in controlling possible deviations. In spite of advances with models (see section 5), and with information technology, we simply do not have the means for modelling the majority of events pertaining to compliance, even in a coarse way. Moreover, there is often lack of detail in the different steps to be taken for compliance reasons, and as Mies van der Rohe, the architect, used to say: 'God is in the detail.'

Sparse data and algorithmic insufficiency prevent us from handling compliance issues to any great extent through computers. Some people may dispute the argument. I would be the first to say financial engineering has made great strides, but the complexity of the instruments and of compliance rules has also increased by leaps and bounds.

For instance, as the Bank for International Settlements points out in its 75th Annual Report, the explicit incorporation of systemic objectives into the design of prudential standards is a relatively recent phenomenon, even if its need has been recognized for some time. Standards that limit the scope for excessive risk-taking at the level of *macroprudential* thinking reflect the notions that:

- Behaviour and rules that are individually rational may lead to undesirable aggregate outcomes, and
- Retrenchment from risky positions in response to elevated measures of market risk may be a prudent approach from the perspective of an individual institution, but a generalized sell-off could trigger a self-reinforcing chain of actions leading to high market volatility.

Input from IFRS accounting can reinforce the risk methodology a financial institution or any other equity uses by presenting risk control with a more reliable and analytical input. The new accounting input, including fair value, can be instrumental in improving the quantitative and qualitative tools employed for:

- Valuing financial instruments, and
- Measuring risk to the bank's net profit as well as its equity.

Both regulatory capital and economic capital calculations would profit. For starters, economic capital is a metric designed to estimate the amount of financial staying power needed to absorb the potential losses arising from exposures to outlier risks at any given time. This must be computed to a statistical level of confidence determined by the board, with the aim of remaining at the highest creditworthiness.[2] For instance, among well-managed banks,

- Internal limits, and
- Exception reports

are expressed in terms of the economic capital usage. They calculate economic capital covering credit risk, market risk, operational risk, liquidity risk, and other exposures. Models used for credit risk compute the probability of default of individual counterparties; correlations of losses associated with individual counterparties; and the loss that the institution would incur as a result of default(s).

The relevance of these references to IFRS compliance is self-evident. *If* the bank property implements the new accounting standards through solid project management (discussed in Chapter 6) and by means of a high level task force, *then* it would no longer be that easy to cook the books (though this can always happen if top management condones it, even worse, requests it). When accounting data and statistics are clean, other things being equal, risk control becomes so much more effective.

5. Learning to live in a world populated with models

One of the major cultural changes, and at the same time technical changes, the task force should address is the company's need to learn how to live with models. Several engineering companies have done so since the 1930s. The models at the time were water basins, where harbour projects and hydroelectric dams were studied. There were also wind tunnels for aerodynamic aircraft design studies.

Physical models are still around, but after World War II they started giving way to digital differential analysers. In 1951, when I served my apprenticeship at

Electricité de France, through an EDF scholarship, I was studying powergrids with them and found it to be a rewarding experience. Simulation provides both:

- Insight, and
- Foresight.

Digital differential analysers were a hybrid, half physical and half mathematical, engine. As simulators they were a precursor to digital simulation done by means of mathematical models and digital computers. Simulation has been the gateway of mathematical analysis into finance.

All simulations are based on analogies.[3] These analogies are made of a number of working assumptions reflected into algorithms and heuristics. Algorithms may not be capable of duplicating actual life, but they are approximating it. Therefore, results obtained through modelling have inherent limitations. For instance, in finance, unlike a real life performance record, simulated returns do not represent actual trading. Still they can be very useful for:

- Prognostication
- Experimentation, and
- Management control reasons.

The first lesson in learning to live with models is that when analogous systems are found to exist, or are constructed to map into them some other system's behaviour, then studies done in one of them – the *simulator* – can help in making inferences about the other.

- The benefit is better vision, and
- The cost is a lower accuracy than observation made in real life.

For instance, since the trades have not actually been executed, the results obtained through modelling may have over- or under-compensated for the impact of market factors. When this happens, it is mainly due to the hypotheses we have made, scarce data we have available, or plain algorithmic insufficiency.

This leads to *model risk* and it constitutes the second lesson in learning to live in a financial world populated with models. All domains, from engineering and physics to finance, are exposed to varying degrees of model risk. Financial market factors we often study through simulation are:

- Changes in volatility
- Liquidity constraints

- Product pricing
- Extreme market events
- Changes in exposure
- Capital at risk
- Fee schedules
- Transaction costs, and more.

Many people think of the Monte Carlo method as being the only simulator. ('Monte Carlo' is the name Dr John von Neumann gave to Lord Raleigh's random walks – a stochastic process developed in the late 19th century.) The method makes possible studying the behaviour of patterns as diverse as the:

- Decay of atomic particles, and
- Prepayment of a pool of securitized mortgages, which is also a process of decay over time.

Modelling and simulation does not really need to be awfully complex, neither should one shy away from learning how to develop and use models. For instance, *actuarial* models are today second nature in the insurance industry, so much so that really nobody thinks of them as being mathematical artifacts. This is the third important lesson, in connection to learning to live with models.

When it is used for the purpose of discounting cash flow from a financial instrument inventoried in the bank's portfolio, an actuarial model provides a good example of fair value computation requested by IAS 39. However, let us take good note of the fact that:

- The actuary makes no claim as to any special ability to predict interest rates.
- What he or she does is to compute compound interest, by knowing how to apply mathematics to practical problems.

Actuaries make wide use of *present value*, in which future money flows are discounted. This means they are valued in a current time frame by taking into explicit account the time value of money. The basic formula for present value of a dollar in future years is:

$$(1 + i)^t$$

where:

$$t = \text{the number of years hence}$$
$$i = \text{the effective annual rate of interest}$$

Present value calculations can also involve discounts for other factors, but invariably the time value of money is present. Many investors, too, have learned to differentiate between discounted and not-discounted *cash flows*, gross and net interest, before tax and after tax, nominal, effective, and real rates of interest, as well as internal rates of return. A more sophisticated study on present value will account for yield curves, as well as for

- Relationships between interest rates for different maturity periods
- Effect of exchange rates on interest rate of return of debt instruments, and other factors.

The hypotheses we make should recognize that any specific interest rate has a basic component for time preference. There are also additional components of which we did not speak at this point; but which should be accounted for in a detailed study on risk and return. For instance, inflation expectations, and possibility of default.

The reader will appreciate that we are still in the early days of rocket science in the world of finance. If we look back a few centuries, we will see that in the 17th century, physics entered into a new era, thanks to the use of mathematics. In a manner, toward the end of the 20th century finance took a similar giant step through contributions of certain brilliant individuals.[4] This has been preceded by the use of mathematics in economics, which started at the end of the 19th century.

While one might suggest that IFRS and simulation are two distinct and unrelated subjects, such a suggestion would rest on very shaky ground. First and foremost, as we saw in Chapters 1 and 2, Fra Luca Paciolo who expressed the rules of accounting, which he developed as a system, in his 1494 book *Summa da Arithmetica Geometria Proportioni e Proportionalita*, was a mathematician.

But there is much more to the connection an IFRS project should have to models and simulation, and this is for two reasons. One is a priori and the other a posteriori of IFRS. As we have already seen on several occasions in Part One:

- Fair value estimates are done partly by marking to market and partly by marking to model.

If the task force leaves the concept and practice of modelling and simulation out of the sphere of its basic activities, *then* its work will be half-baked. The company will not be able to satisfy fundamental IFRS, and most particularly IAS 39, requirements in an able manner. It needs no explaining that this should *not* be the case.

- Since IFRS provides a modern, dynamic, and fairly accurate accounting infrastructure, it would really be a pity not to use its produce to the fullest possible extent.

The example on possible benefits offered by section 6 is on personal productivity. As we will see in this example, doing away with trivia and time-consuming administrative duties requires accurate accounting and statistics, a good deal of modelling, as well as the use of knowledge engineering artifacts like expert systems and mobile agents. The task force should include such deliverables among its priorities.

6. Using the new accounting system to improve personal productivity

Being *productive* means many things: fruitful, fertile, rich, fecund, plentiful, abundant, prolific, dynamic – as well as imaginative, creative, inventive, resourceful, profitable, rewarding, generative, ingenious. The term productive is an adjective. *Productivity* is a noun. The underlying process is one of efficiency in industrial production, or in the service industry.

Greater productivity obtained through an interactive, accurate, and timely accounting and statistical system, is a payoff that can cover all IFRS-related expenses and leave a profit to the company. A strategy targeting managerial production is akin to that followed by well-managed firms in the mid- to late 1990s in connection to the Year 2000 (Y2K) problem, when they used the solution they had to implement as an opportunity to renew their information technology.

Therefore, greater individual productivity by exploiting the opportunities offered by IFRS should be at the top of the task force's list of objectives. Here is a practical example. In 1990 Banker's Trust studied the way its managers and professionals spent their time, and what it found out was:

- That 33% of their time was truly productive
- While 67% went on trivia and administrative activities.

After that, the executive committee decided that new information technology investments would be tied to inverting these percentages: making 67% of managers' and professionals' time productive and leaving only 33% wasted on trivia and administration – available technology did not allow any further shrinkage of that share. A similar goal should prevail among task force aims, with regard to managerial and professional productivity in two domains:

- Management accounting, and
- Financial accounting.

The primary objective of *financial accounting* is that of providing financial information to people and entities outside the business: shareholders, bondholders, bankers, regulators, and other parties. To a considerable extent the techniques, rules, and conventions according to which financial accounting figures are collected and reported reflect the requirements of these outsiders and, as its title implies, IFRS is primarily oriented to their information needs.

By contrast, *management accounting* is concerned with accounting information that is useful to the firm's own management. This is the theme of Chapter 8. The problems we shall discuss are those of the use of accounting figures in the recognition, or solution, of management problems. On the other hand, *management* is also responsible for the content of financial accounting reports.

Professional productivity is important in connection to both management accounting and financial accounting. Not many companies appreciate the importance of productivity on their bottomline, yet its impact can be major. Two questions come to mind when industrial engineering studies document wide differences in productivity of competing companies:

- Is company management too lenient, and the professionals themselves untrained on how to improve their performance?
- Or do the differences lie in the quality of capital equipment, in the development and installation of new technology, and in obsolete methods?

According to certain studies, differences in management practices account for much of the gap in total office productivity – a finding not too different from that concerning factory productivity. Moreover, higher management quality scores correlate with higher returns on capital employed, as they do with sales per employee, sales growth per employee, and other measures of personal output.

The European Central Bank made a study of productivity in Euroland's banking industry and its conclusion has been that there are indications that the slower pace of productivity growth observed since the mid-1990s reflects an insufficient use of new methods and tools, particularly of productivity-enhancing technologies. The way ECB sees it:

- Productivity has increased in sectors that produce information and communication technologies.
- But it has declined in many other areas of the economy, pointing to structural rigidities that prevent or hinder change.[5]

This should be an alarm signal for the task force. IFRS conversion is a major investment, and there should be a return attached to it. Such a return is in direct proportion to effective dissemination of new technology and improved production processes across the firm. Against this background, reforms that stimulate innovation, investment, and productivity, and promote the use of new productivity-enhancing technologies, are of critical importance.

In an organizational sense, one of the reforms that must enter into an overall plan for greater efficiency is the flattening of the company structure, by eliminating intermediate management layers through expert systems and on-line datamining. It is not the job of the IFRS task force to do so. What it should do is to provide the incentives and infrastructural support that would make it possible.

Notice, however, that reorganization can also have a downside, particularly so if it is only done for reorganization's sake. This does not happen only today. 'We tend to meet any new situation in life by reorganizing,' Petronius Arbiter, a 1st century Roman satirist had remarked, 'And what a wonderful method it can be for creating the illusion of progress while producing confusion, inefficiency and demoralization.' The Romans, too, had efficiency problems to cope with!

An example of what the task force can contribute is the *commissioning* of a new and effective management accounting system, which will significantly contribute towards results along the Bankers Trust frame of reference (see Chapter 8). This is one of the basic reasons why in section 2 I insisted that the members of the task force should be innovative and creative thinkers who:

- Are open to new ideas
- Are willing to take risks and able to communicate with all levels of management, and
- Have corporate-wide knowledge, perspective, and respect.

To achieve this aim of contributing towards greater productivity, the chairperson and members of the task force must have sufficient clout, and use their work stature to make some tough decisions. Beyond this, for reasons already explained, good understanding of business and technology trends, as well as a willingness to learn quickly, are most welcome traits.

Another interesting example of the productive use of IFRS accounting is the ability to provide a timely and accurate *customer mirror* with every counterparty the bank has. Box 7.1 shows the component parts of a customer mirror I designed some years ago for the retail and small business trade of a commercial bank. Wholesale trade requires a more sophisticated approach which:

- Capitalizes on the fair value component of IFRS, and
- Provides account managers in the institution with a clear picture of risk and return assumed with every client relationship. (See also the virtual balance sheet in Chapter 15.)

Along with the stimulus it should provide regarding productivity of people, the task force should also be looking after the productivity of money. Its job is not to make investments, but to provide the infrastructure necessary that those who do make investments can:

- Deliver a better job for the same time they are spending
- Or, produce the same results for less time and lower cost.

CalPers, California's state employees fund, presents a good example. It grew from $28.6 billion in fiscal year 1984–5 to $161.4 billion as of fiscal year 2004–5 – an

---

Box 7.1 Component parts of a customer mirror

1. All transactions done with the customer, by channel
2. Cost of each of these transactions to the bank
3. Risk assumed by type of instrument and by transaction
4. Monetization of risk the bank has taken with these transactions
5. Customer collateral, and unsecured loans
6. Fees the bank charged for the transactions
7. Other fees pro rata, like portfolio management and safekeeping
8. Volume of and income from cross-sales in relationship banking
9. Strengths and weaknesses in historical customer relationship
10. P&L with this customer, seen as a profit centre

increase of 564% in managed money. In those two decades, the average return was 11%, which is well above the average of most privately run funds.

- In the past decade, 76.2% of CalPers' growth has been made from investments.
- An additional 12.7% came from employee contributions.
- Employers, that is California's state agencies, provided only 11.1%.[6]

But at the same time CalPers is highly cost-conscious. Its administrative cost is 18 cents per $100 invested, while in the typical pension fund costs are higher by nearly an order of magnitude, and the brokerage and securities firms charge $2 per $100 invested.

A prerequisite to providing the right infrastructure for productivity of people and money, as well as for cost control, is understanding of a broad range of market requirements, application complexities, and advanced technologies and techniques. Moreover, cost reduction that facilitates competitive pricing throughout the lifespan of a financial product is crucial to success. (More on cost control in Chapter 8.)

Notes

1 BIS 75th Annual Report, Basel, 2005.
2 D.N. Chorafas, *Economic Capital Allocation with Basel II: Cost and Benefit Analysis*, Butterworth-Heinemann, Oxford and Boston, 2004.
3 D.N. Chorafas, *Systems and Simulation*, Academic Press, New York, 1965.
4 D.N. Chorafas, *Rocket Scientists in Banking.* Lafferty Publications, London and Dublin, 1995.
5 ECB, Monthly Bulletin, March 2005.
6 EIR, 18 March, 2005.

Part 3

Management Accounting and the Budget

Management Accounting
and Corporate Governance

1. Introduction

President Lyndon B. Johnson is famous for his penetrating remarks. A story making the rounds in Washington is that an assistant tried to impress upon the US President the need to attend a lecture by a well-known economist, who was presenting his latest theory on federal budgets, employment, and growth. Johnson refused. 'He is also a Democratic Party fund raiser,' insisted the assistant. 'Yes,' said Johnson, 'but the theories of economists are like somebody who is pissing in his pants. To him, but only to him, it's hot stuff.'

And there is another Washington story about economics and economists. This concerns another US president: Harry Truman. President Truman had his way of reacting to the rather ambiguous advice he got from economists. 'I am looking for a one-armed economist,' he is rumoured to have said in a cabinet meeting at the White House. When asked why, he answered: 'So that when he gives me an opinion, he does not immediately add "... on the other hand ...".' Between them, these two presidential stories do indeed provide a take on what management accounting seeks to achieve:

- To provide *shareable* hot stuff on the facts and figures for decision-makers, rather than individually assembled incompatible numbers, and
- To assure that data are complemented through qualitative information, detailing an array of options, as well as their likelihood, so that alternatives are available for decisions to be taken in an informed manner.

Traditionally, the accountant has been thought of as a person engaged in reporting the financial facts of an enterprise, from a dispassionate and fully objective viewpoint. This view defines the accountant as a recorder of facts so that the finances of business may be written down in a reliable, systematic way. This simplistic view of accounting, and of accountants, forgets that there are many problems which have to be met and solved in carrying on such duties. Examples are:

- Interpretation of transactions in terms of their materiality
- Recognition of contingencies regarding revenue credits
- Probable useful life of depreciable assets, and
- Management implications embedded in financial reports.

From this viewpoint, the results of the accounting process are statements which set out income, profits, losses, assets, liabilities of the enterprise for a given period, as well as its financial position at given dates. This necessarily involves subjective judgment. Moreover, what the above bullet point stated is more or less the traditional conception of accounting; modern accounting must go much further.

Parts 1 and 2 of this book have explained why the International Financial Reporting Standard (IFRS) is a good basis for modern accounting. Since it has become the accounting standard in the 25 countries of the European Union, IFRS can serve regulatory general accounting, financial accounting, and *management accounting* (see section 2 for a definition).

This plurality of services is important inasmuch as accounting operations are not separate and apart from other activities in the business, for instance those relating to management decisions. Quite to the contrary, they are highly interconnected with them. Chapter 7 brought to the reader's attention the difference between management accounting and financial accounting. Here is a comparison between management accounting and general accounting.

- *General accounting* reflects this interconnection in a *precise*, detailed manner looking after compliance to rules and regulations, and seeing to it that what is written in the books squares out.
- By contrast, *management accounting* must be *accurate* rather than precise, reflecting internal company rules, showing trends, informing management, and serving internal control procedures.

Financial accounting essentially sits at the junction between these two bullet points. On the one hand, the making of financial statements is part and parcel of business operations; on the other, formatted in an order of magnitude way, these records are action-oriented senior executives' tools. Management cannot depend upon mere memory or hunch in making decisions. Financial records are, indeed, an integral part of business activity.

- The recording process should not be maintained only for general accounting purposes.
- It must also be designed for, and used by, senior management to help in business operations day-to-day and in the longer term.

Management accounting's rationale lies in the fact that both tactical and strategic decisions must be made when they are of consequence. To a significant extent they must be formulated with reference to future activities, because what has been done cannot be undone though its recurrence may be avoided. Moreover, managerial decisions must be made promptly when they are called for, even if the information available for such decisions is incomplete or inconclusive.

2. Management accounting defined

In order to improve the reader's perspective of what accounting, and most particularly management accounting, is and is not, it is advisable to consider its content, objectives, and procedures from at least two viewpoints. Far from being contradictory, these viewpoints complement and enhance one another.

- The first view of accounting is that accounting serves to measure, record, classify, and present financial effects of business transactions and of inventoried positions.

Addressed to an entity's own management, its regulators, as well as creditors, investors, and general public, accounting reports comprise income statements, balance sheets, ledgers, and other records. These may be accompanied by analyses that present reasons for changes in specific asset, liability or equity accounts. This may be enriched by supporting computations or subclassifications. And they may incorporate comparisons, ratios, or other relevant information in tabular or graphic forms of presentation.

- The second view of accounting, with which this chapter is particularly concerned, is that its information and its procedures are intimately connected with the processes of management of an enterprise. Indeed, accounting is a part of management.

Management accounting requires digested data streams and other information able to reflect an integrated set of activities related to the books and records of the firm. Contrary to general accounting, it is not interested in deals with a large mass of detail but, rather, in their relevance to actual handling and carrying on of operations; also on information regarding the way in which things are done.

Because *financial accounting* produces statements that convey information to investors, banks, government agencies, and other interested outside parties, it has to be regulated. Personal accountability for compliance rests on the shoulders of whosoever signs or countersigns the financial statement. By contrast, management accounting is an activity useful to the entity's own management, in being in charge of business operations. Hence,

- It does not need to be governed by the 'generally accepted principles', that are so important in the case of financial accounting, but
- Concepts behind management accounting are most similar to those of financial accounting: usefulness and objectivity being examples. What is different are the principles of *content* and *presentation*.

This difference is readily explainable in terms of the criterion of usefulness. Still, although such difference exists, most elements of financial accounting are also found in management accounting. Moreover, readers of both types of reports need assurance that what they read:

- Is prepared according to some known set of ground rules, and
- Is based on reasonably objective and verifiable information.

To understand those two points, one must appreciate that data upon which a large part of the fact-finding associated with managerial decisions is based are largely accounting data. Strategies, policies, and management plans are seldom established without some reference to accounting records. The same is true of supervision of business activities – hence the linkage between management accounting and internal control. Indeed, internal control brought out the need for maintaining appropriate records permitting management to:

- Fix responsibilities
- Facilitate smooth and effective division of authority
- Reduce errors, fraud and waste.

The functions of an internal control system are not merely to provide data for financial type events, and make sure that all transactions, and persons or units accountable for them, are recorded. Rather, internal control is aimed at guaranteeing error-free, efficient, and smooth performance of regular operating activities, providing feedback on failures and exceptions.[1]

Failure of internal control to perform this task represents a burden on operations and opens up loopholes. Basically, it makes little difference whether or not internal control is viewed as the province of an accountant. As shown in Figure 8.1, general accounting, management accounting, and internal control are interlinked and they also relate to auditing and risk management. This is a crucial reason behind the regulators' decision that auditors should now examine, and express an opinion on, both:

- The company's books, and
- Its internal control system.

The message to be retained from this extension of auditing responsibilities is that a mere record-keeper cannot contribute much to the solution of internal control problems. The managerial accountant must be much more than a person who keeps financial records and submits quantitative reports. He or she must view

Figure 8.1   Accounting closely relates to management control

situations, and data from the viewpoint of *decisions* against which such information is to be marshalled. This imposes several requirements related to accounting
standards, as well as responsibilities assumed by the accounting division.

- The standards must incorporate managerial information elements
- Data must be available when needed, hence in real time[2]
- Facts and figures must be complemented with qualitative information
  which explains and, may be, prognosticates.

Every one of these bullets is important to management accounting because it
impacts on systematic collection and presentation of facts about operations
within the enterprise; provides assistance to internal control; and helps in interpretation of costs and risks in terms of organizational units of responsibility
and/or with respect to different managerial decision problems.

Furthermore, information available through management accounting makes possible post-mortem evaluations of what has or has not been achieved by existing
accounting systems and procedures. The debate on the consequences of the
insolvency of Enron provides an example. The collapse of the US energy trader,

in December 2001, attracted international attention because the Enron case had consequences both:

- For the company itself, its investors and its employees, and
- For its auditing firm, Arthur Andersen, for its role in concealing Enron's shady business practices.

Basically, Enron has been not only a managerial scam but, as well, an accounting and auditing scandal, which triggered an international debate on its causes and consequences. A similar statement is valid about other cases we have briefly reviewed in Chapter 1, like WorldCom and Parmalat.

Reports to tax authorities and (for quoted companies) to regulators and the general public, incorporate elements from both general accounting and management accounting. Rules governing them have been chosen so as to avoid future market disruptions like those that ensued in the aftermath of a general loss of confidence in published company financial statements. While fraudulent business activities and wilful violation of rules may have been partly to blame for Enron's collapse,

- Fundamental flaws and gaps in accounting and auditing have also been revealed, and
- These revelations brought to light that corporate governance practice, too, was wanting.

Unguarded gates in the system of internal control, financial reporting, and regulatory supervision, as well as loopholes control, related to US GAAP, created incentives for Enron either to circumvent or abuse existing rules. As a result, Enron conducted many types of business for the sole purpose of being able to present a favourable financial statement to the market. For instance, it:

- Established non-consolidated special-purpose vehicles
- Manipulated its accounts
- Used credit institutions in doubtful deals like prepays,[3] and
- Ended up with fraudulent statements that masqueraded so well it took a long time to uncover the fraud.

With the complicity of its auditors, Enron misrepresented facts and figures to all stakeholders – investors, regulators, and its own employees, many of whom were also shareholders and depended for their retirement on their company's pension fund. Italy's Parmalat is another example of a company that lied to all stakeholders till it collapsed.[4] This fraud, too, was accomplished with other parties' complicity – and, as we saw in Chapter 1, the case is still on trial.

The silver lining behind Enron, WorldCom, Parmalat and so many other companies which have cooked their books, is the documentation these cases provide in linking general accounting not only with auditing but also with management accounting and with internal control. These links are substantiated by both qualitative and quantitative criteria. Section 3 brings into perspective another dimension: that of organization and structure, as well as its impact on the accounting unit.

3. Management organization and sought-out results

Except in the very smallest of companies, there is a division of tasks of management among a number of departments and business units; and therefore of persons, since companies are made up of people. It is the task of organization to ensure there is specialization to make maximum use of the aptitudes and abilities of people, for the various operations of the firm. The divisionalization, or other form of organization that arises from this specialization of duties, represents a structure which consists of:

- Units of attention, or
- Centres of managerial interest.

This divisionalization also entails a number of problems, many of which have relevance to the accounting operations – starting with the fact that the latter must reach the lowest level of supervision. In manufacturing, the lowest level of supervision is the foreman. In an office environment, such as banking, the lowest level of internal supervision is the section head. In both cases,

- The highest level of supervision is the chief executive officer (CEO), and
- Above the CEO stands the board of directors to whom he or she reports.

Top to bottom, all levels of supervision, both at headquarters and in the subsidiaries, must benefit from management accounting support. Planning and control provides a good example on how this should work.

- *Planning* is the process of deciding what action should be taken in the future.

The area covered by a plan may be a small segment of the entity, or it may be the whole enterprise. The decision as to whether the price of one product should be increased by, say, 3% is a plan; and so is a decision to merge the company with another firm.

The essential characteristic of a plan is that it involves a decision about action to be taken in the future. Planning is therefore to be distinguished from *forecasting*, which is an estimate of possible evolution; for instance, in market demand, in inflation, in general economic well-being, or in matters concerning the entity internally.

- *Control* is the process through which management assures itself, as far as is feasible, that what the company does conforms to plans and policies.

Accounting information, particularly cost accounting, is most useful to management in evaluating the efficiency of employees in doing their jobs. Merits assigned in the aftermath of *appraisal* of performance may result in salary increase and/or promotion. Demerits may lead to reassignment, corrective action of various kinds, or even dismissal.

Accounting information assists in this appraisal process, even if an adequate basis for judging individual performance cannot be obtained from accounting records only. Organizational activities, discussed at the beginning of this section, also require reliable information for planning and control. The performance of a responsibility centre must be judged in terms of its inputs and outputs registered through accounting. Since output is often divided into *quality* and *quantity* components three key questions need to be considered simultaneously:

- How much was accomplished?
- How good was its quality compared to specifications?
- How much did it cost? (See section 7)

Actual results must always be compared with some standard showing what is expected. Part of the importance of giving due consideration to all three aspects of performance, identified through these bullet points, lies in the fact that divisionalization must be evaluated in terms of its deliverables. Results obtained in real life are the only way to test an organizational solution.

Divisionalization should never be made at random, and the same principle is valid about establishing the inputs and outputs of the accounting system. Two notions closely connected to organizational theory are: The *span of control* and *layers of supervision* – they are connected to one another. Span of control defines how many managers report to a superior. Layers of supervision are counted top to bottom: from the CEO to the lowest level. Other things being equal:

- The larger is the span of control, the fewer are the supervisory layers.
- Lean organizations have very few managerial levels; not more than five. Badly managed firms may have fifteen.

Ideally, the *accounting unit* should be a subsection of the lowest level of supervision because this can assure both detail and greater accuracy. A basic aspect of the difference between financial and managerial accounting lies in the unit of accounting taken as the very basis of operations. Here again the distinction can be made top to bottom.

- For regulatory financial reporting, the firm is viewed as a single entity, in terms of which financial data is marshalled to show the position, or effects, of operations as a whole.

The company's financial reporting is a summation of general accounting data whose detail is found in the aforementioned smallest units of operation (and supervision). This detail is most important, as well, for managerial accounting. Costs and risks cannot be controlled in a summary manner.

- For management purposes, however, the notion that the firm is a single entity is not very useful because most critical decisions are not of the type that can be related to overall enterprise data.

Activities such as extending credit or making capital investments require detail – and, associated to it, maintenance of records to make readily available specific information. Typically, such information cannot be obtained except by following the transactions involving a particular customer or business unit, as well as its subdivisions.

Along a similar line of thinking, valuing assets or setting a selling price for a given product or service (see Chapter 10) cannot be done in terms of income statement aggregates. Some costs are variable with output, and some are related to factors other than output. All costs are important (see section 7), and it must be possible to track them to their origin.

- The proper appraisal of cost, as well as of risk and return, involves much more than mere aggregates or summary data.

A good way of going to the heart of costs and risks is to set up accounting units at the level of detail about which management wants information from accounting, also specifying the kind of information that is wanted. Moreover,

- Information that is wanted in the future may vary considerably as management requirements evolve and reorganizations reshuffle the units.

Therefore, it is desirable that the accounting structure follows the smaller subdivision(s) of the smaller organizational unit. Another factor leading in this direction of greater detail is that the scope of managerial accounting may shift considerably, and likewise the kind of information that will be wanted as operations evolve. Greater detail of accounting records also makes feasible information that may be accumulated for both:

- Regularly recurring, and
- Exceptional special-purpose, reports.

One of the prerequisites applicable to both general and managerial accounting is that the accounting function itself must be kept in the hands of persons separate from those who perform various activities, from R, D&I to manufacturing, marketing, distribution, and after-sales service. When this is done, the system of accounting serves as an independent reporting agency. Subsequently, the auditing process is checking all the activities of the firm in such a way as to bring to the attention of operating executives deviations or other data demanding immediate attention.

- Continuous review and reporting of conditions by an 'independent agency' is an effective means of making sure that operating executives do not overlook their responsibilities.
- In this sense, management accounting provides an overall check upon the entire organization, thereby contributing to better governance and performance.

This is done not by giving orders or attending to details of supervision, but by bringing various parts of the picture of the enterprise's progress and achievement to the attention of the proper officers. Precisely because of this function, which is vital to good corporate governance, companies should welcome IFRS and its rigorous rules and clauses. The alternative is drifting.

4. What should and should not be expected from an expert accountant?

The knowledge the accountant has acquired through his or her study and experience is manifested in several ways. At the very least, the accountant knows the procedures for recording all accounting aspects of business transactions – doing so quickly, efficiently, accurately, and in a way that minimizes the opportunity for fraud or theft.

It is self-evident that the expert accountant does more than that. For instance, he or she knows a great deal about their own company, the type of data that is vital, that information managers and professionals have found useful, the meaning of compliance, the way in which transactions must be recorded and retrieved, and so on. These are largely matters connected to world 'experience', for which books and classroom teaching are not satisfactory substitutes.

The expertise of a good accountant goes beyond techniques for summarizing, arranging, and presenting information so that it meets the needs of various requirements and types of users. For instance, he or she knows the legal principles that govern financial reporting. And because tax considerations play a major part in many decisions, they should be fully reflected in both financial and management accounting.

Moreover, the expert accountant knows, or can find by referring to texts and handbooks, generally accepted ways of handling different specialized types of transactions, of valuing inventory, searching for hidden costs, and diligently looking to detect fraud or abuse. For example, costs should be collected and measured only to the extent that they are *material*.

- Reporting a long list of cost elements, many of which have only minor impact, obscures the few really important ones.
- This can happen when the cost report is a standard form containing a long list of cost items that are reported uniformly for each responsibility centre.

The better way to proceed is that the company's control system is tailor-made to reflect materiality in each profit centre, and for the company as a whole. For instance, for cost control reasons $1000 may not be material for the firm as a whole – but it is material for a small business unit. The proper organization work is done by keeping in mind the significance of every expense. (More on cost-findings in section 7.)

Costs must always be classified into controllable and uncontrollable. The term *controllable costs* refers to those under the responsibility of profit centres. *All internal* costs are controllable by someone in the organization. This, however, is not true of costs like taxation, or bills or fees paid to third parties, which are mainly controllable at the time a purchasing contract is signed.

In principle, negotiating about procurement of goods and services is the responsibility of the purchasing department. It is not the expert accountant's job, though he or she may help in the negotiation by providing facts and figures. Both purchasing and accounting, however, is management's responsibility, and the same is true about:

- Assuring that deliverables follow the plan
- Abiding to agreements that have been made, or
- Providing appropriate coordination to capitalize on the synergy of different divisions in a joint effort.

An example of the aftermath of lack of coordination, particularly in connection to deliverables, is provided by the European Commission's Financial Services Action Plan (FSAP). This was adopted with good intentions but poor management in 1999. The so-called *Lisbon Agenda* of the European Commission launched FSAP as the core of a programme to make Europe the world's most competitive economy by 2010.

The FSAP initiative constituted a major overhaul of the European Union's existing regime for financial services, aiming to promote the development of a truly integrated financial market with homogeneous securities markets regulation. To meet that objective, FASP:

- Affects the corporate governance framework, and
- Pays particular attention to transparency and disclosure, tightening periodic information requirements for issuers.

When the FSAP agreement was originally made, those in its favour said it would be a big boost to realization of the single EU market for financial services, and also prove a strong impetus on other related issues. But the accounting criteria for judging the results have not been forthcoming. As the elapsed years document:

- Expert accountants cannot contribute to FASB's success, because this is beyond their job description.
- Neither can expert accountants take any initiative in strengthening specific arrangements for financial stability, another FSAP goal.

Because of what it promised it would deliver, FSAP originally found considerable support in the main European financial market. However, a few years down the line, in March 2005, financial experts expressed the opinion that it has become something of an orphan – and its deliverables have been both minimal and irrelevant.

The mood changed for several reasons. One is lack of clear initiatives able to promote FSAP's implementation. Another is cost. Companies have generally found the costs of change to be far higher than expected, partly because Europe's regulatory regimes are so different from one another. For instance, the UK's code of market conduct had to be changed to take account of the EU market abuse directive.

Experts also say that the insurance mediation directive is the worst example of a measure that:

- Has imposed huge costs on British insurance brokers, and
- Has offered highly uncertain benefits in return.

Bureaucracy, too, made its contribution. In the hands of the European Commission, what began as a liberalizing initiative has turned into a mess of 42 directives or regulations, several among them contradicting one another. To make matters worse, most of these '42' are characterized by impenetrable detail. In fact, contradictions became unavoidable as there has been a shift:

- Away from an approach based on mutual recognition of each other's regimes
- To a platform of ill-studied harmonization of incompatible regimes, which resulted in lots of friction.

Another lesson from FSAP's failure is the simplicity required to characterize written instructions on inputs and outputs of the accounting system, down to the level of the most elementary accounting unit. If IFRS had been available when FSAP was set up, the need for homogeneous financial accounting and management reports might have been met.

Added to these problems is the fact that too much effort has been devoted to harmonizing small retail markets. Another reason for disillusionment with FSAP is the continuing parochial behaviour of many EU governments and central bankers. For instance, Dr Antonio Fazio, the governor of the Bank of Italy, has stood in the way of European banking consolidation by ruling out takeovers of Italian banks – but had no objection to the takeover of a major German bank by an Italian bank.

Let's face it. The European union is totally lacking *unity of command*. Moreover, the success of any project greatly depends on the executive who will father it and see it through. Nobody was really in charge of FSAP, which depended largely on good intentions – but, as this real-life case study documents, good intentions wear out fast.

5. Why financial reporting and management accounting correlate

There is a saying in business that accounting reports frequently substitute for supervision. This is only half true. Essentially, management accounting reports are worthwhile supplements to the supervisor's own eyes and ears. This is the case at all echelons of management. Particularly at the vertex, comprehensive reporting plays a crucial role in terms of:

- Planning, and
- Control.

At the same time, however, it is no less true that financial accounting has its limitations, of which the reader must be aware. Managers cannot really be in charge unless they know where the limits are. The limits are the plan. Financial reporting is part of the control activity. Four issues are brought into perspective in connection to management accounting and financial reporting:

- Budgets, which establish the financial plan for a term period (see Chapter 9)
- Valuing assets and liabilities, which is much more an art than a science (see Chapter 10)
- Subjective judgment entering into accounting policies and practices (see section 6)
- The need for forward-looking statements to drive the business in a dynamic market (see Chapter 12).

Let's start with this last point. Theoretically, accounting is concerned with *factual* measurement, in money terms, of operations undertaken by the enterprise. Historically, accounting records and financial reports are considered largely as summaries of what has happened, without too much emphasis upon the interpretation of data they contain in terms of:

- Why things have happened, or
- How they may be expected to appear in the future.

In practical terms, parallel to this policy of reporting on past events, for which there exist accounting inputs and statistics, there has been the accountant's traditional and conventional emphasis upon historical costs. With the accruals method (see Chapter 1), historical cost has been the basis for:

- Stating assets
- Evaluating liabilities, and
- Measuring expense.

Both good governance of an entity and shareholder value require that management accounting reports and financial statements are *forward*-looking – which brings into consideration the second bullet point, on subjective judgment.

Contrary to historical figures, which essentially constitute *hard data*, or statistics (noun, singular), forward-looking statements talk about the likelihood, shape, and weight of future events. This is *soft data* involving opinions, with the entries into the management report characterized by different levels of dependability – each with 'yes' or 'no' probabilities attached to it.

An example of a forward-looking exercise is the valuation of assets and liabilities at current market value. In a dynamic market, this is necessary in order to get an appreciation of how solvent a company is. As far as the whole enterprise is concerned, a currently popular algorithm is:

$$\frac{A}{L} > 1$$

where:

> A = assets at fair value using market capitalization as proxy
> L = liabilities at book value, because these represent commitment the company must face, no matter what its market value may be.

This is, of course, an approximation, but it is useful because management decisions must always be forward-looking in the sense that history is irrelevant except in so far as it may be a basis for forecasting. The cost of the approximation is that what is prognosticated may not materialize, therefore inducing management error.

In a way, it makes no difference whatever what the historical cost of a transaction, and risk associated to it, may have been when the decision is made as to whether this transaction should be hedged. Similarly, in manufacturing, last year's costs have no relevance to the selling prices of current and future periods, except as:

- They may provide a reasonable basis for current interpretation of profit margin(s), or their future adjustment, and
- They can be used in applying rigorous cost control procedures, because costs matter greatly (see section 6).

For management purposes, the financial data must be related to the use to be made of them. Therefore, while the origin of data for general accounting and management accounting purposes is very similar, their massing, reporting, and timing requirements differ. For instance, along with the need for detailed information concerning certain aspects of operations, there is a difference between financial and managerial accounting in terms of timeframes.

- General accounting has a periodicity fixed by the law of the land, through prevailing rules, regulations, and even customs.

The basic figures for the preparation of conventional financial reports arise from general accounts, by summarizing major data classes concerning enterprise operations. Revolving around the general ledger, accounting practice has built a complex set of procedures and records closely integrated with operations, but designed to accomplish a number of objectives not associated directly with enterprise management.

Classical general accounting includes the preparation of documents or business papers commonly referred to as *vouchers*. These are original documents and memoranda designed to accomplish various tasks, one of which is to keep the accounting department informed as to what has occurred in various parts of the firm's activities; another, to provide documentation for general ledger entries.

Being the basis for all accounting records and tabulations, vouchers support the accounting data as classified and presented in various kinds of subsidiary ledgers, analyses, and reports. They also permit implementation of a system of internal checks and controls. By contrast, common tools of financial reports and of management accounting are balance sheets and income statements. This is not surprising because:

- Regulatory financial reporting responds to legal and supervisory requirements targeting the governance and solvency of the entity, and
- Management accounting responds to the entity's internal criteria for good governance as well as for management control.

To be truly helpful in this mission, management accounting must be ad hoc, polyvalent, and deliverable in real time (see Chapter 15 on real-time balance sheet). At the same time, it is important to recall the difference made in the Introduction regarding general accounting's need for high precision, while good accuracy is enough to satisfy management accounting requirements.

Another principle to keep in mind is that, quite often, incomplete details of an operation obtained promptly and submitted to management may be more useful than complete information that is available only after a considerable lapse of time. The requirement of *current relevance* in terms of risks, costs, prices, productivity, and sales conditions has attracted management attention because in a dynamic market it is key to competitiveness and the survival of the firm.

Take costs as an example. The costs that are important and relevant to a decision are those that will be different when the choice is made in one way rather than in another. In terms of productivity, what management accounting is after is deviations from planned performance expressed in the form of:

- Variances from standard costs and other question-raising data.
- Budget estimates that are not matched by actual costs because productivity is lagging.

From the intelligent raising of questions as to why deviations occur may be found better ways of accomplishing the tasks that are to be done in the firm. From this viewpoint, management accounting should be the source of questions to answer in a factual way. In the broader sense, management accounting is the trigger for asking the questions senior executives are curious enough to want answered (see also section 7).

6. Impact of subjective judgment on accounting figures

No matter which might be the jurisdiction or prevailing accounting standard, the way to bet is that a consolidated financial statement will include certain amounts based on management's best estimates. As such they are judgmental. Hypotheses and estimates derived from partly objective and partly subjective information, are used in determining items like:

- Provisions for sales discounts and returns
- Amounts recorded for contingencies
- Depreciable and amortizable wares
- Recoverability of inventories produced in preparation for product launches
- Guesstimates on environmental liabilities
- Assumptions about pension and other post-retirement benefits
- Taxes to be paid on income.

Because of uncertainty inherent in such estimates, actual results may differ, sometimes significantly, from projections being made. In section 5, this difference has been characterized as being the cost of forecasts – a notion that applies widely. Notice that variations in accounting estimates can have a potentially significant impact on financial statements.

Take as an example revenue recognition. Revenues from sales of products are typically recognized when title and risk of loss passes to the customer. But there are exceptions. For instance, in the United States revenues for domestic pharmaceutical sales are recognized at time of shipment, while for many foreign subsidiaries revenues are recognized at time of delivery.

Recognition of revenue requires reasonable assurance of collection of sales proceeds, and completion of all obligations. Domestically, sales discounts are issued to customers directly at point of sale or indirectly through an intermediary wholesale purchaser. Revenues are recorded net of provisions for sales discounts and returns, which are established at time of sale. This is a fairly objective procedure.

More subjective issues arise in connection to the provision for aggregate indirect customer discounts, which covers chargebacks and rebates. Chargebacks are discounts that occur when a contracted customer purchases directly through an intermediary wholesale purchaser. The intermediary, however, as an independent entity may apply its own discount policy – to all clients, or only to those in its priority list.

Unrecognized net loss amounts reflect experience differentials primarily relating to differences between expected and actual returns, as well as the effects of changes in actuarial assumptions – which are mostly judgmental. Expected returns are based on calculated market-related value of assets. US GAAP requires that gains and losses resulting from actual returns that differ from the company's expected returns must be recognized in the market value of assets. Other jurisdictions follow different rules.

One of the major judgmental issues is the valuation of intangible assets. These consist primarily of client lists. Under SFAS 142, US GAAP, intangible assets which have finite lives continue to be amortized over their estimated useful lives and are subject to impairment testing under the provisions of SFAS 144 'Accounting for the Impairment or Disposal of Long-Lived Assets'. The latter requires that intangible assets other than goodwill be tested for impairment whenever events or changes in circumstances indicate that the company's carrying amount may not be recoverable. In these cases, senior management must assess whether future cash flows related to the asset will be greater than its carrying value at the time of the test. Accordingly, the process of evaluating a potential impairment is based on estimates and it is subjective.

- Sound accounting principles require that the measurements being made are objective and dependable

- But market values change rapidly and some of the factors included in metrics are qualitative, therefore judgmental.

This should always be kept in mind when comparing accounting systems. Within the context of this reference, an important part of a sound financial reporting procedure is the proper definition of significant financial events.

Well-managed banks analyse their performance on a reported basis determined in accordance with prevailing regulatory directives, accounting standards, and a normalized basis which excludes from the reported amounts certain items termed *significant financial events*. A rigorous policy sees to it that management uses figures adjusted for significant financial events based on underlying operational performance of their business, insulated from the impact of one-off gains or losses such as:

- Non-recurring items
- Event-specific issues in a market sense
- Industry-specific material items
- Company-specific, but not industry-wide specific issues.

Examples of issues treated as significant financial events include the gain or loss on the sale of a major subsidiary, and restructuring costs associated with a major acquisition or downsizing. Notice that significant financial events are not a recognized accounting concept under US GAAP, and many other national financial reporting rules. When this is the case, they must be handled with care, within available guidelines and in accordance with compliance rules.

It is always a sound policy to clearly identify all adjusted figures as such, properly disclosing both the pre-tax amount of each individual significant financial event and the net tax benefit (or loss) associated with each significant financial event in each period. In regulatory financial reporting business risk is typically reflected into the accounts only through its effect on profit and loss. To the contrary, in management reporting business risk must be shown as the result of either:

- The company's own action or inactions, or
- Competitive forces that need to be properly identified.

For instance, financial institutions face intense competition in all aspects of their business from asset managers, retail banks, other commercial banks, investment banks, brokerages and other investment services firms. The management accounting report should clearly show lost revenue by class of competitors and, sometimes, individual competitor firm.

Attention should also be paid to the fall-out from trends in the industry. For instance, the trend toward consolidation in the global financial services industry is creating competitors with:

- Broader range of products and services
- Increased access to capital, and
- Greater pricing power than classical banks.

At the same time, all companies are faced with operational risks. These are largely dependent on their ability to process a large number of transactions, appeal to diverse markets, trade in different currencies, and be the subject of many largely incompatible legal and regulatory requirements. As a result, any weaknesses in their systems and procedures can have a negative impact on the results of their operations, which will show up in their financial reporting – and it should be explained through facts and figures in management accounting.

7. Effective use of management accounting: a case study on cost-finding

The accounting system as a whole is valuable to management not because it answers questions, but because it raises them. An effective use of management accounting is more concerned with *why* things are as they are, rather than with *what* they are – which is the province of general accounting.

Raising questions about what might not go right is so important because the more dynamic is the market, the less sure management is that answers it has adopted in the form of plans for operations are those that they should be. The after-effects of business decisions are always finely balanced as:

- Market conditions change
- Competition increases, and
- New products take the market away from the old.

In a way, senior executives are in the position of scientific experimenters. Certain things about the company's operations are fairly well understood, and on the basis of that understanding hypotheses are developed in the form of strategic or tactical moves. But other things are uncertain, and hypotheses about them may not be well documented.

- Whether or not the hypotheses being made are sound can be determined by observing the results that follow their application.

- This is, however, a course full of risks. Like the scientific experiment that fails, an unsuccessful plan is merely a challenge to the invention of better hypotheses for future experimentation.

But can the company afford to follow an after the facts approach? *If* not, *then* the better solution is proactive experimentation, with a most careful evaluation of cause and effect. Cost structures offer themselves to such an approach (more on this later). Chapter 7 focused on the need for cost control. The theme in this section is cost-finding.

Management accounting contains stuff which, when properly exploited, helps in deriving business intelligence. This leads to finding means of improving corporate governance. It may also allow events to be uncovered that should not have happened in the first place. For instance, violations of company rules that should be sanctioned internally, rather than waiting for regulatory action and associated penalties.

Mid-March 2005 the Securities and Exchange Commission filed a civil lawsuit against the former CEO of Qwest, Joseph Nacchio, and six other former executives of the firm. They have been accused, among other things, of fraudulently reporting $3 billion in revenue to seal a merger with another telecom company in 2000. The SEC wants the executives to repay bonuses and options accrued during the period. Qwest would have been much better off *if*:

- Its internal control system had reported such misbehaviour to the board, and
- The board had taken immediate disciplinary action, rather than waiting for the regulator to intervene and penalize the firm.

Such a proactive stance would have been in accordance with the principle that management's rationale is that of planning, directing, and exercising control. In this connection, management accounting is important inasmuch as it is facilitating control action. Cost control provides an example.

The problem of cost-finding is one of the great puzzles in practically every enterprise. Cost standards, and data concerning costs, are obviously a large part of management accounting, and they also constitute a considerable part of the domain of economic analysis. Moreover, cost data has a significant impact on company governance.

For starters, the form in which cost data is most frequently encountered is as *units cost*, not as abstract and general interpretations of outlay, or resource allocation. A unit cost is cost of 'something' that has to be compared to a standard in order for management to decide if it is high, low, or just right. This short paragraph tells us that a cost control system rests on two pillars:

- Established standard unit costs, and
- Timely reporting of actual unit costs.

The latter are provided through management accounting, fulfilling the requirement that cost planning and cost control presuppose the existence of a reporting mechanism, bringing forward values that permit comparison of current measurements against standards and get immediate results. Comparing an actual cost to a standard provides ratios that can be readily understood by anyone concerned.[5]

The unit cost may correspond to a component of a product or service. It may target production chores, an administrative duty, the cost of a function, a process, an activity, a method of doing something. The fact that there can be many different kinds of cost units increases the flexibility to costing operations.

- Costs are related to efficiency, production processes, price policy, financial activities, and any other issue whose cost matters.
- The fact that costs nearly always have to be thought of as 'costs of something' makes it necessary to specify the item with which cost is associated, if the cost figure is to mean much.

The problem of establishing standard costs and selecting cost units for systematic treatment in an accounting system, is that stereotypes of rules and procedures will not do. There is need for a great deal of adaptation – all the way to using cost information with respect to the various purposes to be served.

- Some costs are fixed over relevant ranges of activity
- Others vary in pattern with respect to output, scope of operations, quality level, and other independent variables.

Costs may be controllable or noncontrollable, avoidable or unavoidable, linear or nonlinear in their statistical behaviour, efficient or wasteful. There are many ways of classifying costs, and by consequence cost data, just like there are many questions that can be raised about them. From the managerial viewpoint, there is also an emphasis upon the behaviour of costs, particularly those:

- Running out of control, or
- Putting the firm in an unfavourable position versus competition.

Therefore, it is to be expected that management accounting makes full use of replacement costs, efficiency ratings, and competitive data in preparation of meaningful and useful reports for corrective action. Moreover, the concept of unit cost has to be further elaborated so that it involves not only the notion of a unit with which the cost is associated but is also a connection, a causal relationship between:

- Cost figure, and
- Cost unit.

Such association of money with units of production, distribution, service, or any other activity tends to express the idea that there is a kind of cause-and-effect relationship between cost measurement and the object to which this cost is coupled. Beyond this the cost of a given unit is part of the continuum, or larger aggregate to which that unit belongs. For instance, the process of production is an assimilation of various kinds of economic services. A similar statement is valid about sales, trading, and other jobs.

Cost accounting, which is an integral and important part of management accounting, is made more complex by the fact that costs are often incurred jointly, in the sense that the absence or alteration of one or more of them may make the aggregate cost difficult to analyse. Some costs are incurred simply because:

- Other costs have been incurred, or
- An entire range of factors must be provided to obtain desired results.

The combination of resources essential to the processes characterizing a company entail that very often costs are joint and inseparable at the very point at which they are incurred. In many cases, failure to note the jointness of cost at point of incurrence produces cost figures that are difficult to interpret, or outright irrelevant. Another challenge in costing is the assignment of costs to time periods. This, too, is largely a joint cost problem.

One way to allocate costs that cross products, processes, and time periods is by means of conventions characterizing costing. For instance, a basic convention of product cost-determination is the distinction between *direct* and *indirect* costs, the former identifying costs incurred at product units in terms of physical accompaniments.

For instance, in manufacturing the working rule is likely to be a requirement that a given cost must be physically identified with the operation or product unit, if it is to be considered a direct cost. If it cannot be so identified, it is an indirect cost.

Indirect costs bring up the issue of their assignment to units of product or service, usually based upon assumed relationships between cost incurred and the things that can be related to the product or service. This is essentially a subjective measurement. There is no single best method of assigning indirect costs to productive units. Company rules usually prescribe how the allocation should be done. Once this is decided, it should be mapped into the management accounting report.

Notes

1   D.N. Chorafas, *Implementing and Auditing the Internal Control System*, Macmillan, London, 2001.
2   D.N. Chorafas, *The Real-time Enterprise*, Auerbach, New York, 2005.
3   D.N. Chorafas, *Corporate Accountability, with Case Studies in Finance*, Macmillan/Palgrave, London, 2004.
4   D.N. Chorafas, *The Management of Equity Investments*, Butterworth-Heinemann, London, 2005.
5   D.N. Chorafas, *Operational Risk Control with Basel II: Basic Principles and Capital Requirements*, Butterworth-Heinemann, London and Boston, 2004.

Budgeting: A Case Study on Financial Planning

1. Introduction

The *budget* is a financial plan. A formal written statement of management's plans for the future, expressed in quantitative terms. The financial allocations the budget makes, as well as statistics derived from them, chart the course of future action. For this reason, the budget should contain sound attainable objectives rather than approximations or mere wishful thinking. Beyond being a financial plan:

- The budget is a *planning model* and the means used for its development are planning instruments.
- As a formal form of planning, the budget works well when the company has the proper methodology, solid cost data and management resolve to keep within budgeted figures.

An alternative view of the budgetary process is that this year's budget is just a downpayment for things to be done in the years to come. Each of those years will have its own budget. A company's business is not a snapshot but a sustained effort over time.

Chapter 7 and Chapter 8 have explained the reason why a great deal of attention must be paid to costs. The whole process of financial planning is based on them. *Costing* makes the budget an orderly presentation of projected activity for the next financial year, based on the amount of work to be done.

While budgeting is the process of planning, and provisioning financially, the overall activity of the enterprise for a specified period of time, usually a year, it is no *carte blanche* to spend money. The most important objective of this formal planning process is to:

- Fit together the separate financial plans made for various segments of the entity
- Assure that these plans harmonize with one another, and
- See to it that the aggregate effect of all of them on the whole firm is satisfactory.

The earliest financial plans were *imposed budgets*; they were edicts promulgated by management which, in effect, implied that the different departments and business units shall do 'such' and 'such'. The results obtained from these imposed budgets were frequently unsatisfactory because different parts in the organization tended to:

- Resent them, and
- Disregard them.

The more modern trend in budgeting is in the direction of allowing the department head, or business unit chief – which means the people held responsible for performance – to have a considerable voice in the preparation of the budget. This makes the budget an interactive process between headquarters and organizational units.

A general principle of financial planning to assure a budgetary agreement is to ask for the participation of the person whose performance is to be measured, in the process of setting the standard. Beyond this, practically every industrial sector has its own particular features as far as budgets, and the budgetary process, are concerned. For instance, typically, a financial institution has two budgets:

- An *interest budget* which covers the cost of money.

This includes interest paid to current account deposits (if any), savings, time deposits, debt instruments, different other IOUs and, of course, money bought from other banks and institutional investors or loaned by the central bank. No two credit institutions have the same profile of bought money and of deposits.

- A *non-interest budget*, which covers everything else – the so-called *overhead*.

This 'everything else' is a mixed bag. In it are included salaries and wages of managers, traders, loans officers, investment advisors, tellers, secretaries, and all other personnel. Also the cost of real estate, utilities, information technology (IT), telecommunications, and so on.

Once again, no two banks have the same ratio between interest budget and non-interest budget, as percentages of total budget. At UCLA, my professors taught their students the total budget divides as two-thirds for interest budget, one-third for non-interest budget. This is, however, an average figure.

Another criterion differentiating one bank from another is the overhead – which, in banking jargon, essentially means personnel costs. Well-managed banks do their utmost to keep this overhead below 50% of the non-interest budget. In poorly managed banks, the overhead reaches 75% or more – leaving peanuts for other important services like state of the art IT, networks, and first class branch offices which, in spite of the Internet, are the windows of the bank to its client population.

Manufacturing, too, has its own standards, with different main budgetary chapters than those prevailing in banking. These are divided into research and development, capital investments, procurement, marketing, sales, after sales service, and administrative activities (which are again called 'overhead', but the meaning is that of expenses other than direct labour and direct materials).

Whether we speak of banking or of manufacturing, the level of activity in each channel, and corresponding costs, conditions the budgetary allocation in direct and indirect expenses. The reader will recall that all costs matter, but indirect expenses are those where management should pay great attention, and keep them in control.

2. The budget as financial information system

The process of financial planning is a direct contribution to effective management. Many experts believe that budgeting contributes more to good governance than any other process or tool at management's disposal. This is true because each of a company's primary functions is directly served by budgeting – *if* and when careful study, investigation, and research have been undertaken in order to determine:

- Expected future operations, and
- Costs associated to them.

As financial plans, budgets are based on forecasts. Budgets can only be as good as the forecasts and standard costs used in making them. The forecasting and planning premises entering a budgetary process increase management's ability to rely on fact-finding, lessening the role of hunches and intuition in running the enterprise.

Budgets based on last year's activity multiplied by 'something', are irrelevant. In fact, one of the best ways available to prune a budget is the so-called *zero budgeting*. This puts everybody working for the enterprise on an 'active status', with the requirement to justify the reason and deliverables of his or her job, before this job is again budgeted.

Jobs performed within an entity must have a synergy. Organization-wide coordination through budgetary procedures is facilitated when each level of management participates in the preparation of the budget. The introduction brought the reader's attention to the need for co-involvement.

Top management should be setting and explaining objectives and projected levels of activity, but each organizational unit must establish its budget under these guidelines – subject to subsequent approval by headquarters. On the other hand, according to a very sound principle I learned when I was consultant to General Electric:

- Approval of a budget is *no* authorization for spending money; it is only a financial plan.
- Beyond a certain level, each expenditure must be individually approved, and all expenses must be controlled for compliance to the plan.

'We watch every dollar like a hawk,' said Microsoft's CEO when, in a Washington, DC, conference, he was asked what was his company's secret in being so successful beyond the genius of Bill Gates. As I never tire of repeating, costs matter a great deal. This must be a company dictum appearing on the desk of every executive, because it is not embedded in the balance sheet and income statement (P&L).

Modelling the company's cost structure is important, as is experimentation with alternative courses of action, but there also exist other prerequisites. One of the crucial issues with budgeting is a steady input of information directly to the database. This is necessary to permit realistic financial planning and management control. Inputs can come:

- *Top down* from senior management to the divisions, departments, operating units and back to top management, or
- *Bottom up*, elaborated at operating unit level, and from there sent to the department or to top management for approval.

The best alternative is an interaction between these two, since it leads to a financial plan which contains the salt of the earth. It starts with top management guidelines, then goes close to lower management level where the budget will have to be subsequently applied. As underlined in the Introduction, participation down the line in budgetary processes motivates the people who will later on have to work with that budget.

Companies that have chosen the hierarchical top-down approach argue that the problem is the amount of time required by an iterative process. This amount of time, they say, can be long and the task may not be well coordinated. This can happen, but it does not need to be that way. Rather, the solution is that budgetary planning is executed interactively on-line through:

- Models
- Computers, and
- Networks.

Various options have been provided to facilitate the input task in financial planning, thereby enabling a manager to concentrate his or her efforts on those accounts that do warrant careful analysis. Short-cut methods are not necessarily the best solution, but for the information of the reader these include:

- An annual, quarterly and monthly amount to be prorated according to the actual number of days in each period.

The aim is to have projected amounts created automatically by the system, using forecasting techniques and standard costs. The downside is that this may perpetuate budgetary mistakes.

- A percentage increase or decrease over the current year's actual and projected data, to temper system-generated business forecasts.

Such entries may be coarse and will need to be subsequently refined, but as they stand they could serve as starting points. This is the opposite approach to zero budgeting.

- Combination entries, with distributions resting on algorithms that reflect marked variations or seasonal fluctuations.

The models used to produce this information are typically run by computer. They work interactively and can provide results in real-time. These results, however, needed testing and pruning, by applying Microsoft's dictum. Where this approach can help is in control of Plan *vs* Actual.

In spite of what was stated in Chapter 7 about model risk, computer-based artifacts can be instrumental in preparation of financial plans, all the way to subsequent analysis for control reasons. An example is interim profit and loss evaluation, based on information derived from the financial plan and operating statistics. This helps in producing ad hoc interactive reports:

- From evaluation of cost factors
- To a critical view of customer profitability (see the discussion on customer mirror in Chapter 7).

As a result of a real-time, interactive budgetary process, the activities of each unit of production, and of each department can be better integrated with those of related operations in the same area, nation-wide and internationally. But as the Introduction has underlined, though managerial planning and coordination are important, they must be accompanied by control.

In conclusion, budgeting contributes to effective management planning and control by providing the standard(s) against which the entity's actual performance will be evaluated and variances revealed. This needs to be done both for each operating unit and for the company as a whole. Hence, in both a detailed and in a consolidated way. Members of the board, CEO, and his immediate assistants must always keep in mind that financial planning and control is an integral part of management accounting (see Chapter 8).

3. Analysis of financial information

Any data stream and all databased information elements should be analysed, indeed tortured, to reveal their secrets. Statistical tools like the test of hypothesis, the four momenta of a distribution (mean, standard deviation, skewness, kyrtosis), *t-test* of the mean, and chi-square for analysis of variance, should be used to this end. This should not be a manual job but one performed by knowledge artifacts (expert systems and agents[1]), with results brought to management's attention.

Operating characteristics (OC) curves are excellent both for reasons of analysis and for mapping the results of experimentation. The OC curve in Figure 9.1 is used for loans approval. On the ordinate is probability of acceptance of giving a loan; on the abscissa is creditworthiness.

Classically, the answer to a loan request is 'Accept/Reject'. Risk adjusted return on capital (RAROC), developed in the mid-1980s by Bankers Trust, is using OC curves and sequential sampling to change this to 'Accept/Maybe/No'.

- Every time credit analysis suggests a lower rating, there is an add-on rate over prime rate.
- This can be seen as a reinsurance, which compensates for risk taken with credit grade, but still permits giving the loan.

Closely associated to the OC curve is the risk being assumed, α, or Type I error, better known as *level of confidence*, widely used today in banking. It is the risk of rejecting a good loan applicant. β, or Type II error, is the risk of accepting a bad applicant. Every sampling plan, or other statistical procedure, has its own operating characteristics curve.

Another statistical tool management must master is Latin squares. They help in experimental design. The Monte Carlo method provides a powerful tool for

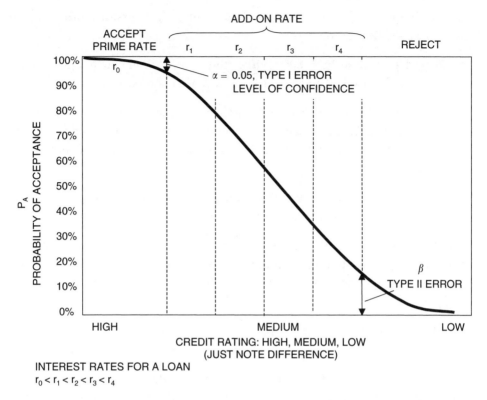

Figure 9.1   Accept/Maybe/Reject: using an operating characteristics curve in deciding on a loan

simulation. Pareto's law permits the evaluation (and capitalization on) the relative weight of two factors. Statistical quality control charts by variables and by attributes are excellent tools for controlling whether a process operates within:

- Tolerances, and
- Control limits.

All these tools are important to analytics connected to budgeting, because budgeting is a dynamic process. It is no futile exercise, where numbers once written are put in the time closet, remaining invariant. Both the development of the financial plan and its evaluation should be done interactively on-line, enriched with statistical analysis tools and using three-dimensional graphics for visualization.

While the final judgment is done by the responsible professional, many of the analytical chores must be automated. Knowledge artifacts help in tearing apart the annual, monthly or other financial plan, line by line, and item by item. They also assist in the parallel maintenance of different budget versions, providing on-line services for simulation.

- Recorded in cash-flow accounting, the annual financial budget transactions can be used as a basis for Plan *vs* Actual comparison.

Every budgetary allocation made in the financial plan must be tested against actual results. Plan/Actual is key to management control because it reveals compliance to the financial plan and/or deviations. Short of this, the budget is a half-baked procedure.

- Critical evaluations must be made along the lines of profitability, cost over-runs, and other budgetary evaluation criteria.

The outcome of analytical procedures enables us not only to control current expenditures, but also to prepare more accurately the new budget which should be checked through stress tests with margins learned through Plan/Actual analysis. This leads to the issue of:

- Algorithmic and heuristic support for budgets, and
- The need to adopt flexible, and adjustable procedural solutions.

Budgetary procedures must be homogeneous through the enterprise and the same is true of Plan/Actual controls. In terms of financial information, no divisional accounting system is an island. To function properly, all units, and their budgets, have to work in synergy.

The methodology we develop for financial planning should pay due attention to the control procedures we will follow – and to the synergy with the budgets of other units. In the manufacturing industry, for instance, the purchase order subsystem works in conjunction with inventory management, production planning, and accounts payable subsystems.

Moreover, it is necessary to have an integrative view of all accounts, starting at the system design level. The budgetary methodology which we establish must be mapped in a way that ensures that the different financial and accounting subsystems interact and relate among themselves in a seamless manner:

- An analytical approach to budgetary decisions is of critical importance to the company's profits and competitiveness.
- The solution we adopt must be able to smoothly transfer the most up-to-date information on Plan/Actual from module to module, to the decision-maker.

Provided we have properly elaborated the model which we employ, budgeting helps to establish a series of relationships between activities across the enterprise. In a financial planning sense, the actual relationships, or linkages, between individual elements of business units determine the structure of our budgetary model.

As an example, the interest budget discussed in the Introduction covers the money paid to depositors, other banks (bought money), the national bank (for emergency loans), and other sources. The costs associated to each source of money, at each time a transaction takes place, constitute information elements to be interlinked for computation of *cost of money* to the institution.

The Introduction also stated that the non-interest budget addresses *all other expenditures*. For instance, in a financial institution significant non-interest expenses are salaries and wage benefits, investments in high technology (communications, computers, software), real estate and occupancy costs, utilities, external and internal publications and other information elements on costs to be interconnected for:

- On-line real-time response, to
- Ad hoc queries about Plan/Actual expenditures.

No matter what is the type of query concerning budgetary appropriations, or Plan/Actual evaluations, the linkages among information elements must be seamless. This has prerequisites of an organizational and structural nature. Able solutions to budgetary analysis tend to share two basic characteristics:

- A definition or statement of which elements connect to one another, and
- An explanation of the manner in which the elements comprising the model are related.

The rules behind these two bullet points are of general applicability though, basically, not all budgeting and budgetary control solutions are the same. Differences exist particularly in the flexibility with which budget updates and modifications can be made, as well as the accuracy characterizing the financial plan at its origin.

With greater flexibility in terms of design and analysis of financial information, it is possible to customize detailed budgetary data by dynamic linking of a series of selected budgetary chapters and sections. This must be designed to happen in an ad hoc manner, in response to on-line queries connected to:

- A specific end-user
- A profit centre or cost centre
- Locality of operations

- Client relationship(s)
- Or, any other variable important to management.

In a design sense, procedural solutions which are adaptable to evolving planning and control requirements help in establishing the major categories in budgeting. Every industry, and within the same industrial sector every organization, has budgetary procedures of its own. No two approaches are exactly the same, though during the past 15 years the use of commodity software for financial planning and treasury operations has introduced a kind of common denominator.

There is no industry-wide standardization of items concerning budgetary inputs and outputs; for the aforementioned reasons there are no major differences either from one to another financial institution. The differences in terminology are also small. Some banks use Net Interest Income, others favour Net Interest Spread, Net Margin, Interest Differential, or Effective Interest Differential. Standards about the monitoring of net interest margins and other variables are wanting.

- In the banking industry, the typical margin reports are for periods covering six months to a year.
- But leading financial institutions suggest that waiting so long for the evaluation of such vital information does not show quality of management.

This explains the attention paid in the implementation of fully on-line interactive information systems whereby net interest margin can be steadily monitored, thereby permitting critical evaluation of conditions of imbalance. Provided the database is properly designed and available on-line, expert systems should be used to help management in its mission to control margin imbalance and volatility. Knowledge engineering artifacts can focus the executive's attention on the salient problem.

4. Elaboration and upkeep of a budget

Financial plans can be *short-term*, *medium-term* or *long-term*. Short-term financial plans are made for up to 3 years, but sometimes can go to 5 years; long-term plans go beyond that. At the junction of short and medium term is the *rolling year*, a budget made for up to 2 years, with the average being 18 months.

The projected life cycle of a financial plan is very important. The shorter it is, the greater must be the detail. The establishment of procedures for annual budget should account for the fact that this is a *short-term* financial plan. All outlays and schedules advanced by the annual budget have definite *functions* and *meaning* for the purpose of:

- Planning, and
- Controlling expenditures.

What the annual budget presents is a formal, detailed plan of all operations of the business for the defined future period which it targets. Although some of the aspects of preparing and stating the plan's details vary from one company to another, the overall process can be described simply as:

- A forecast of all transactions that are expected, as well as their costs, and
- An estimate of all fixed costs and overheads, after having cut out the fat.

Well-managed organizations appreciate that the proper preparation of a projected financial plan is made in an iterative way, between headquarters, departments, and business units, as briefly described in section 2. Subsequent to an initial tentative schedule, the different entries are evaluated, altered if necessary, and accepted as next year's financial plan.

In banking, this statement is just as valid of the interest budget as it is of the non-interest budget. In fact, both of them share some major conceptual and design issues in regard to projected, forthcoming transactions. The most important are:

- Costs
- Risks, and
- Returns associated to them.

For example, changes in margin during the budgetary period must not only be included in the interest budget but also appropriately explained. This is a good example of Plan *vs* Actual evaluation in a financial environment which includes significant uncertainties – as well as of risk and return analysis.

A similar statement can be made about marginal interest spread, including recording of the rates for the major groupings that are used in determining net interest margin. Such information allows management to quickly monitor changes, taking corrective action when necessary.

The message these paragraphs convey is that the budgetary process is not a one-way street, just piling up expense after expense and asking for funding of the resulting balances. Quite to the contrary, it is a two-way process which can be properly executed only when there is a total view of:

- Planning premises
- Developing requirements, and
- Control procedures.

Moreover, even the most carefully elaborated interest budget will become obsolete if it is not steadily upkept. Updating is no hit and run job. A comprehensive solution to budgeting means a valid approach to planning and control in a distributed, complex business environment. And there is need for detail. A good way to look at requirements imposed by updating is to examine them in a multidimensional manner by:

- Organizational unit
- Market in which it operates
- Money market realities
- Trend in currency exchange
- Product or service being financed
- Customer relationship being supported.

Wisely set procedures for budget management will be focusing on *value creation*, not on mechanics. To promote value creation, we must appreciate that the elaboration of budgets and making of analytical studies, have many issues in common. The aim is to provide factual and documented evidence on the transition which takes place from financial plan to actual results – by customer, product, market and organizational unit. Their synergy permits us to:

- Streamline the planning process
- Improve the credibility of financial procedures, and
- Help to reduce costs of production and distribution of services.

Moreover, whether for planning purposes or for management control reasons, the on-line interactive presentation of budget information should be *future oriented*. Past statistics are interesting, but we should never forget that, to a large extent, the budget is executed in the future.

On the side of the non-interest budget, a case to study with care is flexible or *variable budgeting*, which consist of a series of financial plans geared to different rates of activity. For instance, the cost of production and distribution of financial services may be estimated at several possible levels of output and operating expenses. Another interesting approach is *alternative budgets*.

- In preparing alternative budgets, careful consideration must be given to the effect of changes in volume on each budgeted chapter.
- The process of alternative budgeting is no excuse for high overhead. The method must ensure that, in all cases, overhead is kept in control.

Financial plans geared to changing levels of activity contrast with the very common practice of inflexible budgeting often based on best guesses that cannot stand the test of time. The processes of flexible and of alternative budgeting have, however, prerequisites. Their implementation requires correct identification of the activity basis that will be applicable to each of the alternative financial plans:

- Hours of work
- Standard costs
- Units of production
- Financial performance, and so on.

Section 2 made reference to *zero budgeting*, popularized in the late 1970s, during the years of the US Carter Administration. As the careful reader remembers, it supposes that the different chapters of the budget regarding the current year are zeroed out. Each department, down to the smallest unit, has to re-justify its existence, otherwise it will receive no funding in the next financial plan.

As a variation of flexible budgeting, some organizations follow the policy of maintaining and reporting on *multiple budgets*. Zero budgets and multiple budgets should not be confused. For multiple budgeting purposes companies prepare:

- A *historical budget* established on the basis of last year's performance adjusted to accommodate new forecasts.
- A flexible *current operating plan*, which reflects the major revisions on the original 'historical budget'.
- A budget focusing on variances between Plan and Actual data from the past three years, as a projection on possible new deviations.
- One or more alternative budgets, prepared on the hypothesis of *major exogenous events* which radically alter budgetary considerations and allocations.

During the Cold War years, for example, several American companies had ready alternative budgets. For example, *if* there had been an outbreak of war, *then* the corresponding financial plan was ready to be applied.

Similarly, alternative scenarios can be built for major economic events such as inflation, deflation, and stagflation. Once the budgetary process has been modelled and mapped into the computer, there is a wealth of experimentation which can be done practically at no extra cost, permitting the evaluation of different scenarios and their aftermath.

In conclusion, a great deal of financial analysis can effectively be done by means of budgeting models that are flexible, easily updateable and provide input to management control. Technology helps in making interactively available copies of versions of the current year's budget. That is the:

- Original budget and all revised plans, whether they are updated quarterly or more frequently
- Variances from original budget and proposed, or preliminary, new operating plans.

This approach can also be taken in terms of projections for one or more future years if our company budgets for the medium term. It also facilitates walkthroughs of past budgets, providing a retrospective look at past years. Since medium-term budgets are based on forecasts, emphasis is not placed on hard data but on *soft data*, including hypotheses and calculation of the probability of different events taking place.

5. Practical experience in setting a budget

The message of section 4 is that budgeting is both a systematic and a flexible study of facts, costs, and other figures. The many factors influencing a company's future development must be accounted for, with due consideration not only of errors in appreciation but also of the vagueness and uncertainty involved in all projections. Hence, the multiple financial plans of which we have spoken.

We have also seen the reasons why before a budget is set up, facts and figures must be thoroughly checked and confirmed. Too many people in management are too much inclined to overlook details or to accept a rather low degree of accuracy, because of expediency or lack of interest in making a budget. Because of expediency, managers often fail to scrutinize the background reasons for costs.

- Some budgetary calculations are taken for granted, or reckoned on assumptions of little value to the end result, and
- Even if the reasoning behind other spending assumptions is logical, there is the risk that budgetary allocations are based on wrong facts.

A financial plan requires not only correct facts about future activities, and carefully normalized costs, but also a well-tuned underlying system of values.

Pragmatism should dominate. There should be no excessive optimism if today sales are booming, whereas if sales are low the sort of pessimism which brings disinclination to take on new commitments is to be avoided.

No reasonable financial plan can be based on the optimist/pessimist type of unstable attitude. Only by objectively considering each and every important factor liable to affect future activities, in each product line, can a satisfactory picture be formed of the problems lying ahead.

- The budget system should be built to a pattern that puts every fact and figure in its proper perspective, according to its true worth.
- Relations between the various levels of management, as well as the different divisions, should instil a dynamic rather than a formal, moribund approach.

Speaking from experience, this is the right strategy in all budgetary decisions, one that can be significantly assisted through mathematical modelling. Knowledge artifacts should be available to assist in handling the details of each budgetary chapter; and seamless access to distributed databases. An interactive visualization can be instrumental in setting up and controlling budgets.

Steady interactivity with databases is important because, among other key reasons, by reflecting the results of past decisions, through Plan *vs* Actual analysis, accounting figures can help management to avoid repeating past mistakes. Taken together,

- Budgeting
- Accounting, and
- Statistics

provide the major part of the background information needed for formulating policy and reaching decisions. This is the sense of using a corporate memory facility (CMF) prior to making financial commitments. A corporate memory facility is different from the other databases because its theme is *decisions*.

The information elements in CMF are management decisions on all important issues of the entity's business, starting at board and CEO level and covering the levels of senior management:

- Why has a decision been made?
- Who participated in it?
- Which were the alternatives at the time?

- What was the expected return from that decision?
- What was the expected return from the alternative courses of action?

Post-mortem walkthroughs 1, 2 or 3 years down the line help management in better focusing future decisions. Budgeting is not the only activity benefiting from this experience, but it is one of those reaping the more important gains.

Not only *cost and return* should be examined in this way but also *risk and return*. One of the best-known approaches to risk analysis with fallouts to the overall conduct of the business was implemented many years ago by General Electric. It led to abandoning the single-option deterministic system and replacing it by estimates of a range, of *bandwidth*.

In a way similar to the flexible budget we examined in section 4, this approach does not lead to a single result but to a spectrum of risk and return results, with different probabilities. Its first implementation was made in the GE budget for 1970 and contained three parts:

- Risk analysis
- Results probability
- Budget partition.

The analysts module serves in determining the bandwidths of factors influencing profits. Not only does it register the expected value but also the limit values which can be *exceeded* or *fall short* at the 90% level of confidence (99% is better). The 90% level means that in the longer run, in one out of ten cases the estimated value can exceed the higher limit or fall short of lower limit values. This is part of *management by exception*. Fluctuations can always happen, but in the stated example:

- This does not mean that budgetary costs altogether rise or fall by 10% (not even the out-of-control chapters vary by such a huge amount).
- What it does mean is that one out of ten budgeted items can present a variation outside its limits due to uncertainties which prevailed when the budget was set.

Influencing factors are political and economic sensitivities, price and standard of living indices, market volume, the company's own market share, variations in sales price, cost of material, wages, salaries, and other important issues. Operational efficiency is under the control of management. This, however, is not true of other factors, as shown by the example in section 6, which explains how the method of budgetary bandwidth works.

6. A case study with the budgetary bandwidth method

Take, as an example, a manufacturing company which converted its budgetary procedures to the bandwidth method, briefly outlined in section 5. To better appreciate the concept, think of a normal distribution characterizing each budgetary chapter, like that in Figure 9.2. The limits are set at a 90% level of confidence.

The classical approach to budgeting will only consider the expected value. By contrast, with budgetary bandwidth at each departmental and divisional level, management must specify by what percentage a given higher or lower value can deviate from expected value. Also, what would be changed by such variation in regard to profits and losses. This company decided to use *residual income* as the reference for profits, as does GE.

- Tribute is calculated from the rate of interest, multiplied by the average capital requirement of a given project.
- The result indicates how much the new profit, decreased by capital interest, is influenced through deviations from *expected value.*

This is the first basic step. The second part of the planning formula contains a probability analysis of turnover, highlighting costs and revenues. Besides the most probable result, the highest and lowest limits are indicated within a 90% probability range.

- Probabilistic examination at 90% might show that the profit can change to a loss.

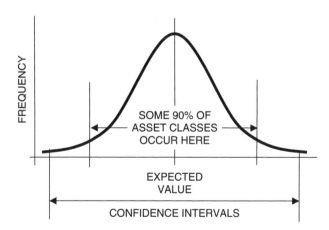

Figure 9.2   The budgetary bandwidth method is based on expected value and confidence intervals

- This immediately leads to much closer scrutiny of this particular item of business, in terms of variation from expected value.

A third step in the methodology specifies the assumptions underpinning the budget, as well as the degree of probability which they have. For instance, the head of a product line must decide on product-related values, and integrate them into the financial plan for the next year. In this regard, he must specify not only the most probable values but also their expected range. This is a refined form of flexible budgeting, of which we spoke in section 4.

The Vice-President Manufacturing has a similar job to do, in terms of budgetary bandwidth chores. Each factory must prepare a budget proposal and send it to headquarters. Factory budgets will be integrated by the VP Manufacturing, and this integration should include their expected value and limits. The best approach is to use expert systems which, at corporate levels:

- Screen budgetary proposals
- Verify their chapters, one-by-one, and
- Compare likely items bringing deviations to attention.

Knowledge artifacts should be used to integrate the forecasts sent by the sales division to total sales by product and by marketing territory. Other expert systems should compare sales projections with production plans. While the factories have (most likely) used data similar to such projections, it is always advisable to make a higher level integrative control. A good deal of this effort must be automated through knowledge engineering.

For evident reasons, the finance department should have a role in this evaluation of production plans versus sales forecasts. And the input of the firm's economics research unit will be valuable in estimating the effect of economic conditions on market demand, as well as the cost of materials and labour.

The fourth step is aggregating several factory budgets with their bandwidth (expected value and limits) into an integrated manufacturing budget. A good approach for doing so is the use of possibility theory – the stochastic method we have examined in Chapter 4. Possibility theory is superior to probability theory in accomplishing this objective because it provides an efficient tool to integrate different budgets into one, while probability theory has no means for doing so.

Some people would say that a top-down budgetary solution would not have presented integrated problems. However, this chapter has pressed the point that the best policy is to ask for input from those executives, and their units, who have to live with the budget. The goal of an interactive effort is to provide the best approximation to what would be revealed, in the future, as real budgetary requirements, therefore guaranteeing more satisfactory results by:

- Elaborating an organization-wide cost distribution
- Showing variables in sales, production processes and costs
- Helping to control expenses by pinpointing overruns through Plan/Actual analysis, including expected value and limits.

There are, also, other issues that can benefit from the outlined methodology. The *cash budget* forecasts direct and indirect cost outlays, balancing them against receipts or other sources of funds. Before the estimated income statement and future balance sheet can be prepared, account must be taken of effects of operations upon the cash position of the organization. This is necessary for two reasons:

- The timing of cash receipts and disbursements will have an important bearing on the amounts of receivables and payables in the projected balance sheet.
- The amounts of money needed to execute transactions, and for financing costs, must be determined if the estimated income account is to be complete.

The *capital outlays budget* defines the investments the organization plans to make during the coming financial period. It is possible to forecast such disbursements by estimating projected investments as well as accrued direct and indirect costs at the end of each month of the budgeted period. Here, again, a methodology of expected value and limits improves the accuracy of the capital budget.

Only tier-1 companies take this approach. The others assume that only slight differences will exist between the budgetary estimates (at the end of the various months) and the different disbursements. *If* only minor differences exist between the successive accruals, disbursements will tend to equal the budgeted labour, materials, and other costs. But nothing can guarantee that *if*.

The need for cash forecasts and cash outlays which allow for a bandwidth is one of the key references that help document the fact that the process of budget preparation entails the making of many analytical decisions. These concern relationships and functions which should be maintained in the operations of any company – whether a financial institution or a manufacturing firm.

Regarding manufacturing proper, a basic premise in drawing up the *production budget* is that production costs are made up of the outlay spent on materials, labour and overhead. The materials estimate can be obtained by taking the quantity already decided upon when drawing up production schedules, and transforming it into costs by using standard cost figures – with tighter limits than in sales.

The *purchasing budget* is based on the quantity necessary for production, plus a small allowance for losses, scrap, substandard goods, and so on. Estimates should take into consideration the stocks of raw materials expected at the beginning of the period and at the end of it, using mathematical models to minimize investments in inventories.

Take the sales budget as another example. The best way is to budget the quantity and not the value of the goods to be sold, in view of the effect of possible price fluctuations. This quantity must be brought down to salesman level, by means of individual *quotas*, where expected value is the assigned quota. Projected sales figures should be calculated:

- By single product and for groups of products
- By territory in which the company operates, and by salesman in this territory.

Grouping should be based on similarities in *product description* and *selling channel*, and can vary according to the firm's line of business. One overriding factor in budgeting the sales quantity is to be very detailed as well as objective, based on:

- Sales forecasts validated through appropriate studies, and
- Translated into individual quotas and higher commissions beyond the assigned quota.

Overheads should be determined with the aid of the rule that administrative costs must rise much slower than production and be absorbed by the cost centre to which they belong. Each department must prepare a budget of the nonrecoverable expenses it will incur in the form of costs connected to trivia and administration. (The sense of overhead in manufacturing is not the same as that in banking, discussed in the Introduction.)

Finally, a crucial policy regarding budgetary practice is the unification process which should bring together the different departmental budgetary estimates. It has already been stated that no divisional accounting system is an island. There must be *a master budget* which:

- Summarizes all estimates for all departments
- Portrays the anticipated result of all forecasts

- Leads to a projected profit and loss statement, and
- Establishes a balance sheet which will result from the fulfilment of those estimates.

This master budget will be transmitted to the financial department and from there to the senior executives who constitute the budget committee, for their consideration. The budget committee may approve the estimate as made, or *optimize* expenditures in connection to expected results. Optimization does not mean saving a piece of coal, but using its heat the best way while it burns.

7. Qualitative factors, quantitative parameters and break-even

Qualitative factors are most crucial both in an a priori financial analysis of aftermath and in post-mortems. Their aim is to provide a critical view in a *detailed* or *consolidated* way depending on the particular study being conducted. The capital and credit required to put the various operational budgets into effect should be carefully examined – along with the expected benefits from carrying out some of the budgeted business transactions (more on this later). That's where vision comes in.

The quantitative side of the research targets an algorithmic or heuristic solution which makes experimentation feasible. The incorporation of *parameters* sees to it that the model become more specific, transiting from a generalized to a custom-made version. Through parameters, the budget analyst can experiment on changes that affect the simulated budget's behaviour.

- The simulator's input corresponds to the set of states provided by its parameters.
- The experimenter observes effected changes through the model's output, and records expected value and limits.

Deterministic or stochastic models are written to map any particular product, process, or operation in the planning phase, through the appropriate use of parameters. These parameters vary around an expected value and many experimenters reflect nothing but this central tendency. But as this chapter has demonstrated, that is wrong because qualitative factors see to it that there are:

- A distribution of values, and
- Management-implied limits.

Every product has its own characteristics and therefore its own parametric requirements. For instance, in scheduling the production of lamps, breakage is a parameter. Neither all types of glass nor all machines have the same breakage rate, hence if the scheduling algorithm includes breakage (as it should) then the multiplier of this factor will vary by specific lamp and machine type.

- Any one production system can be regarded as the coupling of its parts, and the same is true of a financial system.
- The use of parameters can also permit the combination of transformations, making feasible combining different schedules together.

For instance, a sales forecasting model can be made parametric, using parameters to specialize it by market. Other parameters may address seasonality. Lamps, for example, are a highly seasonal product. An increase in the number of parameters makes the construction of prediction algorithms so much more challenging.

No budget-making process should forget the importance of profit margin. Many companies have found that good results are obtained by *breakeven analysis*, which shows fixed costs and variable costs, the latter connected to varying quantities of output. The breakeven reflects:

- Total cost, and
- Total revenue from sales

as the intersection of these two lines. Profit and loss in regard to a given output, sales volume, product prices, costs incurred in connection with the different transactions, all influence the *cost* and *revenues* lines. That is what theory says, and to a significant degree theory is right – but not quite.

The difference comes from qualitative factors which may guide management's hand towards certain decisions altering breakeven analysis. For instance, slow-moving sales can lead to major discounts even at high season. This has an evident impact on the wisdom of looking at breakeven under two conditions:

- Expected value, and
- Upper and lower limits.

It is wise not to start with a high sophistication in modelling. The first effort should be kept along relatively simple lines aimed at gaining experience. More complex versions should come later. However, from the start the mathematical model we build should carefully reflect not only budget construction but also the:

- Existence of alternatives, and
- Their evaluation against one another.

Also from the outset one should define the job a breakeven analysis should fulfil. Another 'must' is investing in training and familiarizing management with the operation of the budgetary model. Equally important is the strategy of soliciting comments for improvement, and incorporating these suggestions into the budget analyser.

Documentation is particularly important in system development as it is in budgeting. All documentation objectives should be computer-based. This will be a significant improvement over current practice where trivia and administrative duties consume a lot of time because documentation is still paper-based, apart from being (quite often) incomplete and obsolete.

8. Insight provided by budget analysis

Whether or not in a conscious manner, management uses budgets, balance sheets, and income statements for the same purpose aeronautical engineers employ physical models and digital simulators of aircraft. The budget predicts the *anticipated* outcome of a business strategy, and:

- *If* the projected results are unsatisfactory
- *Then* management can alter some of the variables, and financial allocation made to them.

Because proper budgetary analysis helps in providing insight, as a financial plan the budget must play a much more dynamic role than the one it is usually allocated in business and industry. For instance, the sales budget (see section 6) provides the basis for a polyvalent projection of income by:

- Indicating the physical quantity of units expected to be sold over a given period, by price tag
- Providing an analysis of these units by market and currency, in case of multinational operations, and
- Presenting a quantitative estimate on which to compute market risk, country risk, currency risk, and associated hedging possibilities regarding income.

The reader's attention has also been brought to the fact that budgetary analysis helps in walkthrough on managerial decisions, regarding issues involved in allocation of funds as well as in performance. This makes feasible a factual level of experimentation in regard to a number of queries that invariably arise with all issues connected with financial allocation.

Spreadsheets have been used since the early 1980s in providing an interactive means for answering *What If* queries. The challenge now is to include sophisticated knowledge artifacts, therefore more intelligence, into the software. In budgeting and budgetary control, like in so many other activities, expert systems are 'assistants to' the executive, and therefore his friends. Their presence should supplement, not substitute human judgment.

Simulation of financial allocation and expected performance should be based on alternative scenarios. Corporate financial models are instrumental in projecting the economic results. They accomplish this mission by translating the budget process into a series of algorithms which permit experimentation.

- Assumptions made about the future, and expressed in an algorithmic form, are tested against real-life scenarios.
- The results obtained can be interactively investigated so that corrective action is taken in time to bring the budgetary process into shape.

'The purpose of any organization is to achieve output,' Dr Andrew S. Grove, Intel's former Chairman, once said; whether it is widgets being manufactured, bills mailed out, loans processed, or insurance policies sold. 'Yet, in one way or another we have all been seduced by tangents and by the appearance of output,' Grove suggested.

To separate the real output from the imaginary, we need measurements and metrics. This is precisely the function to be fulfilled by a *budgetary analyser*. The more classical and less sophisticated types of budget analysers are simple quantitative models. Because, however, qualification is important with any financial plan, more recent approaches introduce a certain number of judgmental factors, including risk and uncertainty (see section 4 on alternative budgets and section 6 on budgetary bandwidth).

The budget analyser is not just a quantitative tool, as many people believe. Sophisticated approaches involve both qualitative and quantitative factors, with the output expressed in expected value and limits, according to the General Electric method (see section 5). Whether we talk of budgets, or of anything else, numerical values are important – but they are only part of the story. The necessary supplements are:

- Qualitative factors, and
- Personal vision.

In his excellent book *Adventures of a Bystander*, Dr Peter Drucker mentions a story about Henry Bernheim, the man who started from nothing and made one of the most important merchandising chains in the United States at the end of the 19th century. Bernheim had sent his son to the then new Harvard Business School to learn the secrets of management – both theory and quantitative methods.

'But father,' said the son when he returned from higher education, 'You don't even know how much profit you are making.' 'Come along my boy,' answered Henry, and he took his son on an inspection of the flagship department store's top floor to a sub-sub-basement which was cut out of bedrock. There, at rock edge, lay a bolt of cloth. Contrary to what business schools teach, there were no statistics around, no budgets, no balance sheets, and no income statements. Just the bolt of cloth. 'Take away all the rest,' said the father, 'It's the profit. This is what I started with.'[2]

Notes

1   D.N. Chorafas and Heinrich Steinmann, *Expert Systems in Banking*, Macmillan, London, 1991.
2   Peter F. Drucker, *Adventures of a Bystander*, Heinemann, London, 1978.

Valuing Assets: The Challenge of Being 'Right'

1. Introduction

As every businessman knows, it is essential that company assets are properly *valued*, and that their value is not only computed in a fairly accurate manner, but also stated in terms that reflect the dependability of numbers being given. This is the fundamental sense underpinning *fair value*, which must be individually calculated for every asset. It cannot be guesstimated in an overall averaging process.

From the viewpoint of modern managerial accounting, it is the *detail* of a specific asset or liability that makes the difference between fairly accurate and rather inaccurate value estimates. Whether for planning or for control, the presentation of managerial information must not only look reliable, but also be reliable. Otherwise, it is worse than nothing.

Through policies, practices and procedures in valuing assets under different accounting regimes, as well as by means of case studies, this chapter demonstrates how and why both US GAAP and IFRS serve as infrastructure for reliable value information to be used in management accounting. In essence, the new rules:

- Bring general accounting, financial accounting, and management accounting closer than they have ever been before, and
- Open new management accounting perspectives through high technology, as will be documented in Chapter 15 with the real-time balance sheet.

Valuing assets through fair value provides a common denominator for practically all types of reports. Single-handed, it does not make everybody a great entrepreneur. On the other hand, as it should be recalled, the corporate raiders of the 1970s and 1980s made good use of their ability to *value* a company's assets better than the market did. Along with this, they capitalized on innovations in financial instruments. On both sides of the Atlantic, with borrowed money they:

- Set about buying companies undervalued by the market, and
- They created usually leveraged conglomerates which they sold at a premium.

For evident reasons, corporate raiders preferred dull, undermanaged businesses in unglamorous sectors of the economy, particularly when they saw firms valued by the stock market according to historic prices of their assets, rather than their (more valuable) potential to generate cash. And they got ahead of the curve by realizing that fast-growing debt markets were willing to lend large sums against *future cash flow*. Behind the corporate raiders' success lay the fact that:

- The right valuation at the right time creates business opportunities, and
- In the markets of late 20th century buying an undervalued firm, even through lots of debt, could quickly pay for itself.

Another important element in the success of corporate raiders in the 1970s and 1980s, and through the 1990s, was that they saw many big firms were not run in a way to maximize shareholder value. Mismanagement, or at least poorly focused management contributed mightily to these companies' low valuation. This was especially true of diversified, strategically driven conglomerates which had lost their original animator – and therefore their soul.

The message the previous paragraphs convey is that quality of management is one of the crucial elements in giving assets their value – as well as in recognizing undervalued assets. In the hands of sharp, hard-working operators, firms were run to generate more cash. Managers in the new team that took over were loaded with incentives, and they were left to get on with the job, usually involving determined cutting of such superfluities as lavish corporate headquarters and inordinate perks. The cash generated by these restructured companies went to:

- Repay debt used to fund the acquisition, and
- Deliver rich dividends to shareholders, essentially the raiders themselves.

Corporate raiders were tough operators who created their wealth by upping the value of diversified portfolios of holdings, many of them formerly sleepy businesses. And they paid for the deal almost entirely by selling many of the acquired companies' subsidiaries, leaving themselves with that part of the business that made a significant operating profit margin.

- These raiders were often likened to dealers who bought a load of junk, tarted it up and sold it with sugar-coating.
- This was partly true, but the real reason for their success was their ability in revaluing undervalued assets, creating wealth, for themselves, their companies and society as a whole.

Available evidence suggests that the originator of the fair value '*plus*' approach has been Harold Geneen, though Thornton of Litton Industries also competes for the title. Geneen's value concept went all the way down to sales. At ITT, sales had no point unless they were profitable. Too many managers were dazzled by volume, and talked proudly about how many people they employed. Geneen's answer to that was: 'Nonsense, all nonsense.'[1] (More on Geneen and the raiders in section 5.)

2. Tracing fair value accounting to its origins

Chapter 8 has defined what management accounting is and is not, as well as the advantage a company gains by bringing closer together management accounting and financial accounting. It is therefore a 'plus' that in European and other countries applying IFRS, listed companies have to use fair value for presentation of their consolidated financial statements. To obtain a wider appreciation of fair value accounting, and get insight into possible consequences, including:

- Customer relationships
- Types of products offered
- Risk management practices, and
- Financial staying power

it is wise to look back in time at the very origins of the method in the post-World War II years. Also, at the debate which took place at the time, prior to its conversion into regulatory requirement. This first time fair value accounting became the letter of the law is in connection to US GAAP in the late 1990s.

As the Introduction brought to the reader's attention, in the last three decades of the 20th century valuing assets in a way different than classical *book value* has been the strength of corporate raiders, who were able to see further than others. Because being ahead of the curve is one of the secrets of success in business, it is good news that fair value has become the generalized new accounting regime which can affect every entity and every process. This includes:

- Banks as financial intermediaries
- Insurers as providers of basic social services, and
- The distribution of financial risks among economic agents.

At the very origin of the new financial reporting regime have been the hearings by the US House Banking Committee, Subcommittee on Capital Markets, Securities and Government-Sponsored Enterprises. Held on 1 October 1997 they focused on implementation of proposed new rules for financial reporting formulated by the

Financial Accounting Standards Board (FASB). Effective as of 1 January 1999 these rules required that all publicly traded corporations, including banks, report their derivatives holdings on their balance sheets *at fair market value*. That is the first official case on record.

During these hearings, then FASB Chairman Edmund Jenkins testified that his board's primary focus was to put into effect rules that would require all firms, whether financial or industrial, to report their derivatives holdings, on balance sheet and off-balance sheet (OBS), by marking them to their current market price. This started the fair value accounting ball rolling. Jenkins' testimony included important references to:

- Why it *is* important to use market value in financial reporting, and
- Why accruals no more fit the modern economy's requirements.

The evidence was fair and well documented. The way the FASB chairman put it: 'If ever a case can be made for reporting something in more detail, it is for derivatives. ... Different companies may report very similar activities differently, and even an individual company may report similar activities differently. ... Gains and losses (on derivatives) are not explicitly disclosed today, and their effect on earnings is difficult, if not impossible, for an investor or creditor to determine. Again, we believe that the public has the right to know.'

What Jenkins did not say, but today can be added with certainty, is that the company's senior management, too, has not only the right to know but also the responsibility to appreciate all the details about recognized but not yet realized gains and losses. This is as true with derivatives as it is with all other instruments in the institution's:

- Trading book, and
- Banking book.

Fair value evidence brings regulatory financial reporting and internal management accounting very close together. Moreover, as far as public scrutiny is concerned, years of implementation of fair value accounting in the United States, following the issuance of Statement of Financial Accounting Standard No. 133 (SFAS 133), have demonstrated that Edmund Jenkins was right.

The more its critics riot against fair value, the more they (unwillingly) prove that the FASB thesis has been sound. Its board was unconvinced by the argument that 'derivatives are just hedges'. True enough, reporting recognized but not realized profits and losses from derivatives on balance sheets, impacts upon reported earnings. This, however, happens because of:

- The huge amounts of red ink treasurers and bankers have recorded with derivative financial instruments, and
- The fact that with accruals red ink was hidden from public view, but it is now becoming transparent by writing them at fair value into the balance sheet.

A day prior to Jenkins' testimony, on 30 September 1997, the *Wall Street Journal* reported that during the third quarter of that year, Salomon Brothers, the investment bank, had lost at least $200 million in derivatives. At the time, experts at Wall Street said the actual money lost could be much higher – and Salomon was only one of the top eight US financial institutions active in derivatives.

An interesting statistic to keep in mind is that in 1997 the top eight US derivatives-holding commercial banks had $22.6 trillion worth of derivatives in notional principal amount, against only $93 billion worth of equity. The derivatives holdings of non-financial corporations were also very large, and growing rapidly as more and more entities thought that they had discovered a new Eldorado off-balance sheet.

How rapid has been the growth of derivatives exposure can be attested by the fact that, according to published figures, at the end of 2004 the derivatives exposure of just one bank, JP Morgan Chase, stood at $45 *trillion* (in notional principal). This is 200% higher than the derivatives exposure by all eight top US commercial banks just seven years earlier.

At the time of the 1997 hearings, FASB also exposed in the US House hearings that several companies had adopted the curious way of *reporting losses* as *increases* in valuation of their assets. That's creative accounting at its best. The American accounting standards setter stated, at the House hearing that: 'The information about derivatives and hedging reported in financial statements today is incomplete, inconsistent, and just plain wrong.'[2]

At the time, Edmund Jenkins responded to repeated calls for non-transparency in derivatives trades made by the guilty parties, by saying that 'gains or losses on derivatives that qualify for hedge accounting should have little or no effect on a company's earnings because they will be offset by comparable losses or gains on the thing that is being hedged – and the result is little or no volatility in earnings.'

Seven years of experience with fair value financial reporting in the United States has proven that:

- Balancing-out is true *if*, and only *if*, hedges are not speculations – as is so frequently done.

By contrast, if the hedge is not matched by, and does not move in the opposite direction from the underlying instrument, then:

- At best the hedge operation was not an *effective hedge*, and
- At worst it was mere speculation masquerading as hedge.

It is, in fact, a common practice that the hypothetical hedge is in reality a speculative investment, or trade, which ended in money losses, as many of them do. The answer to those gamblers evidently is that banks as well as all other quoted companies should not be speculating with their shareholders' and depositors' money.

It is quite interesting to keep in mind that, during his 1997 testimony, Jenkins revealed some creative accounting practices which alter the true value of balance sheet reporting. But contrary to the thesis by FASB and the Securities and Exchanges Commission (SEC), the Federal Reserve was not happy with the new regulations making it mandatory to reveal to regulators, investors, and the general public the whole extent of a public company's exposure – and for good reason.

3. New rules are the aftermath of financial markets developments

Quite often, a basic reason for differences of opinion between central bankers and regulators is one of mission. Accounting standards setters and regulators are tasked with protecting the interests of investors and the general public from all sorts of fraud. Central bankers, on the other hand, see this as only one of their obligations, often subordinate to:

- Preserving intact the financial fabric, and
- Avoiding the need of having to use taxpayers money to salvage defunct credit institutions from bankruptcy.

Seen under this perspective, one can appreciate why, while testifying on behalf of Fed Chairman Alan Greenspan, Federal Reserve Board Governor Susan Phillips said during the 1997 US Senate hearings that 'the desirability of meaningful disclosure is not the issue', adding right after that: 'These problems can be mini-mized by placing market values in meaningful *supplemental disclosure*, rather than by forcing their use in the primary financial statements ...'

- This essentially meant continuing the reporting of huge derivatives expo-sure off-balance sheet, and
- Keeping the torrents of red ink a closely guarded secret from investors and regulators rather than promoting transparency.

What the Fed and the banks had been fearing from on balance sheet reporting of derivatives gains and losses is that this would uncover their large derivatives losses, and put an end to their hide-and-seek game. Similar silly arguments, which border on lack of business ethics, have been heard in 2004, in Europe, with IASB's decision to make recognized but not realized derivatives gains and losses transparent. 'Replacing historical cost with fair value accounting will lead to uncertainty in financial statements,' warned a senior partner of a Big Four accountants firm. A sweet answer to such a statement is: 'Don't make me laugh.' More to the point, however, is the fact that certified public accountants should not be pulling dirty tricks.

Speaking at a conference in London, in late 2004, Allister Wilson, senior techni-cal partner at Ernst & Young, raised doubts about the 'practical impact' of accounts prepared in accordance with International Financial Reporting Standards (IFRS). In his words: 'Income statements will now be the residual whereas previously the balance sheet was the residual. Historical costs have been replaced with fair value.'[3]

This was the 'right sort' of music to the ears of executives of companies who wish to keep their derivatives losses hidden from the public eye. But Wilson should have known better about the importance of revealing recognized but not yet realized gains and losses. He works for a global certified public accountant who has years of experience with SFAS 133 in the United States. And he should have been aware not only of Jenkins' testimony, but also of Levitt's.

Faced with rapidly developing financial markets, a surge in the number of unknowns, fast and wide product innovation, and mounting risk, regulators have been happily sticking to their guns. In 1997 in the United States, Arthur Levitt, then chairman of the Securities and Exchange Commission, testified at a Senate hearing that SEC will enforce the FASB accounting rules (outlined in section 2) for the 15 000 American companies which are public.

To make the reasons for this decision, as well as his point, clear to the US legislators, Arthur Levitt warned that FASB must remain independent, and that he was there 'to shield it from political pressure'. 'It is very inappropriate for the Congress to suggest any further delays. I believe that we would be playing Russian roulette with our markets,' Levitt stated firmly – a statement that also applies with IFRS.

In 2004, David Tweedie, chairman of IASB, proved to be just as firm. Speaking at the same conference with Ernst & Young's Wilson, he told the attendees that businesses will find the transition to IFRS tough, but reiterated the need for a global set of accounting principles. Tweedie also added that 92 countries will permit financial statements produced in accordance with IFRS after the 1 January 2005 start date – and he described IAS 39, *Financial Instruments: Recognition and Measurement* (see Chapters 4 and 5), as 'the bane of my life'.

Whether we talk of FASB or IASB, of SFAS 133 or of IAS 39, the long-term aim of bringing fair value into play, in the balance sheet and income statement, is *transparency*. The law of the land now is to actualize the financial reporting standard. As has been explained on several occasions, accrual accounting:

- No longer reflects rapidly evolving business conditions, and
- It fails to inform stakeholders on assumed mega risks.

Moreover, writing down derivatives losses in a 'supplemental disclosure', as Susan Phillips suggested to US legislators, might make sense if the amounts involved in these trades and portfolio positions were a trifle – a minor exception compared to the balance sheet. This, of course, is not the case. Derivatives deals, by all sorts of public companies and most particularly by big banks, are a *multiple* of their assets and a *high multiple* of their equity. At that size:

- They eat up the entity's balance sheet for breakfast, and
- Hiding them in 'supplemental disclosures' is tantamount to placing a nuclear bomb under the world's financial fabric.

All managers and professionals should appreciate that the fundamental mission they have been entrusted with is to assure the survival of the enterprise for which they work; not just some temporary profit numbers. The problem of course lies in defining fair value in assets and liabilities, appreciating the fact that financial reporting:

- Is much more about predicting future staying power (see Chapter 12)
- Than massaging numbers to beautify the past.

Cognizant people in the derivatives business know very well that the fight over the FASB's and IASB's accounting standards is more than just an issue over 'this' or 'that' rule. Bringing to light the full exposure assumed by public companies might tell the world that the global financial system is not far from being bankrupt – a bankruptcy hidden by the old accounting framework, which has repeatedly failed to adequately reflect economic reality.

There is no wonder that the investor community increasingly demands greater transparency. The prerequisite is that firms provide information that really reflects the impact of their trades, and of prevailing economic conditions, on their financial position. Hence the need for fair value approaches, where valuation rules are applied depending on management's *intentions* in holding certain assets and liabilities.

- This is precisely the intentional process corporate raiders used to make their fortune.
- This is, also, the scope of management accounting information chief executives and their immediate assistants should want to have for better governance reasons.

Ironically, it is precisely because of *better governance* that accounting reforms are likely to have a profound impact on business and industry, and most particularly on the banking sector. Neither is IAS 39, which roughly corresponds to US GAAP's SFAS 133, the only financial standard that needs to be enacted, in order to gain advantages in governance.

Much can be learned about further requirement from accounting standards applied in the United States during the past few years, as well as from Financial Accounting Standards Board Interpretations (FIN). FIN 45 'Guarantor's Accounting and Disclosure Requirements for Guarantees, Including Indirect Guarantees of Indebtedness of Others', was issued in November 2002. It addresses:

- Disclosures to be made by a guarantor in its interim and annual financial statements, about its obligations under certain guarantees that it has issued, and
- Clarifies that a guarantor is required to recognize, at inception of a guarantee, a liability for fair value of obligation(s) undertaken in issuing the guarantee.

For its part, FIN 46 'Consolidation of Variable Interest Entities, an Interpretation of Accounting Research Bulletin 51 – Consolidated Financial Statements', was issued in the United States in January 2003. It provides new criteria for determining whether a company is required to record assets and liabilities on its balance sheet. Notice that the more complex the accounting rules become, in order to reflect the greater sophistication of financial instruments, and of entities holding them or trading in them, the greater the need for interpretations by supervisors so that companies are not gaming the system, and it becomes feasible to maintain a level playing field for all entities. This is precisely what both US GAAP and IFRS are targeting.

4. LOCOM and Replacement Value

To its credit, IASB has incorporated into IFRS not only rules but also some of the *methods* which should be followed in financial reporting. For instance, financial instruments like deposits, loans, bonds, or derivatives must be divided by the bank into two main portfolios (books).

- Instruments that are intended to be held to maturity, or for longer-term investment purposes, are allocated to the *banking book*.

These continue to be accounted for at cost, or at the lower of cost or market (LOCOM) method. Generally, this approach can be considered as a more conservative variant of historical cost valuation, hence it is an important prudent principle for accounting purposes under the old regime.

- By contrast, instruments in the *trading book* are in principle held for short-term trading, and they must be marked to market.

This second point essentially amounts to an increase or decrease in the inventoried instrument's valuation, which has many benefits associated to it. The after-effect of increased transparency and improved quality of accounting information is earlier corrective action by management; better appreciation of exposure assumed by shareholders; and timely intervention by supervisors if a bank incurs excessive risks which put it in peril.

Some of the IFRS critics say that, for trading book class of instruments, it would have been enough if the new accounting rules had asked for *replacement value* reporting. What these critics forget is that replacement value is based on present value plus add-ons which should take into account risk premiums to be delivered for default risks and deferred earnings.

In fact, *if* it is properly done, the calculation of replacement value would be tougher than that of fair value. It will also be an excellent exercise for management accounting reasons, because it constitutes an important input to good governance. Many companies appreciate its importance and those best managed see to it that:

- For traders, replacement value results are shown at least daily and even better *intraday* – with accuracy being more important than precision.
- For trading lines, these results must be both accurate and precise; available daily, weekly and monthly, with profit and loss calculated just as frequently.

There are many applications with which the replacement value method can be effectively used. For instance, the result from counterparty risk can be calculated by means of gross present value. For this purpose, the gross result before operating costs is determined by means of the algorithm:

Gross Result = present value of the receivable contracted premium
+ counterparty risk cash account
− present value of the required premium based on current assessment

Both for the interest rate business and for other trades, in the case of inventoried transactions whose life cycle ranges over several years, the delivery of counterparty risk premium can be made on an annual, quarterly or more frequent basis – as well as at termination of the transaction. Many banks arrange it so that for trading line products the risk premium is paid up front.

As far as assumed exposure is concerned, counterparty risk is an important factor in any transaction, especially so in over-the-counter derivatives trading. With exchange-traded products counterparty risk is negligible because changes in the value of positions are being offset by means of daily adjustments to required margins. With OTC and other deals of a bilateral nature a valuable indicator of current exposure to counterparty risk is derived from gross and net replacement values of contracts outstanding.

- *Positive replacement value* is the marked to market value of all receivables under derivatives contracts with third parties outstanding – without allowing for master netting or collateral arrangements.
- *Negative replacement value* is the sum of all liabilities to customers under contracts outstanding, also without netting.

As these examples document, the use of new definitions of financial value, and their associated metrics, improves the classical means for projecting credit risk such as the credit quality of counterparties. Negative replacement value tells a great deal about exposure towards any one counterparty with which a master netting agreement has been concluded.

Those who have opposed IFRS because it has increased the complexity of keeping accounts, should take note of these references. As we will see in greater detail in section 7, the accounting system is the messenger. What has really increased by leaps and bounds is not the rules of accounting, but the complexity of the financial business itself.

Moreover, the wider use of replacement value speaks volumes about the relative merits of fair value *vs* accruals. The reader should always remember that slow-moving accounting rules which (in most cases correctly) put greater emphasis on precision than on accuracy are not the best way for internal management accounting.

- Regulatory reporting requires precision that is attainable when the report is due quarterly or annually.
- But management accounting must be *intraday*, capitalizing on US GAAP and IFRS. (More on this in Chapter 15.)

This distinction basically concerns two types of assets and liabilities: (i) those that are realized, and (ii) those that are recognized but not yet realized, though they are reported in the balance sheet and profit and loss statement (income statement). Among other interesting outcomes this leads to the concept that economic capital funds are on both sides of the balance sheet (see Chapter 14). It also results in the three classes of accounting for assets and liabilities shown in the framework illustrated in Figure 10.1.

5. Taking advantage of vision provided by fair value 'plus'

The Introduction made reference to how some exceptional individuals, essentially speculators by nature, took advantage of their better vision of a company's worth to acquire it, turn it around, and use it as cash cow – or sell it at huge profit. The statement was also made that a good part of the concept underpinning this strategy should be credited to Geneen and Thornton.

A standard acquisition procedure with both empire-builders has been to tell the owners that everything will stay the same, and then to tell staff to double earnings.

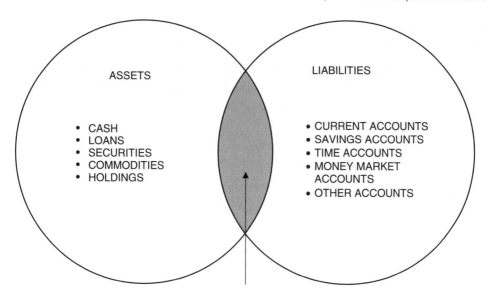

• DERIVATIVE FINANCIAL INSTRUMENTS

Figure 10.1   The original balance sheet taxonomy of assets and liabilities has been enriched by a class of items which find a home only after establishing their fair value

Most evidently, this goal cannot be met by working 'as usual'. Neither were the new owners willing to be lax with

- Lost sales
- Lagging products, and
- Variances from budget.

Once asked why he was so eager to buy other companies, Thornton answered: 'We don't buy companies. We buy time.' The time element, sales distribution, and total cost have been dictating the choice. The CEO is not on top of the company's central issues by watching book value. He definitely needs:

- A realistic estimate of fair value 'plus'
- Where 'plus' means an added value over fair figures, the entrepreneur feels that it is there, and it can be exploited.

In imposing his Basic Acquisitions Policy, in March 1965, Harold Geneen told the ITT board: '... our primary interest in any acquisition is its rate of growth for the future.'[4] Since ITT was growing at a rate of 10% or better yearly, in compound numbers, any firm being acquired had to have the potential of growing more than that in the aftermath of the new management's efforts.

Every empire-builder, of course, has his or her own criteria for cherry-picking. Britain's James Hanson provides an example different to that of Geneen. In the 1980s, with a string of well-placed deals, the share price of his company outperformed the UK's top 100 firms by 368%, a 'first' in Europe. Eventually, however, the warlords get tired and lose their grasp. Or, in the case of public companies, they are forced to retire. By the mid-1990s, Hanson's company shares were falling in a rising market. The intense scrutiny of some takeovers led many investors to question the sustainability of its profits, which had come to depend in part on complex tax deals.

The message the reader should retain from this story of rise and fall is that – through assiduous picks and turnarounds, based on fair value 'plus', James Hanson had built a transatlantic business that, at its peak, employed 90 000 people. Most importantly, his strategy of rewarding managers for maximizing shareholder value and focusing on cash generation became standard business practice, imitated by other corporate raiders who:

- Improved upon it
- Capitalized on financial mistakes of current management, and
- Created a new basis for dynamic asset valuation and revaluation of a going concern.

The principle is that in many companies management is wanting and rationality in decision-making has gone on leave. An example, which recently came to the public eye, is that of Banca Popolare Italiana (BPI), Italy's tenth largest bank, whose balance sheet, if marked at market prices, will further reduce its weakened assets.

Reportedly, gambling on the value of its assets BPI has promised to pay Deutsche Bank Euro 330 million for 30 million shares of Bipielle Investimenti (BPI's own subsidiary). Deutsche had bought these assets in 2003 for only 198 million euro, but at the end of 2004 they were worth a mere 174 million euro[5] – roughly half BPI's derivatives commitment to the German bank.

Other entrepreneurs, however, make a fortune out of their wizardry in developing new financial products. With some rocket science added to it,[6] this new development basis has become known as *financial engineering*, providing a different, more market-oriented way of valuing assets. The original rocket science part was contributed by Lewis S. Ranieri, who has been one of the first to recognize that:

- Mortgage securitization is a mathematical art, and
- There is a market for securitized loans, starting with mortgages.

To develop more sophisticated instruments, Ranieri hired PhDs who designed collateralized mortgage obligations (CMOs), which turn pools of 30-year mortgages into collections of 2-, 5-, and 10-year bonds, albeit at a level of higher-up risk. Today securitization is applied to a wide range of receivables from credit card balances to auto loans.

Taken together, these examples make the point that the fair value of assets depends a great deal on business vision, management quality, mathematical modelling, and experimentation, as well as the novel way an entrepreneur approaches the market. Valuing assets is an art:

- With many preconditions, even if every artist exercises what he or she considers to be their prerogatives, and
- With factors that both qualify and quantify embedded value.

One of the major challenges is to establish the fair value of a company's debt. Today, this is determined using pricing models reflecting one percentage point shifts in appropriate yield curves. Estimating the fair value of investments calls for a combination of pricing and duration models.[7] Duration is a linear approximation that works well for modest changes in yields and generates a rather symmetrical result.

In conclusion, whether we talk of valuing assets or debt, we stand a better chance by targeting order of magnitude accuracy than trying to provide greater precision. This is no good for financial reporting, but it is perfect for management accounting.

6. A case study on differences between IFRS and US GAAP

The evidence presented in the preceding sections, as well as in several of the preceding chapters, should leave the reader in no doubt that fair value is superior to book value and accruals. This is true both in regard to the support provided by an internal accounting management information system (IAMIS), and in regard to market information by means of financial reporting.

More irrefutable evidence is provided by the fact that in all major countries accounting standards setters have adopted the fair value principle. The downside lies in the fact that the norms are not quite homogeneous – though this may be changing, as we saw in Chapters 2 and 3. The case study in this section dramatizes the impact differences in fair value standards have on compliance.

Bank Beta is a global financial institution operating in all major markets of the world. Because of its activities in North America, years ago, it adopted US GAAP in parallel to the accounting system prevailing in its country of origin. To prepare itself for the new accounting rules in its home market, Bank Beta did a dry run with IFRS, including IAS 39. The case study in this section is concerned with five issues:

- Restructuring provisions
- Financial investments
- Employee benefit plans
- Retained earnings adjustments
- Derivative instruments and hedging.

Under IFRS, restructuring provisions are recognized when a legal or constructive obligation has been incurred. Restructuring provisions, for instance, may cover personnel, IT, the entity's premises, and other costs associated with combining and restructuring operations. They may also reflect the impact of increased precision in the estimation of certain leased and owned property costs.

In its home country, prior to IAS 39, financial investments were classified as being either current or long-term. Management considered current financial investments to be held for sale and carried them at lower cost or market value (LOCOM), discussed in section 4. By contrast, Bank Beta accounted for long-term financial investments at cost, less any permanent impairments.

Under US GAAP, the credit institution's financial investments have been classified as available for sale under 'debt and marketable equity securities'. They were accounted for at fair value, with changes in fair value recorded in the balance sheet with:

- Gains and losses recognized in net profit in the period sold, and
- Losses recognized in the period of permanent impairment.

After January 2005, for IFRS to US GAAP reconciliation, debt and marketable equity securities have been adjusted from LOCOM to fair value, and classified as available-for-sale investments. Unrealized gains or unrealized losses relating to these investments are also recorded in the balance sheet.

Under IFRS the bank's private equity investments and non-marketable equity financial investments are included in financial investments. For US GAAP, however, non-marketable equity financial investments are reclassified to assets, and private equity investments are shown separately on the balance sheet.

This is an interesting case in terms of conversion and diversion characterizing the two standards. The accounting for financial investments classified as available for sale is now generally the same under IFRS and US GAAP. There are, however, two exceptions:

- Private equity investments and non-marketable equity financial investments, are classified as available for sale and carried at cost less other than temporary impairments under US GAAP, and
- Write-downs on impaired assets can be fully or partially reversed under IFRS *if* the value of the impaired assets increases. Such reversals of impairment write-downs are not allowed under US GAAP.

Another important reference concerns retirement benefit plans and generally employee benefits. Under IFRS the entity must recognize pension expense based on a specific method of actuarial valuation. This is used to determine the projected plan liabilities for:

- Accrued services
- Future expected salary increases, and
- Expected return on pension plan assets.

Pension plan assets are recorded at fair value, and are held in a separate trust, to satisfy plan liabilities. Under IFRS, the recognition of a prepaid asset is subject to certain limitations, and any unrecognized prepaid asset is recorded as pension expense.

Notice that under US GAAP, pension expense is based on the same actuarial method of valuation of liabilities and assets as under IFRS, but there are differences in the amounts of expense and liabilities, due to different transition date rules, and stricter US GAAP provisions for recognition of prepaid assets.

Moreover, under US GAAP, if the fair value of employee plan assets falls below the accumulated benefit obligation, an additional minimum liability must be shown in the balance sheet. And if an additional minimum liability is recognized, then an equal amount will be recognized as an intangible past service cost.

In regard to other employee benefits, under IFRS Bank Beta recorded expenses and liabilities for post-retirement medical and life insurance benefits. These have been determined under a method similar to the one described under retirement benefit plans.

Under US GAAP, expenses and liabilities for post-retirement medical and life insurance benefits are determined under the same methodology as under IFRS. Here again, however, there are differences in the levels of expenses and liabilities incurred due to different transition date rules and the treatment of other activities.

The handling of retained earnings adjustments should also attract the reader's attention. With IAS 39, an opening adjustment has to be made to reduce retained earnings by reflecting the impact of new hedge accounting rules, re-measuring assets to either amortized cost or fair value as required under the standard. For US GAAP purposes, the first adjustment has not been required because all derivatives were previously recorded in the income statement. By contrast, the second adjustment has been recorded in profits and losses.

In connection to derivative instruments held or issued for hedging activities, Bank Beta applied no hedge accounting under US GAAP reporting. Therefore, all derivative instruments were carried on the balance sheet at fair value, with changes in fair value recorded in the income statement. In the course of a dry run, the bank first accounted for derivative instruments hedging non-trading positions in the profit and loss statement, using the accrual or deferral method. Then it experimented with IAS 39 and SFAS 133.

Under IAS 39, the bank has been permitted to hedge interest rate risk based on forecasted cash inflows and outflows on a group basis. For this purpose, accounting accumulated information about financial assets, financial liabilities, and forward commitments. Such information has been used to estimate and aggregate cash flows. Also, to schedule the future periods in which these cash flows are expected to occur.

Amounts deferred under previous hedging relationships that no longer qualify as hedges under IAS 39 were amortized against net profit over the remaining life of the hedging relationship. Such amounts had to be reversed for US GAAP as they have never been treated as hedges.

Appropriate derivative instruments were used to hedge the estimated future cash flows. Notice that SFAS 133 does not permit hedge accounting for hedges of future cash flows determined by this methodology. Accordingly, for US GAAP such items continue to be carried at fair value, with changes in fair value recognized in net trading income.

Finally, in addition to differences in valuation and income recognition, there are also other differences between IFRS and US GAAP. These are essentially related to presentation. One of the differences is *settlement date* vs *trade date* accounting. The bank's transactions from securities activities are recorded under IFRS on:

- Settlement date for balance sheet, and
- Trade date for P&L statement purposes.

This results in recording a forward transaction during the period between trade date and settlement date. Forward positions relating to trading activities are revalued to fair value and any unrealized profits and losses recognized in net profit.

By contrast, under US GAAP, trade date accounting is required for spot purchases and sales of securities. Hence, all transactions with a trade date on or before the balance sheet date, and with a settlement date after the balance sheet date, must be recorded at trade date for financial reporting purposes.

7.   Contrary opinions on IFRS and cherry-picking

Those who take a contrary position say that no matter what 'might be' its benefits, fair value accounting raises substantive concerns – which they try to identify through contradictory statements. For instance, because changes in economic environment and risk profile are better accounted for, the fair value's net result would be to increase volatility of earning, assets and liabilities reflected in financial reporting.

The first half of this argument on the fact that both risk profile and changes in economic environment are *better accounted for* through fair value is very positive in regard to IFRS. This is precisely what can make both financial accounting and management accounting much more:

- Relevant
- Accurate, and
- Informative to its user.

The second half of the contrary, that *fair value increases volatility* of earnings, assets, and liabilities, confuses the messenger with the wrong-doer. IFRS is simply the messenger, who says that the type of instruments in the banking book and in the trading book are such that market changes greatly impact on:

- The entity's asset values, gains, and losses, and
- On the volatility characterizing its assets and liabilities.

According to the same critics, this volatility in the profit and loss account 'may even be misleading, with the result that unrealized profits are taxed', a cost which may not be offset by the tax deductibility of unrealized losses. This is, of course, a fool's argument, essentially amounted to the statement: Better to have losses in order not to pay taxes.

By contrast, a better documented contrary argument is the fact that determining the fair value of instruments like inventoried derivatives, which have no relevant market price, could be difficult, except by marking to model. As has already been discussed:

- Models involve assumptions leading to model risk, and
- Different models could give very different results for instruments with comparable risk features.

Furthermore, the reader should appreciate that the value resulting from a modelling procedure is only as good as the data used as input, and as sound as the algorithms of the model itself. Most banks lack model experience and, moreover, all too often they use too short a time perspective for estimation of model parameters. This works against the accuracy of model results. There is also the fact that different entities can use:

- Different models, and
- Significantly different assumptions underpinning their valuation procedures.

When this happens, the resulting fair values, and their effects on the profit and loss account, may not be comparable across different financial institutions or other firms. And because value estimates always involve subjective judgment, both external auditors and supervisors find it challenging to verify whether fair values obtained through modelling are reliable.

True enough, what the last couple of paragraphs have stated is the negative side of the fair value approach. But *if* the critics had a better method to propose, all they needed to do is to come forward with it, rather than suggest either of two totally unacceptable alternatives:

- Staying with the meaningless book value, or
- Espousing opaque proformas, the greatest cheat of them all.

Still another argument advanced by critics is that a deterioration in a bank's credit rating would result in a reduction in value of its own bonds. This will decrease the fair value of its liabilities and, if the value of the assets were to remain unchanged, it would simultaneously result in an increase in shareholders' funds calculated as the difference between the fair value of the assets and liabilities.

This particular argument divides into two parts. The one is the effect of credit downgrading on the bank's liabilities – which might have a perverse aftermath *if* banks see their credit downgrading as a way to improve their balance sheet. The counter argument to such a statement is that banks simply cannot afford to do so; they have to maintain a high rating in order to:

- Attract funds, and
- Be considered worthy partners by correspondent banks and other parties.[8]

The likelihood of a misleading improvement in the entity's solvency position resulting from deterioration of its own credit risk is a different case – both counter-intuitive and controversial from a supervisory viewpoint. It might allow banks to game the system in respect of regulatory capital requirements, *if* supervisors don't watch out for this case, and consequently apply the brakes as well as the penalties.

To better appreciate whether or not this particular issue might become a loophole, it is advantageous to recall that no matter what the supervisory regime or accounting system, banks always found incentives for cherry-picking. For instance, under the accounting framework, which (for European firms) had been valid till the end of December 2004, the economic value of instruments:

- Was only recognized at the moment they were actually realized
- Therefore, a bank might have had an incentive to realize certain transactions purely to boost its accounting profit.

A frequent practice in this regard has been that assets which show substantial latent surplus values, such as hidden reserves, are sold to offset poor results for core business activities. Both new regulatory regimes, like Basel II, and new accounting rules, IFRS being an example, are designed to stop institutions and other entities from manipulating their financial results.

Another sound test of a new accounting system is how entities implementing it would react to economic shocks. Take as an example an unexpected change in interest rates (leaving for a moment the derivatives portfolio out of consideration). In principle, an interest rate change will have a different impact on the accounting value of items in the banking book under accruals and fair value approaches.

- An interest rate increase would result in a lower economic value of fixed value instruments.
- By contrast, a reduction in official interest rate would result in an increase of the economic value of fixed interest investments.

Under fair value accounting, value changes will be recognized in the financial statements. This is not true of accruals accounting, because value changes resulting from interest rate volatility will not affect the value of loans.

For securities in the banking book, when the lower of cost or market valuation is used, the recognition will only occur in the case of an interest rate rise. Even this valuation, however, will not recognize the latent value increases resulting from an interest rate decrease, which is not the case with IFRS.

In practically all entities today, and most particularly in the case of big banks with trillions in inventoried derivatives investments (in notional amounts), forgetting about the impact of derivatives on balance sheet and P&L is an oversimplification tantamount to a lack of management accountability (see section 8). The impact of derivatives gains and losses is so great that it can tilt the balance in terms of:

- Creditworthiness, and
- Financial staying power.

In more classical investments like equities and bonds, price declines could be absorbed, up to a point, by hidden reserves. But there are no hidden reserves big enough to cover huge derivatives losses as Barings Bank and tens of other documents. Therefore, it is right that under IFRS all price declines must be fully reflected in the profit and loss account – leaving no way for cherry-picking.

To better appreciate this message, let us apply a similar approach to the credit institution's deterioration in credit quality. In principle, deterioration in credit-worthiness of a financial asset, such as a loan or a bond, will be reflected in lower than expected cash flow.

- *If* the fair value of the instrument were to be calculated by discounting its expected cash flows,
- *Then*, its fair value would decline in parallel with the credit downgrading.

Prior to IFRS, in most jurisdictions the value of an asset was (usually) adjusted through creation of a specific provision, when that asset has been non-performing. A certain event reflecting deterioration in quality, like delay in interest payments or outright default, has to occur prior to such an adjustment. As a consequence:

- *If* provisioning decisions are perfectly forward-looking and reflecting likely changes in expected cash flows,
- *Then*, the accounting effects of accruals and fair value accounting, on credit risk, will be more or less identical.

Notice, however, that forward-looking provisioning is handicapped by cost-based accounting and tax regulations, which tend to narrowly define impairment and non-performing loans. Typically, the loan loss provisions have largely been backward-looking – a default which has not been corrected through Basel II because of abandoning the expected losses (EL) formula. Another current practice which has to change is that:

- As a rule credit ratings and probabilities of default are estimated in a point-in-time
- This limits vision to the short time horizon of one year, which is totally inadequate.

Only the better-managed banks use a longer time horizon for their credit risk assessment, taking into account expected average performance of a borrower over an economic cycle. In terms of management accounting, if not also for financial accounting reasons, the longer horizon is by far the better solution. Short-time estimates need to be revised most frequently, and can lead to volatility in statements greater than what might result from IFRS. Surely even a blind man could see this – yet IFRS critics don't.

8. What the critics forget: top management's accountability

It makes no sense to abandon the proverbial long hard look the board, CEO and senior management should take of all operations under their watch, for the sake of 'simplifying' accounting procedures, or keeping some of assumed exposure out of public eye. What all opponents of rigorous accounting rules should appreciate is that those entrusted with governance are *personally accountable* for obtained results: Good or bad.

Precisely for this reason, Chapter 1 presented a short but comprehensive list of recent scams, from Enron and WorldCom to Parmalat, which boomeranged and hit CEOs and their immediate assistants on the head. Daewoo, the Korean conglomerate, provides another example of management irresponsibility by exploiting loopholes in:

- Accounting systems, and
- Financial reporting rules.

In 1999, the high-flying Daewoo Group, the South Korean *chaebol*, collapsed with debts of *$80 billion*. Mid-2005, after running for six years as a fugitive, Kim Woo-choong, the former founder, animator, and CEO of Daewoo, returned home to South Korea to face arrest. He has been accused, among other things, of inflating the group's assets by $41 billion. Daewoo once employed 200 000 people worldwide and had sales of $60 billion.

Chief executives who are wrong-doers are not the only parties facing penalties and possible prison terms. The long hand of the law has now reached the formerly exclusive club of board member. Company directors therefore should be personally interested in analytical, timely, and accurate:

- Financial accounting, and
- Management accounting which provides advance notice of impending disaster (see also Chapter 15 on real-time management reports, Chapter 16 on interval control, and Chapter 17 on the Audit Committee).

A severe blow to the idea of a secure and unchallengeable director's seat was delivered in January 2004 with the announcements that ten former directors from each of two big firms, WorldCom and Enron, had agreed to pay a collective $18 million and $13 million, respectively, of *their own* money. Behind these settlements is the desire to tie up lawsuits launched by enraged shareholders against:

- Board members, and
- The firms which were supposed to have them under their watch.

While directors have often been sued by shareholders, these settlements are almost unprecedented. Moreover, other board members are currently the targets of high-profile lawsuits. In the past, shareholders' and regulators' claims against board members were covered by directors' liability insurance. This no longer seems to be enough, and therefore the payments agreed by the WorldCom and Enron directors sent a warning as well as thrill of fear through boardrooms.

Whether an insurance company or individual directors themselves pay for damages, a major question which arises when a company and its directors are sued for mismanagement or fraud is one of personal accountability. Each year, America's biggest firms spend a few million dollars each on premiums to cover the directors and officers in case disgruntled shareholders, employees or regulators take them to court, but:

- The amount of money at risk rises fast, and
- Rather than being reactive depending on an insurance, it is much better to be proactive and in charge of the situation, through fair value accounting.

During the first quarter of 2003 claims worth more than $1 billion were paid by, or came due from, insurers who wrote coverage for directors and officers (D&O). Now directors depending on reactive approaches must become used to opening their own wallets in order to pay for damages beyond what insurers would cover. Notice that in the cases of Enron and WorldCom insurers of the scandal-shattered companies are expected to pay out the bulk of the money:

- $36 million for WorldCom
- $155 million for Enron.

What ten former non-executive directors of WorldCom agreed to settle is *in addition* to insurance. The $18 million will come from their own personal wealth, though they neither admitted nor denied wrong-doing. Some estimates suggest this is equivalent to 20% of their personal assets, leaving aside their principal homes and pensions. The same is true of ten of Enron's former directors, who will cough up $13 million – a disgorgement of insider-trading gains, plaintiffs say.[9]

It comes as no surprise that these settlements have sparked a hot debate about whether it will now get harder to find qualified directors for company boards. Also, whether the two settlements will embolden America's class-action lawyers to redouble their efforts – till tort legislation is revamped, which does not seem to be around the corner.[10] According to some estimates, in America alone plaintiffs are seeking *$60 billion* to *$80 billion* in class-action suits that are yet to be settled.

Independent directors play a vital role in company management, but also in its mismanagement. Therefore, institutional investors are increasingly interested in seeing officers and directors considered to be malefactors make due financial contributions out of their own pockets.

Insurance should be a matter of last resort, rather than one of blind reliance. Moreover, for insurance companies, too, the rise in the number and size of lawsuits means that rates for D&O coverage will go up, even if a couple of years ago (in 2003) they fell by 10%, because of tough competition. Start-up insurers in America and Bermuda have rushed to provide D&O cover and cut the coverage prices. But is this a viable solution?

In conclusion, no matter what different IFRS may be saying, the best way to solve a great problem is to treat it boldly as a whole, to go to the root, and settle its solution upon a sound foundation. In business, the sound foundation upon which top management decisions can be based is reliable and timely financial and operational information. This is precisely what IFRS and US GAAP aim to provide.

Notes

1   Robert J. Schoenberg, *Geneen*, W.W. Norton, New York, 1985.
2   EIR, 17 October 1997.
3   The Accountant, www.lafferty.com, October 2004.
4   Schoenberg, *Geneen*.
5   *The Economist*, 13 August 2005.
6   D.N. Chorafas, *Rocket Scientists in Banking*, Lafferty Publications, London and Dublin, 1995.
7   D.N. Chorafas, *The Management of Equity Investments*, Butterworth-Heinemann, London, 2005.
8   D.N. Chorafas, *Economic Capital Allocation with Basel II: Cost and Benefit Analysis*, Butterworth-Heinemann, London and Boston, 2004.
9   *The Economist*, 15 January 2005.
10 D.N. Chorafas, *Operational Risk Control with Basel II: Basic Principles and Capital Requirements*, Butterworth-Heinemann, Oxford and Boston, 2004.

Business Ethics Add Value to Financial Disclosures

1. Introduction

Chapter 10 has brought to the reader's attention that accountability for good corporate governance squarely falls on the shoulders of senior management. In practically every jurisdiction, the top of the organizational pyramid is the party ultimately responsible for reliable financial reporting. The Basel Committee on Banking Supervision says that responsibility for financial reporting may also rest with the board of directors[1] – who should be the first to appreciate that honesty is the best policy.

Paraphrasing the old Roman dictum about Caesar's wife, the members of the board, CEO, and senior executives should not only be ethical people, but also should be seen as being so. Ethics in business is not the past but the future, and it is destroyed through *creative accounting* practices.

The reasons for creative accounting are well known, and all of them are counterproductive (see section 2). It is the directors' and CEO's responsibility to ensure that such practices are alien within the organization under their watch. Legislation helps in bringing a sense of accountability, an example being the 2002 Sarbanes–Oxley Act in the United States which made the CEO and chief financial officer (CFO) personally responsible for the accuracy of what is written in the company's financial statement (see section 3).

Organizations are comprised of people, and it is a human trait to boast more than one has or does. But directors, the CEO and CFO should know where the brakes are. Even with an objective and accurate presentation of financial information in the consolidated quarterly and annual reports, inference about a company's worth and financial staying power is not an easy matter. As far as equity valuation is concerned, the analyst's work is very similar to that of the archaeologist.

- The archaeologist tries to make inferences and reconstruct a civilization through its surviving evidence.

To obtain some information on which to base his or her hypotheses, the archaeologist studies the shape and nature of a container through fragments which may have decayed, or may be insufficient. Yet, this practically is all there is available in terms of evidence in archaeology. Quite similarly,

- The financial analyst looks at past accounts which may be obscure, or altogether unreliable, because of 'creative' ways of financial reporting.

More recently, the analyst also looks at the quality and ethics of corporate governance for clues on what went right or wrong with the accounts. The storm which shook up Tyco started when Wall Street got wind that Denis Kozlowski, its CEO, had cheated the State of New York on taxes due for artwork he had purchased, by shipping the wares to Maine and, through a U-turn, bringing back the art to his residence in New York City.

In a much broader sense, events such as the collapse of energy trader Enron, cable operator Adelphia Communications, international carrier Global Crossing, and the second largest US long-distance carrier WorldCom, or for that matter Italy's Parmalat, have cast doubt on the reliability of accounting practices. Many parties have come under fire:

- Accountants
- Auditors
- Rating agencies
- Financial analysts, and
- The entities' own top management.

These and many other meltdowns, have directed new attention to the ills of personal greed, lousy accounts, and inadequate surveillance. The consequence has been a loss of trust that needs to be won back, and this will not be easy. A long list of scams has demonstrated that company CEOs and CFOs can manipulate accounts to suit their own finances, rather than shareholder value or the interest of their employees and of the general public. Proof has been provided that:

- Accounting standards become easily the subject of manipulation.
- Hence the need for legislation to see to it that prison terms beckon for wrong-doers.

Even investors have attracted criticism for accepting published corporate profit figures at face value. Over-reliance on audited financial statements, and on creditor protection acts, ended by emptying many portfolios of their wealth, hitting particularly hard those who can least afford to lose their hard-won money. Everybody can profit from ethical financial reporting practices and the purging of creative accounting gimmicks.

2. Stamping out the practice of creative accounting

Ethics and good business sense correlate. The market accords a *transparency premium* to the share price of companies who are willing and able to provide clear, consistent, and informative disclosure about their operations and financial results. Such disclosure must go beyond the general line of how the company works, to:

- Include the risks that are taken
- Provide an accurate understanding of economic drivers, and
- Accurately describe the detailed financial results of the business.

Creative accounting negates each one of these three points. In fact, the term is a misnomer because what takes place is neither 'creative' nor is it 'accounting' in the sense defined by Fra Luca Paciolo (see Chapter 2). The practice of changing the numbers in company books to hide losses, beef up profits, or otherwise manicure financial statements is:

- Corrupt
- Quite often patchily done
- Eventually leading to abysmal results, and
- Always demonstrating a disregard for business ethics.

Ethics means *virtue* and as Socrates once said virtue is knowledge that cannot be taught. It is knowledge that is constantly evolving and often goes beyond formal legal and regulatory requirements, though these help to sustain business ethics. Market discipline, one of the three pillars of Basel II, means growing demand for more responsible personal and corporate behaviour (see section 7).

It is part of the ethical stance of top management to ensure that within each reporting period disclosure is consistent and comparable. Also, that between reporting periods the books are always kept in accordance with rigorous accounting standards. It is also top management's responsibility to see to it that financial information is presented in as simple a manner as possible, consistent with readers' ability to understand the company's performance.

Unbiased reporting standards are all-important in substantiating a strong commitment to corporate responsibility, recognizing the demands placed by different stakeholders: shareholders, bondholders, employees, regulators, and the general public which patronizes the company's products and services. A frequently encountered problem, however, is that corporate responsibility means different things to different people. The best way to tackle this issue is to press the point that:

- Core corporate responsibility starts and ends with ethical corporate governance, and
- The guardians of ethical corporate governance are the directors, CEO and CFO.

Corporate ethics make good business sense, as events in the early years of the 21st century demonstrate. Unable to depend on financial statements and unwilling to take risks, investors pulled more money out of equity mutual funds in June and July 2002 (after WorldCom's bankruptcy) than they did in the weeks after the tragic events of September 11, 2001.

Weary of the lack of corporate accountability and failures of judgment, before buying stocks again many investors want to see CEOs effectively sign off on their books and assume personal accountability for what is being reported. The US Congress has aptly passed the Sarbanes–Oxley Act and the Bush Administration has been right in its decision to hunt down culprits.

- Doubling prison terms for CEOs guilty of financial fraud
- Freezing improper payments to corporate executives
- Forcing managers who benefit from creative accounting to forfeit their gains, and
- Setting the Securities & Exchange Commission to ban convicted chief executives from ever serving on a board.

The capital market, too, became more cautious. Securitization of corporates with scant disclosure of embedded risk is one of the practices that contributed to the widespread after-shock of the big bankruptcies. Many banks exposed on loans to Enron, WorldCom, Parmalat, and other defunct firms sold securitized products to institutional investors and to their retail clients. Also, experts say, to recoup some of their losses, they went short on these companies' equity, essentially using inside information in making their moves.

The good news is that the scams which shook business, industry, and the markets during the past ten years have had the effect of issuing a wake-up call. The new mood reflects a recently prevailing notion that the culture of a corporation can produce malfeasance. Eventually, the consequences for an accused company can be severe. As an article in *The Economist* suggested, in the aftermath of Enron:

- Many clients have deserted Andersen, the accounting firm
- Thousands of employees have lost their jobs, and
- The whole international network of one of the Big Five has crumbled.[2]

Like an auditor, a financial entity or any other business that operates under the scrutiny of regulators might find it difficult to survive a criminal probe. Bankers Trust paid dearly for its derivatives scams. Its indictment became its death warrant.

274

Yet banks and other financial companies sometimes act in a way that invites regulatory action, if not outright public wrath.

This policy of cheating through creative accounting and other murky deals is simply senseless, and something is needed to save managerial wrong-doers from themselves. Cooking the books is a criminal act – though a government prosecutor might choose a civil over a criminal charge because it carries a preponderance of evidence rather than proof beyond reasonable doubt. While penalties imposed in a civil case are less severe than those in a criminal one, *reputational risk* is roughly the same, and so is the aftermath.

The events that took place in the go-go 1990s, and came to light after the stock market bubble burst in 2000, document that many players are no longer in charge of their actions. Pessimists say that the system itself has been corrupted and needs urgent repair. This requires a long list of changes going deep into the business community and its practices.

- Self-regulation might have been preferable, but does not seem to be doable.
- Therefore, legal measures are needed to redress the balances of business ethics. The letter of the law is the only alternative to a runaway system.

Firms must meet the public demand for transparency and ethical behaviour all of the time, not just in sporadic cases (see section 4). They must take their responsibilities seriously, and put shareholders' interests first. This is not happening today, as a myriad of examples documents. We will study some of them in this chapter.

A strategy of personal and corporate accountability needs to show results for the efforts being undertaken in a clear and unambiguous manner. Measuring ethical performance is therefore essential, and it should be done through comprehensive and generally accepted criteria and standards. Both IFRS and Basel II have contributed a great deal in this direction, but the best example of legal framework is the Sarbanes–Oxley Act in the United States.

Moreover, while the written law is important, it is not everything. Only jurisprudence, which will take years to develop, will establish tolerance levels for violators, and will answer questions regarding assertions about effectiveness of management control. In the meantime, however, the regulators must provide some interpretations that could help to reduce the cost of compliance without diminishing the effectiveness of the law.

While only a few years old, Sarbanes–Oxley is already having a positive outcome. A near-consensus on Wall Street is that the new legislation succeeded in improving stock market performance of large American companies. A noted 'plus' in financial disclosure has come in spite of growing complaints from corporate America that the pendulum has swung too far, resulting in excessive compliance burdens. Looking for factors that gave investors greatest transparency in judging behaviour, a mid-2004 study by Governance Metrics International (GMI) confirmed academic studies showing a link between share price performance and adherence to best practice in corporate governance.

3. The application of the Sarbanes–Oxley Act in the United States

In July 2002 the Sarbanes–Oxley Act was passed in the US Congress, establishing rigorous corporate governance rules. It set specific expectations as to the reliability of financial statements of firms whose shares are traded on US stock exchanges. The Act requires chief executive officers and chief financial officers to certify the dependability of such statements, as well as if they have:

- Effective systems of internal control related to external financial disclosures, and
- Procedures able to notify both external auditors and the entity's Audit Committee (see Chapter 17) when significant control deficiencies are detected.

The Sarbanes–Oxley Act also obliges a firm's external auditor to report on the reliability of management's assessment of internal controls. This is a requirement which has raised important questions. For instance, How many and what type of control deficiencies the CEO and CFO can not report to external auditors and the Audit Committee without violating the Act? What is the threshold over which the Securities and Exchange Commission (SEC) and civil courts will act?

This law took effect in 2005 for US companies with market capitalizations of more than $75 million. A statistic that is worth retaining is that more than 1000 quoted US companies, including some majors, said that they would restate their accounts. Moreover, about 8% of the companies affected have:

- Reported material weaknesses in controls, and
- Indicated that the law addressed a real problem.

A number of those companies have discovered errors in their financial statements caused by both accounting and managerial weaknesses. But many companies also complained that costs were too high and that auditors forced them to go through expensive procedures, rejecting tests of controls done during the fiscal year and saying all tests must be done again at year-end.

Following these findings, the Securities and Exchange Commission provided a more relaxed definition of what is *material* in deciding whether a weakness in controls needs to be reported at all. In general, it said, companies should determine materiality based on annual totals for the entire entity, not on the impact an item might have on a quarterly report or on results of one part of the company. But SEC also added that in some cases, such as when one or two segments of a company are very important to investors, the definition of materiality has to be expanded.

Michael Oxley, of the US House of Representatives, co-sponsor of the Act named after him and Senator Paul Sarbanes, said in early 2005: 'How can you measure the value of knowing that company books are sounder than they were before?' Oxley, the chairman of the House of Representatives' financial-services committee, acknowledged that the Act imposed real costs on firms, but he commented that this is 'an investment for the future'.[3]

Oxley is right. In 2005 as for the first time companies have been filing the reports required by section 404 of the Sarbanes–Oxley Act, came some good news. For instance, fewer big American companies were reporting problems with their internal controls than had been expected. Moody's stated that about 5% of the companies that it rates had reported material internal control weaknesses up to 1 April 2005, compared with the 10–20% that the market thought would be the number.

In fact, Moody's has taken a positive view of the impact of section 404 of Sarbanes–Oxley, saying that, to its perception, companies are strengthening their accounting controls and investing in the infrastructure needed to support quality financial reporting. Because of the Act, firms now have to make some major accounting decisions for themselves. As a result,

- They are reinvesting in accounting personnel, and
- They look more closely at their business processes, fountainhead of their original accounting data.

According to the rating agency, the most serious control problems which have been encountered do not lie with the reported delinquents, but with the late filers. These are the companies that were unable to get their reports to the SEC on time, a group which includes notorious cases such as AIG, the world's largest insurer, Delphi, the automotive components manufacturer, and Fannie Mae, the colossal US government agency for mortgage discounting and securitization.

AIG, Delphi, and Fannie Mae have been no newcomers to troubled financial reporting, which proves that Sarbanes–Oxley has been successful in flushing out weak cases. Sometimes, it is a rash of unintended consequences that dominates the aftermath of new legislation, but in this case, the consequences so far observed have been wanted – and the same is true of a significant increase in financial transparency.

4. Transparency is the best disinfectant: a case study with WorldCom

This is the third occasion in the course of this book when I have mentioned the famous dictum by Dr Louis Brandeis, the US Supreme Court Justice, that 'Sunshine is the best disinfectant'. Paraphrasing Brandeis' dictum, when it comes to financial reporting by business entities, and all other organizations, sunshine is not just the best disinfectant, it is the only one that makes sense.

Sunshine, and therefore, transparency, should be a basic characteristic of every accounting standard and financial reporting regulation. Indeed, not only IFRS and US GAAP but nearly all standards of accounting have been established to promote disclosure. The aftermath of steady innovation is difficult enough to appreciate, without the true risks being obscured or hidden. In Enron's case, and many others, shareholders were cheated because they:

- Received misinformation about the true debt, profits, and losses of the company, and
- They were misled by a corporate policy of always disguising its financial data.

A similar story has happened with WorldCom. During 2001 and the first quarter of 2002, just prior to crashing, the company counted as capital investments (Capex) some $3.8 billion that it had spent on ordinary everyday expenses. This makes a big difference because, for accounting purposes, capital investments are treated differently from other expenses.

- Capital spending is money used to buy long-lasting assets, such as fibre-optic cables or switches that direct telephone calls.

The cost of capital investments is spread out over several years. For instance, if WorldCom spent $35 million on switches it expected to last 7 years, this money would be booked as $5 million expense for 7 years. In contrast, if it spent $35 million on office space, it had to count all of that expense in the period in which it occurred. Switching everyday expenses into the capital budget is one of the perverse ways of creative accounting.

The company said, to its justification, that the expenses that were counted as capital expenditures involved *line costs*, which are fees WorldCom paid to other telecom players for the right to access their networks. But line costs are ordinary expenses. Creative accounting comes in because counting such expenses as capital investments boosts net income:

- Eventually expenses are counted in one quarter
- But capital expenditures are spread out over years, sugar-coating the P&L.

The regulators, investors, and the general public have been misled and cheated by this sort of false accounting. WorldCom originally reported net income of $1.4 billion in 2001 and $172 million in the first quarter of 2002. After bankruptcy, it was found that it had lost money on both occasions.

Another creative accounting practice in which WorldCom specialized has been the massaging of its cash flow. What it did affected cash generated from operations – a closely watched line in financial statements. The company originally reported that its operating activities in 2001 produced $7.7 billion in cash. After bankruptcy, it was revealed that its cash flow really was $4.6 billion.

Where WorldCom, and so many other companies, have been masters in managing accounting data is with earning before interest, taxes, depreciation, and amortization (EBITDA). This is one of the areas where creative accounting has a big impact. WorldCom originally reported that its EBITDA for 2001 was $10.5 billion. After bankruptcy it was found this figure really was $6.3 billion. Moreover, in the first quarter of 2002 it reported EBITDA of $2.1 billion but in reality the figure was $1.4 billion; the company was in much worse shape than investors thought.

This sort of swindle in financial reporting was not the sort of thing that happened only once. Rather, it was a steady business practice. Yet, over long stretches of time creative accounting cannot be done without the external and internal auditors' complicity.

WorldCom's external auditor was Arthur Andersen. Immediately after the event the now-defunct auditor said its work for the company complied with all accounting standards (!). The fake numbers came to light through a probe conducted by

WorldCom's new auditor KPMG, as well as by WorldCom employees who had had enough with the prevailing culture of duplicity in financial accounts.

As this example, and so many others, document, *transparency* in financial reporting means not only releasing accurate and timely information, but also structuring this information in a way that it tells nothing but the truth. This 'truth' about the financials of a company must be presented in a way that board members, risk controllers, regulators, investors, and the public can understand and act upon it. This is the role of rigorous accounting standards like IFRS and US GAAP.

Notice that sometimes variations between different accounting standards may be exploited to conceal the true financial figures. In early 2000, Nomura Securities published a comparison of American and Japanese financial reporting in the 1980s and 1990s. This pointed out that Japanese banks, and other companies, tried to conceal their financial problems:

- Through shady accounting practices, and
- By capitalizing on loopholes in financial reporting standards.

For instance, during the bubble of 1980s in the Japanese stock market, firms depended for their financing almost entirely on banks which, in turn, relied on shares and property as collateral for lending. That left banks completely exposed to falling asset prices. The thunderbolt which hit the Nikkei 225 after the bursting of the bubble left the whole Japanese banking industry comatose – in which state is has practically remained until today, 15 years down the line.[4]

Contrary to the Japanese, the better known US companies depend for financing on capital markets. Capital markets, however, will not be cheated for long, though this happens from time to time as the Enron and WorldCom examples suggest. In the years to come, borrowing in the capital markets must be characterized by increasing transparency, as major investors are now carrying out more analytical accounting investigations than ever before. This means that companies must not only adopt reliable reporting practices, but also show greater discipline with capital investment decisions in the economic environment(s) in which they operate. At the same time, new global capital adequacy guidelines must be matched by careful domestic reform. This is written in full understanding that globalization and technology have:

- Changed the credit dimension
- Made markets more dynamic, and

- Forced companies to take more risk which should be fully reflected in their income statement and balance sheet.

Central bankers and regulators also depend a great deal on reliable financial reporting. The European Central Bank (ECB) regards transparency as a crucial component of its monetary policy framework. ECB says that transparency requires central banks to clearly explain how they interpret and implement their mandates. This helps the public to monitor and evaluate a central bank's performance. But it also requires an understanding of the analytical framework used for its internal decision-making on monetary policy and assessment of:

- The state of the economy, and
- The economic rationale underlying monetary policy decisions.

In the case of a central bank, for example, transparency is strongly enhanced by means of a publicly announced monetary policy strategy. A comparable criterion of transparency for a commercial bank would be a public announcement to all stakeholders of the level of risk the institution is willing to assume, including:

- Leveraging
- Loans
- Investments
- Trades other than derivatives, and
- Derivatives trades.

Not only companies but also nations should observe the transparency principle, which they often don't. South Korea, Indonesia, Thailand, Brazil, Mexico, Argentina, and other countries might have avoided sudden exchange-rate crises and panics *if* investors had a more accurate idea of the country's foreign reserve levels. Also, investors might have steered clear of the abyss *if* firms in these countries had been forced, by their regulators, to disclose:

- The size of their foreign liabilities, and
- Their financial staying power when confronted with huge debts.

Lack of transparency encourages governments, companies, and people to indulge in reckless behaviour or use second rate criteria which minimize outstanding risk. An example from the 1990s has been lending short-term to Asian borrowers because such loans carried a lower risk-weighting in the scales established by Western regulators, which proved to be a big mistake.

5. Off-balance sheet and proforma are creative accounting practices

Creative accounting has many aspects, both qualitative and quantitative. The February 1997 (2/97) issue of *McKinsey Quarterly* makes reference to certain relatively simple ideas which can lead to major if temporary financial advantages.[5] A good example to keep in mind is the effect of manipulating financial results by means of off-balance sheet (read: derivatives) deals: 'The deployment of off-balance-sheet funds using institutional investment money ...'

- 'Fostered (Enron's) securitization skills ...', and
- 'Granted it access to capital at below the hurdle rates of (other) major oil companies.'

A second reference from the same source helps to explain how some types of negotiating and manipulating skills lead to new opportunities, altering the way work is traditionally done: 'Enron was not distinctive at building and operating power stations, but it didn't matter; the skills could be contracted out. Rather, it was good at negotiating contracts, financing, and (obtaining) government guarantees – precisely the skills that distinguished successful players (in a virtual economy).'

The tie-in comes from the fact a virtual economy provides plenty of opportunities for creative accounting which, in turn, strengthens 'negotiating skills' of an unscrupulous management. Credit (or rather debit) for some of Enron's moves goes to a team that developed an electric power and natural gas hedge fund, and contributed to the engineering of:

- The huge California power price spike, and
- The unforgettable (as well as unforgivable) California power blackout.

Other big companies, too, don't shy from creative accounting practices and the ephemeral benefits they provide. Mid-January 2005, Nortel Networks released restated results from 2003, which *reduced* prior reported profits by some $300 million. As a justification, the well-known telecom equipment manufacturer blamed several former executives for using 'inappropriate' accounting methods to:

- Inflate profits, and
- Beef-up their own bonuses.

Where were Nortel's internal control procedures, which should have reported the scam? Where was the vigilance of the board's Audit Committee? Apart from the fact that this creative accounting scandal, like so many others, is indecent, a dozen senior executives who said 'they had not been directly involved' will nevertheless return $8.6 million in bonuses over the next three years. Five Nortel board directors stepped down.[6]

One of the best case studies on the many colours of creative accounting is AIG's 2004 proforma reporting. *Proforma earnings* has been the brainchild of EBITDA. Proforma is a 1990s manipulation of operating earnings, with the resulting unreliable financial reports popularized by dot.coms. The way proforma is being used tends to exclude basic costs like marketing and interest, among others, thereby giving a fake picture of profitability.

Over time, like the spider crab, which has been renamed the Alaskan king crab and become an instant success, proforma was rebaptized as *adjusted earnings*. When the reader hears about adjusted earnings, he or she will do well to remember this is merely a new term for proforma, invented after the latter has:

- Highly disappointed investors, and
- Led to lots of money being lost.

Proformas are creative accounting gimmicks; they are financial statements which do not have to conform to the US GAAP. They are not approved by regulators, they do not conform to accepted accounting principles, and they are unreliable, but curiously enough accepted by a market thirsty for 'good news'.

There is nothing better than a real life case study to demonstrate what companies can do when they are free to choose the metrics and methods through which they report their financial results. American International Group (AIG) is one of the biggest and best-known companies in the insurance business.

- It is the largest American insurer, and
- It seems to be cherry-picking in its financial reporting.

On 11 February 2004 AIG announced a 68% increase of net income. This boosted the company's stock, which had anyway been rising for a whole quarter. Struck by the huge gains in profits, David Schiff, of *Schiff's Insurance Observer*, took a closer look at the impressive profits being announced and found that:

- *If* AIG had used the same methodology as it had in the past,
- *Then* it would have been up a far less impressive 15% in profitability terms, instead of 68%.

The way *The Economist* had it, this most interesting discovery prompted Schiff to take a deeper look at AIG's record.[7] What he found is that when, in the fourth quarter of 2002, AIG began its net income announcement, it provided investors with an adjusted number that:

- Excluded realized losses on its securities portfolio, and
- Featured a large charge-off for miscalculating previous losses.

The pivot point of this resetting of financial facts and figures was that a 3% increase in net income could be viewed as a 12% increase. By contrast, *if* financial and accounting gimmicks were put to test, and as David Schiff says the various superfluous adjustments were left out, *then* in reality AIG's earnings declined by 4% in that year.

With this significant finding regarding AIG's 2002 financial accounts, David Schiff went back over four more years of AIG accounting to find that the insurance company has been able to improve the appearance of its profits growth in 19 out of the 20 preceding quarterly financial statements. The miracle was achieved by shifting the emphasis in its presentation of results between four different measures of profits (the cherry-picking). While stating net income, the company:

- Sometimes offered an adjusted figure highlighting realized investment returns
- In other times, it highlighted various losses, and
- In still other cases it did neither, so that quarter-to-quarter financial results were no longer comparable.

The net effect of this cherry-picking has been the creation of a far more positive impression of the company's growth which, as expected, misguided investors. The miracle was achieved by manipulating the freedom provided by proforma statements, that commonly appear at the beginning of company reports and public announcement.

The price is *legal risk*. In early 2005 American International Group filed its annual report, after three previous delays, and restated net profit for the past five years, reducing it by $3.9 billion – which is a large sum. In the sequel, the State of New York brought a civil lawsuit against the insurance giant and its former chief executive officer, accusing them of manipulating financial statements.

In conclusion, as AIG's case and a myriad of others demonstrate, proformas have been invented and used to paint a company's financial performance in an overly flattering way. In 2003, as part of the new Sarbanes–Oxley legislation (see section 3), the SEC passed rules to crack down on proforma abuses.

Companies who had lost no opportunity to mislead investors made reference to the new regulatory requirements noting that:

- Their proforma statements were not in accordance with GAAP, and
- A reconciliation or restatement would be made at some later date.

The management of these companies could never use the excuse that 'senior executives did not know ...'. As David Schiff pointed out, in AIG's case, the NYSE's manual for listed companies writes clearly in black and white that 'changes in accounting methods to mask' unfavourable news 'endangers management's reputation for integrity'. But who cares?

6. Expensing stock options is good business ethics

Stock options are a peculiar instrument of executive compensation, as well as a form of creative accounting at senior management level. Although lavish stock options make a mockery of shareholder value, and they have been largely used for self-gratification, with little or no link to performance, until very recently they have not been recognized as expenses in income statements. Like EBITDA, stock options are:

- A way of not lowering reported earnings, and
- A loophole in financial reporting favoured by companies across the board.

This loophole is evidenced by the fact that once stock options are vested or exercised they obviously reduce per share earnings, as companies simply issue more shares to meet their option obligations. This is a practice which hurts stock prices, is generally against shareholder interest, and constitutes a way of disguising financial statements.

Companies try to cover this loophole in two ways. One is *buybacks*. By regularly purchasing more of their own shares than they currently need for option exercises, companies prevent such dilution in ownership from coming to light. At the same time, share buybacks tend to push up stock prices. Thus:

- Enriching people holding stock options, and
- Pleasing shareholders who might otherwise be upset by huge executive option awards
- But, at the same time, depriving shareholders of a regular dividend.

As we have seen in Chapter 3, the rules of IFRS ensure that companies can no longer bury stock option handouts as footnotes to their financial statements. The new accounting rules make management responsible for showing the full value of all stock options it grants to itself and the employees. This section elaborates on the effects of this requirement.

The other way to cover up equity dilution through non-expensed options is to play with *derivative financial instruments*. Eventually, this means significant derivatives losses. On 24 September 2002, the shares of EDS, the computer services company, plunged for a second time in a week:

- The first drop was 52%
- The second another 43%.

Investors confidence was shaken by the company's huge losses with derivative products, a gamble which was not part of its core business. The way it has been reported, EDS used derivatives to try to reduce the cost of issuing shares, under its employee stock option plan.

That is far from being the only case. Storebrand, the Norwegian insurance company, did the same – with equally disastrous results. In EDS' case, the cost from sour derivatives was $225 million, and these losses made it more difficult to fund the upfront cost of large insourcing deals. Apart from the damage done to shareholders, EDS also attracted SEC's attention.

For how long can this loophole, particularly exploited in the last two decades, remain open? Stock options dilute ownership but at the same time the rising volume of buybacks reduces the number of outstanding shares of large companies. In the United States this has happened at the rate of about 1% a year over the 1994–99 timeframe – the stock market's boom years. At Wall Street, financial analysts suggested that it:

- Produced a steady upward pressure on share prices, and
- Magnified its own impact by being factored into market expectations.

The steady growth of stock options and buybacks meant that companies devoted more and more of their earnings to buying their own shares, reducing dividends to historically low levels. During the bubble of the 1990s, payouts to shareholders has been mainly done through rapid appreciation of stock price – essentially a Ponzi game, since profits depended on other investors buying up inflated stock.

By 1999, total payout through dividends and buybacks had hit 80% of cash flow, which led to more and more leveraging of companies. Because at the same time they continued to spend a big chunk of their earnings on capital investment, they went deeper and deeper into debt. In retrospect,

- This led to serious weakening of the companies' financial staying power, and
- In the early years of the 21st century management had to concentrate on repairing the balance sheet.

A most significant challenge to the option mania, leading to a change in corporate accounting, was proposed in April 2004 by the Financial Accounting Standards Board (FASB), when it asked companies to deduct option costs from their earnings. The aim has been one of changing the secrecy practice, where options costs:

- Are footnoted in financial reports
- But do not have to be subtracted.

FASB's initiative could not have come at a more opportune moment. It followed on the heels of an announcement that Intel more than doubled the number of stock options granted to Chief Executive Craig Barrett in 2003, when the top chipmaker's profit surged 81%. Intel also paid Barrett a bonus of $1.5 million, up 41% from a year earlier.

As this and many similar examples demonstrate, expensing options provides more complete and surely more transparent information to investors regarding what is being done with their money. Technology companies, however, say that expensing hurts their earnings, their stock price, and their ability to compensate employees. This is only half true.

After the stock market crash of 2000, a new way to make a living in Silicon Valley has been *equity-only* jobs. Employees and workers received stock options and a letter of intent to hire them in the future, rather than wages and benefits. This sort of employer–employee relation has been on the rise, especially among laid-off information technology workers who no longer want to wait indefinitely for paying jobs.

The *San Francisco Chronicle* wrote on 22 December 2002 that equity-only jobs are often with start-up IT companies. One, however, should not confuse the start-ups that try to survive by paying in equity share, with the pillars of technology, like Intel, lavishly awarding options beyond fat salaries and other benefits. Moreover, California officials have warned that:

- Equity-only agreements violate state labour laws, and
- Labour laws stipulate that all workers must be paid at least the minimum wage.

There are evident reasons why big outfits fought the expensing of options tooth and nail. In 2003, communications equipment companies would have seen a 117% drop in net income had they expensed executive options, and the income of semiconductor firms would have dropped 102%, while the S&P 500 overall went south by 8%.

It needs no explaining why, in the United States, fearing they would have to write such figures in their income statement, instead of inflated current profits, companies put their lobbyists in motion. On 20 July 2004, the US House of Representatives voted 312–111 to block the proposed FASB rule that would require the accounting of employee stock options as corporate expenses. Instead, expensing would be limited to stock options for:

- The chief executive, and
- The next four highest-paid officers of a company.

Among the dissenting voices to this legal sustenance of stock options greed at the expense of shareholders has been Rep. Paul Kanjorski (D–Penn.), who argued that this lop-sided vote threatens the independence of the FASB. Moreover, Kanjorski said, stock options have contributed to recent financial storms on Wall Street, noting that a decade ago the Congress strong-armed FASB into abandoning an effort to adopt a rule requiring stock option expensing. It is to the credit of IASB that expensing stock options became a rule with IFRS.

7. Companies respecting themselves account for all their expenses

It needs no reminder that companies respecting themselves, their stockholders, bondholders, and the general public account in their income statement for *all* their expenses. Based on this principle, different entities have chosen different methods in accounting for executive options. For instance, in 2002 Crédit Suisse Group has decided to:

- Adopt the fair value method of expensing stock option awards as of 1 January 2003, and
- Modify its practice with regard to the use of stock options, so that awards are reasonable and documented.

Stock option awards continue to be part of Crédit Suisse compensation plans as a means of retaining key personnel, but this is now happening at a lower level than in preceding years. In addition, the bank has introduced three-year vesting for all option awards granted in future compensation cycles, which is a commendable practice.

Other companies dropped stock option grants altogether. On 8 July 2003, Microsoft said that it would no longer grant stock options. Instead, it will rely on potential awards of stock to its almost 50 000 employees. There has been a very good reason for that decision.

- In the decade from 1991 until mid-2000, Microsoft's outstanding shares increased from 4.2 billion to 5.3 billion.
- Over that same period, the company issued about 1.6 billion new shares under its share option schemes and it bought back 677 million.

The share buyback cost the company $16.2 billion but, at the time, that figure did not appear as an expense in Microsoft's profit and loss statement. Microsoft had the courage to be transparent on these figures. A myriad of other companies who did the same, or even worse, kept such numbers close to their chest so that shareholders do not know how much money is taken out of their pockets.

Microsoft has also changed its accounting practices, adopting a standard that tries to accurately assess the impact of stock grants and stock options on the company's balance sheet. Beneath this and similar actions lies the fact that the unaccounted treatment of options makes it hard for investors to form a clear judgment of a company's financial strength. This can be particularly serious in the high-tech industry, where lack of transparency as well as other issues has greatly contributed to the share price bubble.

Microsoft's practice is an excellent example for other firms to follow – particularly those companies who, over the past two decades, relied very heavily on the stock market to pay their executives and CEOs, at the owners' expense. For instance, a 1999 study in the United States by Bear Stearns, the investment bank, estimated that operating profits at computer networking companies:

- Would have been 26% *lower* under fair value accounting, and
- This would have meant a similar or larger drop in the market value of their shares.

Along the same frame of reference, at Wall Street analysts calculated that while the shareholder takes all the risks he or she gains only 75% of the profits. Taking high fees of this sort, which skim the cream off the top, has become very similar to the policy followed by hedge funds. The exact figures are that:

- In the general case options trim 10% off annual company profits, and
- For technology companies this rises to between 20 and 25% – and it can go up to 50%, as in the case of Intel.

As we saw in section 6 with EDS, bumper bonuses and derivatives losses correlate. As Warren Buffett aptly suggests, derivatives are so complex, and based on outcomes so distant, that parties on both sides of a given bet are able to book a notional profit. That essentially means big trading bonuses today, and who cares about future losses which:

- Destroy shareholder value, and
- Bring to its knees the company which bets its future?

Moreover, senior management tends to award executive options for results it did not deliver. Only few people have the decency to give back these options after having second thoughts about their wisdom. On 23 January 2003, Tom Siebel, chairman and chief executive of the software company that bears his name, handed back $56 million worth of stock options to head off concerns that their excessive use was hurting other shareholders. As Warren Buffett puts it:

- If options aren't a form of compensation, what are they?
- If compensation isn't an expense, what is it?
- If expenses shouldn't go into the calculation of earnings, where in the world should they go?

The answer to be given to this question on how to account for stock options varies by jurisdiction. Mid-July 2000, in the UK, the Accounting Standards Board (ASB) delivered a common sense approach with its proposal that share options should be measured at fair value at their vesting date, spread over the performance period and recorded in the profit and loss account. The message behind the ASB thesis has been that both companies and their stakeholders should appreciate that options are not a free lunch. They are a *claim on future profits* and, therefore,

- They should be valued at the point they become available to the employee, and
- They should be accrued over the period the services are provided.

The UK Accounting Standards Board initiative obliged companies to scale back profits to reflect the cost of options given to employees or used to pay for services such as consultancies, with their value computed by using the Black–Scholes formula.

Finally, the irony of lavish executive stock options is that they can turn to ashes. Starting with the 2000 burst of the stock market bubble a large number of options sank beneath the water. By mid-October 2000, as the market turned south in a big way, 52 CEOs at 200 of the better-known US companies were holding worthless stock options.

- When issued, these were worth billions of dollars
- But all that value was wiped out by the drop in their companies' stock prices.

One of the worst hit was C. Michael Amstrong, then chairman and CEO of AT&T, who saw the value of his $26 million in stock options vanish with the 61% slide in the company's stock price. The fate of other self-rewarding CEOs was not much different. Some of the big beneficiaries could wait for better times, but others could not. As reported in the press – according to regulatory filings – Bernie Ebbers, then president and CEO of WorldCom, had to sell 3 million shares in his long-distance communications company to meet a margin call from his brokerage account, because the value of his stock had dropped so much.

- All of Ebbers' stock options granted in the past three years had become worthless by mid-October 2000.
- Then, mid-2002, came WorldCom's bankruptcy, and by 2005 Bernie Ebbers was in court on a long list of fraud counts.

The horde of CEOs who lost their options perks grew in the September/October 2000 timeframe. At the top of the list, right after Amstrong, were: Alan McCollough, of Circuit City, with $25 million; Lawrence Weibach, Unisys, $23 million; Daniel Carp, Eastman Kodak, $17 million; Leo Mullin, Delta Air Lines, $14 million; Donald Carty, AMR, $9.4 million; David Novak, Tricon, $6.6 million; David Whitwam, Whirlpool, $6.5 million; Steven Rogel, Weyerhaeuser, $5.8 million, and Charles Holliday Jr, DuPont, $2 million.

Nor was such a debacle limited to year 2000. Senior management and other employees at the world's largest investment banks 'lost' nearly $30 billion in the October 2001 to September 2002 timeframe, from the fall in value of equity they held in their companies. This figure is based on the fall in share price of 10 of the largest investment banks. However, given that share prices in 2001 were already far lower than at the end of the bull market in 2000, overall losses have been significantly higher.

One of the worst affected firms in the aforementioned timeframe has been the Crédit Suisse Group. It saw a 60% dive in the value of its shares, wiping $32.7 billion off the company's capitalization. Crédit Suisse employees owned about 5% of the firm, which makes it easy to calculate their losses. (However, as we saw at the beginning of this section, Crédit Suisse has since changed its accounting practices related to executive options.)

With a late 2002 share price below $20, about 92% of JP Morgan Chase's options were also below the water line. Analysts estimated that staff at JP Morgan Chase, including the chief executive, had lost nearly $4.25 billion on the value of the shares that they owned in their employer. At Goldman Sachs, bankers lost $5.44 billion. At the time, Goldman's staff owned more than 40% of the firm – by far the largest employee stake of any of the large investment banks.

According to certain estimates, staff at Citigroup have lost about $7.8 billion between them, but because the company employs so many people, their wallets are unlikely to have been as badly hit as bankers at JP Morgan Chase and Goldman Sachs. Another estimate has been that at Morgan Stanley and Merrill Lynch possible staff losses stood at $4 billion and $2.6 billion respectively, based on 15% ownership.[8] The story these numbers tell is that, apart from being a less-than-ethical practice, fat stock options are also a gamble. Options are derivative instruments anyway; and it is better to expense them at fair value.

Notes

1 Basel Committee, *Supervisory Guidance on the Use of the Fair Value Option by Banks Under IFRS*, BUS, Basel, July 2005.
2 *The Economist*, 15 June 2002.
3 *The Economist*, 21 May 2005.
4 D.N. Chorafas, *After Basel II: Assuring Compliance and Smoothing the Rough Edges*, Lafferty/VRL Publishing, London, 2005.
5 *Business Week*, 8 July 2002.
6 *The Economist*, 15 January 2005.
7 *The Economist*, 6 March 2004.
8 *Financial News*, 21–27 October, 2002.

Forward-Looking
Statements, Models,
Earnings, and Goodwill

1. Introduction

Forward-looking statements are forecasts focusing on the likely evolution of the company's business. As such, they contain no statistics but projections. Mainly they are projections relating to the implementation of strategic initiatives in a particular country or worldwide, the development of new products and services, or a contemplated expansion of operations.

- All of these factors relate to future business developments and economic performance.
- What they have in common is *business risk* as well as management risk, which is inseparable from projections being made.

With the exception of financial reporting on goodwill, forward-looking statements are not regulated. They only represent management's judgment and future expectations concerning the development of the company's operations in the market(s) in which it is active, as well as risks associated to the operations. Part of the risks are uncertainties and other factors that could cause actual results to differ materially from expectations. Such factors include, but are not limited to:

- General economic trends
- Changes in local and international markets
- Changes in currency exchanges rates and interest rates
- Competitive pressures and technological developments
- Changes in the financial position or creditworthiness of the firm's customers, obligors, and other counterparties
- Legislative and political developments including the impact of terrorist attacks
- The aftermath of management changes and of other key factors that could positively or adversely affect the entity's financial performance.

Even with these reservations, forward-looking statements have become fairly popular. Increasingly, in addition to historical information and statistics, Annual Reports by exchange-listed companies contain statements that reflect management's beliefs, objectives, and expectations. Among other things, these relate to:

- Revenue growth
- After-tax profit margin, and
- Return on stockholders' equity.

They also reflect on the company's ability to sustain and improve its competitive position, as well as management's intentions to be implemented in the year or years to come, including restructuring initiatives, cost control measures (usually expressed in downsized head counts), and other factors affecting the company's profitability.

For instance, important factors that may cause differences in terms of future expectations include, but are not limited to, the company's success in building a closer relationship with its clients; the effect of client procurement patterns on company revenues and earnings; changes in revenues and profit margins due to market fluctuations; volatility affecting the securities market and economy as a whole.

Other factors with an impact on performance are primarily internal. Examples are the company's inability to attract and retain key personnel; timing and impact of changes in the company's level of investments; changes aiming at technological leadership; computer system failures; security breaches, and so on.

Projected political, regulatory, and legal changes, too, can have a significant impact on the message conveyed by the forward-looking statement. This is the case of pending legislation, regulation, or changing industry practice which may favourably or adversely affect the company. Moreover, results of litigation may be onerous; and the effects of competitors' pricing and intensified industry competition may lead to lower profit margins than those experienced in the current year.

Like all forecasts (see section 2), forward-looking statements are not fail safe. While they represent the senior management's judgment and future expectations concerning the development of the company's business, a number of risks and uncertainties could cause unexpected developments and end with results that differ materially from projections. At the same time, however, they provide a warning about the likelihood of different events and their probable consequences.

2.   Forecasters and Forecasts

In the 17th century, physics entered into a new era thanks to the more extensive use of mathematics. In the second half of the 20th century, this has been repeated in finance thanks, to a substantial extent, to the contributions of rocket scientists and the skills they brought with them from aerospace engineering, nuclear engineering, and physics.[1] Historically, the use of mathematics in finance has been preceded by its use in economics, which started at the end of the 19th century. The work of Vilfredo Pareto in analysis and of Leon Walras in macro-economics are examples of the beginning of this trend.

Not everybody is convinced that mathematical analysis can make a real contribution to economics and finance, yet given the growing complexity of the financial business and mountains of assumed risk, this is the way to bet. As a participant at one of my London seminars remarked, 'The world is full of frustrated geniuses and misunderstood factors.' This is a valid opinion, particularly in connection to the unknowns characterizing risk factors. Discussions speculating on what would or might have happened in 'this' or in 'that' case, and models written to reflect on such hypotheses, are usually pretty meaningless unless their reason is to elaborate scenarios about:

- What *might* happen in the future under specific projected conditions, and
- How one can develop appropriate countermeasures to likely but not certain negative events.[2]

To get prepared for evolving economic and financial conditions, management needs forecasts. In fact, forecasting is the first of the six main functions of management, the others being: planning, organizing, staffing, directing, and controlling. Forward-looking statements, whose definition has been given in the Introduction, are essentially management forecasts made public.

The art of forecasting gained momentum in the post-World War II years, and by the end of the 20th century the practice of *professional forecasting* had been institutionalized. The February 2005 Monthly Bulletin by the European Central Bank (ECB) published the results of the 26th Survey of Professional Forecasters (SPF), conducted by the ECB in late January of that same year. The SPF gathers expectations for the whole of Euroland, particularly in connection to:

- Inflation,
- Economic activity, and
- Unemployment.

These projections are contributed by experts affiliated to financial or non-financial institutions based in the EU. Given the diversity of the panel of participants, the ECB warns that aggregate SPF results can reflect a relatively heterogeneous set of subjective views and assumptions. Still, these prognostications are valuable.

For instance, in terms of inflation expectations for 2005 and 2006, the ECB report states that compared with the previous survey, inflation expectations of 2005 were unchanged while those of 2006 were revised downwards by 0.1 percentage point. SPF panelists now expect Euroland's inflation to gradually decline over the two years ahead.

The European Central Bank's Monthly Report of February 2005 also points out that over the coming months a large majority of forecasters expect the lagged upward impact of recent oil price developments to be partly counteracted by a number of other factors, including:

- Moderate wage increases
- Continued strength of the euro, and
- Downward base effects from administered and food prices.

In their way, forward-looking statements by corporations resemble the economic forecasts of which we just saw an example. They are based on assumptions and tentative statements which may or may not materialize. Forecasts, however, should not be confused with *creative accounting*, which is a totally different ballgame (see Chapter 11).

Because prognostication is an art, a crucial question regarding its dependability is whether hypotheses made by expert forecasters have been right or wrong, and how much external events influence outcomes. For instance, in mid-May 2005:

- Italian workers went on strike asking for an 8% wage increase, at a time when Italy's GDP caved in
- Some food prices spiked upsetting earlier projections, and
- The dollar significantly strengthened against the euro with a negative effect on oil prices.

Forecasts are *always* subject to error, whose effects should be analysed. Indeed, ECB's Monthly Report of February 2005 presents a very interesting graphic, which can be seen in Figure 12.1. The theme is probability distribution of accumulated autonomous factor forecast errors. (This is connected to an autonomous factor forecast project for interest rates, and hence is different from the inflation forecast which has been the subject of the preceding paragraphs.)

Forecasts on future performance are *simulations*, and simulations are working analogies based on a number of assumptions that may not be capable of duplication in actual life (see section 6 on simulated performance of the housing market). Therefore, simulated results have inherent limitations of which the reader must be aware.

Unlike a real life performance record, like that of financial statements targeted by IFRS, simulated returns do not represent actual statistics. Since the events to which reference is made have not yet happened, the result may have over- or under-compensated for the impact of market factors such as:

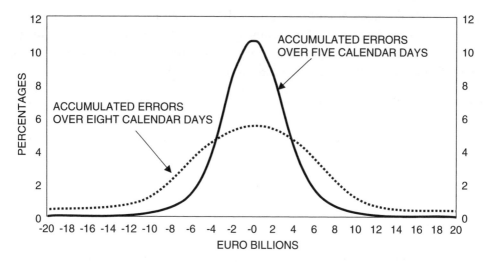

Figure 12.1   Probability distribution of accumulated autonomous factor forecast errors, based on daily data for the period 8 January to 8 December 2004 (*Source:* European Central Bank, Monthly Bulletin, February 2005, p. 69)

- Changes in volatility
- Liquidity constraints
- Extreme market events, and other reasons.

Some simulations may also have a built-in bias because they have been designed with the goal to prove some point. This is, in fact, the only case when a forward-looking statement might border on creative accounting, albeit at prognostication level.

With the aforementioned exception, forward-looking statements should be welcome, provided their reader understands their inherent limitations. These are often expressed in their wording, through references such as management 'expects', 'anticipates', 'targets', 'goals', 'projects', 'plans', 'believes', 'seeks', 'estimates'. Variations of such words, and similar more elaborate expressions, are intended to identify the risk involved in the contents of a forward-looking statement. Its reader should always keep in mind that:

- Forward-looking pronouncements are not guarantees of future performance, and
- The uncertainties and assumptions which they contain are difficult to verify in advance.

Not only actual outcomes and results may differ materially from what is forecast, but also because forward-looking statements are not regulated, senior management does not have any obligation to update publicly – whether as a result of new information, changes in assumptions, or otherwise.

The reader should notice that, in the general case, the risks, uncertainties, and assumptions involved in a prognostication include: tougher competition by other companies including new entrants; rapid technological developments and changes and the firm's ability to continue to introduce new products and services; and the likelihood that some of the current products will no longer be cost-effective.

Other worries are credit concerns regarding customers for which the company provided financing; continuing customer demand for the company's products and services; reliance on resellers and distributors; timely implementation of restructuring programmes and financial plans, as well as the firm's:

- Ability to recruit and retain talent, and
- Ability to control costs and expenses.

Behind other differences between forecasts and real life may lie governmental and regulatory changes, volatility in local and global securities markets, swings in currency exchange rates and interest rates, competitive pressures, and technological disasters. All of these, and other major factors, can adversely affect projected business and financial performance and, in consequence, earnings figures.

3. Forward-looking statements require lots of experimentation

Forecasts can be qualitative, quantitative, or both. Those that are qualitative are based on expert opinion, as the ECB example in section 2 documented. Quite often qualitative estimates are economic, but they may also involve product development timetables, estimates on market demand, and sales projections. On the other hand, forecasts might be based on quantitative models, benefiting from experimentation to substantiate expert opinion.

As advice based on long years of experience, simulation results should not be taken at face value. Several caveats should be borne in mind, such as the aforementioned possible existence of nonlinearities and asymmetries, and the fact that models do not include all variables that impact on real life output (see the case study on models for fair value estimates of real estate in section 7). Hence, as a matter of policy, quantitative approaches:

- Should always be subject to thorough testing, and
- They must be enriched and substantiated through qualitative approaches (more on this later).

Quantitative analysis has been promoted by advanced modelling procedures developed by mathematicians, physicists, engineers, and economists. It has also significantly benefited from cheaper and cheaper computing power which made it cost-effective to generate complex simulations, serving the main object of computing which is:

- Foresight
- Insight
- Analysis, and
- Design.

This is much more important than the automation of numerical calculations. The basic reasons for experimentation are better understanding of the problem; analysis of alternatives in terms of risk, cost, and reward; as well as a more objective and better documented basis for decisions.

Forward-looking statements benefit from what has been outlined in the preceding paragraphs, because through experimentation management can provide faster response to developing situations. It also acquires the ability to test novel methods or solutions. Both qualitative and quantitative approaches should be used for experimentation reasons. In financial analytics:

- Qualitative results are largely based on fundamental research
- While technical analysis and charting is, to a large extent, quantitative.[3]

In connection with forward-looking statements, a qualitative approach would typically look into the company's ability to successfully implement its new strategic direction, including alliances and other factors, such as the ability to focus on products and services which permit it to:

- Take advantage of the most desirable opportunities in the firm's industry, and
- Implement product rationalizations in a manner that does not disrupt the link to its customers.

Qualitative analysis may as well address governmental and public policy changes that may affect the level of new investments; changes in environmental regulations; protection and validity of patent and other intellectual property rights; as well as reliance on large customers and significant suppliers (section 6 presents a case study on assessing real estate prices in the housing market, which includes both qualitative and quantitative evaluation).

Serious undertaking of qualitative research should look at the longer term, which is always a challenge. Italy's Finsiel, the software company, provides an example on the aftermath of failing to do so. In the early to mid-1990s Finsiel:

- Had a billion dollar turnover, and
- Was one of Europe's biggest information technology services firms.

The company's problem has been that its business came almost entirely from lucrative technology contracts from Italy's public sector. Diversification was wanting, and likely future developments were not given due attention. Eventually, Finsiel's tight grip on the Italian public sector market was forced open by European Union directives on tendering.

In the mid-1990s, there has also been a negative fallout from *Tangentopoli*, the targeting of a myriad of scams by Italy's judiciary. Finsiel's power in the Italian software market waned, and the Rome-based firm went into decline all the way to becoming an acquisitions target. In March 2005, Finsiel found a new owner, Gruppo Cos, which specializes in call centres – a line of business basically different from Finsiel's historical strength.

On the border line between qualitative and quantitative research lie issues such as the company's credit rating; ability to provide customer financing when appropriate; continued availability of financing, expressed by financial resources in amounts and on terms required to support future business; compliance with covenants and restrictions of the firm's bank credit facilities; and outcome of pending and future litigation. All these issues impact upon the outcome projected by a forward-looking statement.

Within the perspective of qualitative evaluations mentioned in the preceding paragraphs, issues relating to the projected income statement are predominantly quantitative. Here, the first and foremost subject forecasters should keep in perspective is that in practically every company profit and loss is a nonlinear algorithm of risk factors, because:

- It is the result of all changes in fair value of positions, and
- A reflection of business risks assumed by the firm in the course of its operations.

Moreover, the market values being used may themselves behave in nonlinear fashion – particularly in connection to the derivative financial products nearly every firm nowadays has in its portfolio. There is also the effect of neglected risk, market disruptions, imprecise risk metrics, and stress circumstances (see Chapter 16).

Another uncertainty entering into an earnings simulation is that of complex correlations across risk types. Whether in the manufacturing industry or (particularly so) in banking, correlations and weights are most often subjective, and imprecise. They are what some analysts call 'tricky things'. Yet, it is not really possible to simulate a business environment without them.

In spite of these limitations and uncertainties entering into the production of a forward-looking statement, senior management must come up with a fairly detailed analysis. A plan is shown in Box 12.1. Every chapter has its challenges which must be addressed, even if at the end management may only publicly release some compound figures. In a growing number of cases, it is also becoming necessary to compute projected profit and loss, along the lines of a long supplementary list as shown in Box 12.2.

Box 12.1 Main chapters of a profit and loss statement

Operating income
Interest income
Interest expense
Net interest income
Credit loss expense/recovery
Net interest income after credit loss expense/recovery
Net fee and commission income
Net trading income
Other income
Total operating income

Operating expenses
Personnel expenses
General and administrative expenses
Depreciation of property and equipment
Amortization of other tangible assets

(Continued)

Box 12.1 (Continued)

Writedown of goodwill, if impaired
Total operating expenses

Operating profit before tax and minority interests
Tax expense

Net profit before minority interests
Minority interests

Net profit
Basic earnings per share
Diluted earnings per share

Box 12.2 Supplementary list with off-balance sheet and other items

- Litigation
- Fair value of financial instruments (required by IAS 39)
- Financial instruments risk position
  - Interest rate risk
  - Credit risk
  - Currency risk
  - Liquidity risk
- Pledged assets
- Contingent liabilities
- Operating lease commitments
- Retirement benefit plans and other employee benefits
- Equity participation plans
- Additional disclosures required under US GAAP and SEC rules (for a non-US company listed in the US)

---

4. Measuring earnings: uncertainty and bias of current metrics

The objective of this section is to bring to the reader's attention the difference that prevails between reliable and unreliable financial statements in connection to earnings. Typically the former are following rules established, or at least approved, by supervisory and regulatory authorities of the Group of Ten (G-10) countries. US GAAP and IFRS are examples.

The not-so-reliable statements are mostly ad hoc inventions of different firms, which might have fitted better into Chapter 10, which addressed creative accounting and other practices designed to misinform investors. On the other hand, it is always a good policy to present the reader with a contrast between what constitutes:

- Dependable financial reporting, and
- Partly or fully unreliable statements of operations which are essentially traps.

Starting with the fundamentals, the more classical way to measure a company's performance over the year is *net income*. Also known as *reported earnings*, or the *bottom line*, this is highly regulated by means of officially set accounting principles. In the United States net income is the number the Securities & Exchange Commission accepts in its filings.

An alternative measurement, the *operating earnings*, is an adjustment of net income that excludes certain costs deemed to be unrelated to ongoing business. Operating income, however, can be misleading both because of these exclusions and for the reason that, to the untrained eye, it looks very much like a GAAP figure: the *operating income* stands for revenue, minus the costs of doing business.

Nearly synonymous to operating earnings is another metric: *core earnings*. Neither of the two is calculated according to rules established by the Financial Accounting Standards Board (FASB). Therefore, when they find their way into forward-looking statements, they bring to them an aura of creative accounting along the lines discussed in Chapter 10. Investors beware:

- Operating earnings and core earnings are more or less defined by the company reporting them.
- As such, they can include or exclude anything the management of that company wishes.

The net result is that they cannot serve for a serious analysis, let alone prediction of financial health. Even more liberal in interpretation is another reporting scheme, to which reference has been made in Chapter 10: *EBITDA* (earnings before interest, taxes, depreciation, and amortization). It does not really mean much, yet it is widely used. EBITDA can reach a level of absurdity by leaving out of the equation all costs. Why only ITDA and not ITDAML, where M stands for all material costs and L for all labour costs.

Like proforma, EBITDA practices were originally developed and used by industry sectors that carried high debt loads, and wanted to hide them – like cable TV (CATV). The easy solution has been to simply leave them. When the stock market curiously accepted this, other industry sectors found it a convenient means for financial misinformation. EBITDA is a curious financial reporting 'standard':

- Unacceptable to the regulators
- But acceptable to some investors who risk their money with unreliable metrics.

Notice that over the years other industry sectors developed their own form of earnings statements which suited better their reporting needs. An example is the real estate investment trusts (REIT), a pioneer of engineered earnings with its *funds from operations* (FFO) reporting. FFOs, however, seem to have backfired and by now some REITs have begun to revert to plain US GAAP earnings reports.

Sometimes with nonregulatory financial reporting even the form of presentation may give rise to uncertainty regarding the meaning of contents. An example is the *earnings press release*. This consists of an earnings number flashed in the headline, which may or may not be calculated according to rules: Press releases are by no means financial statements reviewed by regulators. They are mainly for public relations reasons:

- Aimed to catch investors who don't do their homework, and
- They usually employ pro forma numbers which, as we have already seen, are unreliable.

In contrast to what has been outlined in the preceding paragraphs, *the statement of operations* focuses on regulatory reporting of net income, and it is audited by certified public accountants (CPAs). Hence, barring Andersen-type risk, it is reliable. Another piece of financial reporting is *the statement of cash flows*, to be found in quarterly reports filed with SEC:

- It provides a good measure of a company's financial health, and
- It is much less vulnerable to massaging than press releases, proformas, FFOs, and EBITDAs.

Of course, the master piece of reliable financial statement is the *balance sheet* (see Chapter 13), when prepared according to IFRS, US GAAP, or other official standards which respect their readers. The balance sheet highlights an entity's assets and liabilities and its cash in hand, and it can be accompanied by footnotes.

I always read the footnotes of companies in which I invest (or plan to do so), but consider them to be a questionable practice. Sometimes they address huge items which turn the balance sheet on its head; as, for instance, derivatives risk. And most often they are skipped by investors because:

- They are cumbersome, and
- In many cases the message they convey is unclear.

Yet, footnotes have their fans, including regulators and standards setters (see Chapter 10). For instance, under US GAAP *Footnotes* can be found only in SEC filings, particularly in the annual report. Quite interesting also is the disclosure under *reversals*, because it indicates that:

- A company overestimated how much it would have to spend, and
- It is crediting that excess back into its earnings, sometimes also restructuring its reserves (more on this later).

In this and similar cases, not only have the earnings figures been manipulated in such a way as to become unrecognizable, by leaving out whole chapters of items such as costs, but also costs still being included are subject to massaging. A case in point is *special charges*. This is a general term for anything a company wants to highlight as 'unusual' – therefore, something to be supposedly excluded from future earnings projections.

As we will see in section 5, an overused term is *goodwill*, written in the assets side of the balance sheet; and with it, *goodwill impairment*. Goodwill is a way of writing down the premium a company paid over the fair market value of the net tangible assets it acquired. As such, it has been regulated in different ways by different accounting standards, in different jurisdictions. For its part,

- Goodwill impairment has a very liberal definition, and
- This is often used to downsize the exorbitant price paid for acquisitions.

The *alter ego* of goodwill impairment is *asset impairment*. It stands for charges taken to bring goods a company paid a high price for down to their current market value. In terms of financial reporting, asset impairment should have been a much more dependable figure than goodwill impairment, but it is not necessarily so. Several companies that bought Internet and other stocks during the late 1990s at highly inflated prices are taking these charges on venture-capital funds.

Another of the major cost articles confronting a going concern is *reserves for restructuring*. It stands for an accrued expense to cover future costs of closing down an operating division or plant – also for downsizing the personnel. These are usually projected costs (of forward statement type) and do not necessarily represent current cash outlays. The trick is that:

- Restructuring reserves are often overstated, and
- When this happens, they become a boost to earnings in following years because they are reversed.

Finally, still another key component of the top list of reported costs is *write-downs*. It stands for lowering the value of an asset, like a plant or equity investment. Write-downs are usually seen as bookkeeping exercises that take care of a real cost incurred long ago, that now proves to be unwise. Frequently, behind a write-down is money spent unwisely. But they may also represent reductions because of banking or some other fees.

It does not take a genius to realize that analysts and investors are at a loss because of the *earnings chaos* which results from the disturbing trend among companies of calculating according to their own idiosyncratic ways. What is surprising is an increasing willingness among financial analysts and investors to accept nonstandard computations in financial reports, trusting them as representative of an entity's real earnings and true balance sheet values – altogether forgetting about the myths behind some of the figures.

5. The Regulation of Goodwill and Goodwill Impairment

Section 4 defined the accounting charge of *goodwill* as the excess of purchase price over fair value of identifiable net assets acquired in business combinations accounted for as purchases. Goodwill, however, also includes other items such as: brand name(s), patents, some sorts of managerial or professional expertise – and a big ego.

The definition of goodwill and its proper handling in accounting terms has long been a nonregulated entry in the company's books, which therefore was widely abused. But things have changed both in Europe, with IFRS, and in the United States. Compliant handling of goodwill came first in America, and for this reason the present section addresses this, original change.

In June 2001, the Financial Accounting Standards Board (FASB) issued Statement of Financial Accounting Standards No. 141 (SFAS 141), *Business Combinations*, and SFAS 142, *Goodwill and Other Intangible Assets.* The latter requires business combinations initiated after 30 June 2001 to be recorded using the purchase method of accounting. It also specifies the types of acquired intangible assets that must be recognized and reported separately from goodwill. With SFAS 142:

- Goodwill and certain intangibles are no longer amortized
- Instead they are tested for impairment at least annually, and this is reflected in the firm's financial statement.

Following the SFAS 142 implementation, starting with fiscal years that began after 15 December 2001, lots of companies experienced their largest write-offs ever. Some entities capitalized on the fact that SFAS 142 permitted them to write off as much goodwill as they wanted in fiscal year 2002 – which after that they had to categorize as goodwill – and account for it at least every year. Said the senior executive of one company participating in research: 'We regularly review assets that are not carried at fair value for possible impairment indications. If impairment indicators are identified we make an assessment about whether the carrying value of such assets remains fully recoverable.'

Here is an example of how Microsoft commented in its 2003 Annual Report, in connection to its compliance to SFAS 142: 'SFAS 142, "Goodwill and Other Intangible Assets"', requires that goodwill be tested for impairment at the reporting unit level (operating segment or one level below an operating segment) on an annual basis (1 July for Microsoft) and between annual tests in certain circumstances. Application of the goodwill impairment test requires:

- Judgment, including the identification of reporting units, assigning assets and liabilities to reporting units.
- Assessing goodwill to reporting units, and
- Determining the fair value of each reporting unit.

'Significant judgments required to estimate the fair value of reporting units induce estimating future cash flows, determining appropriate discount rates and other assumptions. Changes in these estimates and assumptions could materially affect the determination of fair value and/or goodwill impairment for each reporting unit.'

As the opening paragraphs of this section brought to the reader's attention, goodwill had been a well-known huge loophole in financial reporting practices. Only after Enron filed for Chapter 11 in December 2001 did money managers start to scrutinize the companies' books as never before, dumping stocks when they suspected even a hint of bad accounting or abuse. Also because of Enron's bankruptcy, market regulators took a closer look at corporate accounting and goodwill handling practices.

For their part, following FASB's new reporting standard, many companies felt that taking big write-offs during a recession would keep them from taking smaller ones later on. (That could have distracted shareholders, as the economy revived.) Therefore, many American companies intentionally depressed their results in 2002 which, among other things, could allow them to inflate financial results in 2003 on a year-on-year basis.

JSD Uniphase was the first to take a huge write-off of over $50 billion in late July 2001, the largest ever in US corporate history. Other companies were not too far behind. AOL Time Warner had $126.9 billion in goodwill as of 30 September 2001 and analysts expected it to take up to 50% that amount in write-off in 2002. Richard Parsons, the company's then new chief executive officer, suggested his firm wanted to keep its accounting for assets in line with what investors think those assets are worth.

Also, as of September 2001, Viacom had $71.3 billion of goodwill, a huge sum approaching its market value of $78.3 billion. Qwest Communications International had done even better than that. Its $30.8 billion goodwill was swamping its $23.5 billion market value.

AT&T, too, took a large write-off for goodwill, and other companies are expected to do so. Among other entities loaded with goodwill were Verizon, to the tune of $44.1 billion; WorldCom, at $40.6 billion; and Philip Morris at $33.1 billion. Notice that the biggest goodwill addicts were found among technology, media, and telecoms (TMT).

When making an assessment of goodwill impairment, well-managed entities compare carrying value to market value. As an alternative, some companies employ the *value in use*, by discounting expected future net cash flows generated by brand names and other goodwill assets to present value. Determination of the value in use requires management to make assumptions and employ estimates which have to be:

- Reasonable, and
- Supportable in the existing market environment.

If the fair value, or value in use, of a reporting unit exceeds its carrying amount, goodwill of the reporting unit is considered not impaired, but it is impaired in the opposite case. Hence, it becomes necessary to measure the amount of impairment loss, comparing implied fair value of the reporting unit's goodwill with the carrying amount of that goodwill.

For instance, a cable franchise intangible can be determined as the difference between fair value of the cable business and fair value of the cable businesses' tangible and intangible assets. The value of use of a cable business can be determined using various valuation techniques including discounted cash flow, analyst estimates, and comparable market analyses.

Intangible and other long-lived assets must also be reviewed for impairment whenever events such as product discontinuance, product dispositions, plant closures, or other changes in circumstances indicate that the carrying amount may not be recoverable. In reviewing for impairment, management must compare the carrying value of such assets to the estimated undiscounted future cash flows, expected from the:

- Use of the assets, and
- Their eventual disposition.

When the estimated undiscounted future cash flows are less than their carrying amount, an impairment loss must be recognized equal to the difference between the assets' fair value and their carrying value. Some companies record adverse changes in their planned business operations affecting a reporting business unit, or a significant portion of it, as well as other unforeseen developments as an impairment of their recorded goodwill.

In conclusion, prior to SFAS 142 and IFRS, because goodwill and certain other intangible assets were having, at least theoretically, indefinite lives, they were amortized on a straight-line basis over the periods the firm benefited from them. What has changed with SFAS 142 is that goodwill must now be tested for impairment on an annual basis or between annual tests if:

- An event occurs, or
- Circumstances change that would reduce its fair value below its carrying amount.

6. Assessing real estate prices in the housing market: a case study

The two greater challenges with forward-looking statements are guesstimating earnings and valuing assets. On this second issue, the real estate market provides an example. The two most popular approaches with house price valuations are:

- Asset pricing, and
- Structural economic model.

Asset pricing capitalizes on analogical reasoning, that is on the similitude assumed to exist between an equity investment and a house investment (see section 3). This hypothesis about an existing analogy is based on the fact that whether one buys a house or an equity, he or she receives cash flows, respectively:

- Rental, or
- Dividend payment.

As the 20-year trend curves (1984–2004) in the values characterizing UK real estate and equities markets shown in Figure 12.2 document, there is some historical basis for such hypothesis. With the exception of the 1995 to 2000 equities bubble, equity prices and house prices tend to move in unison – with the latter trailing the former.

In the opinion of many financial analysts, the price of a house should not be too different from its discounted cash flow, plus a factor accounting for appreciation or depreciation of the asset's value. These variables are reflected in the following models

$$\frac{P}{R} = \frac{(1+R_g \pm \Delta V)}{(F+H-R_g)} \tag{12.1}$$

where:

P = price of the house
R = discounted cash flow from rent
R_g = growth rate of rent(s)
ΔV = change in value of the house
F = risk-free rate of interest
H = the house's risk premium

Equation (12.1) is the modified version of an algorithm by the European Central Bank (ECB). In ECB's opinion, favourable financing conditions and expected

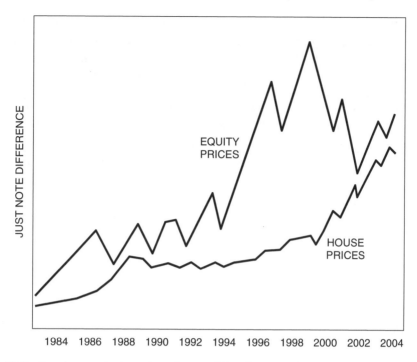

Figure 12.2   Trend curves in the values characterizing the UK real estate and equities markets

capital gains in the 2004–5 timeframe seem to have supported strong demand for housing. On the other hand, the rapid pace of increase seen in some countries since the mid 1990s – particularly Ireland, France, and Spain – calls for close monitoring, given the potential implications for these economies and the region as a whole.[4]

One of the key reasons why central banks are interested in housing prices is that developments in residential property prices are an important factor in the assessment of underlying monetary policy decisions aimed at maintaining price stability over the medium term:

- Changes in residential property prices may affect households' consumption behaviour
- Wealth effects are sensitive to paper profits from residential investments.

Moreover, the housing market has a two-way relationship with credit developments: it indirectly affects inflation through an increase in rents, and an avalanche in foreclosures severely tests the financial fabric. One of the nightmares of the

Great Depression of 1929–33 was Sheriff's sales and home foreclosures. While governments talk up the merits of an *ownership society*, and brag that the number of new homeowners is the highest in history, this nightmare might return with a vengeance.

For instance, on 30 May 2005, the *Washington Post* wrote that there are fears of 'Depression-era' numbers of foreclosures in Pennsylvania. A report by the Pennsylvania Banking Department, released in March of that same year, pointed to such fears. This has been a study prompted by the concern that Pennsylvania was ninth among states in the number of foreclosures in 2003, and fourth in the category of subprime loans. The latter are the high-interest, high-risk loans addressed to lower-income borrowers with no good credit standing.

Therefore, given the polyvalence of objectives to be met by marking to model housing prices, prior to discussing how the variables entering into the construct can be estimated, it is important to notice an important limitation of the asset pricing method. Note that this limitation also prevails in many other cases of thinking by analogy.

While both the equity market, as a proxy of asset prices, and the housing market have historical boom–bust cycles, these are not necessarily an image of one another. A recent IMF survey analysed periods of bust in housing and equity markets, reaching the following conclusions:[5]

- Housing price busts appear less frequently than equity price busts. (This can easily be seen in Figure 12.2).

Housing price peak to trough periods last, on average, longer than equity price busts: 4 years *vs* 2½ years, respectively. Price declines during housing price busts are in the order of around 30% *vs* 45% for equities. Both statistics are positive for housing. The negative is that, again on average, some 40% of housing price booms are followed by busts; for equities this stands at 25%.

- During housing price busts, bank-based financial systems incur larger losses than market-based financial systems; the opposite is true for equity price busts.

During the post-World War II period, nearly all major banking crises in industrial countries coincided with housing price busts. Moreover, output losses associated with asset price busts have been substantial. The loss incurred during a typical housing price bust is near to 8% of GDP. The loss associated to equity price busts is roughly 4% of GDP.

Financial analysts are aware of this broader impact and its likely aftermath on the economy. Therefore, they take a close look when confronted with house pricing booms, and bubbles likely to lead to subsequent busts. Spikes and/or a steady upward trend in house prices prompt them to look into just where the froth and the risks in the housing market are located.

For instance, a mid-2005 study by Merrill Lynch found that more than half of the top 50 US cities are showing signs of overheating, with housing prices far outstripping personal income gains. At the top of the list were Miami, New York, Los Angeles, and Denver. Furthermore, as this study indicated:

- The overheated local markets represent such a big slice of economic activity that the growth of the US economy, as a whole, could suffer if the housing market were to falter, and
- It was estimated that GDP growth would be trimmed by one-half of a percentage point in 2005, and more than a full percentage point in 2006, if house prices were to simply level off.[6]

The analysts concerns were well-grounded because both in the United States and in the UK increases in real estate wealth have been an important driver of economic growth in recent years. In America, average house prices have soared by more than 40% since the Fed started cutting interest rates in early 2001; and mid-2004 to mid-2005 home prices have been looking even frothier as yearly growth has accelerated in pace.

- Rising real-estate net worth accounted for 70% of the rise in overall household wealth in the past five years, and
- An increase of 1 dollar in housing wealth boosts consumer spending by 6 cents, an impressive 6% increase.

The Merrill Lynch study concluded that housing wealth has accounted for about $50 billion a year in US consumer spending over five years, adding about one-half of a percentage point to real GDP each year, on average, since 2000. The brokerage firm has developed a housing model using the house price index (HPI), real mortgage rates, real disposable income, and a proxy for the housing stock. The model shows that, by a wide margin, interest rates are the key factor driving house prices and they have six times more influence on home prices than does income growth.

7. Models for fair value estimates of real estate

Let us now look into challenges and opportunities associated with estimating the variables in equation (12.1) above, as well as ways and means for improving upon this algorithm. A good proxy for risk-free rate of interest, F, is a long-term bond by the US, UK, or other Western European government. More difficult is to evaluate in advance the house's risk premium, because it depends on:

- Technical factors, like steady maintenance, and
- The public's propensity to buy *new* houses, a trend evident in the United States
- A possible deterioration in the appeal of the neighbourhood, and similar variables.

By contrast, it is not difficult to have a fairly good estimate on ΔV, based on macro-economics (more on this later) as well as the house's location and its appeal to future home owners for primary residence or as a second house. Notice, however, that estimates of ΔV include uncertainties due to social factors and government policies. Also, most evidently, interest rate and taxation.

Moreover, in its present form equation (12.1) by no means covers all important factors affecting house prices. It can be made more sophisticated by including into it:

- Transaction costs associated to real estate (as distinct from taxation)
- Liquidity affecting the market at large, and the housing sector, in particular
- Borrowing criteria and facilities available for mortgage lending
- Changes in land prices which have an evident effect on the price of houses
- Changes in construction costs, and[7]
- The population's propensity to change houses every X years, X being a one-digit or low two-digit number.

All of these factors help to explain either lasting differences or spikes between house prices and rents. For instance, the French socialist government's implementation of the 35 hour week increased construction costs by 20% in the year it became effective. In terms of rotation in ownership, on the French Riviera, British and American owners tend to change their secondary residence every 5 or 6 years, while Greeks and Russians keep their real estate out of the market for 20 or 30 years.

Moreover, as it now stands, equation (12.1) presupposes that homeowners can quickly change rents to accommodate an increase in house prices. Generally speaking, this is not a valid hypothesis because national regulations existing in some jurisdictions prevent them from doing so.

Neither is it possible to exclude a priori that there is, or will be, a misalignment in house prices. When such a misalignment exists, this is often due to the fact that one or more of the hypotheses entering into equation (12.1) does not hold when tested in the market. Or, alternatively, conditions have changed and one or more of these hypotheses is no longer valid.

In spite of these shortcomings, the factors entering in equation (12.1), and even better an improved version of it incorporating the foregoing references to other variables affecting the P/R ratio, could serve as a predictor. It is appropriate to notice that, so to speak, the accuracy of a model is elastic. As an example, factors other than government regulations to be taken into account, in the relation between house prices and rentals, are:

- Household disposable income, and
- Equity market bulls or bears (see also the discussion in section 6).

To substantiate this statement, Figure 12.3 and Figure 12.4 provide statistics from Japan. The pattern in Figure 12.3 presents the ratio of house prices to rents. That in Figure 12.4 maps the ratio of house prices to household disposable income. Both of them convey a significant message:

- The more a model reflects what is happening in real life
- The more complex and less controllable this artifact becomes.

So much for the *asset pricing* approach. For its part, the *structural economic model* for house price valuation can be seen both as a self-standing simulator and as a worthwhile complement to the asset pricing model (which, in my judgment, is the better alternative).

Basically, the structural model involves estimation of supply and demand for the housing market, as well as certain empirical factors. Take the French commercial real estate market as an example. Among professionals, the value of commercial real estate, particularly in an area for shops and retail outlets, is generally computed in either of two ways:

- Economic performance measured in revenue and profits
- Established evaluation tariffs, if any, and their variables.

In the case of economic performance, the investor searches for accounting elements and statistics that allow him or her to form an opinion about the real

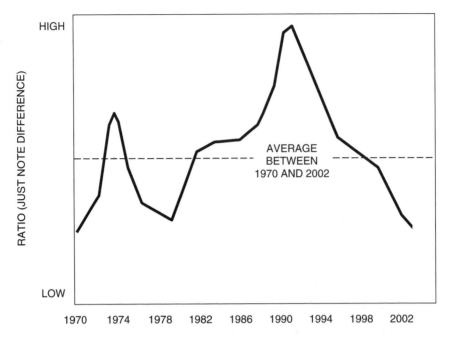

Figure 12.3 Ratio of house prices to rents in Japan (*Source:* European Central Bank, based on its own statistics and statistics by Japan Real Estate Economic Research Institute)

estate's likely value, subject to certain ranges. For instance, a restaurant is generally sold at a price between 50 and 200% of its annual turnover; while a marketing outlet for foodstuff masters a much lower ratio – between 10 and 25% of annual turnover.

The downside of this approach is that tariffs permitting a more accurate evaluation are not always available. Their development requires a diagnostic study which considers location – as well as commercial activities taking place at that location – plus a number of technical, financial and juridical elements associated to the commercial real estate and its use.

The alternative to these practical inputs, when they are not available, is a theoretical evaluation. A hypothesis underpinning the structural economic model is that supply of housing is usually determined by the profitability of housing construction. In a free economy, this is a reasonable assumption. The downside is that supply is relatively inert in the short term, quite often leaving demand as the main force driving house prices at a one year, or so, time horizon. Furthermore, housing supply might be relatively slow to adjust to demand, even in the longer term.

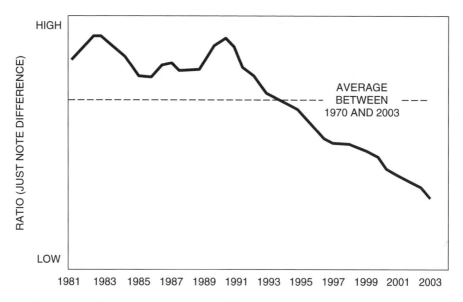

Figure 12.4 Ratio of house prices to household disposable income in Japan (*Source:* European Central Bank, based on its own statistics and statistics by Japan Real Estate Economic Research Institute and national accounts)

As far as the demand side of the equation is concerned, as we have seen in Figure 12.4, a key factor is household disposable income. Prevailing mortgage interest rates also have a major impact on growing or dampening demand (see section 6). Housing demand is also influenced by demographic trends.

Some experts suggest that a measure of *affordability* should also be used, beyond the ratio of house prices to household disposable income. Affordability is a fairly complex factor taking into account: disposable income, interest rates, future prospects of employment, and some social variables. When interest-adjusted affordability declines, this might indicate a change in house price dynamics.

As the last few paragraphs have shown, a structural economic model is not simpler than that of asset pricing, and it also involves more tentative statements than asset pricing. The downside of using only a structural model lies in the fact that available explanatory variables are often limited, and they might not take all relevant information into account. Also, as with all econometric approaches, this one:

- Is based on average behaviour, and
- Averages are typically misleading in the presence of structural changes in the demand or supply of housing.

Precisely because housing values are affected by a plurality of factors, house prices should be assessed by different approaches; cross-checking information obtained from various models, such as asset-based and structural; looking for discrepancies between the two; then targeting improved versions whose results may converge.

Convergence might be obtained by homogenizing common factors, such as borrowing costs and increased or decreased fragility of borrowers – as a function of changes in interest rates, employment, and other variables. A good example is what was observed in the early 1990s during the Swedish banking crisis.

The Swedish case is particularly relevant in connection to the commercial real estate market. Though commercial real estate and private housing are often seen as two different markets, a British research finding by a major British bank suggests that the two correlate up to 88%. This correlation is most significant to the structural economic model. The Swedish real estate crisis has affected the banks' expected cash flows from borrowers through:

- A deterioration of their intrinsic repayment capacity, and
- Lower values of real estate collateral, in case the debtors defaulted.

Therefore, in equation (12.1), the evolution of expected future cash flows should also reflect *credit risk* since it leads to lower asset values. This is another example of improvement which may help to provide greater accuracy to be obtained from a given model.

Finally, the prevailing accounting standards for financial reporting should also be taken into consideration. The combined effect of value changes would need to be fully reflected in financial statements under fair value accounting (FVA). By contrast, under historical cost, if specific provisioning behaviour of the bank is disregarded, credit quality deterioration would have no impact until impairment – a fact that can mislead investors in their asset allocation decisions.

Notes

1 D.N. Chorafas, *Statistical Processes and Reliability Engineering*, D. Van Nostrand Co., Princeton, NJ, 1960.
2 D.N. Chorafas, *Modelling the Survival of Financial and Industrial Enterprises: Advantages, Challenges, and Problems with the Internal Rating-Based (IRB) Method*, Palgrave/Macmillan, London, 2002.
3 D.N. Chorafas, *The Management of Equity Investments*, Butterworth-Heinemann, London, 2005.

4   ECB, Financial Stability Review, June 2005.

5   T. Helbling and M. Terrones, 'When Bubbles Burst', *World Economic Outlook,* IMF, April 2003, Chapter II. Busts are defined as bottom quartile peak to trough real price decreases. The authors base their results on a sample of 14 countries (for housing prices) or 19 countries (for equity prices), between 1959 and 2002.

6   Merrill Lynch, *Global Research Highlights,* 17 June 2005.

7   For instance, the implementation of the 35 hour week by the socialist government in France, in the early years of the 21st century, increased construction costs by 20% in one year.

Part 4

Corporate Governance and the Balance Sheet

13

Balance Sheets and Income Statements as Management Tools

1. Introduction

A *balance sheet* (B/S) is a written representation of *assets* and *liabilities* of an individual, a partnership, a quoted company, or other entity, such as a city. The term B/S is not crisp, its best definition being expressed as a list of balances in assets, liabilities, or net worth accounts. Notice that this definition, by the American Institute of Certified Public Accountants (AICPA), is accurate, but it is not so meaningful in management terms.

A more meaningful statement about the balance sheet is that it shows sources from which funds, presently used to operate the entity, have been obtained; for instance, owner(s) equity and other liabilities. It is also meaningful to state that the B/S documents the types of property, and property rights, on which funds are currently used. These are the assets (see section 2).

Just as important is to bring into perspective that a balance sheet may be made in an honest manner, or be subject to creative accounting by 'cooking the books' (see Chapter 11). When it is honestly made, and the representation of its details is correct, the balance sheet portrays the financial condition of the entity to which it belongs.

- The assets and liabilities in a balance sheet, and profit and loss (P&L) *income statement* show, at year's end, the results of the exercise.
- By contrast, as Chapter 9 explained, the *budget* is a financial plan, which must be carefully established *a priori*, documented, and approved to become effective.

The yearly closing of the balance sheet, for financial reporting reasons, is based on accounting conventions – like those advanced by IFRS (see Part One) or US GAAP. This is a different way of saying that accounting and reporting through financial statements is, to a substantial extent, regulated by standards setters and supervised by government authorities.

Well-managed companies are driven by a strong focus on their balance sheet and P&L; also on the B/S of other companies in which they may be investing or to which they extend a line of credit. As an investment advisor pointed out in a recent discussion, 'We never invest our client's money in leveraged companies. We look for strong, free cash flow, low relative debt to asset ratios, high tangible book value, and solid sales growth, among other metrics.'

Top tier companies appreciate that the balance sheet can become a great management tool. Quite often, however, financial information tends to be misrepresented or misinterpreted, for a variety of reasons. The most frequent is that management is dishonest, and what is shown in the B/S and P&L has little to do with the facts. Enron, Global Crossing, WorldCom, Adelphia Communications, Parmalat and many other firms are testimony to this.

The profit and loss statement, too, is an important tool of management. The problem is that quite often definitions are blurred, either in textbooks or in the mind of managers. Many entrepreneurs can never grasp the difference between *sales* and *profits*; when they say *revenue* they mean either one, says Peter Drucker.[1]

Another reason for misinterpretation of financial information is the limited imagination of analysts. It is almost second nature that when we see a new phenomenon we try to fit it into the framework we already have. This might have been acceptable at the beginning of the Industrial Revolution, but today, it is an aberration. Until we have made enough tests and experiments, we don't know whether there is really a difference between 'this' and 'that' figure.

Still another reason for misinterpretation is that while background and foreground business factors have changed, the B/S may show the same figures over and over again. Sometimes both companies and markets have more than one way of doing things, but:

- They repeat their story over time, and
- The accounting system fails to capture the ongoing change, or does so with considerable latency.

The opposite also may be true. Data reported in financial statements may look different, while it describes aspects of the same thing. There is a larger picture underneath, from which things can be broken into parts, but these parts don't differ more than the fingers of the same hand.

These are good enough reasons to make one most careful when reading balance sheets. Expert investment advisors suggest that there are other important facets of the research process beyond analysing numbers. To get insight, equity analysts talk to the management of companies they study, and also participate in conference calls.[2]

- Moreover, they make extensive use of macro information, and
- Examine industry background, trends and prospects.

This qualitative approach to analysis diminishes in noting the importance of having available reliable B/S and P&L. Focusing not on one year but on 10 and 20 years of balance sheet reporting allows identification of the upside and downside of the company's prospects. On the other hand, a factual and documented process of prognostication, or detection of events as they develop, requires qualitative input.

2. Assets defined

The assets of a small enterprise, like the corner drugstore, might consist of only a limited number of items which are rather easy to classify. By contrast, the assets of a large corporation might consist of millions of items. It is in the classification of the various items in assets that the judgment and experience of an analyst first comes into play.

The proper classification and identification of assets and liabilities is a prerequisite to their proper valuation (more on this later). Figure 13.1 shows a parallel classification and identification system I developed with the management of Osram, the international lamp company, to lead to better management accounting, sales forecasting, production planning, and inventory control.[3] Similar principles apply to the classification of balance sheet items.

Classification of assets and liabilities into the B/S is based, to a significant extent, upon conventions that find their origin in the seminal work by Luca Paciolo in 1494. Though, over more than five centuries, Paciolo's approach has considerably evolved, some of the original conventions remain, like the requirements that assets and liabilities balance out. (These days they rarely do. We saw why in Chapter 2.)

Assets are typically divided into current, medium- and longer-term. (Some companies only make two divisions: current assets, and the others.) Adam Smith, the economist and philosopher of capitalism, is credited for having best defined *current assets* (CA). In his *Wealth of Nations*, published in 1776, he explained, 'The goods of the merchant yield him no revenue of profit till he sells them for money, and the money yields him as little, till it is again exchanged for goods. His capital is continuously going from him in one shape, and returning to him in another, and it is only by means of such circulation, or successive exchanges, that it can yield him any profit. Such capital, therefore, may very properly be called circulating capital.'[4]

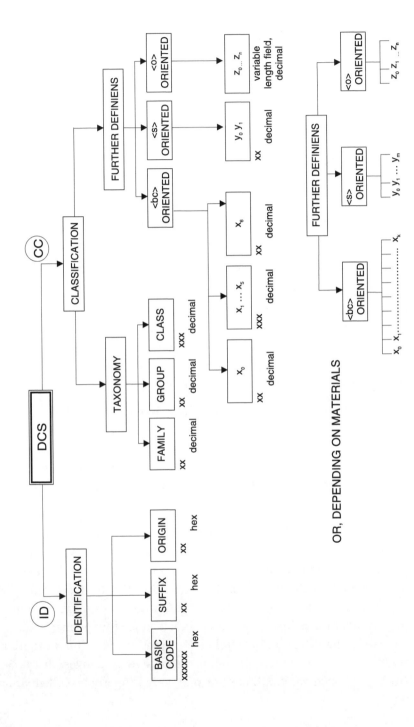

Figure 13.1   A bird's eye view of the parallel code system, including taxonomy, further definiens, and identification used in the case study

What Adam Smith called *circulating capital* is essentially what is today termed *current assets*, with the added notion that the current assets timeframe is less than one year. A characteristic of current assets is that they are circulating through the business rather rapidly, reflecting the recurring circular flow:

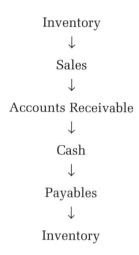

Inventory

↓

Sales

↓

Accounts Receivable

↓

Cash

↓

Payables

↓

Inventory

Another essential characteristic that distinguishes current assets from other balance sheet items is their flexibility. Management has more frequent opportunities to make decisions on the recommitment of funds labelled as current assets than with medium- or longer-term assets. However, a crucial question with current assets is how they are measured. This happens in two different ways:

- Cash, temporary investments held *in lieu* of cash, and accounts receivable, are measured essentially at market value.

The reader should however notice that for receivables this implies that the company can make a reasonable estimate of its bad debt losses, and other factors impacting their fair value.

- Classically, inventories and prepaid assets have been measured at cost. This is the accruals method, changed into fair value with IFRS.

The rationale behind accruals has been that items in this group are held for the benefit of operations in future periods. By consequence, their value to the business is that their existence reduces the necessity for making outlays for similar goods and services in the future. Except for differences in terms of life cycles, items in this group have been essentially taken as similar to fixed assets.

Fixed assets in the balance sheet are *longer-term assets*, such as machinery and buildings. With accruals these have classically been subject to a statement of unexpired costs, which means costs that have not yet been charged against operations. (More on this when discussing intangibles.)

Notice that fixed, longer-term assets are commitments that weigh heavily on the income statement. A factory running at only 70% of capacity has to be depreciated *as if* it has been working at 100%, while the money it earns through production are at a much lower level. Assets carry with them responsibilities; they are not just 'rights'.

While financial analysts look at both current assets and longer-term assets, it is the former that interest them the most. According to many economists the proper classification of current assets is the most important in a balance sheet, as current assets (CA) largely determine the going solvency of a business concern. Precisely for this reason, the ratio of current assets over current liabilities (CL, see section 3)

$$\frac{CA}{CL} \qquad (13.1)$$

is known as the *acid test*. The problem with this ratio is that what comes into it is not quite standardized. A more extended definition of current assets incorporates all assets moving, in the orderly and natural course of business, onward through production, distribution, and payment of goods, until they become cash or its equivalent. As we will see later on, current assets are:

- Cash available for current operations
- Temporary investments readily convertible into cash
- Receivables created by the sale of goods and services
- Inventory of merchandise
- Advances on merchandise
- Marketable securities, and so on.

By contrast, medium-term assets are those maturing within more than one but less than three years, or five years depending on jurisdiction and company policy. Long-term assets are maturing beyond that. Laws and rules governing depreciation of equipment, factories and other assets provide a good basis for this distinction.

An interesting class which cuts across the aforementioned categories are *intangible assets*. (Goodwill is part of them, see Chapter 12.) Their particularity is that they are not available for the payment of debts of a going business, and they often weigh most significantly in case of liquidation. Fixed assets (of which we spoke in the preceding paragraphs) are not part of intangibles, but share with them the longer-term perspective.

Intangible assets are rarely found in balance sheets of small firms, but big companies may have plenty of them. In alphabetical order they include: bond or debenture discount, brands, catalogues, contracts, copyrights, designs and drawings, development items, formulas, franchises, goodwill, leaseholds, licences, mailing lists, patents, processes, subscription lists, trademarks and treasury stock when carried as an asset.

According to option theory, by buying or holding the equity of a company investors are essentially purchasing an option on its assets. For this reason when it comes to mark to market the assets of an enterprise quoted on the stock exchange, a proxy to their fair value is its *capitalization* (number of issued stock multipliers by their market price). This lies behind the second crucial ratio:

$$\frac{A}{L} = \frac{Capitalization}{Liabilities\ at\ book\ value} \tag{13.2}$$

where A stands for assets, capitalization is the proxy of the market value of company assets, L stands for liabilities, and these are counted at book value. When this ratio is below 1, the company is insolvent. The market votes for it with its dollars, pounds, euro, or whatever is the local currency, to express its feelings about the entity's assets.

3. Liabilities defined

The definition and interpretation of *liabilities* involves a subtle point. The items included on the right side of the balance sheet are indeed claims against the entity's assets, but they are only those claims which are recorded with an offsetting debit to an asset or another equity account. What is important to appreciate in this connection is that these are *not* necessarily all obligations which the company knows it must pay.[5]

The *liabilities* of a small firm, for instance a newsstand, might consist of only two items: accounts payable for merchandise, and net worth. Big companies, by contrast, have a long list of accounts payable, as well as bank loans, provisions for taxes, due to officers and directors, accruals, debt instruments payable over the years, and various classes of outstanding equity. As with assets, liabilities, too, need to be classified, though this job is simpler. All items on the liability side of the balance sheet can be grouped into three broad classes:

- Current liabilities
- Deferred liabilities, which may be divided into medium-term and longer-term, and,
- Equity, or net worth.

Current liabilities (CL) are those whose settlement is due within a year, or shorter time period such as 3 or 6 months. (The definition of short term is depending on jurisdiction.) Equity is an example of long-term liabilities, but there may be others, like 10-year bonds issued by the entity for longer-term financing, or medium-term 3–5-year loans taken from banks.

All sorts of short-term obligations are usually incurred in the normal course of business, and they must be paid on fairly definite dates. Too much short-term financing is a negative, both because of the stress it puts on the treasury and because it indicates the firm cannot get longer-term financing. Indeed, the term *current liabilities* basically designates obligations whose liquidation is expected to require:

- Use of existing resources classified as current assets, or
- Creation of other current liabilities and associated obligations.

Most current liabilities are contracted for items that have entered into the operating cycle, such as payables incurred in the acquisition of supplies to be used in production of goods, or in providing services for sale. Examples of current liabilities are notes payable to banks, trade acceptance for merchandise, other accounts payable, loans payable, accruals, deposits, reserves for taxes, reserves for contingencies, dividends declared but not paid, and more.

Whether it is shorter- or longer-term, in the general case debt means leveraging, and this is an item which should attract considerable attention in every analysis. Management must be prudent with short-term debt, such as loans taken for payroll purposes, purchase of merchandise, premium of an insurance policy, rent, utility bills, and so on. On the other hand, whether debt is short-term or long-term, the liability is definite and:

- While values on the asset side shrink
- Obligations never shrink; rather, they accumulate.

Hence, it is not unusual for the liability side to increase when debts are discovered which apparently were casually overlooked. In the study of individual items that make up current assets, it is easy to see that each of these items is inflated purposely or by oversight. In the study of current liabilities, the problem is just the opposite. Whoever prepares the balance sheet occasionally omits from current liabilities items that the analyst must find out and include – or, overstates them. This can happen:

- Because of oversight, or
- As a policy to cook the books, condoned by senior management.

Whatever the reason may be, it is fraud. It is also counterproductive because it shows a company in financial difficulty which wants to show the market that it is profitable and growing. Eventually the fraud is unmasked and the bubble bursts, but not before investors lose money.

A similar statement about financial difficulties can be made when a company pledges assets to banks or other creditors for short-term credit. Entities that are in healthy financial condition have no reason to do so. Hence, whenever certain assets are pledged, that very fact is an indication that some creditor, who has presumably made a more or less intimate study of the financial condition of the firm, is dissatisfied and has insisted upon the pledge of some type of security to protect their claim.

All told, the study of liabilities is more revealing about a company's financial staying power than the study of its assets. This is one reason why market *capitalization* can serve as proxy of the value of assets, but liabilities must be studied in detail. The pattern of how liabilities have been created, and how they are served, provides significant insight on the quality of a company's management.

Analysts who care about their work and their findings must look for smoke on the right side of the B/S. *If* there is smoke *then* there may be fire, and therefore it is not unlikely the company will face a blaze in its accounts in the near future. Some 80% of the answer to a query 'How healthy is the company's balance sheet?' can be found through careful examination of its liabilities.

4. Modelling the balance sheet

The term *comparative balance sheet analysis* stands for the study of the trend of the same items, or computed ratios, in two or more balance sheets of the same business enterprise on different dates. It is also the study of the trend of proportions extracted from B/S figures, as of the different dates, and used to create a pattern of the entity's financial behaviour.

Comparative balance sheet analysis is most comprehensive when based on a balance sheet model that remains invariable between time periods, thus making comparisons possible. Also, it is most desirable that successive yearly balance sheets represent the financial condition of an enterprise at the same point in the natural business year cycle. To be successful in a comparative B/S study, the analyst must realize that:

- Financial figures must be strictly comparable, and
- He or she should always find out why they are not comparable, if it so happens.

This calls for appropriate modelling of assets and liabilities, starting with their classification in the manner discussed in section 2, keeping that classification steady. It also requires a balance sheet model which more or less remains invariant. Box 13.1 presents as an example the different chapters of a consolidated B/S. The theme of Box 13.2 is critical balance sheet ratios to be targeted in an analysis.

The strategic aspect of A&L modelling is a direct after-effect of the fact that a company's balance sheet represents its financial state, complemented by its profit and loss calculations (see section 5). Both are important to all of its stakeholders: the shareholders, bondholders, management, employees, regulators, and investors. Tactical aspects, on the other hand, are mainly concerned with the:

- Mechanics of modelling
- Use of the construct for predictive or evaluative purposes
- Risks with incorrect entries to the B/S, whether because of error or fraud, and
- Risks taken with models because of their imperfect fit with real-life performance.

Good news first. As we have already seen in Part 3, models written for analysis and simulation have the major advantage of making mental processes explicit. They help to expose inconsistencies in these mental processes, and make possible rethinking of variables and patterns. They also contribute to determining future implications ahead of time.

Box 13.1   A consolidated balance sheet.

ASSETS

- **Current assets**
  Cash and cash equivalents
  Short-term investments
  Accounts receivable
  Other receivables
  Prepaid expenses and other current assets

- **Longer-term assets**
  Property and equipment at cost, net
  Investments including available-for-sale securities
  Goodwill and other intangible assets, net
  Other assets

LIABILITIES

- **Current liabilities**
  Accounts payable
  Accrued expenses and other liabilities
  Accrued personnel costs
  Deferred income taxes

- **Longer-term liabilities**
  Bond issues
  Longer-term loans
  Irreversible commitments

- **Stockholders' equity**
  Preferred stock
  Paid-in capital
  Unrealized gains on available-for-sales securities
  Cash flow hedges, net
  Retained earnings

Box 13.2   Critical balance sheet ratios

- Annualized Revenues per Employee
- Working capital
- Acid test (current ratio), CA/CL
- Book value per share
- Assets/liabilities test (A/L), with proxy capitalization
- Cash per share
- Days of inventory
- Debt to capitalization
- Earnings per share
- Inventory turns
- Quick ratio
- Sales to total assets
- Return on sales
- Return on equity
- Working capital

In this sense, models developed for balance sheet presentation and those written for analysis can provide a rich source of information on financials, including latent problems. The risk involved derives from simplification, which comes with abstraction. Seen independently from one another, each of the financial ratios shown in Box 13.2 is too weak in terms of provided information for decision purposes. But these ratios can present a more complex pattern when taken in unison, provided that:

- Their meaning is clear
- Their computation is fairly standardized, and
- We are confident in the way they have been recorded or estimated; in short, in their accuracy.

Let's take a closer look into a ratio providing investor information which falls at the P&L side. Earnings per share (EPS) is one of the time-honoured criteria, and quite often analysts look at the price of a stock as 10, 20, 30 times or more earnings per share. Both the Financial Accounting Standards Board (FASB) and the International Accounting Standards Board (IASC) issued new standards for computing EPS, which primarily deal with the denominator used in its calculation, since always on the numerator is net income (see section 5 on the difficulty of estimating it properly).

Earnings per share has been classically employed as a metric for stock valuation. More recently, however, two value-added metrics were introduced: *EPS Change* (year-to-year) and *Consensus EPS*. Earnings per share and its add-ons are calculated not only on an annual basis but also quarterly, based on the company's financial reporting, or at shorter intervals as information becomes available.

This may help provide better focus; on the other hand, add-ons make the computation more complex. Under Financial Accounting Standards 128 (FAS 128), the computation becomes simpler, but at the same time FAS 128 requires two EPS statistics, and the spread between the two figures can be wide:

- FAS 128 substitutes basic earnings per share (BEPS) for primary earnings per share (PEPS).

BEPS is net income available to common shareholders divided by the weighted average number of common shares outstanding. The other figure is fully diluted earnings per share (FDEPS) which, generally, will be the same or higher than the previously calculated figure referred to as diluted earnings per share (DEPS). Inversely:

- DEPS will be higher than FDEPS when stock prices rise at the end of the period.

DEPS continues being calculated using the *if converted* method for convertible securities, and treasury stock method for options and warrants. But between FASB and IASB the specifics of this calculation diverge, and moreover the impact varies by company.

An added complexity is provided by the proliferation of metrics due to the policy entities follow in retained earnings. Growth companies typically pay no dividends, therefore two further metrics, *dividend rate* and *dividend yield*, are not important to them, but they are used with companies paying dividends, a growing breed. Just as important are cash flow measurements. Two metrics applicable in this connection are:

- Cash flow/share
- Price/cash flow.

Strictly speaking, these are not balance sheet items, but they are critical issues to analysts and investors, and the place to find information about them is the balance sheet and income statement. This brings back into perspective the question of which values are written in the B/S and P&L. Or, more precisely, how these have been computed. The principle is that what matters is *fair value* which, as we have already seen, is market value established by a willing buyer and willing seller under other than fire sale conditions.

5. The profit and loss statement

As every manager and every accountant should know, the first step in counting profit and loss is to clarify the meaning of *net income*, which is the basic item on any income statement. Generally speaking, net income is taken as equal to the difference between *revenue* and *expense*. The problem is that there exists no general agreement on the method of measuring each of them. This leaves room for considerable differences of opinion about the:

- Real meaning of net income, and
- The dependability of the estimate of net income, for an accounting period.

Expert accountants say that dependability of net income estimates depends primarily on four factors: the length of accounting period; the extent to which events relating to the current period are separated from events affecting prior or future accounting periods; the amount of longer-term assets owned by the company; and, most evidently, stability of prices.

The fourth of these factors is squarely addressed by IFRS, through the fair value option. The other three largely depend on the jurisdiction – the laws, regulations, and supervisors' opinions prevailing in the country in which a company reports profit and loss. As far as both financial reporting and management accounting are concerned:

- Estimates of net income for a day, week or month are likely to be much less reliable than estimates for a year, and
- Estimates for a year are less reliable than estimates covering a longer period, such as the medium term.

Both bullets should be interpreted on an 'other things being equal' basis. Moreover, no matter what the first bullet states, it becomes increasingly important (and popular) to compute intraday P&L for management accounting reasons, albeit admitting the possibility of a 3–4% error. (See Chapter 15 on the virtual balance sheet.)

To appreciate the importance of the accounting period, the reader should recall that while the expenses assigned to a period are supposed to relate to revenues realized in that period, more frequently than not it is not practicable to attempt such matching. For example, it is usually difficult to estimate the portion of the cost of a long-lived asset applicable to a given accounting period. For these reasons:

- The net income reported on the income statement is unlikely to correspond exactly to the true increase in the owners' equity during an accounting period, and
- In fact, the true *monetary* income of an entity can be known only after this entity has been completely terminated, its assets disposed of and its liabilities paid.

Notice, however, that there is also *non-monetary* income, such as personal satisfaction service rendered to society, but this is not part of regulatory financial reporting requirements. On the other hand, certain of the individual items on a P&L statement may be quite reliable. The sales revenue figures are usually a close approximation to actual sales revenue.

For instance, amounts for many expense items, such as wages, suppliers, and utilities, are close approximations to actual expenses. To the contrary, depreciation is most often only a rough approximation, while some special adjustments reported as non-operating expenses may be little more than guesswork.

Somebody, of course, must be responsible for facts and figures. With or without the Sarbanes–Oxley Act (see Chapter 11), from initial financial planning estimates to the master budget, balance sheet, and income (profit and loss) statement, the processes which come into play involve *managerial responsibility*.

- Personal accountability has to be engaged, from lower level to higher level management, and
- This is true not only at the vertex of the organization but at every level of the process of financial reporting.

Not only must the company's financial plans and reporting requirement adhere to proper accounting principles, they must also be characterized by *cost-effectiveness*. Attention should be paid to the fact that many costs tend to get out of control, as they accrue continuously and have to be settled by cash payments.

- It is a rare case where bureaucracy and its out-of-control expenditures are deliberately planned.

- Typically, bureaucratic costs grow up and, if they are not curtailed, they run out of control.

Including the reliability of figures and the issue of costs, the managerial responsibility involved in the preparation of profit and loss statements calls for a great amount of care and rigorous evaluation. The P&L at year end is a snapshot, whose contents accumulate day after day. Hence the need for a conceptual view of how to derive added value from the resources available to the firm.

These are the dynamics of the computation of income statements. Regarding the mechanics, there is no mystery as to how to prepare a profit and loss report. Keeping always in mind what has been said about caveats to net income, an easy way to compose the P&L statement is through a few simple equations:

$$\text{Gross margin} = \text{Net sales} - \text{Cost of goods sold} \qquad (13.3)$$

$$\text{Net result} = \text{Gross margin} - \text{Nonrecoverable expenses} \\ - \text{Administrative expenses} \qquad (13.4)$$

For a manufacturing company, *net sales* represents the revenue on sales. That is the gross sales amount minus all discounts and price reductions. *Cost of goods sold* is based on current costs of direct materials (DM), direct labour (DL), and overhead (including utilities, rental, depreciation, and so on) at factory level.

Notice that while the budget is the financial plan kept internal to the entity, the P&L statement is not only an instrument reporting to stakeholders, regulators and the public, but also an internal control device. For many leading-edge organizations, the procedure of tracking and testing P&L is critical to establishing and maintaining a system of internal controls, enriched with financial analyses which highlight *high performers* and *low performers* among the company's business units.

If the financial plans and the internal management accounting system have been established on sound principles, *then* P&L will provide a sound basis for evaluation of performance. From an internal control perspective, for each department, section, and project, there should be available:

- Projected budget figures
- Authorizations to spend money, and
- Actual results for the given period.

These three sets of figures can form the basis of comparative analysis in *performance reporting*, from cash estimates to expenses, all the way to Plan/Actual (see Chapter 9) and costs versus obtained result. In fact, using high technology, P&L evaluations can be made ad hoc, which is serving the purpose of being in charge of operations. Questions confronting company management are:

- How detailed should the monitoring be?
- How to judge whether subordinates are performing the delegated task in an effective manner?, and
- How to increase or decrease our frequency of monitoring, depending on quality and steadiness of results?

Senior management can answer these queries if it is capable of both *quantifying* and *qualifying* the tasks under its control. That is precisely the area where financial algorithms, heuristics and scenario writing come into the picture, as a way to clarify what enters into the different chapters, how these chapters relate among themselves, and the notions which exist behind their variation.

In conclusion, the mathematics of P&L statements are simple, but the data coming into them are not always reliable. Sometimes hypotheses being made have not been properly tested. Yet, their effect is to alter the P&L information elements, at times misinforming the reader. In other cases such elements are largely guesses.

6. B/S and P&L complement one another

In the background of what is stated in section 5, lies the fact that P&L statements are not more than the mathematical interpretation of policies, experience, knowledge, foresight, and aggressiveness of the management of an enterprise. They are also influenced by qualitative factors concerning issues which, superficially, look as if they are purely quantitative. Examples are:

- Income
- Expenses
- Gross margin
- Operating profit, and
- Net profit or loss.

Provided that it has been computed in a reliable and ethical way, the final net profit or loss is the ultimate measure of the skill of management. The time lways comes when an entity that is taking losses must lock its doors and disappear.

For all practical purposes, the income statement is of special importance not only to the firm's own management and (for quoted companies) to the authorities, but also to investors and financial analysts who are interested in obtaining a longer-range view of an enterprise. The reader should appreciate, however, that for investors and analysts, the P&L is really an *interim* report.

- Profits or losses are not necessarily the result of operations during any short period of time.
- They are a longer-term aftermath of a progress of decline, with part of the pattern based on assumptions as to future events.

This is one of the reasons why creative accounting intended to beef up the balance sheet and impact P&L, like deferred tax allowances (DTAs), is an aberration (see Chapter 2). One quarter's or one year's massaged assets and income figures is a scalar point in a financial situation made out of wishful thinking – and being totally undocumented.

Even a true P&L statement means nothing when examined on the basis of just one or two years. Only 10, even better 20, P&L years can give a pattern in which some degree of confidence could be placed. It is also important to notice that P&L and balance sheet should be examined in unison in order to discover what is the entity's financial staying power.

- Investors in the firm's debt instruments and preferred stock, as well as stockholders (common stock), are inclined to pay more attention to the income statement.
- By contrast, short-term creditors, such as suppliers of raw materials and merchandise, and credit institutions that extend 3–6 months' unsecured loans, generally pay more attention to the condition of the balance sheet.

The reader should moreover appreciate that the B/S and P&L don't necessarily move the same way. As the overview in the 75th Annual Report 2004/2005 of the Bank for International Settlements (BIS) stated, in the course of the two half-years:

- Its balance sheet grew significantly to stand at special drawing rights (SDR) of 180.5 billion, representing an increase of 7.5%.
- But the result of lower average interest rates depressed income from securities financed by the Bank's equity, and net profits declined by 25% compared with the previous financial year.

On the other hand, both balance sheets and P&L statements can be manipulated. In their excellent book *Security Analysis*, Graham and Dodd devote eight chapters to 'Analysis of the Income Account'. Their *analysis* is only nominally concerned with variations in the expense items and their relations to net sales. Basically, it is aimed at acquainting the reader with *artifacts* and *window dressing* designed to:

- Misrepresent earnings, and
- Conceal losses from the public eye.

As we have seen in a certain length in Chapter 11, creative accounting is the practice of mishandling the intricate problems involved in corporate accounting. 'There are unbounded opportunities for shrewd detective work, for critical comparisons, for discovering and pointing out a state of affairs quite different from that indicated', Graham and Dodd suggest.[6]

Because creative accounting is pervasive, every bondholder, stockholder, creditor, speculator, and analyst should realize that net profits have been and still are subject 'in extraordinary degree to arbitrary determination and manipulation', according to Graham and Dodd. The three devices most commonly used for reaching this unethical goal are:

- Making charges to the surplus (retained earnings) account, instead of to the income statement, or vice versa.
- Overstating or understating depreciation, depletion, amortization, and other reserve charges, and
- Different proforma pronouncements, including EBITDA, manipulated to suit the CEO's and directors purpose(s).[7]

Ethically managed companies appreciate that income should not be distorted, or artificially stabilized, by creating arbitrary reserves either by appropriating income or surplus or by overstating expenses in certain periods. Moreover, expenses or losses arising from contingencies thus anticipated should be reflected not as reductions of the reserve, but in the income statement of the period in which they are recognized.

Also, as we saw in Part 1, new accounting rules promoted by IFRS bring forward specific regulations on how to handle recognized but not realized P&L associated to derivatives. Growth statistics of on-balance sheet and off-balance sheet items document that this requirement by IFRS, as well as by US GAAP, not only makes sense but has also become a 'must'.

The rush towards 'more assets' and 'more liabilities' through derivatives started in the early 1990s. This rush has gained a great deal of momentum over the years, with many of the characteristics of a bubble. In research I carried out in the late 1990s, German commercial banks have given the following statistics on their business growth:

- On-balance sheet business increased by 1.7% per year.
- The now traditional currency and securities futures progressed by 4.9% per year.
- But the growth rate of other derivatives, essentially the more risky, stood at 12.5% per year.

What has happened thereafter in credit institutions' balance sheets? The answer is that they continued their leveraging in derivative financial instruments, widening the gap between the real and virtual economy. Their off-balance sheet growth at the time was 700% greater than the on-balance sheet. Today, it is a high multiple of that. When derivatives become the tool of mega-speculation, accounting standards setters and regulators are right to insist that fair value should gain the upper ground.

7. Financial planning, cash flow, and book value

In the post-World War II years the majority of big companies used to depend on a classical form of annual financial planning: projections targeting medium range 5-year plans, and a detailed yearly budget. In many large organizations, however, the 5-year plans were a 'me too' exercise. They would largely sit on a shelf and collect dust. Only short-term financial instruments got the limelight.

- The budget
- Balance sheet, and
- Income statement.

Since the mid-1980s, however, this has started to change, at least among well-managed firms whose senior management is now taking a look 10 years into the future. As longer-range plans are being elaborated, top executives and independent analysts in the industry get together to give the board their opinion on the future state of the industry sector the company is in. During these roundtable sessions, senior management mainly looks at four factors:

- Economic
- Social

- Technological, and
- Customer demand.

This emphasis is well chosen and it rests on the appreciation that each one of these factors can affect the company's strategy in a significant manner.

A case study helps in giving some muscle to what the previous paragraph stated. In 1985, a well-known copier company established the vision that, by 1995, the world would have gone digital and become networked. This prognostication, which proved to be accurate, enabled the entity to capitalize on new opportunities:

- Moving almost all of its R&D budget out of light lens and into digital, colour and networked products, and
- Ensuring that marketing, as well as all of its business units, were tasked with convincing customers to switch to digital machines.

The policy underlying this approach to an evangelical-type sales campaign was that the opinion of customers follows a longer-term trajectory; it does not change instantaneously. And a changing trend must be explained to customers ahead of time, in order for the company to be ahead of the curve. Moreover, the company has to refocus its activities and finance its changeover to the projected new line of technological evolution. This requires plenty of management guts, and also a great deal of financing. The faster the market and technology move, the greater become the financing needs. It is not surprising that, since the mid-1980s, a great deal of top management interest has concentrated on cash flows – almost on a par with the interest in profits. The term 'cash cow' has been coined to identify those product lines with good cash flow, which would provide the resources to finance other product lines

- With better 'future prospects', in the 10-year perspective
- But currently strained for liquid assets, both because *their* market is not yet zooming, and *their* R&D and marketing expenses are high.

As the balance sheet has a model, which we have seen in Box 13.1, well-managed companies develop and use a consolidated cash flow model. As Box 13.3 shows, this divides into five main chapters, summed up as an increase or decrease in cash and equivalent instruments.

There is evidence that cash flow estimates and realized profit figures tend to correlate. Theoretically, profits and cash flow are independent variables. Practically, as shown in Figure 13.2, behaviour of the cash flow variable has moved in tandem

---

Box 13.3   Consolidated statements of cash flows

- **Operations**
  Net income
  Cash provided by operations
  Adjustments for non-cash and non-operating items:
  - Non-cash restructuring charges
  - Loss on derivative instruments
  - Loss (gain) on sale of other investments
  - Depreciation and amortization
  - Charge for acquired research and development
  - Amortization of compensatory stock options
  - Equity in losses of investees

  Changes in operating assets and liabilities, net of acquisitions and dispositions:
  - Trade accounts receivable
  - Other receivables
  - Prepaid expenses and other current assets
  - Other assets
  - Investments including available-for-sale securities

  Accrued expenses and other current liabilities
  Deferred revenue and other liabilities

  (Continued)

---

with net profit. (The figure uses statistics from a major Swiss bank, from the early to mid-1990s.) This correlation does not necessarily hold true in connection to return on equity (ROE).

A basic reason why the tracking of cash flow by main source is so important is that money is needed to finance management's plans. *If* internal resources don't suffice, *then* the company has to take loans thereby leveraging itself – and there are limits beyond which leveraging becomes most unhealthy. (See also section 3.)[8]

Another fundamental reason for looking carefully into cash flow is that it constitutes the reference on which will be measured the *intrinsic* value of the company. (As we have seen in Part 1, the intrinsic value is one of the methods helping in calculating fair value.) Generally speaking, there exist three metrics that can give an idea of what a company is worth, each with its own opportunities and challenges.

Box 13.3 (Continued)

- **Investing activities**
  Cash used in investing activities
  Purchase of property and equipment
  Product development costs
  Proceeds from sale of investments
  Purchase of investments
  (Purchase of) proceeds from short-term investments, net
  Purchase of minority interest
  Net (payments) proceeds for acquisitions/dispositions
  Other investing activities

- **Financing activities**
  Cash provided by financing activities
  Proceeds from issuance of common stock, net
  Principal payments on debt
  Payment of deferred finance costs
  Proceeds from issuance of debt

- **Cash and equivalents at beginning of year**
  Cash received during the year
  Cash paid during the year

- **Cash and equivalents at end of year**

- **Increase (decrease) in cash and equivalents**

- *Market value*, measured through the proxy of capitalization for the whole firm – or directly observed market value by inventoried position or business unit.
- *Intrinsic value*, computed as the discounted value of cash that can be taken out of the firm during its remaining life.
- *Book value*, an approach based on the classical accruals method whose results nowadays are not really meaningful.

While alert investors appreciate that book value does not mean much, this is still used as indicator when the equity price lags behind. Take Deutsche Bank book

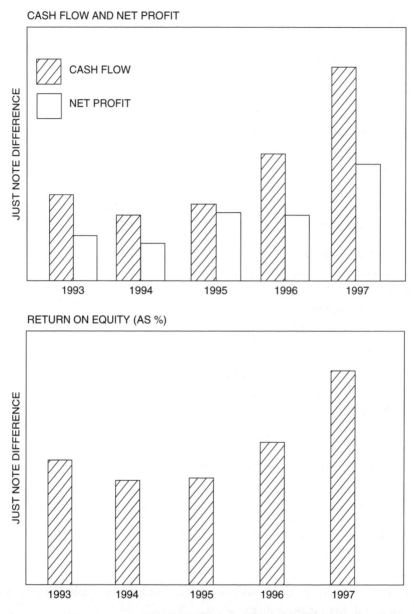

Figure 13.2   Cash flow, net profit and return on equity tend to correlate

value as an example. Mid-2004, as Deutsche's equity lost more than the stocks of its peers, analysts said the price-to-book multiple needed almost to double from its level of about 1 to 1.9 before large-scale deal-making would be feasible. (For starters, a price-to-book multiple below 1 means that the price of the company's common shares is less than its break-up value.)

In this same case, other analysts expressed the opinion that, in a way, the mark-down in the credit institution's share price was harsh. Josef Ackermann, Deutsche Bank's CEO, did a restructuring which helped the bank enjoy a 20% pre-tax return on equity in the first half of 2004, up from 15% a year earlier. And the investment arm of the bank was doing rather well – but markets are hard critics.

Because book value may be way off the mark of what it intends to represent, tycoons use it to turn things to their advantage. In the late 19th century the clash between Andrew Carnegie, the majority owner of Carnegie Steel, and Henry Clay Frick, the president of his companies and third major partner, was one of per-sonalities. Eventually Carnegie evoked a partners' agreement, known as the Iron Clad, to eject Frick and purchase his interest at book value.

- First, at a board meeting the move was seconded and approved.
- Then Carnegie strode into Frick's office and delivered the news, along with a settlement.

The news was that the board had voted to enact the Iron Clad, and the transfer of Frick's stock would be made at book value. The book value of Carnegie Steel was $25 million, giving Frick a mere $1.5 million for his 6% interest; whereas from Frick's viewpoint, the company's *real value* was at least $250 million, a selling price agreed a year earlier but never executed, which would make his interest worth $15 million in 1899 money. (Eventually Carnegie Steel was sold to Dr J.P. Morgan for $480 million – nearly double of what was offered by the failed takeover, and 20 times its book value.)

The problem often encountered with instrument-by-instrument market value is that quite often there is no direct observance of market value against which to mark portfolio positions. This has been explained in Part 1, and it is further doc-umented by 2005 Basel Committee research on 'reference market' for trading book positions. The research demonstrated that:

- Between 0.2% and 28% of total trading book positions have no reference market.
- But on net basis, this rises to between 80% and 85%.[9]

In the opinion of some of the experts, even what constitutes a 'reference market' is not well defined. Generally, it includes direct price comparison; comparison to market inputs, according to market convention; and comparison to observable inputs, involving a range of models. But there are also other definitions.

Where no active market exists, the practice is that of marking to model. Therefore, the Basel Committee examined the credit institutions' valuation method, price verification procedures, and evaluation of reserves. The regulators also looked into challenges faced by banks in valuing their positions, and in gaining experience from the implementation of a fair value policy.

8. Accuracy, transparency, and the market's perspective

Reliable financial reporting must be the rule, whether balance sheet and income statement are written for submission to regulatory authorities and exchanges, for compliance reasons; to inform the market at large; or only for the proprietors of a firm. The best disclosure rules are those characterized by:

- Significant accuracy, and
- Extraordinary transparency.

Both bullets are pillars of good governance. By increasing information about the risks being assumed by different entities, one also increases their incentives to act prudently and reduce the likelihood of failure. Critics say that the idea of exercising market discipline is theoretical, because extraordinary disclosure needs to be supported by measures to reduce the contagion effect. This is true, but it does not contradict the need for accuracy and transparency.

The goal of balance sheets and P&L statements, which reflect an entity's true financial situation, is not to mitigate the contagion effect but to reveal their financial staying power, cash flow, and profitability. Contagion, and therefore systemic risk, is the central banker's and regulator's problem. Its solution needs the backing of a lender of last resort, as well as deep market-oriented reforms which might make banks better able to cope with trouble. At the same time, accounting and regulatory rules which are:

- Rigorous, and
- Homogeneous

help in exercising damage control. Part 1 has explained how and why IFRS provides the rigorous rules which are necessary for reliable financial reporting and, by extension, for market discipline. From a regulatory viewpoint, market discipline is Pillar 3 of Basel II, the new capital adequacy framework by the Basel

Committee on Banking Supervision.[10] Pillar 3 rules require globally active banks to disclose a range of information about:

- The risks they take
- The way they assess these risks
- Their regulatory capital position, and
- Behavioural issues that reinforce regulatory supervision.

Cornerstone to all four bullet points is the fact that the new capital adequacy rules call for a significant amount of transparency in regard to the individual bank's level of risk, and the quality of internal risk management. From a system viewpoint, for a publicly listed financial institution, market discipline is a multiple feedback loop providing:

- Evidence of a company's practices and their results
- Information on ongoing changes in seeking to survive in a highly competitive environment, and
- Steps taken in response to market reaction to the disclosure.

Current reporting requirements at the New York Stock Exchange (NYSE) are a proxy of how the new disclosure standards for market discipline might work. A foreign company listed on NYSE must comply with disclosure requirements of the Securities and Exchange Commission (SEC) as well as the NYSE's own, including additional disclosure at half year to meet specific SEC or US GAAP requirements. However, though necessary, tougher disclosure requirements imposed by just one exchange are not enough to answer the worries of a globalized economy. Globalization has seen to it that the network is more important to it than an individual exchange on its own.

For this reason, at the Bank for International Settlements the Basel Committee now has a new peer, the *Markets Committee*, which groups senior officials from the G-10 central banks responsible for market operations. Its bimonthly meetings provide an opportunity for participants to exchange views on:

- Recent developments
- Structural changes in foreign exchange, and
- Events related to the different financial markets.

The Markets Committee also considers short-run implications of particular current events and their impact on the way markets are functioning. This includes a range of issues like: reasons for recent large movements in the major bilateral exchange rates; low level of both nominal yields and implied volatility exchange rates; similar considerations in major bond markets, as well as the aftermath of the search for yield on credit spreads.

The Markets Committee also examines the effect of the presence of hedge funds; the financial market impact of changes in pension fund regulations; influence on market functioning of the growth of electronic trading platforms; and financial market impact of accumulation in foreign exchange reserves by different countries. The key objective is information-sharing among central banks.[11]

What the preceding paragraphs outlined is that regulators now pay more attention than in the past in looking at things from the market's perspective. With this in mind, a different way of looking at Pillar 3 is as a set of rules that concentrate on the expansion of disclosure requirements by credit institutions for better regulation of the global financial system. In the longer term, this expansion is enabling the complementary use of market mechanisms for prudential supervision.

There are reasons to believe that in the supervisors' mind the central theme of Pillar 3 is that the markets should be able to sufficiently assess the risk profiles of all players – starting with credit institutions. Experts suggest that, precisely for that reason, the European Union will most likely give national supervisors the authority to require banks to:

- Disclose more frequently, and
- Use specific means of verification and examination.

At the same time, more emphasis is placed on an objective presentation of own funds, capital requirements for individual risk categories, and risk profile pursuant to Pillar 1 and Pillar 2 of Basel II. Part of the same drive for greater transparency at market level is to provide sufficient explanation for conspicuous changes in individual items. This can help in avoiding misinterpretations.

Those in favour say that over time Pillar 3 will prove to be a valuable contribution to improving communication between the banking industry and the financial market at large. Discipline will be enhanced through more frequent, detailed, and accurate disclosures, because lack of it gives rise to many rumours which are usually damaging to an equity's market standing.

In conclusion, the financial stability of a company hinges, to a large degree, on its level of indebtedness, cash flow, and profitability. To a significant extent, financial soundness is an enterprise-specific determinant of risk premium. As we have already seen, a company's financial staying power can be approximated through the ratio of assets over liabilities with:

- Assets taken at capitalization, and
- Liabilities assigned at book value.

Because the market is a tough critic, equity price movements tend to reflect this ratio. The probability of default owing to overindebtedness increases with the volatility of the firm's equity. These relationships are factored into an estimating algorithm by taking account of implied volatility of the share price, computed by using options.

My professors at UCLA taught their students that the most successful entrepreneurs don't just take risks; they also appreciate the need to control the exposure which they take. Xenophon (430–354 BC) once wrote 'Whoever wants to keep alive must aim at victory' – and in business victories can be won both by exploiting opportunities and by exercising timely damage control.

Notes

1 John J. Tarrant, *Drucker*, Warner Books, New York, 1976.
2 D.N. Chorafas, *The Management of Equity Investments*, Butterworth-Heinemann, London, 2005.
3 D.N. Chorafas, *Integrating ERP, CRM, Supply Chain Management and Smart Materials*, Auerbach, New York, 2001.
4 Adam Smith, *The Wealth of Nations*, Modern Library, New York, 1937.
5 Robert N. Anthony, *Management Accounting*, Irwin, Homewood, IL, 1956.
6 Benjamin Graham and David L. Dodd, *Security Analysis*, McGraw-Hill, New York, 1951.
7 D.N. Chorafas, *Management Risk. The Bottleneck Is at the Top of the Bottle*, Macmillan/Palgrave, London, 2004.
8 D.N. Chorafas, *Economic Capital Allocation with Basel II: Cost and Benefit Analysis*, Butterworth-Heinemann, London and Boston, 2004.
9 Basel Committee, *Trading Book Survey: A Summary of Responses*, BIS, Basel, April 2005.
10 D.N. Chorafas, *Economic Capital Allocation with Basel II: Cost and Benefit Analysis*, Butterworth-Heinemann, London and Boston, 2004.
11 BIS, 75th Annual Report.

14

Economic Capital Is on Both
Sides of the Balance Sheet

1. Introduction

One of the basic prerequisites of good corporate governance is the existence of reserves able to cover worst-case events with liquidity. The bank should hold such liquidity in order to enhance its financial staying power. This is the role economic capital, also known as respectability capital, must fulfil.

The nature of worst-case events changes over time. During the first three and a half decades of the post-World War II years, major risks commercial banks faced were associated to their role as financial intermediaries. In consequence, regulatory capital requirements were sized-up in a way that permitted them to confront losses from loans.

But by the early 1980s the type of risks had significantly changed because trading in derivatives grew fast, and along with it came a new, more pervasive type of exposure. In the 1980s and up to the mid-1990s, derivatives trades were written *off-balance sheet* (OBS) with the result that they were only lightly regulated. Moreover, by being written off-balance sheet they did not alter to any great degree the assets and liabilities side of the B/S discussed in Chapter 13. Then came two major changes:

- The 1996 Market Risk Amendment by the Basel Committee obliged banks to report to regulators their trading exposure through value at risk (VAR),[1] and
- Starting with the American, British, and Swiss regulators, supervisory authorities required that derivatives gains and losses are recognized in the balance sheet, even if they are not yet realized.

Both Basel II and IFRS have strengthened and formalized this requirement. This is a change which evidently has a major impact on the balance sheet. Moreover, Basel II redefined the need for capital by distinguishing between expected losses (EL) and unexpected losses (UL).[2] *Regulatory capital* is practically what is required for expected losses, while unexpected losses must be covered through liquidity provided by *economic capital.*

Economic capital is signalling to the market that the bank has endowed itself with enough resources to enhance its financial staying power. For every practical purpose, economic capital is *risk capital* which must be calculated for unexpected losses and extreme events. Briefly stated,

- *If* regulatory capital is the minimum amount necessary to have *a licence*
- Then, respectability capital is the minimum amount needed by a unit, and the bank as a whole, to be accepted as *business partner.*

The Basel Committee says that with the advanced internal ratings-based (A-IRB) approach to regulatory capital, banks will be also provisioning for unexpected losses. This, however, does not necessarily mean for extreme events – though some institutions may do so for respectability reasons.

Extreme events find themselves at the tail of the risk distribution – and can be statistically targeted in terms of likelihood of appearance. As Figure 14.1 shows, economic capital covering risks at the 99.97% level of confidence is key to obtaining an AA credit rating from the independent rating agencies. This 99.97% signals to the market that the bank is a creditworthy business partner.

From a qualitative point of view, capital is referred to as economic because it treats positions solely on an economic basis. This means in a way irrespective of differences in accounting issues, or of regulatory nature. Economic capital is risk capital because it is the amount of money needed to remain *solvent* under extreme:

- Market
- Business, and
- Operational conditions.

It is also the basis used to calculate the economic return on a given set of activities, on the basis of capital assessed for and allocated to them. The growing focus on economic capital has raised the crucial question as to which side of the balance sheet it comes from. Many bankers believe that economic capital originates on the 'assets' side alone. That's wrong.

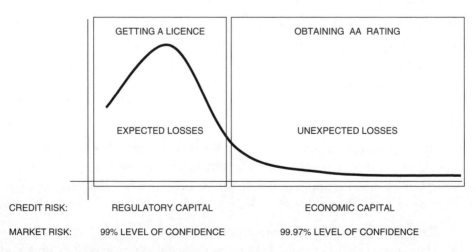

Figure 14.1   Getting a licence and obtaining AA rating are two different objectives

2.   Paciolo's Balance Sheet Needs Thorough Revisiting

Some years ago, when he was chief risk management officer of Barclays Bank, Alan Brown suggested that commitment to financial staying power assumes that the bank's management worries about exposure. Also, that the whole organization will be risk-prudent not just once in a while, but every day. Traders, investment specialists, loans officers, and other professionals cannot allow themselves 'to be a little cavalier at the end of the day'.

Neither is past experience sufficient in detecting new and rapidly changing types of risk. Even if managers and professionals are very prudent with the exposures they assume, the market may move against their best hypotheses, and this likelihood brings into the picture the duties of two people who will be required to find a solution, without any loss of time:

- The treasurer, who must make available required liquid assets, and
- The chief risk management officer who, with his people, must exercise damage control.

Neither of these executives can afford to take a fire brigade approach. Solutions must be experimented with, properly tested, and holistic. A few years ago, a study by the Bank for International Settlements (BIS) underlined that many firms are increasingly seeking to take a consolidated and enterprise-wide view of risk.[3] This, BIS says, is welcome but difficult because:

- The underlying time horizon associated with different risks is variable.

For instance, market risk must be measured daily, while credit risk is usually addressed yearly, and operational risk can be longer term.

- The correlation between different risk types may be very difficult to measure.

Yet, in spite of that, the credit institution must aggregate these separate metrics of risk into one comprehensive number, or a pattern, if the target is aggregate exposure and its control. And:

- There are inherent difficulties in developing precise estimates of benefits from diversification.

Precisely because of these difficulties, integrative solutions are still in their early stages. The reasons identified in these three bullet points require that the bank must have enough liquidity to face its developing exposure(s), with every type of risk taken into account.

Theoretically, this is doable, provided we test our hypotheses, control the models we are using, and are sure about the data we employ. Practically, the three issues just raised are *ifs*. The computation of economic capital has the characteristics of an art, rather than of a science.

This is precisely the reason why, in modern banking, we think and talk in terms of levels of confidence. Exposure estimates must be covered at a high level of confidence by appropriate liquidity in order to confront financial stress. The accounting system being used adds more than a grain of salt to the computation of cash equivalent resources, which needs to be done in order to assure the bank has respectability capital.

With IFRS, as with US GAAP, at origination and maturity of an instrument, fair value and book value have a comparable effect on the bank's financial statements, but for the period in between, fair value will result in more volatility. Is this good or is it bad? Those who say it is bad, don't realize that:

- While the accruals method provides less volatile numbers,
- This happens because risk is *uncoupled* from the real value of the instruments, which must be liquidated to provide liquidity.

This is precisely why the reaction of insurance companies to IFRS, which we studied in the case study in Chapter 2, is irrational. Failure to show embedded volatility in financial accounts is like lying to oneself, which should never be the case. Moreover, the volatility of the instruments in the bank's portfolio is not limited to their absolute value, but also includes *sign reversal*. Derivatives provide an example.

- When a contract is in the money, it is written in the assets side of the balance sheet.
- But when, after the market changes, it is out of the money, it moves to the liabilities side of the balance sheet.

As we have seen in Chapter 2, balance sheet accounting was developed by Luca Paciolo in 1494. But more than five centuries down the line, Paciolo's pace-setting concept does not hold as well as it used to. At the time of the great master, there were no complex and highly price-sensitive financial instruments of the type we have (in great abundance) today.

By all evidence, the first truly important issue to affect established balance sheet structures has been the fact that newer and newer derivative financial instruments do not fit so neatly in the assets or liabilities two-way classification because:

- They possess aspects of both, and
- Over time, as the market shifts, they change their position: from assets to liabilities and vice versa.

Even when they find themselves a pigeonhole, some entries may not be there for long, because they are volatile. While this becomes transparent by marking to market, what the reader should understand is that:

- A fact, and
- Reporting on that fact

are *not* the same thing. What IFRS does is the reporting part. The 'fact' is the derivatives positions deliberately taken by banks, insurance companies, and other entities. Fair value accounting can lead to additional volatility in the B/S and profit and loss statement, over the lifetime of these instruments, only because such instruments happen to be volatile.

This is easily illustrated by looking at the balance sheet of a bank in the case of an external interest rate shock. A very important paper has been published by the European Central Bank, with a couple of balance sheet assumptions such as (i) no hedging and (ii) a maximum maturity of instruments of ten years. In the absence of an observable or relevant market price, this article states, the fair value of bonds and loans can be approximated by calculating the net present value of their expected cash flows. Such calculation consists of:

- Discounting the cash flows of the particular instrument over the remaining lifetime
- Using a discount rate that reflects the risk-free rate, plus a risk premium.

The effect of an interest rate shock on the fair value of the instruments can, then, be simulated by changing the discount rate.[4] *If* they were priced correctly, at origination, the computed value of these instruments will normally be equal to their nominal value. However, as market conditions change, the computed value will also change. It will:

- Decrease if interest rates rise, and
- Increase if interest rates fall.

In either case it will no longer be equal to the nominal value. Under IFRS, a positive change will be recognized in the bank's income statement as a profit. Under the accruals accounting the portfolio would remain at its earlier book value equal to the nominal value. On the other hand, if this were a leveraged derivative instrument, its value could well become negative. In that case rather than being written on the assets side of the balance sheet, it would belong to the liabilities side – defying and reversing its earlier B/S classification.

3. Regulatory and Economic Capital Are Made Up of Both Assets and Liabilities

One of the most frequently discussed very positive effects of Basel II is that over time it will lead to a much bigger emphasis on *risk management*. The reason is that in order to face dynamic capital adequacy requirements, banks need to significantly upgrade risk sensitivity and risk control systems. At root, that is what the advanced internal ratings-based (A-IRB) method is all about.

Many bankers say, and they are right, that another fallout will be much greater attention paid to *risk-based pricing*. Some credit institutions even suggest, at least in private discussion, that they may exit product lines where the risk and return ratio is dubious or highly uncertain. According to expert opinion, Basel II:

- Will also have a significant effect on junk bonds and on distressed debt, and
- This might lead to the emergence of banks specializing in low credit quality counterparties.

Besides that, in all likelihood, the unloading of distressed debt, through massive securitization or direct sale, by credit institutions will hit hedge funds, which control about 70% of very low rated issues in the United States. If this happens, a secondary after-effect of Basel II will be some sort of realignment among financial institutions in terms of the product line each one of them targets.

Still other experts talk of a beginning of quantification of business risk and of reputational risk, including associated control measures. In their opinion, this is likely to follow the implementation of the new capital adequacy framework by the Basel Committee. The reader should notice that:

- All these opinions and hypotheses are reasonable and plausible.
- But they are not complete, in the sense that they are missing one of the vital ingredients of the ongoing change.

When the economic and financial history of this decade is written, much will be made of the fact that the original form of Luca Paciolo's balance sheet cannot accommodate *economic capital* on just one side, as happens with *core capital*, which is part of the bank's liabilities. The reason is very simple, and it lies in the fact that, as section 2 has stated, many new financial instruments don't quite fit into a prestructured pattern of A&L.

Before going further in this discussion it is appropriate to appreciate that the foregoing statement will eventually be true also for *regulatory capital*, as the latter admits Tier 3, which is capital for trading. But mainly the two-sided balance sheet approach concerns economic capital, given that its sources vary widely.

It needs no explaining that this would be *a different book* – one that borrows from both sides: A&L. What's more, in all likelihood legally valid solutions would vary by jurisdiction. For example, under German law economic capital includes:

From assets:
> + contingency reserves pursuant to section 240F of commercial code
> + unrealized reserves, maximum of 1.4% of weighted risk assets
> + reserves up to 45%, pursuant to German income tax act

From liabilities:
> + liabilities represented by participation rights
> + longer-term subordinated liabilities
> − market management positions in securitized own participation rights/longer-term subordinated liabilities

Other jurisdictions have different criteria in answering the query 'which side of the B/S?'. Under Japanese law a big chunk of regulatory capital comes from assets, as supervisors permit all banks to write in Tier 2 up to 45% of unrealized profits from securities. Even more ridiculous is the supervisors' permission to accounts for deferred tax assets (DTAs) as regulatory capital. That's simply monkey money.[5] In this sense, even the T-2 capital does not come from the same side of the balance sheet.

Some experts say these are rough edges which will be smoothed out over time. I personally think the opposite is true, as new financial instruments are developed every day and many of them do not fit the classical A&L classification. This sees to it that a pattern is developing akin to that in Table 14.1. Based on this pattern,

Table 14.1   On which side of the balance sheet does capital adequacy responsibility fall?

Capital	B/S
T-1	L*
Hybrid t-1	L, (A)
T-2	L, (A)
Hybrid t-2	A, (L)
T-3	A

L = Liabilities; A = Assets; L, (A) stands for primarily liabilities and secondarily assets; the opposite is true of A, (L).

it is better to look at regulatory capital and economic capital as providing a fourth dimension to accounting:

- General ledger
- Balance sheet
- Income statement
- Regulatory and economic capital.

The good news is that this fourth dimension is proactive. 'The difficulty for risk control in financial institutions,' said a senior management officer, 'is that this is a reactive job. Even if we see that an inordinate risk is taken, it is hard to prohibit certain trades.' This statement is true, but there are three forces which may change that landscape:

- The advanced internal ratings-based (A-IRB) method, which is obliging proactive examination of creditworthiness.
- The IFRS, and US GAAP, financial reporting requirement for marking to market, which uses market forces to expose assumed risk.
- Risk-based product pricing and economic capital allocation, which sees to it that banks must assure the liquidity of their positions, in accordance with their risk appetite.

The first of these bullets will oblige banks to use advanced tools for risk management. Internal ratings may prove instrumental in keeping some low creditworthiness customers at arm's length, a change from current policy where banks are becoming attached to the client relationship and to the transaction.

The second bullet will ensure that credit institutions will have to monitor the results obtained by the customer's account, not by means of historical costs and past risks, but through cash flow analysis and by marking to market. This would not permit sales people to handle business through 'dear customer' relationships; or traders to hide risks in assumed positions from the eyes of management.

The third bullet will help to assure that procedures regarding capital adequacy, both in the regulatory and in the economic sense, are strong and steadily updated. With Basel II, banks will have to put their money on the line (Pillar 1) under closer and more detailed supervision (Pillar 2). Moreover, the market will steadily watch through greater transparency (Pillar 3).

In conclusion, *if* we admit that regulatory and economic capital constitute the fourth dimension of financial accounting, *then* as in the case of the budget (see Chapter 9) capital adequacy should be computed for the rolling year and be steadily re-evaluated. Furthermore, both capital adequacy and the budget should be matched through cash flow projections:

- Mid-term, under normal conditions
- As frequently as necessary, under tightened inspection.

It is also appropriate to notice that while balance sheets and income statements are financial accounting tools, capital adequacy and the budget are financial plans. As such, they depend on steady cash flow (see Chapter 13) or, alternatively, on bought money. According to some expert opinions, capital adequacy and the budget overlap. According to other experts, the budget is a subset of corporate capital adequacy.

4. Contradictions in market discipline: a case study with loans provisions

The Basel Committee says that *regulatory capital* is set for public purposes, and it implies some degree of standardization. By contrast, as we saw in sections 2 and 3, economic capital is tailored to the bank's own risk appetite, and it represents private costs of failure. As Figure 14.2 suggests, the dividing line between financial accounting and management accounting follows, more or less, the same dichotomy.

The budget and economic capital, which find themselves on the right side of Figure 14.2, are neither standardized nor regulated. Both address the future whether this is:

- Future cost, the business of the budget
- Future risk, the mission of economic capital.

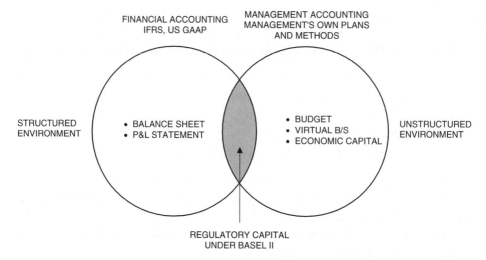

Figure 14.2   Accounting standards setters and regulators promote a structured environment of management reports

Risk, of course, can be monetized, and taking care of private cost of failure through precommitment is a matter of respectability for the credit institution. To make such precommitment a realistic proposition, well-managed banks ensure that economic capital methods assess the amount of money needed to support:

- Well-defined business activities, and
- Exposures that inevitably are associated to them.

Based on such assessments, economic capital can be redefined as the amount necessary to cover losses up to a specified probability: for example, within a 1-year timeframe, in 999 out of 1000 possible scenarios,[6] which means at the 99.9% level of confidence ($\alpha = 0.001$).

The role of respectability capital becomes evident after having defined the level of confidence in an acceptable way, for instance at the level of 999 out of 1000 cases – while VAR only covers 99 out of 100. This creates a buffer of liquidity which becomes necessary to face the twists of the market. Theoretically, at least, this should provide a good frame of reference as far as market discipline is concerned.

The downside is that there exist internal contradictions to market discipline because investors and analysts are classically concerned about earnings per share – and banks are fully aware of it. Reading the fine print of FDIC's Quarterly Banking Profile, for the third quarter of 2004 one sees that while the level of unpayable debt grows, US banks have been drawing down rather than beefing up their level of loan loss reserves.

- Six times in seven quarters (Q4 2002 to Q2 2004), the amount of money the banks set aside as provision for loan losses has declined, and
- The $7.3 billion the banks set aside in the third quarter of 2004 was the smallest since the third quarter of 2000, when the loan portfolio was 23% smaller.

A policy of drawing down loan reserves when credit risk increases is evidently counterproductive, and contradicts everything that has been stated about respectability capital. This situation seems to be more critical for banks with $10 billion or more in assets, *the big banks*, where according to FDIC net charge-offs exceeded provisions for the seventh quarter in a row. Moreover, the overall level of loan loss reserves declined for the fourth time in five quarters.

It is self-evident that when net charge-offs exceed provisions, credit institutions are not adding enough in reserves to cover the loans they are writing off. Indeed, in the third quarter of 2004, the big banks provisions covered only 93% of their write-offs.[7] So much for observance of regulatory capital rules.

An article in *Business Week* has pursued this frame of reference, pointing out that in 2004 banks had an easy way to juice their profits by allocating a little less money to loan loss reserves. Together, the FDIC and *Business Week* references suggest that creative accounting is alive and kicking, because all companies dread profit shortfalls. If nothing else, missing analysts' estimates damages their credibility on Wall Street.

Banks jumped ahead of themselves to trim loans reserves, and therefore regulatory capital, because in 2003 the economy had improved and defaults slowed. With that hindsight, in 2004 many credit institutions decided they did not need as much in reserve as they did in 2003. This was an easy way to increase their earnings per share. 'A lot of banks may do this from time to time to meet estimates,' said Brian Shullaw, senior research analyst at SNL Financial.[8]

This is, however, a policy full of risks because the economy is not static. As credit institutions write more loans, they have to replenish reserves put aside to cover the likelihood of loan losses. Credit conditions are never stable. When economic growth slows and interest rates rise

- Credit conditions worsen, and
- Banks need to set aside even more money than would otherwise be necessary.

Indeed, the 2004 dwindling in loan reserves documents that it was *unwise* to abandon the expected losses (EL) formula of Basel II. This took place mid-October 2003 at the Madrid meeting of the Basel Committee on Banking Supervision, on the hypothesis that banks anyway account for expected losses. What followed in 2004 documented that the hypothesis on which that decision was based was too optimistic. Without an iron-clad algorithm given by regulators which establishes a level-playing field. Credit institutions can play games with loan loss reserves:

- This distorts the true quality of bank earning, and
- It also damages business confidence, as the news of dwindling loans reserves becomes public.

The same *Business Week* article to which reference was made, uses as an example Detroit's Comerica, which had one of the largest drops in its loan loss reserves relative to total assets. Not only did Comerica fail to add money in the fourth quarter of 2003, but it also extracted $21 million from its credit risk reserves.

- That gave it an extra $98 million in income, or 57 cents a share, and
- It allowed the bank's management to beat analysts' earnings estimates by 10 cents.

But is this the reason why a credit institution keeps reserves for loan losses? Another reference by *Business Week* concerns Citigroup, which gained a few extra cents in its income statement from replenishing reserves by a smaller amount than before. This was enough to beat analysts' earnings estimates by 1 cent. In a January 2005 conference call, Citi Chief Financial Officer Sallie L. Krawcheck said that the reserving process was done in mid-quarter based on a mathematical formula. Krawcheck added that: 'We, as a company, work very hard to systemize the process around rigorous analytics,' but then she warned analysts not to expect substantial reductions in provisions in the future.

Eventually, Pillar 3 market discipline might make this practice a relic, because while investors and financial analysts appreciate that victories require taking risk, they also know that reductions in capital adequacy mean greater *financial risk* in the case of adverse change in market conditions. Low reserves are akin to *mispricing* of loans in connection to credit risk.

Mispricing is often done voluntarily, related to commercial risk. An example is *volatility smile*, the guesstimate that future volatility would be benign, which permits the entity to sell cheap options. Sometimes options are purposely mispriced in order to sell them like hotcakes, while forgetting that the synergy of commercial exposure and financial risk can create an earthquake.

5. Facing the challenge of procyclicality through economic capital

Critics say that accounting for procyclicality is one of the dark edges of Basel II. When capital provision accumulated during economic upturns is not adequate to cover risks materializing in downturns, banks are expected to reduce the pace and size of new loans, or recall loans to satisfy regulatory capital requirements. This is essentially the process known as *procyclicality*.

If procyclicality is the problem it is said to be, *then* the best way to handle it is to face it proactively by means of a buffer that upstages capital adequacy (more on this in section 6). This extra reserve is not part of regulatory capital, but can it be considered as one of economic capital's components?

A good question: and the better way to answer it is through a short story. Two monks, this story goes, one Jesuit, the other Benedictine, couldn't agree on an argument whether it is allowed to smoke while saying prayers. The Benedictine said 'yes'; the Jesuit, 'absolutely no'. To get an official answer, they asked the pope for an audience. First spoke the Jesuit, who asked: 'Is it permitted to smoke while praying?' The Pope's response was 'No!' The Benedictine posed his question next, but phrased it differently: 'Is it allowed to say a prayer while smoking?' The Pope answered: 'Yes, a prayer is always welcome.'

Reserves for procyclicality, too, should be welcome as part of economic capital which, as it should be remembered, is a precommitment the bank is doing on its own initiative, in order to face adversity in the future. Apart from other benefits, this approach will answer those who criticize Basel II for creating a close relationship between assumed risk and capital required to provide liquidity in case of adverse market conditions. Moreover, a reserve addressing procyclicality promotes the main strengths of Basel II which are:

- Risk-based pricing of financial instruments, and
- A much greater sensitivity to assumed risk, projected into capital requirements.

For starters, the best way to look at procyclicality is as an after-effect of the economic cycle. 'In dealing with the financial cycle, a key objective would be to ensure that adequate defences are built up in upswings so as to be relied upon when the rough times arrive ... A range of instruments would seem worthy of consideration. These could include ... variants of forward-looking provisioning for prudential purposes,' according to Andrew Crockett, former general manager of the Bank for International Settlements (BIS).

Critics do not seem to be satisfied with that reply. According to them, the procyclical effects of Basel II might increase in an environment of deeper economic and financial integration, if this makes vulnerabilities and cyclical swings more synchronized. Behind this argument lies the fact that in a globalized economy the frequency and magnitude of procyclical effects tends to grow because:

- International banks are inclined to follow a procyclical policy in all their areas of operations, and
- There is a concentration effect; local banks would emulate the internationals when the latter reduce the pace and size of new loans.

It is hard to argue that this will not happen. It will. But globalization is not the only reason. Mergers and acquisitions in the same country is an even greater force pushing in that same direction, as changes that took place in the American financial landscape demonstrate. During the past 20 years, the US banking system has experienced significant consolidation. Particularly between 1994 and 2002 there have been more than 3300 bank mergers among American credit institutions, with nearly $3 trillion in banking assets being acquired. This consolidation led to considerable increases in *national* concentration among the largest banking organizations. As a result:

- The share of domestic banking assets held by the top five banking groups went from 18% in 1994, to almost 32% in 2002.
- Over the same timeframe, the share of the top 25 financial holdings went from 46% to 61%, which speaks volumes about concentration.

In the aftermath of this consolidation, by the end of 2002 there were about 600 domestic financial holding companies, with about one-third engaging in new activities authorized by the Gramm–Leach–Bliley law. Eighty per cent of these included insurance business, while 40 credit institutions have been involved in broker-dealer activities plus in insurance underwriting and fairly significant merchant banking – permitted by Gramm–Leach–Bliley.

On the other hand, while 3300 banks disappeared, between 1994 and 2002 more than 1300 new banks were opened in the United States, sometimes in response to declines in service resulting from bank mergers. The more significant decline was in retail banking, and that is where many of the new financial institutions addressed themselves.

This example documents two things: even in the same country, mergers and acquisitions tend to bring the surviving entity away from loans intermediation. Then, the gap left in banking loans tends to be closed by new financial institutions, which take advantage of the fact bigger banks concentrate on bancassurance, brokerage, and merchant banking. These new institutions are not swamped by the errors of the past and, if well managed, they can nicely integrate the likelihood and aftermath of procyclicality into their economic planning.

6. The capital buffer solution

As far as regulatory capital requirements are concerned, procyclical aspects have been expressed in the context of the IRB solution where banks use their own estimates of probability of default. They do so based on the borrower's current condition, in a way oriented towards the short time horizon of one year associated with the probability of default (PD).

The problem is precisely this short-term horizon. Economic cycles do not work at that speed, and there may also be spillover effects. One of the risks with procyclicality is that several banks, insurers, pension funds, and other lenders sell the same asset at the same time. This will create considerable volatility, with underlying correlations that exacerbate the initial effect

- Forcing additional sales
- Destabilizing capital adequacy requirements, and
- Having a negative impact on the financial system.

Another likely after-effect is *rebalancing* with more leverage; therefore loading the liabilities side of the balance sheet. Some studies have shown that the practice of rebalancing to fixed weights with leverage creates trading patterns leading to forced liquidation of positions. These have nothing to do with margin calls related to leveraged positions when investors cannot come up with the needed additional margins – but the two have a similar effect.

The motor behind rebalancing with leverage is that total wealth drops faster than equity price(s), necessitating a decrease in risky positions. Another factor economists add to effects of procyclicality is stop-losses: investors cut losses after a fall in price by selling an asset. Some credit institutions and insurance companies are more prone than others to fall into the trap of procyclicality because they are after strong credit (or underwriting) growth. In bank lending, fierce competition leads to:

- Risk underpricing
- Lower quality of borrowers
- Lower level of loan loss provisions to total credit (see section 4).

Not all bankers have been trained to realize that credit growth affects problem loans with about a 3-year lag, and it hits the hardest in a downturn. Many credit institutions have a policy of growing rapidly and increasing their market share, but this is usually done by lowering credit standards which eventually leads to hefty capital requirements.

With all these factors in the background, it is easy to appreciate that the effects of procyclicality are a major concern to regulatory authorities. In Basel II, procyclicality comes under Pillar 2 along with residual risk. Those in favour suggest that the best way to face it is *dynamic provisioning* through capital buffers – which is part of the economic capital concept discussed in preceding sections.

The essence of *capital buffers* is to keep more liquidity than is required along the economic cycle, through special provisioning. This can be instrumental in easing capital requirements at times of distress. The algorithm is fairly simple:

$$\text{Economic Capital for Credit Risk} = \text{Regulatory Capital Requirements} + \text{Capital Buffer} \tag{14.1}$$

This is the policy followed by the Banco de Espana in its regulation of Spanish credit institutions under its jurisdiction. The regulatory capital requirements are those necessary to have a licence. The capital buffer is known as *statistical provision*.[9] Banco de Espana says that apart from its contribution to avoidance of procyclicality, the capital buffer makes banks' managers better aware of credit risk – a fact which shows in:

- Risk appraisal
- Risk pricing, and
- Internal models for risk control.

Banco de Espana also states that, furthermore, the statistical provision also leads to more sound accounting practices. In its way, it corrects excess volatility of bank profits brought about by *ex post* acknowledgment of credit risk.

This last statement, however, is challenged by commercial banks. The latter say that the statistical provision has been advanced by regulators, but Spanish accounting law has not changed to accommodate it. As a result, it ends up being a nightmare for the accountants, internal auditors, and external auditors.

Other central bankers suggest that to mitigate procyclicality, certain elements could be introduced in the measurement of PDs. At the same time, however, they add that measures such as drawing on past experience and using longer-term average PDs represent a theoretically simple but backward-looking approach. To the contrary, *stress testing* (see Chapter 16) can be effectively used to:

- Adjust PDs for the effects of different economic conditions, and
- Permit banks to dynamically evaluate and reestablish their capital adequacy.

Indeed, stress testing is actually proposed in Pillar 2 for these purposes. Its results could be integrated with statistical provision in building up additional capital buffers, beyond minimum capital requirements. Properly studied and implemented, this solution can:

- Provide banks with more flexibility in their lending behaviour, and
- Allow them to avoid any forced cutback in lending in economic downturns.

Enriching equation (14.1) with stress testing can lead to a proactive provisioning method satisfactory to bankers, accountants, and supervisors. Dynamic provisioning would also be desirable from a financial stability viewpoint, because it is based on assessment of expected losses, under both normal and stress conditions.

In conclusion, it is most advisable to give due consideration to the entire risk profile on the loan over the economic cycle not just in the short 1-year term; also, to capitalize on modelling technology with the purpose of creating an early warning mechanism about any future deterioration in any component of the loan portfolio. This would allow a timely response by bank management. Stress testing can help in forecasting difficult conditions, preparing for them in advance, and avoiding abrupt changes in capital requirements and loans policies.

7. Corporate-wide risk management

Risks must be continually monitored, evaluated, and controlled by instrument, counterparty, transaction desk, and corporate-wide. This requires a comprehensive process as well as the understanding that its proper execution leads to more effective management of exposure. Which is the best organizational form?

Some institutions have chosen a centralized approach where risk management and the finance division responsible for economic capital allocation act in unison. Others prefer to assign primary responsibility to the individual business units. These units are expected to manage their risks by adhering to:

- Established internal policies
- Internal control guidelines
- Risk management milestones, and
- Financial staying power expressed in respectability capital.

Explicit internal policies, established by the board of directors, must emphasize the need for balancing risk by appropriate liquidity supported by both sides of the balance sheet (see section 3). Internal controls must be rigorous in all channels, from loans to investments, trading, and the management of inventoried positions in the banking book and trading book.

As has been explained on several occasions, risk management must be exercised by desk, instrument, counterparty, and any other variable important to the bank's staying power. A crucial question to be answered in real time (see Chapter 15) is: What can happen with mispricing inventoried derivatives contracts because of adverse movement in:

- Interest rates
- Exchange rates
- Or, changing market psychology?

Apart from credit risk, interest rate risk and other exposures affecting the bank's portfolio in its home country, foreign exchange risk can negatively impact on the value of foreign assets and liabilities, damaging the bank's balance sheet and P&L.

While adverse market effects are bound to happen and nobody in the banking business can be immune of potential financial losses, management should be in charge at all times. This it can do only through a thoroughly studied system of internal controls which operate in parallel channels to lines of authority like the *sympathetic* and *parasympathetic* systems in the human body.

A basic organizational principle is that the person who is in charge of trading should have no control of the backoffice. This is a well-known principle, but it is rarely observed. Even after the flagrant case of Nick Leeson in Barings Singapore office, which brought down the venerable bank, few financial institutions rethought:

- The structure of their internal controls, and
- The existing conflicts of interest between operations, accounting, and supervision.

Not only must parallel controls form a structured system able to assure independence of opinion, but also control systems should be regularly tested both quantitatively and qualitatively. A good way of testing how the system of internal controls works is analysing credits for risk management. Here is a sample of critical questions:

- Are our credits diversified or concentrated in a few names?
- How are our credits distributed by counterparty? By currency? By interest rate? By maturity?
- What's the pattern of our credits by credit officer? By branch? By foreign subsidiary?

There are plenty of crucial questions to be asked in testing how well the internal controls work: 'Is there any abnormal number of "weak credits"?' How much of the loans business of the bank is done with the same counterparty? How much faster is the derivatives business growing than the more classical business lines like loans, investments, and personal banking?

Other crucial queries for internal control and risk management reasons are oriented towards the traders, loans officers, and senior executives. Is the same credit officer dealing with the same counterparty all the time? Is the same dealer following a similar pattern with the same counterparty in regard to derivative financial instruments?

One of the major contributions of Basel II is the awareness it brought to the banking industry about the aftermath of operational risk, and the capital requirement to confront it.[10] Figure 14.3 brings three patterns to the reader's attention in regard to risk exposure characteristic of a credit institution:

- The more classical one, where credit risk accounted for two-thirds of assumed exposure, and market risk for the balance.
- The portfolio heavily weighted in derivatives, where market risk is in excess of credit risk.

- The pattern of the global money centre bank where business risk is king, because sprawling operations in 80, 100, or more than 100 countries make the institution most vulnerable to political events and litigation resulting from its own mistakes.

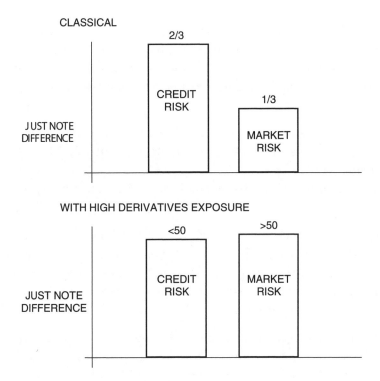

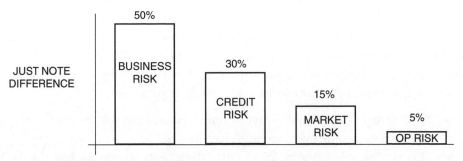

Figure 14.3   Risk exposure according to estimates made by banks

Given its potential magnitude, business risk must be controlled. Respectability capital is the way of doing so at the financial end. The able management of credit risk, market risk, and operational risk is also important. While legal risk has been part of operational risk, its recent magnitude and business impact lead me to put it as part of business risk.

Mid-June 2005, JP MorganChase agreed to pay $2.2 billion to settle its part in a class action lawsuit, led by the University of California, that accused several banks of aiding Enron in defrauding investors before the energy trader went bankrupt in December 2001. A week earlier, Citigroup said it would pay $2.0 billion to settle its part in the suit. Both banks denied any wrong-doing.

Business risk of that magnitude brings our discussion back to the query asked in the opening paragraph of this section about centralization *vs* decentralization of crucial functions. The arguments about decentralization revolve around the fact that a most important tool in any process is on-the-job experience and judgment, enhanced through direct and constant communication. The pros say that while awareness of risk must be continuously emphasized through the company, local exercise of risk control can provide a clear and simple statement as to what should not be done in committing capital.

The arguments about the centralization of risk control start with the fact that risk policies and procedures must be clear, homogeneous, and well understood. If this responsibility is dispersed, inevitably there will be heterogeneity and mis-communications. Some local risk managers may not consider the *unexpected*, and therefore they may not constantly:

- Probe for potential problems
- Test for weaknesses, and
- Identify potential for loss.

To my mind, whether the chosen solution is centralization or decentralization of risk management and capital adequacy duties, the system to be established should be flexible, to permit adaptation to changing environments, including the evolving goals of the institution. Whichever the organizational solution to be chosen, the key objective is that of minimizing the possibility of incurring exposures outside the board's and CEO's guidelines, and supervisory rules. And because there will always be risks arising from rare or extreme events, the bank must have a policy of being adequately equipped with respectability capital.

Notes

1   D.N. Chorafas, *The 1996 Market Risk Amendment: Understanding the Marking-to-Model and Value-at-Risk*, McGraw-Hill, Burr Ridge, IL, 1998.
2   D.N. Chorafas, *Economic Capital Allocation with Basel II: Cost and Benefit Analysis*, Butterworth-Heinemann, London and Boston, 2004.
3   The Joint Forum 'Risk Management Practices and Regulatory Capital', BIS, November 2001.
4   ECB, Monthly Bulletin, February 2005.
5   D.N. Chorafas, *After Basel II: Assuring Compliance and Smoothing the Rough Edges*, Lafferty/VRL Publishing, London, 2005.
6   Basel Committee, The Joint Forum: Trends in Risk Integration and Aggregation, BIS, August 2003.
7   EIR, 14 January 2005.
8   *BusinessWeek*, 21 February 2005.
9   D.N. Chorafas, *Economic Capital Allocation with Basel II: Cost and Benefit Analysis*, Butterworth-Heinemann, London and Boston, 2004.
10 D.N. Chorafas, *Operational Risk Control with Basel II: Basic Principles and Capital Requirements*, Butterworth-Heinemann, London and Boston, 2004.

The Real-Time Management Report

1. Introduction

Typically, at the higher organizational layers of a corporation information gets distilled and reported in summary and/or by exception. Emphasis is on accuracy rather than on precision. By contrast, great detail and precision characterize the information requirements of the middle layer. The advent of on-line real-time response to management information requirements means that this process is about to change.

Whether we talk of budgets, balance sheets, P&L, or any other type of financial information, a basic characteristic of interactive information technology, at both the top and middle layer, is that database access should be ad hoc. Response must be given in real time with fully updated information:

- Using visualization, by turning numbers into figures
- Having built-in intelligence to identify exceptions and outliers
- Detecting evolving features and patterns, such as trends, spikes, heads, shoulders, and confidence intervals.

Knowledge artifacts are necessary to sort, combine, and prove transactions, as well as validate general ledger account numbers, and pinpoint personal responsibilities. Filters should be used in connection to all entries, including accounting, financial, statistical, and other issues. Data input should be on-line under the 'one entry, many uses' principle.

A great deal of attention must be paid to system design. Parametric solutions permit flexible transfer of information from and to various applications. High technology should be used as a competitive weapon, to promote the automation of accounting operations. A modern organization cannot afford the luxury of mediocre technology or of obsolete solutions.

By emphasizing the benefits to be obtained from fully interactive approaches, and by assuring that these are properly implemented, an able management provides itself with the means to develop and sustain successful business operations. A good example is *real-time balance sheet* reporting, the theme of this chapter. Financial models should be designed and implemented with the aim of bridging the gap that often exists between:

- Those people whose job is to develop and supply knowledge, in order to enhance the competitiveness of the firm, and

- Those who must manage output, assuring an uninterrupted flow of high-quality products or services – and of reliable financial information.

Increasingly, the distinction between well-managed and poorly managed entities lies in the ability of the former to experiment prior to commitments. Enriched through real-time response, a dynamic IT system can be instrumental in assuring that the enterprise does not get out of control. A significant part of *what-if* experimentation with balance sheets (see section 2) rests on the foregoing requirements, which have been met by top-tier banks.

For instance, since the late 1990s, Boston's State Street Banks has been able to produce a *virtual balance sheet* (VBS) for its world-wide operations within 30 minutes (in fact, since then, the time lag has shrunk). A virtual balance sheet is management accounting, not financial accounting (see Part 1). It has all the characteristics of a classical balance sheet but it accepts up to 4% error as the price for immediate response.

- This is not acceptable for financial reporting purposes
- But it is perfectly alright for an internal accounting management information system (IAMIS).

Notice that a level of accuracy of ±4% has nothing to do with 'cooking the books'. This is fast response, internal management information. For example, when Saddam Hussein invaded Kuwait on 4 August 1991, the top management of Bankers Trust was able to reposition the bank at the right side of the B/S, by having a global virtual balance sheet at short notice, experimenting on alternatives and using the time window offered by the bank's London operations before the New York market opened for business.

2. 'What-if' experimentation with balance sheets

The serious user of financial or accounting statements is not a passive reader of figures, who does so just to kill time. He or she will typically ask a series of questions aimed at answering professional worries, or at providing the insight necessary for important decisions. Meaningful questions will never be made in the abstract:

- They typically reflect a specific situation
- Inquire on *what, when, who, why* or the way in which things evolve.

Many questions have no straight answer. A factual and documented response to them requires investigation, at least of the what-if type. *What-if* experimentation started in the early 1980s with the spreadsheet and since that time it has made great strides. More than two decades down the line, experimentation has become a 'must'. As an example, we will follow a scenario on the insurance industry. Legitimate questions in evaluating projected profitability are of the kind:

- What if inflation rises by x% over the next two years but premiums only increase half that much?
- What are the effects on the company if the probability of natural and/or man-made disaster rises by y% but, because of competition, premiums remain the same as that of the last period?

Some of the answers to queries of this kind, particularly if there is precedence on x, y, and the other conditions, can be provided by information in the database handled through a spreadsheet. More sophisticated, and better documented, replies will require mathematical models, which map into the computer the:

- Range of operations of the company
- Market and the way the company interacts with its market
- Composition of the company's investment portfolio in fixed income and equities
- Risk-sensitivity of the company's insurance products and effect of rise in probabilities.

Other modules of an experimental system should simulate the money flows that arise as the result of risks taken in underwriting. These flows typically include: premium receipts, claims payments, investment of funds, investment income, expenses, taxes, and dividends. Most of the factors outlined in the preceding paragraphs impact on the:

- Balance sheet, and
- Profit and loss statement.

Experimentation on different probabilities of underwriting risk and return is necessary because the net result of all money flows occurring in a given period of time is ultimately reflected in an insurance company's assets and liabilities. In fact, this statement is valid for any firm, though each has its own ways and means of management analysis for accounting and financial reasons.

Changes occurring in the balance sheet and P&L that result from money flows must be calculated according to IFRS. But for *management accounting* purposes there exist considerable degrees of freedom, and real-time interactive reports should preferably be structured in a way that allow change to some of the para-meters on-line, and further experiment with the obtained interim results.

Clearly, this approach requires considerable system support. Figure 15.1 presents an example from an insurance application which capitalized on networked databases to provide a rich environment for experimentation. Important elements in this process have been aggregate flows such as underwriting profits and total earnings.

- The primary flows, which contribute to aggregate flows, are generally cal-culated from simple basic equations and numerical parameters specified by the experimenter.

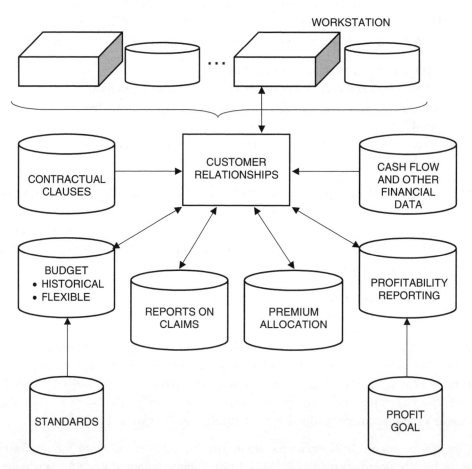

Figure 15.1 'What-if' experimentation requires on-line access to databases and artifacts which stimulate or optimize business conditions

- This contrasts to econometric models which attempt to forecast the values of such items as gross profits, by relating them directly to important economic indicators and their own past values.

Another major domain where experimentation assists management in the insurance industry is claim processing. This is a highly repetitive job but each case has its own characteristics and estimation needs a fair amount of knowledge and calculation. Hence, it is an ideal application domain for expert systems. However, to effectively contribute to profitable results,

- The knowledge-based artifact must operate on-line and access rich databases, and
- Be enriched by knowledge engineering tools that go beyond the capabilities of early constructs, utilizing genetic algorithms, neutral networks and fuzzy sets (more on this in section 3).

A similar approach to that shown in Figure 15.1 can be used in connection to other financial activities, such as loans. In the mid-1980s, Japan's Mitsui Bank was one of the first to build an expert system for *scoring* company loans, which significantly improved upon past practices. It *analysed balance sheets*, using *public databases* and Mitsui's own data warehouse. It also compared companies applying for loans to standard credit criteria, and to one-another. The model reflected on:

- Company profits
- Acid test (current assets over current liabilities)
- Liquidity and cash flow
- Long-term assets
- Capital ratio, and
- Future business perspectives.

Other critical variables, or sensitivities, used by the Mitsui model include company size, annual growth, productivity, and qualitative criteria such as quality of management. This has been one of the early success stories of system solutions capitalizing on knowledge engineering.

Whether in the sciences, in engineering, in insurance, or in banking, experimentation is a culture that characterizes the person willing and able to challenge the obvious, as distinct from the bureaucrat who can only follow the beaten path.

- The experimenter is not after pithy details.
- What he or she wants is better insight and foresight, to be obtained through investigation.

The cornerstone to all experimentation is a principle formulated by Dr Enrico Fermi, the nuclear physicist. What the *Fermi principle* states is that if our assumptions make sense, the errors that they possibly contain will average out; they will not always be loading the results on the same side, therefore helping the process we put in motion in keeping a sense of balance, and therefore of accuracy.

The Fermi concept is very important to management, both in exploiting business opportunities and in controlling exposure. *Our* bank's risk managers never really have all the data they need when a decision is done. The balance is provided through reasonable assumptions. The careful reader will also note that both internal and external auditors operate in a similar way. Therefore the method has polyvalent applications. A person who never made a mistake never did anything; but a person who has no control over his/her actions is an even greater disaster.

3. Analytics is a polyvalent methodology

In her book *How the Laws of Physics Lie*, Nancy Cartwright advances the thesis that *science* does not describe a profound physical reality.[1] It only advances phenomenal models, valid only in a limited space or conditions which, therefore, are fictitious. What this argument forgets is that the added-value of science is the *scientific method* of investigation, and it is largely based on *analytics*.

Insight and foresight, to which section 2 made reference, are boosted through analysis which is served through a research spirit equipped with appropriate tools and a methodology.

- The first major contribution of a methodology is to inspire confidence
- The second, to permit the repetition of experiments
- The third to help in building up a generation of experts.

The real expert is a person who knows how to recognize early enough his or her mistakes, and has the vision and courage to take immediate corrective action. Both for the purpose of recognition, and to make possible a change in direction, the expert must be able to endow himself with what Sam Walton, of Wal-Mart fame, called 'the ability to turn on a dime'.

An expert must be competitive, and competitiveness requires going beyond present-day solutions. That is where developments in mathematics which have taken place over the past 40 years make their major contribution. For instance, fuzzy engineering can be instrumental in helping underwriters assess risks and set appropriate premiums; also, in evaluating the risk taken with each type of contract an application which additionally requires client profiling.

Much of the benefit derived from the use of genetic algorithms is in optimization and scheduling problems. An example of optimization is finding the maxima of functions; scheduling problems involve the combination of different processes in order to obtain the best utilization of plant, or any other facility. Genetic algorithms also help in emulating learning effects, which is an important process in modelling.[2]

- Fuzzy sets are a development of the 1960s
- Genetic algorithms a development of the 1970s.

While spreadsheets were very useful in analysis of financial and accounting information, and they continue being so, as the Mitsui example in section 2 documented, since the mid-1980s the process of analysis has been enriched with an increasing array of tools – including knowledge artifacts. Capitalizing on advances in computers and communications technology:

- Expert systems, optimizers, and risk evaluators work in real time, and
- Their on-line service is providing invaluable assistance to management, from balance sheet analysis to experimentation.

A model written for reasons of experimentation should be objective. It is not the purpose of science, or of the scientific method, to distinguish between 'good' and 'bad'. A spreadsheet is simply calculating the *what-if* outcome of projected decisions taken in conjunction with a specified scenario. For its part, an *optimizer* helps the user find the best solutions in regard to established criteria – varying the numerical values of decision parameters in each run. For instance:

- A genetic algorithm would generate outcomes guided by goals and constraints, the way they are set by the user,
- Therefore, whether for descriptive or optimization purposes, the model must be flexible in its structure, and in terms of the parameters it handles.

One of the more sophisticated models developed in the insurance business simulates a complex combination of risks, reinsurance policies, economic environments, and investments. This is a sophisticated expert system whose output is used by underwriters. One of the modules of the artifact interprets the results provided by the other modules the way a professional actuary would do. Still another module calculates corresponding insurance premiums.

This is a good example on the polyvalent nature of analytics. The proper use of the new tools technology makes available requires an open mind and good appreciation of how the scientific method works. Short of this:

- Results will be limited, and
- The overall experience may end up being a deception.

A wrong way of looking at science is to believe that scientific proof is a matter of showing formal consistency with what is treated as *self-evident* definitions, axioms, and postulates of a given system of thought. Not only is this false, but also the effect of believing in such nonsense impacts in a negative way on the mind of scientists and analysts because it leads to denying the existence of anything outside the bounds of that fixed system.

The alternative to a formal, deductive organization is to abstain from reference to the 'self-evident' by depending on experiments. This means experimentally validating every hypothesis. Behind such an experimental approach lies the fact that, in the real universe, there are no fixed sets of 'self-evident' definitions, axioms, or postulates. Researchers typically operate on the basis of *assumptions*, which they believe to be sufficient up to a point, but:

- They are eager to challenge the 'obvious', and
- They are open-minded about discovering that some of their assumptions might be false.

It is a basic principle of invention and discovery that the most important issue in investigations is that of being on the alert for evidence of changes in previous assumptions. An underwriter, for instance, may simulate the likely aftermath of an insurance policy covering specific events in the global market by calling into play basic building blocks such as:

- Risk classes
- Treaties
- Countries
- Companies, and
- Private clients.

Data filtering, too, can be knowledge-enriched in order to avoid the company's professionals being snowed under with news items and data streams. Typically a major financial institution today receives real-time news wires from many different services, as well as market information that is channelled into the bank every day at amounts that are overwhelming.

Best results are usually obtained through dynamic modelling, simulating the changes in the state of the insurance policy under study, which result from evolving economic environments or most recent trends – subsequently experimenting with the interim results.

In a different example regarding banking loans, financial criteria leading to experimentation can be expressed as a set of rules and numerical parameters which, for instance, determine the solvency margin a debtor must have. In all these cases, the ability to provide *full customization* through the use of knowledge engineering is of major competitive advantage.

4. Virtual balance sheet and budget *vs* actual

Since the late 1990s the better managed financial institutions have started fair valuing their assets and liabilities on a daily basis. Financial statements based on fair value became a 'must' with IFRS, but in this section we are concerned with management accounting done intraday at an acceptable level of accuracy. Both B/S position and P&L become more transparent with fair value accounting.

An interactive virtual balance sheet needs be no different from the classical B/S, unless, for reasons of greater effectiveness in enterprise management, it is provided in a personalized form. Basically, as a policy it is wise to use the standard format which is understood by everybody and required by regulations. As an example, Box 15.1 presents the A&L reporting format according to the European Union Accounts Directive. This, however, may be the pivotal point around which real-time customized versions are built. For instance, a customized version may provide a more detailed and closer look at fair value at the assets side of the balance sheet. This can be most instructive in a managerial sense. Both the *balance sheet* and *profit and loss* statement carry valuable information, and knowledgeable executives and professionals know that in order to get a full message they must:

- Read between the lines, and
- Correlate information elements to make useful inferences.

Box 15.1   Reporting format on assets and liabilities according to the EU Bank Accounts Directive

Assets

- Cash in hand
- Treasury bills
- Loans and advances to credit institutions
- Loans and advances to other customers
- Debt securities
- Equities in portfolio
- Participating interests
- Shares in affiliates
- Other assets (derivatives)

Liabilities

- Amounts owed to credit institutions
- Amounts owed to customers
- Debts evidenced by certificates
- Subordinate liabilities
- Equity
- Other liabilities (derivatives)

Modelling makes balance sheet information available much more frequently in an updated form, accessible on-line as often as necessary. Its contents must be made to reflect an instantaneous picture of the condition of the enterprise as of some particular day. They must also show how, within the ±4% level of accuracy mentioned in the Introduction, the company positions itself in terms of assets and liabilities.

Within this perspective of computational financial analysis comes the process of experimentation discussed in section 2, as well as the need for a polyvalent methodology explained in section 3. Notice that precisely the same principles of steady control that are applicable to the balance sheet are also valid with budgets (see Chapter 9) and with standard costs.

Budgetary compliance, and the functions of controllership associated to it, must be executed on-line interactively. No effective solution to management control can take figures on faith. General statements never get further than the surface. Good governance requires knowing what is behind the figures.

- Fast answers through guesswork, are deprived of documentation, and
- The way to bet is that in the large majority of cases even educated guesses stand a good chance of being wrong.

My favoured dictum in budgeting and budgetary control is that you don't make money – you save it. This is more true of a non-profit foundation than of a profit-making organization, but it applies to corporations as well. If the budget is over-run and the CEO takes no immediate corrective measures, this means he or she:

- Lacks the decisive force to impose a regime of cost-effectiveness, or
- Has no clues about how expenditures can be rationalized.

Every well-managed firm tracks its expenses, because its management appreciates that under no conditions can they be left to run wild. A practical example from manufacturing companies is the control of inventories. Sales and production always favour rich inventories; their job is easier with full stock on hand. But from the viewpoint of cost-effectiveness:

- Large inventories have negative effect on profits
- Therefore, production planning must be tuned to using sales forecasts, and sales management should be eager to contribute such forecasts rather than resisting them.

Another reason behind budget overruns is that in many cases the existence of a standard cost system is looked at as an impedance rather than as an opportunity. From a good governance viewpoint, however, after having established a cost standard senior management should be eager to hold everybody responsible for upholding the financial plan:

- Budgeted levels must be compared with actuals, and
  Woe to the department manager, or section head, who exceeds cost limits.

Abiding to budgets and cost standards should be part of the company culture. It is also a matter of personal ability that one can accomplish one's mission in an able manner; being over budget and over standard cost limits indicates a person elevated beyond his or her capacity.

One of the 21st century reasons why steady and focused cost control is so important is that with globalization most products and services, including banking, have become a commodity in regard to their functionality, quality, price, and delivery. While markets mean more than just budgets and balance sheets, it is no less true that:

- A company that does not watch its bottomline would not be around for long, and
- The position of those who don't care for budgets and cost standards is not merely wrong-headed obstructionism; it is the manifestation of a destructive force.

The message of the foregoing paragraphs, reading between the lines, is that executives and companies who have been fighting against IFRS should appreciate that, apart from all the other reasons already explained, the observance of standards is a matter of culture and of self-discipline. The fair value of assets and fair value of liabilities serves not only in regulatory compliance but also in sound corporate governance. This is the very reason for implementation of a real-time balance sheet as well as on-line budget *vs* actual solutions.

5. The pervasive nature of financial information

The CEO cannot be expected to be an expert on everything. But he or she must be willing and able to get the fundamentals and pick up enough of the jargon to do what the chief executive's job demands. Namely, the ability to:

- Ask the right questions, and
- Accurately evaluate the answers, leading to more questions.

When they are correct and to the point, qualitative comments which are complementing quantitative answers, are instrumental in picturing the company's operations: one-by-one and as a whole. While analytical information on products and services is at the top of the list, financial analysis, too, has a key position in good governance, because:

- Its goals are the soul of the company's existence, and
- The nature of financial information is pervasive, entering into every walk of organizational life.

Personality traits are also important. Above and beyond his or her other qualities, the CEO must be quick both in number crunching and in decision-making. He or she should also assume full responsibility for all decisions made under their authority. All these positive characteristics are strengthened through fair value management reporting.

The internal accounting management information system (IAMIS)[3] the company puts in place must provide consistent and comparable information elements. One way to assure comparability is that all of the company's assets are marked to market. Using both marking to market and accruals for assets and liabilities positions can give results that are uncoupled and misleading. As an example, take a balance sheet which shows:

Assets	Liabilities
100	90 Debt
	10 Equity

Over time, accruals still show 100 in assets, but marking-to-market may show 90 in assets, using capitalization as proxy. Because the debt has not changed, the equity is gone. The company has no more core capital.

This poses serious management challenges (not only problems to accounting), and brings into the picture the need for recapitalization. Short of this, the distance to default can dramatically shorten – and senior management must be immediately informed about it, not at the end of the week, month, or year. The virtual balance sheet provides the needed support for damage control and corrective action.

What about marking to market the liabilities? This is not in the books. Part of the difficulty of fair valuing the liabilities is that while a market for them exists, it is narrow. Some experts suggest using fair value in a way consistent with the market value of heavily traded assets of similar characteristics. But this is possible only in some industries. In the insurance business, for example,

- *If* it is possible to calculate the fair value of life insurance liabilities
- *Then* it is feasible to use the same technique for the calculation of premiums.

In banking, derivative financial instruments, with which most big credit institutions are overloaded, may fall into this class. The same derivatives in the trading book of the financial entity may be classified as 'other assets' when in-the-money and 'other liabilities' when out-of-the money. The difference is made by the instrument's market value (more on this in section 6).

This process, however, has its challenges. Trading positions in financial derivatives may be classical or exotic. What is by now considered classical derivative financial instruments include interest rate swaps (IRS), currency swaps, forward rate agreements (FRA), foreign exchange forwards, options on equities, equity indices, financial futures, and more.

Exotic financial instruments are more novel and more complex. Therefore, they are less understood by market players and, quite often, have legal loopholes. Options providing an example are: all or nothing, average strike, barrier, basket, binary, chooser, nested or compound. Other examples are instruments connected to credit risk exposure, currency rate exposure, down and on, down and out, embeddos, knock-in, knock-out, lookbacks, one-touch, outperformance, path-dependent, preference, quanto, step-lock, synthetic time-dependent, up and in, up and out.

Many, though not all, of the exotics are tailor-made to the client's specs. Therefore, they are difficult to generalize and classify from a credit risk and market risk standpoint. Plenty of customized derivatives are today available or can be developed on request. Some are found in interest and currency markets; others are equity or debt related.

Because the trading environment of exotic derivatives is unstructured, fair valuing them is no easy task. This is, incidentally, one of the reasons why a ±4% accuracy is acceptable with the virtual balance sheet. According to the Fermi principle, there is a good likelihood that derivatives would balance themselves out. The purpose is not to gain precision, but an acceptable level of accuracy accompanied by speed in:

- Management information, and
- Damage control, if the situation warrants corrective action.

The officers of the bank evaluating the appropriateness of portfolio positions, falling into an unstructured environment, must be fully aware of both counterparty risk and of market exposure. For this, they should be equipped with powerful means for risk evaluation as well as for experimentation – more than 'What-if' discussed in section 2. The tools available to senior executives must allow them to:

- Become truly proactive, and
- Adopt a rigorous risk management culture.

It is preferable to provide senior management with interactive visualization, rather than cold numbers. A radar chart can be a first-class medium for communicating on-line information in selected crucial variables. The example in Figure 15.2

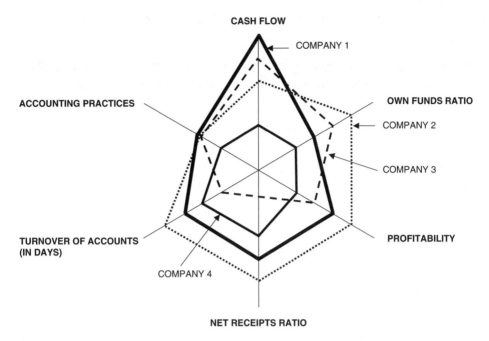

Figure 15.2   A radar chart for crucial variables distinguishing whether a loan is eligible or ineligible for central bank refinancing

comes from an application which rated four different companies against one another in regard to six factors chosen to reflect quality of governance.

In conclusion, as the examples we saw in section 4 and in this section demonstrate, a virtual B/S based on fair value accounting is very important to regulators, bankers, financial analysts, and investors. If we understand the fair value of assets and liabilities, we can assess the worth of company stock. With that knowledge the balance sheet and income statement take *present meaning*, rather than reflecting slow changing data.

6.   Watching over position risk

When a bank concludes a transaction, it assumes an obligation whose value will change – increase or shrink – throughout its duration. The answer to the query 'By how much?' is never known in advance. This rise or fall in value due to price volatility reflects itself, correspondingly, into unrealized but recognized profits and losses – the IAS 39 and US GAAP stuff. It also tells a lot about market risk; but there is also credit risk:

- If the transaction becomes more valuable, counterparty risk will grow.
- If the value of the transaction falls, counterparty risk decreases although market risk increases.

There are also other characteristics of inventoried positions which need watching, each with its own criteria. Long and short positions are an example. The term *long* is used to describe a producer, trader or investor who has an actual commodity position. *Short* describes people and companies who have an obligation to deliver the commodity but do not own it. Hence, they will have to borrow it, or buy it at a later date.

The virtual balance sheet, virtual income statement, and interactive computational finance at large, permit the manager and the professional to keep steady watch *intraday* over recognized but not realized gains and losses. Enhanced through expert systems, this can be a most rewarding experience.

- With every transaction there is one or more crucial parameter(s) whose behaviour must be studied, to be ahead of the curve.
- Globalized markets don't permit easy-going approaches and seat-of-the-pants judgement; and they penalize delayed response to ongoing events.

For instance, with derivatives at any point in time a crucial parameter is the underlier's market behaviour which dictates the value of a position in the portfolio, and therefore the associated exposure. Another critical parameter is maturity. Other things being equal, longer maturities increase the likelihood that a certain price, rate, or market will move. This translates into *position risk*, on which the executive with responsibility must be immediately informed.

Moreover, the wave of change taking place in the banking industry is not connected strictly to derivative financial instruments, even if derivatives have been the vector that brought about a major transition. Also, in the traditional banking business, mainly lending and deposits funding must now face new and complex requirements in the management of embedded interest rate risk. Take as an example position risk in the loans book.

Whether the object of lending is customer needs, mortgages, or the wholesale markets, banks now must account for risks well beyond the well-known credit exposure and 1-year horizon. They must look at their P&L in a more sophisticated way than the simple cost-of-money basis and assume at least a medium-term perspective. Three risks are outstanding in connection to lending:

- *Credit risk* regarding the borrower's trustworthiness, expressed in his or her ability to pay the interest and repay the loan.
- *Interest rate risk*, associated to fixed rate loans, and including mismatch risk which addresses the difference between the interest rate structure of deposits (or bought money) and that of loans.
- *Liquidity risk*, which arises when there is a difference in the maturity profiles of assets and liabilities – particularly of current assets and current liabilities.

Each one of these risks must be thoroughly studied in all its aspects. Interest rate risk in the loans book provides an example. Simulation must include interest rates rising, falling, or steadily holding high or low for an extended time period. Every one of these patterns has an aftermath, and senior management must be:

- Aware of the underlying reason, and
- Sure of its after-effect on the bank's portfolio.

Interest rate risk and liquidity risk are embedded in the bank's loan book, thereby introducing into it market risk. This market risk component is not too different from the one existing in the bank's trading book which addresses the deals the institution makes in equities, bonds, and derivatives.

For better risk control reasons, many credit institutions today make internal interest rate swaps to take interest rate risk out of the banking book, bringing it to the trading book and hedging it. This process, however, is dynamic and the executive in charge of position risk must be fully aware of the impact of intraday changes on interest rates and on market liquidity. Left unwatched, both factors can cause a loss.

- Banking book exposures are typically more long term
- Trading book exposures are shorter term, with positions taken for resale and quick profits.

The virtual balance sheet and virtual P&L statement should reflect changes in the aforementioned risk factors as they happen, intraday. Simulators and expert systems should be available to enable responsible executives to study and analyse the aftermath of hedging or repositioning decisions, prior to reaching them.

Until securitization became a driving force in the retail banking market, particularly for mortgages, credit cards and other receivables, banks held their loans to maturity. They did the same with the securities in their portfolio. But securitization of retail banking receivables has been typically passed by the corporate loans book's securitization, as well as by credit risk mitigation (CRM) by means of a growing pallet of credit derivatives.

Critics say, with reason, that whether we talk of credit risk mitigation, fixed/ flexible interest rate swaps, or any other derivative instrument, there is no assurance that the hedge will be perfect. Indeed, the most likely outcome is that it would be *asymmetric*, leaving the institution with a significant amount of exposure. This underlines the need to know much more about what is happening than just applying the mechanics of a CRM or interest rate swap.

Here is what the 75th Annual Report (2004–2005) of the Bank for International Settlements had to say on persistently low interest rates: 'Several explanations for the low level of long-term rates were proffered. Deteriorating prospects for economic growth provided an explanation in the euro area, Japan, but not in the United States ... Longer-term inflation expectations were exceptionally controlled, but real rates were down as well. Low volatility and reduced risk premiums were also in evidence, but mostly at the short end, leaving longer-term forward rates still unusually low. Other possible explanations included prospective pension fund and accounting reforms, perceived by some market participants as increasing the demand for long-dated assets, and the accumulation of US dollar assets by Asian authorities.'

The BIS Annual Report concluded that it is difficult to quantify the impact of these latter factors, in a way that is valid in the most general sense. On the other hand, each credit institution has its underlying assumption which it uses concerning both the amounts and timing of future cash flows and discount rates. A virtual balance sheet should take note of idiosyncratic factors, because this is the way the bank's senior management thinks.

A similar statement is valid about accounting for counterparty exposure. Changes in credit quality of loans in the portfolio must be taken into account in determining fair values, even if the impact of credit risk is recognized separately by deducting the amount of the allowance for credit losses from both book values and fair values. While some institutions say that this is not necessary, because fair value is market value, and the market has already embedded the aftermath of credit downgrades, there is always a time lag exploited by sharp operators and paid by the laggards.

7. Real-time access to satisfy new Basel directives: SFTs, CCRs and more

Theoretically, the final version of Basel II was published in June 2004. Practically, nothing is really 'final' because both the financial industry and its instruments are in full evolution, making necessary new rules so that regulation is ahead of the curve. This section highlights issues raised by Basel's consultative document of April 2005 on trading activities.[4]

The first subject that should hold the reader's attention in respect to this document is the creation of a family of *securities financing transactions* (SFTs), which eventually may become as important as OTC transaction are today. These SFTs include:

- Securities lending
- Securities borrowing
- Securities margin lending, and repurchase, and
- Reverse repurchase agreements.

Indeed, in this April 2005 consultative document, the Basel Committee compares and contrasts SFTs to OTC derivatives, making the point that generally SFT transactions are undertaken with a counterparty against which a probability of default can be determined. Also, they:

- Generate a current exposure
- Have a random (read: unknown) future market value, and
- Create an exchange of payments, or of financial instruments against payment.

The implication of the factors listed above is that financial institutions will be well advised to use a methodology similar to tracking position risk in the loans book, as explained in section 6. While some of the mechanics will differ, the general systems approach remains valid.

A similar statement is valid in connection to another major issue raised by the April 2005 Basel consultative document: *counterparty credit risk* (CCR). This is the bilateral credit risk of transactions with uncertain exposures, that can vary over time with the movement of underlying market factors – hence the wisdom of tracking them intraday, interactively.

As a term, CCR refers to the likelihood that the counterparty to a transaction could default prior to final settlement of the transaction's cash flows (Herstatt risk). This contrasts to the credit institution's exposure to a loan, because in the latter case credit exposure is unilateral and only the bank faces a risk of loss. By contrast,

- With CCR the risk of loss is bilateral, and
- The market value of the transaction can be positive or negative to either counterparty.

Notice that the treatment of CCR arising from OTC derivatives was first set forth in an amendment to the 1988 Basel Accord. What Basel II does is to update this treatment for transactions booked in either the trading book or the banking book. It also advances repo-style treatment of CCR and other types of transaction.

For starters, the basis of existing treatment of OTC derivatives, known as the current exposure method (CEM), is that of reflecting potential future exposure, calculated by applying a weighting factor to the notional principal amount. However, because the risk-sensitivity of this treatment appears limited, particularly with regard to the internal ratings-based (IRB) method, supervisors propose to enhance this procedure for OTC derivative transactions.

Enhancement is provided by introducing a new treatment for securities financing transactions (discussed in the opening paragraphs of this section). The consultative document referred to advances three alternative methods for calculating exposure at default (EAD) or exposed amount for transactions involving CCR in the banking book or trading book:

- An internal model using expected positive exposure (EPE)
- A standardized method, and
- The existing current exposure approach (CEM).

These alternatives represent points in a continuum of sophistication in risk management, and they aim to provide incentives for banks to improve their handling of CCR by adopting more accurate approaches. Given their dependence on current information, every one of them, particularly so the most advanced, can benefit from virtual balance sheet solutions.

One of the more interesting practical issues connected to CCR, which can benefit from interactive computational finance, is the tracking of *wrong-way risk*. This is a new term introduced by Basel and used for identifying *synergies in credit exposure*. Two types should be distinguished:

- *General wrong-way risk*, which arises when the probability of default of counterparties positively correlates with general market risk.

- *Specific wrong-way risk*, the result of exposure to a particular counterparty, which positively correlates with the counterparty's probability of default (PD).

Real-time access to databases, experimentation, simulation, and the use of knowledge engineering artifacts are valuable tools for wrong-way risk studies. The same statement is valid about the calibration of stress probability of default (SPD) and stress loss given default (SLGD).

The challenge of computing unexpected losses (UL) is a key reason why the requirements for internal loss given default (LGD) calculation in the A-IRB method of Basel II had to be rewritten. Theoretically, but only theoretically, the LGD parameter can be seen as an average, default-weighted, loss ratio – which is taken as not being associated to a particular economic scenario. Practically, this is not the case. As far as the LGD parameter is concerned, the down scenario must be included in estimates. Therefore, it has to be entered into the UL risk-weight function. Along this frame of reference, regulators essentially promote three LGDs:

- *Mean LGD*, taken at lower level
- *Downturn LGD*, taken at crisis time, and
- *Expected LGD*, which accounts for the current economic environment.

The downturn LGD can be calculated from LGDs in time periods characterized by large credit losses. Mean LGD and downturn LGD might be identical in the case of credit exposures where the LGD is independent of cyclical movements. The careful reader will appreciate that these notions open up a huge perspective for experimentation involving all material positions in the loans portfolio (see also section 4).

With Basel II, downturn LGD is applied to non-defaulted loans, both when determining UL and when determining expected losses (EL). This is a simplification which permits banks to use only a single estimated value of LGD to determine the regulatory capital requirements, calculated for each individual category of:

- Assets, and
- Collateral.

Similar notions also apply to probability of default in market downturns or if systemic risk becomes significant, owing to adverse economic or other conditions. This concept leads to SPD, by converting the input probability of default into a stress PD applying an appropriately adjusted UL risk-weight function. The latter would be prescribed by supervisors.

8. The new rules of governance require a paradigm shift

Paradigm shifts exist in all walks of life and of business, not just in technology and in banking. Take as an example Michelin's *active wheel* which is fitted to the front of the vehicle and has an integrated active suspension system, disc brake, and permanent magnet motor. The engine looks futuristic but experts say that it is:

- Only three car 'generations' away, and
- Well within the period covered by the industry's most forward-thinking designers and engineers.[5]

In automotive engineering, the active wheel is a huge paradigm shift from the well-known pneumatic tyre, which has been around for almost as long as the motor car itself. The concept underpinning the classical type has survived even if during that time new knowledge, materials, and industry demands have dramatically changed its characteristics and performance.

The radically new design of an integrated development of tyre and wheel challenges convention with a technology that has the potential to re-write the rules of traction, stability, and comfort. It's puncture-proof, too, says Roger Bishop, editor of *European Automotive Design*. Both designers and users of motor vehicles should take notice.

Among the interesting innovations of the active wheel is the fact that there are no mechanical connections to the energy source, allowing development engineers to remove a number of components including the clutch, gearbox, transmission, anti-roll bar and shock absorbers – which have been standards in auto design. According to Michelin, vehicles fitted with this technology will be able to maintain a stable chassis while turning, because body and wheel angles can adopt motorcycle geometries.

Let's now carry this concept of a paradigm shift into financial analysis. An evident example is the calculation of a company's *distance to default* by proxy. The distance to default point represents the number of asset value standard deviations away from default point (DP). This distance is calculated using option pricing theory, to solve for:

- Unobservable market value of assets, with capitalization as proxy
- Volatility from observable capitalization, and
- Leverage data relative to the firm, and its ballooning liabilities.

Most evidently, the probability of default is related to the firm's indebtedness measured by the *equity to debt* ratio. The default point is the point at which the bank's value is precisely equal to the value of its liabilities. This practically means its equity is zero (see also section 5). The algorithm with which the reader is already familiar, is:

$$\frac{A}{L} = \frac{Capitalization}{Liabilities} = 1$$

If $\frac{A}{L} < 1$, *then* the company is insolvent.

The use of capitalization as proxy in calculating default is a new departure, but at the same time it is part of the old discipline of challenging the obvious. Another paradigm shift in finance is the ongoing trend towards abandoning the 1-year time perspective and generating a 5-year default likelihood estimation. By tying projected, further-out credit scores directly to default probabilities, it can be possible to determine over the medium term pricing milestones:

- For underwriting, and
- For securitization reasons.

The need for a further-out credit outlook for enterprises is evidenced by the fact that while consumer-lending has experienced significant transformation over the past 10 years, middle market lending is still a largely subjective process, one that concentrates on the short term.

The point is that the use of short timeframes for multi-year commitments is no longer admissible at a time of deregulation, globalization, and increasing number and size of risks, some of which may be latent but turn around and hit the creditor some years later. Their unearthing requires the paradigm shift of which we spoke earlier in this section.

Look again at Michelin's active wheel as an example that can provide guidance on how to steer away from old concepts. The new design replaces the tyre and wheel with a composite reinforced tread band, connected to a wheel that is both flexible and deformable through rectangular polyurethane spokes. This structure has the weight-carrying ability, shock absorption, ride comfort and rolling resistance characteristics of a pneumatic tyre. It also features suspension-like properties that are said to greatly improve handling. That is the sort of composite measure that can help to significantly improve upon the current ways and means to which we have become accustomed, but which may well be obsolete.

As far as Basel II is concerned, the *use test* may be a catalyst in the direction I am suggesting. The April 2005 consultative document to which reference was made in section 7 has this to say on use tests: the distribution of exposures generated by the internal model for computation of effective expected positive exposure (EPE) must be closely integrated into the day-to-day counterparty credit risk (CCR) management. The bank could use:

- Peak exposure from the distributions for counterparty credit limits, or
- Expected positive exposure for its internal model for capital allocation.

The internal model's output should play an essential role in credit approval, as well as credit risk management, and corporate governance at large. Notice that use tests have a double meaning. On the one hand, is that results provided by the implementation of Basel II rules and models should be used in decision-making. On the other, is senior management's participation in implementation of Basel II, including analysis of obtained results. This, too, is a paradigm shift as far as top executives are concerned.

Notes

1 Nancy Cartwright, *How the Laws of Physics Lie,* Oxford University Press, Oxford, 1983.
2 D.N. Chorafas, *Rocket Scientists in Banking*, Lafferty Publications, London and Dublin, 1995.
3 D.N. Chorafas, *The Real-Time Enterprise*, Auerbach, New York, 2005.
4 Basel Committee, 'The Application of Basel II to Trading Activities and the Treatment of Double Default Effects', a Consultative Document, BIS, Basel, April 2005.
5 *European Automotive Design*, February 2005.

Internal Control, Stress Testing, and Effective Risk Management

1. Introduction

The design of an internal control system starts with a definition of goals: What exactly are we after in terms of good governance? At which level of transparency do we want the internal control system to operate? How capillary should it be? What do we wish to accomplish? At what level of timeliness and dependability? The next step includes identification of the sources of information that should contribute to internal control. This should be followed by:

- Evaluation of current internal control policies and practices, and
- An examination of the reliability of the existing internal control system.

For internal control to work correctly, it is important that there is no covering-up of problems by 'this' or 'that' manager, at any level of the organization. IFRS contributes a great deal to the mechanics part of internal control by promoting transparency and by bringing fair value into perspective. But top management must also play its part by:

- Assuring the dynamics of the financial reporting system, and
- Seeing to it that the organization's arteries are not clogged through opacity, indifference, inability, or conflicts of interest.

Internal control works well only when decisions, actions, and results obtained by all managers, at every business unit, are characterized by openness, objectivity, and transparency in appraising their own performance and that of others. Everything counted, this is the simple, most valuable index of management's strength.

Take risk management as an example. No effective risk evaluation process can take place without identification of all relevant sources of risk information, and of their accuracy. The preliminary work includes the definition of risk sources, followed by risk limits, risk models and rules associated to credit, market, and operational information. Another 'must' is the examination of facilities used to:

- Perform risk analysis, and
- Exercise control over the entire organization.

Enterprise-wide risk management brings to the foreground the need for a conceptual framework based on sound management practices and rigorous internal control principles.[1] To avoid a fragmented approach, the design of a consolidated internal control framework must ensure that it is:

- Global in nature
- Integrating all units which organizationally or geographically may be separate
- Filtering large volumes of data with internal control objectives in mind, and
- Assuring real-time processing as well as comprehensive reporting at all management levels.

For instance, in connection to risk management, the accurate computation of exposure requires access to a wide range of databases located throughout the organization and its business units. Among other locations, information will be needed in transaction logs, legal contracts, market data feeds, trading systems, pricing models, the corporate memory facility (CMF, see Chapter 9), and back-office records.

Along with the ability to capture, integrate, filter, and report internal control information, a main challenge in an enterprise solution is that operational data provided by different units, and systems, is often rich in detail but narrow in scope. Most organizations find themselves with isolated islands of information, which may or may not have bridges to one another. Business activities are frequently supported by:

- Applications running on different hardware platforms and operating systems
- Information coming from many levels within the institution, often in inconsistent physical forms
- Widely spread files and databases which usually have heterogeneous record and data structures.

As we saw in Chapter 15, real-time update and reporting is another challenge. The volume of updates that will be generated depends on risk events being targeted; when and how these are created by different trades; number of risk factors to be handled; internal structure of the institution (desk, department, business unit); number and form of limits being updated (trading book, banking book, counterparty, country, type of trade); time-handling of required procedures, and so on.

A single trade may generate multiple updates, and each time an inventoried position is modified or priced, most or all of these updates have to be recomputed and reapplied. They also have to be tested and this leads straight into issues connected to testing policies: normal or stress testing followed for risk management purposes. As we will see in this chapter, *stress testing* has become an integral and important part of corporate governance.

2. Enterprise risk and style of management

A primitive-type organization and rudimentary internal controls correlate both between themselves and with substandard accounting procedures. In turn, a fragmented type of accounting, which lacks detail, does not permit pushing profit and loss responsibility down to the smallest operating unit – or the capture of the information necessary for exercising rigorous internal control.

When, in the mid-1950s, Harold Geneen became the executive vice-president of Raytheon, he felt the urgency of putting a network of financial controllers in place. Characteristically, as with DuPont and General Motors, divisional and plant controllers were directed to report straight to the corporate controller, not to the manager of plant or division. Organization-wise, they were connected to the business unit's manager only through a dotted line.

This type of organization runs contrary to embedded interests. Therefore, it needs both a strong will and time to be put in place. Even for a forceful personality like Geneen, who knew exactly what he wanted and how to do it, it took a year and a half to entrench his controls. Then he put forward his return on equity (ROE) objective. The basic goal of the company, he announced, was to get an average 3% profit net of sales.

- With a 3-times turnover this meant 9% return on assets (ROA), and
- Since Raytheon borrowed about half its capital, it represented roughly 18% return on equity after taxes.

To reach his goal Harold Geneen set ratios which, in Raytheon, become a sort of business religion. This was in line with his enterprise motif that *isolated facts meant nothing.*[2] The ratios were carefully selected and structured hierarchically, on the premise that:

- Fifty ratios all presented as being of about equal significance mean nothing,
- They are, practically, 50 numbers of equal *non-value* for running a business enterprise.

At Geneen's Raytheon, which was an engineering company *par excellence*, all three top ratios were related to sales: sales divided by gross plant; sales divided by gross inventory balance; sales divided by accounts receivable balance. All other ratios created a catchment area to feed information into these three.

Another major innovation in management reporting and in exercising internal control, has been the *commentary*, which became the alter ego of facts and figures.

It has been Geneen's belief that 'numbers only' is an approach that does not really provide any insight, therefore being of little value to corporate governance. There is most definitely a need for:

- Explanatory, and
- Analytical comments.

The principle is that no accounting figure being presented to management should be bare-bone; all must be enriched by an interpretation. Notice that a similar principle applies with risk exposure. Value at risk (VAR) cannot be effectively managed just by noting that today it is a 'little higher' than yesterday. The key questions to ask about this figure are Cicero's: *what, why, who* (or by whom), *when, where* and *how*?

- Figures alone don't speak for themselves
- Interpretive comments contribute to clarity, and to understanding.

Additionally, interpretations must provide proof that managers and professionals submitting a report understand the figures' meaning. Such understanding is vital, because without it no corrective action makes sense. At the same time, failure to properly manage and control the risks incurred in daily business would result in damage to the bank's reputation. For this reason,

- Operating limits allocated among business lines must be set to quantify acceptable exposure, and to control their risk appetites, and
- Ways and means must be in place to gauge risk and return relative to each business line, bringing this information immediately to senior management's attention.

This is doable *if* the entity's internal control system keeps a close watch on limits with the aim of protecting the company from unacceptable damage to its assets, its annual earnings capacity, its dividend-paying ability, and, ultimately, its business activities. An entity's ongoing viability is based on these fundamental principles of:

- Cost control, and
- Risk control.

A prerequisite to effective enterprise-wide governance is comprehensive, transparent and objective reporting and disclosure. In this sense, risk control is an integral part of commitment to providing consistent, high quality returns for all stakeholders. Tests are necessary to make the mass of data confess the exposure which has been assumed, alert management to situations requiring immediate correction, and distinguish between what counts and what is not material to the enterprise.

3. Stress testing cost and risk and return

Effective corporate governance depends on achieving an appropriate balance between cost and risk and return, both in day-to-day business and in strategic management. For this reason, cost control and risk control strategies should seek to limit the scope for adverse variations in earnings, as well as negative B/S impact. To a considerable extent, adverse variations can be effectively judged through *stress scenarios* arising from costs and material risks being assumed.[3]

Simple linear models help only up to a point in *cost reduction* and *risk identification*. Stress tests provide more rigorous responses, particularly in relatively new business lines and in complex or unusual transactions; also, in response to external events that affect a vital business activity, such as the continuous monitoring of *our* portfolio, and evaluation of each transaction's P&L. Stress tests should be:

- Administered consistently, and
- Cover all risk categories and their detail.

The frequency of their implementation must be increased after a significant market change, budget overrun, or growth in exposure. But what is really meant by a stress test? The most straight-forward answer comes from engineering: putting a man-made product or system under stress conditions. Usually, though not always, the aim is to make inference about a product's or system's behaviour in a compressed timeframe.

Take quality of incandescent lamps for the consumer market as an example. Such lamps are supposed to work for an average of 1000 hours under 240 volts. Curves relate voltage to useful life, and by testing the lamps under 360 volts it is possible to estimate the statistical distribution of a manufactured lot in a much shorter time, since lamps get used faster under higher voltage. This is *destructive stress testing*.

By contrast, in finance we use *statistical stress testing*. An example is provided by looking at Figure 16.1, which shows a normal distribution curve with a long leg and a spike. Within two standard deviations, s, each side of the mean, x, lies the 95% of the area under the curve. This rises to 99.99% within four standard deviations either side of the mean. At that 99.99% level, it looks *as if* practically

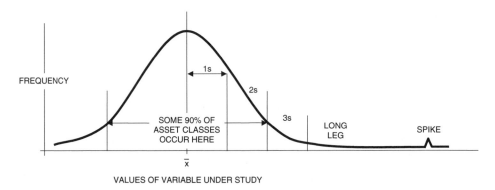

Figure 16.1   The normal distribution curve is an approximation: future events whose impact we study may well be outliers

every event has been covered. But it is not so. The reason is not only that the normal distribution is an idealized case; it is also that statistics depend on past information – while present and future events that we want to study may fall outside these limits as the nature of the distribution evolves.

The effort of trying to capture *now* the after-effect of likely but not so probable future events is served through a method similar to that of testing incandescent lamps. Such events may lie at the long leg of a distribution, and this is investigated through a *stress test* at 5, 10 or 15 standard deviations, depending on what we are after.

Putting assumed exposure in the trading book and banking book under stress conditions provides a certain assurance that future risks involved in transactions can be studied beforehand in terms of their after-effect. This also helps in the sense that some of their characteristics become transparent and subject to appropriate risk evaluation. For this reason:

- Stress loss measures should be most extensively implemented for trading activities, including credit risk, market risk, legal risk, country risk, and other exposures.
- Default stress testing, too, is very important not only for the loan portfolio, with particular emphasis on lower-rated borrowers, but also for investments and derivatives trades.

A *stress loss* framework is a dynamic process which must be continually enhanced and progressively extended to all classes of risk categories. The identification and quantification of risk under stress conditions has become a vital and integral part of a properly tuned internal control, as the introduction has explained.

While sensitivity to risks being assumed is an important, never-ending business, equally critical is the ability to effectively communicate to all levels of management the results of risk tests, so that corrective action can be taken without delay. Delays increase the pain and cost of corrective processes, while at the same time they diminish their effect. A similar statement is valid in regard to cost control measures.

In the general case, whether the theme of analysis is cost control or risk management, an effective communication of stress testing results must be made in a comprehensive manner. This should account for company culture and management style. Key to well-designed management style approaches is the ability to:

- Follow the way executives make decisions, and
- Frame the reported risk in a way that works in synergy with these decisions.

Moreover, valuation models must be used to identify strong and weak positions, accounting for the fact that financial markets are *discounting mechanisms*. This should make us sceptical in regard to the often-made assumption that 'the future will replicate the past'. Except (sometimes) in the very long run, this never really happens.

Because the future holds surprises, managerial and professionals must appreciate the importance of *experimentation* and *simulation*, including the steady development of better methods and sharper tools to avoid the impact of standards fatigue (see section 4). Just as important is a system design that permits the company's internal control system to work both vertically and horizontally – vertically by digging up greater detail, which reveals the hidden side of exposure; horizontally by addressing the risk assumed by:

- Any instrument
- With any counterparty
- By any officer or trader
- In any business units
- In every country of operation, and
- At every time of day or night

The rationale of experimentation, and the way to go about it, has been explained in Chapter 15. Supported through analytics, the enterprise management system must not only reflect on each and every exposure, and on the synergy which exists between them, but also correlate the level of exposure to market liquidity, market volatility, and *our* bank's financial staying power. As an example, Figure 16.2 presents a frame of reference for senior management reporting.

Taking the banking industry as an example, the complexity of this job is increased by the steady innovation characterizing financial instruments. As a result, the entirety of the enterprise risk management problem cannot be analysed, and cannot be accurately modelled, by using only the currently available artifacts. We need methods and metrics able to identify differences between models like VAR required by regulators, and an holistic solution which is future-oriented.

- Determining *our* bank's current exposure is reasonably straightforward.
- Determining *our* bank's potential exposure is much more complex, and it cannot be done without stress tests.

Not only do we need to anticipate which risks might increase beyond prudential limits but we also should consider which new ones enter into the risk and return equation. Once these exposures and their potential magnitude have been identified,

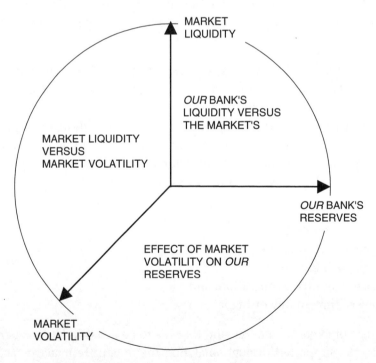

Figure 16.2   Liquidity, volatility, and financial staying power

the next move is to determine the type of information necessary to track them, and keep them in control. Steady vigilance, timeliness, and accuracy are at a premium. In the case of the highly leveraged portfolio of Orange County, for example, prior to the December 1994 meltdown of its treasury most of the repo desks at investment banks which acted as counterparties had not even been calculating daily price change of the collateral. Instead,

- They were marking to market this collateral once per month
- But while doing so they did not know the value of structured notes they sold and neither did they appreciate their counterparty's ability to withstand market stress.

Never believe theoreticians who say that hedging creates a risk-free portfolio. What silly statements like that don't bring into perspective is that even the more perfect hedge can be invalidated because of market changes. As the price of the hedged commodity fluctuates, the investor must alter the composition of his or her portfolio, or be subject to an inordinate amount of risk.

For this reason, only steady vigilance involving alert risk management policies and procedures, which are supported by high technology, can ensure that *our* institution has under control the risks which it is assuming. Let me add that while it is evident that this cannot be done through manual methods, mathematical models and computers will not automatically provide the needed rigorous solution. Snapshots are most often rushes to judgment for which senior management feel guilty later on. Rigorous analytical processes are best supported through long-term stress testing.

4. Stress testing and standards fatigue

One of the fundamental forces propelling stress testing is that previous control methods have been subject to *standards fatigue*. This term means they are no more effective because they have been left behind by innovation in industry sectors, all the way from financial instruments to technological products. To help appreciate this point, let's take as an example:

- Internal control standards, and
- The system of limits in the banking industry.

Readers will recall from previous discussions that the basic role of internal control is to provide management with clear feedback signals about what is going both right *and* wrong within the enterprise.[4] Up to a point, but only up to a point, internal control and auditing procedures overlap, but in the general case they cannot be confused with one another, even if only for the reason that:

- Internal control is steady and holistic
- While auditing digs deep, is intermittent, and often proceeds by sampling inspection.

One of the prudential standards often used in internal control is the system of limits. Some banks, however, have, unwisely, substituted limits by value at risk (VAR), which is absurd. Leaving aside that VAR is an incomplete and obsolete standard,[5] its use for VAR has been established by the regulators for a sort of order of magnitude reporting on *exposure*.

By contrast, internal controls and the system of limits are put in place by the institution. The system of limits is not intended to reduce risk in an abstract or order of magnitude sense. Its goal is the steady and dependable:

- Measurement and
- Pricing of risk.

In a similar manner, the real objective of risk management standards is neither to eliminate failures of individual banks nor to abolish the process of creative destruction that provides the market with its dynamism. Risk measurement *and* risk-based pricing are important prudential standards which must continue to evolve in order to bite. Beyond this,

- They are not intended to replace individual responsibility, and
- Their purpose is to contribute what it takes to enhance it.

Within this frame of reference, IFRS must be seen as an accounting standards renewal which helps both risk management and risk-based pricing. Guidelines related to risk management and capital adequacy do not mean much in the absence of sound accounting conventions (see Part 1), dependable valuation of assets (see Chapter 10), robust auditing practices (see Chapter 17), and a timely, focused system of internal controls. Precisely for these reasons:

- Stress testing is an integral part of the system of rigorous management controls, and
- Increasingly more powerful and more scientific stress tests must match the rate of innovation, to avoid severe financial crises.

Globalization increases the need for stress tests. Efforts aimed at improving financial stability are more likely to be effective if they can test a priori the aftermath of market forces, harness the prudential instincts of serious market players, and promote a code of market practices by providing benchmarks on which practitioners can depend.

Not only in banking but throughout industry, financial innovation means that attaining the objective of sound governance requires a steady evolution of methods and standards. Precisely for this reason, tools, methods, and standards for risk control are no longer as simple as they used to be. The complexity of the financial system makes a simplified approach lightweight, a reason why risk management must:

- Take account of multiple specific requirements, and
- Aim to avoid standards fatigue by means of steady evolution.

Such evolution should be cultural, conceptual, and pragmatic – and this is what stress testing is all about. Properly executed stress tests can be instrumental in convincing economic agents that they will not be protected from the consequences of adverse outcomes because:

- 'This' or 'that' exposure has outgrown its original limits
- While credit risk is on the increase, many banks bend their credit standards and do not respect them, or
- Too many derivatives contracts have turned sour, pulling hedge funds down with them (see Chapter 1).

The many aspects of the financial infrastructure must work in unison to provide the input necessary for effective risk control. Accounting conventions, auditing standards, and reliable financial reporting are not discrete islands but part of the same system.[6] They are internal prerequisites to sound governance, while other prerequisites are external.

Another internal prerequisite is the development of more sophisticated tools and methods. This is often handicapped because of *algorithmic insufficiency*. The term means that the algorithmic approaches we are currently using are no longer able to serve risk management problems of the magnitude with which we are confronted today. (This evidently applies also to the VAR model.) Much more powerful methods and tools are necessary:

- Experimental design helps in investigating contemplated solutions, and
- Stress testing makes feasible the hunt for outliers.

The management of risk connected to derivatives is an example where algorithmic insufficiency has made itself felt. Theoretically, derivative financial products are used by banks and other institutions to limit risk concentrations in their portfolios. Practically, indeed most often, they reach the opposite result leading to concentration of exposure. Only the best governed entities appreciate that one of the major problems with innovative financial instruments is that they have not been fully tested under adverse circumstances.

Stress tests for liquidity provide an example. Usually contracted over the counter, derivatives are instruments having questionable liquidity under virtually all circumstances. This runs contrary to the principle that capital markets need liquidity for timely settlement of their obligations. Hence, the need for steady stress testing liquidity positions.[7]

- Estimates of value at risk based on historical price volatility are not a good guide to potential losses under nervous markets, and
- Liquidity in the underlying markets can dry up unexpectedly, leaving economic agents more exposed than they expected to be on the basis of estimates by classical models.

Therefore, it is no surprise that well-managed institutions look at stress testing as a way to overcome these limitations. Testing the long leg of risk distributions plays an important role in identifying potential vulnerabilities and in supporting senior management's efforts to deal with them. Survival requires spotting gaps in the institution's financial staying power ahead of the curve. This is one more reason why stress testing should be an integral part of enterprise risk management.

5. Stress testing is a holistic methodology

Sections 3 and 4 should not have left a doubt in the reader's mind that every credit institution, and every other entity with major financial stakes, must have in place rigorous stress testing policies, procedures, and processes. These should be used in an able manner for the assessment of risk, as well as of capital adequacy. As part of its stress testing programme, a bank:

- Must measure its solvency target over the life of all trades, loans, and investments in its portfolio, and
- Compare results against the measure of limits to exposure set by the board, and by regulators under Pillar 2 of Basel II.

Here is the viewpoint of the Bank for International Settlements (BIS), expressed in its 75th Annual Report (2004–2005): 'Mirroring the development of stress testing methodology at the level of individual firms, many central banks are now developing the infrastructure to perform robustness tests of the financial sector as a whole, relying on both micro and macro indicators. Such exercises often combine three elements:

- Macroeconomic models, built to guide monetary policy decisions,
- Models of the financial condition of households and the business sector, and
- Surveys of the potential impact of different scenarios on the performance of financial institutions and markets.'

BIS points out that in some jurisdictions, this infrastructure is used not only to carry out routine assessments of financial sector vulnerabilities for prudential reasons, but also to provide input into decisions concerning monetary policy. Once in place, stress testing technology lends itself to ad hoc exercises that are more focused on the analysis of specific risks; for instance, risk arising from abrupt decline in asset prices.

Adding to this important reference to polyvalent use of stress test methodology, an article by Olivie Mahul, of the World Bank, published by the Geneva Association, emphasized the contribution stress tests provide in agricultural risk assessment.[8] *Catastrophe modelling*, Mahul says, is an evolving science which assists policy-makers and other stakeholders in managing the risk from natural disasters.

The problem is that existing models, however, mainly focus on the impact of rapid onset disasters such as earthquakes, floods and hurricanes. While such emphasis is important, it is not sufficient; for instance, the assessment paradigm must also be used in connection to slow onset disasters like drought. The catastrophe risk model Mahul built has four modules:

- A *hazard module*, defining the frequency and severity of a peril, at a specific location, based on historical events.
- An *exposure module*, which values assets at risk (like crops, and livestock), then computes the value for all types of exposures.
- A *vulnerability module*, quantifying the damage caused to each asset class by the intensity of a given risk event at a site, and
- A *damage module*, translating losses estimated in the vulnerability module into monetary loss – that is, the bottomline.

The latter module produces risk metrics like annual average loss and probable maximum loss, providing policy-makers and risk managers with essential information necessary to be in charge of their risks in future time periods.

Another noteworthy model mentioned in the same paper addresses itself to agricultural risk financing, a domain that has so far received much less attention than it deserves. This model deals with that part of risks which cannot be mitigated with cost-effective preventive measures but, to the contrary, they would be financed through:

- Farmers' self-retention
- Private financial markets, and
- Governments by means of an appropriate layering of risks.

Three layers are distinguished in this connection: top, mezzanine, and bottom. The *bottom layer of risk* includes high frequency but low impact (HF/LI) events, that affect farmers from a variety of mainly independent happenings. Losses relating to this layer are mainly caused by inappropriate management decisions, including adverse selection problems.

The *mezzanine layer of risk* includes less frequent but more severe types of exposure, affecting several farmers at the same time. Examples are hail, frost, floods, and drought. In this connection, the private insurance industry has shown its ability to cover resulting losses, but the insurers themselves may be exposed to fairly major aggregate insured losses.

In the *top layer of risk* are low frequency but high impact (LF/HI) events. These are essentially catastrophic risks that have not yet been properly studied and, even worse, have not been well documented. Yet, their probable maximum loss can be very large, and so is the corresponding insurance premium.

Farmers are usually unwilling to purchase the top layer risk insurance not only because of cost but also because they tend to underestimate their exposure to catastrophic risks. Or, alternatively, they rely on post-disaster emergency relief – which sometimes is unavailable and in other cases it comes too late. By concentrating on the higher impact of lower frequency events, stress testing can look into mezzanine and LF/HI events:

- Through scenario analysis, or
- By means of simulation.

A banking industry example of hypothetical scenarios involving stress testing by using changes in portfolio value, looks at changes that would occur at end-of-day positions given a certain level of volatility. Changes in volatility are expressed either through absolute asset values or by percentiles. Through scenarios we also model default or event risk, to achieve greater accuracy in estimates of exposure.

As an example, a simulation involving stress tests may address future changes in economic conditions that could unfavourably impact on the firm's credit exposures. Or, they may target an assessment of the bank's ability to withstand changes such as:

- Economic or industry downturns
- Severe market events, or
- Market illiquidity conditions.

A credit institution must also stress test its gross and net collateral counterparty exposure, including jointly stressing market risk and credit risk factors. Stress tests of counterparty risk should consider concentration risk to a single counterparty, or groups of counterparties, as well as correlation risk across market risk(s) and credit risk(s).

As these examples demonstrate, stress tests are becoming increasingly more sophisticated. According to the Basel Committee, banks using the double-default framework – involving the likelihood of simultaneous failure of obligor and guarantor – must consider as part of their stress testing framework the impact of a deterioration in the credit quality of protection providers. For instance,

- The impact of guarantors falling outside the eligibility criteria relating to an A-rating, and
- Consequent increase in risk and in capital requirements.

Additionally, stress tests should account for credit risk concentrations that have an adverse effect on the creditworthiness of each of the individual counterparties making up the concentration. Notice that such concentrations are not addressed in Basel II's Pillar 1 capital charge for credit risk, but they are becoming part of Pillar 2. And while credit risk concentrations may be reduced by the purchase of credit protection, banks are well advised to stress test whether the concentration remains because *wrong-way risk* is greater than that reflected in the calibration of a double default treatment.

6. Relative risk and relative capital

The estimations of expected risk and risk-based return of assets in *our* institution's portfolio, including combinations of different exposure factors, is one of the basic tasks of enterprise risk management. Therefore, the solution that we adopt for internal control reasons should be able to provide dependable information along this frame of reference. The bottomline is that what we expect from stress testing is to:

- Reveal latent and hidden exposures associated to assets and liabilities, and
- Enhance, in the longer term, *our* institution's financial staying power, in relation to risks that have been and continue being assumed.

These two points bring into our perspective the concepts of *relative risk* and *relative capital,* which are a new development in enterprise risk management and, also, in banking supervision. Changes introduced in 2005 by the Basel Committee to the rules regarding capital adequacy through Basel II, practically align *relative* capital requirements quite closely to *relative* risk. This strategy is significant for several reasons, the most important being that:

- It strengthens the soundness of financial institutions by making their capital requirements dynamic, and
- It lessens some of the distortions that have arisen under the original 1988 Capital Accord and its fixed 8% capital ratio.

Risk management should capitalize on the fact that the concepts of relative capital and relative risk, as well as of risk-based pricing, have entered financial disclosure and supervisory review. As such, they are contributing to an earlier recognition of risk-related problems by markets, banks, and supervisors, essentially leading to faster and better focused corrective action.

Because they help an institution in being ahead of the curve, stress tests have an important role in connection to a dynamic approach to capital adequacy, guided by relative values. They can be effectively used to lead to worst-case scenarios in relative risk, and they can assist in prognosticating regulatory capital requirements through time – in line with the evolution of *measured risk*. Dynamic adjustments:

- Increase the bank's staying power
- Prompt towards a more considered exposure, and
- Help in decreasing systemic risk in the financial system.

The degree to which such potential is realized depends on how closely *measured risk* tracks *underlying risk*. A high degree of accuracy is not easy to obtain through general rules, because each bank has its own characteristics. Therefore, every entity must establish its own modelling solution, though supervisory guidelines help. As Chapter 14 brought to the reader's attention, one of the options that has been applied is a regulatory approach which acts as a *built-in stabilizer*, limiting the *procyclical* nature of the financial system. Spanish commercial banks are doing so, under directives by the Spanish central bank.

An alternative to relative capital matching relative risk is to require a provision to be created whenever the interest margin on a loan does not cover the expected losses arising from possible default. This can be based on the rating of a client firm plus a careful watch on credit volatility, assisted by the rating pattern established by independent rating agencies.

- *What if* the rating of a major counterparty changed from AA to A? to BBB? to BB?
- *What if* 25% or 50% of *our* bank's counterparties in the banking book and trading book moved downwards in credit rating?
- *What if* 5%, 10%, 15% of *our* counterparties defaulted? Where will this leave *our* banking book? Our trading book?
- Which emergency measures will be necessary? What kind of leading indicators should be used? From where will come the required capital reserves to weather the storm?

These are quite legitimate queries in the framework of an enterprise risk management system.[9] The answers to be provided can be elaborated through scenario writing, and they must be most carefully thought out. While provisions might generally not be required at origination of a loan or a derivatives trade, they might become subsequently necessary if the borrower's credit quality deteriorates. This is an outcome of the dynamic nature of the market.

With this notion of synchronization between relative risk and relative capital, provisioning rules can be designed to act as the flywheel of the financial institution's survival course. Stress level can be thoroughly simulated. The drawback is that while today we have practically unlimited computing power,

- Our data sources are not well organized, and
- The information elements in our databases are often incomplete or obsolete.

Speaking from personal experience, it is highly recommended that a rigorous risk analysis *looks at data* and its adequacy, as well as whether its form can be effectively exploited. Equally important is to be able to map the longer term pattern of counterparty dependability, including its leverage and the type of risks which this relationship involves. This issue will be more closely examined in section 8, using as background detail from the virtual bankruptcy of Long Term Capital Management (LTCM).

LTCM treated money like a commodity. There is no objection to this approach, but at the same time it failed to apply adequate controls related to this commodity, its ups and downs and its risks. The information LTCM provided to its senior management on assumed risk was dismal. There was nothing like a real-time balance sheet (see Chapter 15) to provide fingertip measures of liabilities versus assets.

By assuming an inordinate amount of risk, and at the same time being totally blind to worst-case scenarios connected to future market realities, and their impact on the company's A&L, management can make all the wrong decisions. It can transform its operations into an abyss of exposure, just by doing the wrong things. While the LTCM partners had the feeling of being 'active', in reality their foremost activity was self-destruction.

- LTCM was a highly leveraged firm but its accounting was terrible.
- The management reporting structure was in shambles and the partners depended on phone calls to know what was going on in their own company.

This is indeed the best way to kill a firm, with leadership being reduced to the role played by a prima donna. Compare this to the many positive examples presented in this book on real-time information technology, and fair value accounting for all financial assets and liabilities. By marking to market and marking to model (provided the models are thoroughly tested), fair value can be evaluated intraday, and used not only in risk control but also in solving another current problem: the difficulty in forecasting *distant events*.

Provided a company is creditworthy and far-sighted, the use of longer horizons is most appropriate to raise capital, restructure the balance sheet, and take proactive risk management measures. This is another reason why in quantifying and qualifying credit risk and market risk through fair value, an institution is able to position itself against market forces, using objective capital requirements associated with each risk class, and including projected frequency and likely impact of each risk event.

7. Synergy between fair value accounting and risk management

Accounting systems and their standards are no ends in themselves. They are means whose function is reliable presentation of financial data. This is aiding our understanding of the many different aspects of business operations, at the level of each individual business unit and of the company as a whole.

Technology has facilitated the production of accounting information, and its presentation at a faster pace than at any time in the past; but in the large majority of cases the contribution of technology has been kept at a 'discrete islands' level. There is no holistic enterprise view. Only tier-1 institutions have seen to it that:

- Technology provides the necessary enterprise-wide passthrough, and
- Enables accounting, auditing, internal control, and risk management to work in synergy.

Companies that pioneered the synergy to which I refer did so because they appreciate that successful implementation of enterprise-wide solutions is inseparable from the able usage of a streamlined accounting system. The synergy between internal control, risk management, auditing, and accounting can be appreciated from different perspectives:

- Fair value accounting makes realistic measurements, and thereby aids a process of improved management supervision.
- Fair value is steadily used as raw material for internal control communications, conveying business facts to senior management, and
- In a broader sense, accounting provides the tool for planning and controlling the distribution of the fruits of enterprise, while targeting preservation of assets.

All three bullet points converge towards the fact that the contribution of enterprise risk management to the success of the institution lies in the making of intelligent measurements of the financial significance of events occurring in the conduct of business. Then comes the study, analysis and interpretation of these measurements, as well as their utilization in the exercise of informed judgments.

Real-time solutions of which we spoke in Chapter 15 are not just the better way, they are the only way to solve ongoing problems and reach factual decisions. As an example, Figure 16.3 presents the building blocks of a risk management procedure for foreign exchange operations established in the early 1990s at Bankers Trust. This solution integrates the different trading modules in existence into a comprehensive risk and return presentation. Among other issues, these modules, and models going with them, address:

- Market liquidity
- Market volatility

- Credit ratings for counterparty risk
- Risk embedded in inventorying multi-currency securities
- Risk associated to derivative instruments, and
- Pricing mechanisms in conjunction to exposure.

Each measurement that leads to a management decision to change a course of action in the interest of more effective risk control contributes to overall performance and therefore to profitability. The collective weight of all such decisions which can be found at the junction of risk management and fair value accounting is a prominent factor in good governance.

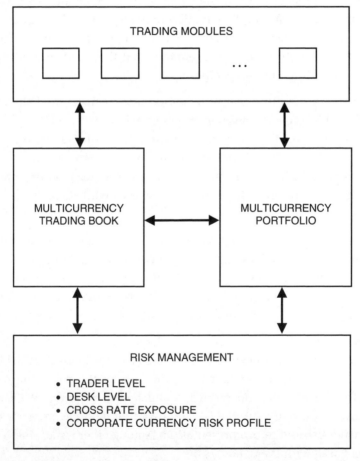

Figure 16.3 Risk and return in foreign exchange should be computed at any time, in any currency, for any counterparty

To a considerable extent, the secret of achieving the best possible balance in the exploitation of business opportunity lies in the assumptions we make about risk, and in the limits which we establish. In many cases, the observance of limits is a matter of positive and negative incentives.

Commissions paid to traders and other professionals play the positive incentives role but they frequently become perverted because they push towards assuming greater levels of risk. Commissions have a role to play in motivation, but economic rewards must be related not to one but to two factors:

- Individual effort and personal initiative
- Risk control, not only at present but also in the future, throughout the instrument's lifecycle.

Compensation irrespective of achievement is deadly because output is bound to fall to the level of the poorest workman. Professionals must have the promise and prospect of commensurate returns as an inducement to show initiative, but the preservation of assets must always be topmost in the list of goals. Fair value added accounting provides the information to meet both objectives which, at first sight, might look contradictory.

Risk management, too, must have a reward for its capacity of successfully keeping exposure under control. This also should happen in proportion to achievement. Additionally, the meeting of aforementioned challenges requires both *forward* and *post-mortem* thinking, a dual approach which finds itself at the junction between accounting and risk management. There is a new term identifying the ability to look back into past management decisions and commitments:

- The term is *traceability*, and
- The initiative in this direction has been taken by leading organizations.

Knowledge management projects assist in obtaining traceability. Their tools include expert systems, agents, and corporate memory facility (CMF), into which are registered all decisions, as well as their reasons and aftermath. We have spoken of the importance of CMF in Chapter 9. Expert systems[10] and agents[11] must be specifically designed for risk control, because such artifacts have provided commendable results. Precisely for this reason, top-tier companies are working to steadily improve them. By contrast, companies destined to fail are doing just the opposite.

8. Learning a lesson from the bankruptcy of the Rolls-Royce of hedge funds

Economic historians who, 50 years hence, write about events of our times will probably say that the 1997 crisis in East Asia was the first of many bubbles that burst in the second half of the decade of the 1990s, with the IMF running to the rescue with ready cash. By contrast, the salvage of Long Term Capital Management (LTCM) in September/October 1998 was undertaken by the Federal Reserve of New York, through brokerage, using the hedge fund's stakeholders as lenders of last resort.

Like any other company, hedge funds fail, and the way to bet is that the more leveraged they are the greater is the likelihood they will lead themselves to bankruptcy. Chapter 1 has presented several examples of hedge fund failures in 2005, but the best of all still remains LTCM which, in its time, was known as the Rolls-Royce of hedge funds.

Central banks do not have to do hedge fund bailouts, because these are not regulated entities. All bailouts are signs that lenders want their money back even if they have to put up more capital. When the payout is done with taxpayers' money it poses two main problems:

- The moral hazard as a forerunner to other rescues, and
- The fact that those who made the mess walk away with their capital intact, or nearly so.

As billion dollar losses multiply, the banking system is discovering that it cannot maintain its current level of loan-making activity to the hedge funds and to corrupt or inefficient sovereigns. Knowledgeable people on Wall Street have also been worried about a longer-term aftermath. In 1998, the magnitude of LTCM's exposure and its underline high leverage were seen as the reason why the New York Fed had no choice but to organize the rescue of the hedge fund, as Dr Alan Greenspan made clear in his testimony to Congress:

- *If* the fund went bust, and its positions were liquidated in a firesale
- *Then* the panic would have turned the banks' trading bets into a nightmare.

Since derivatives and other leveraged instruments are revalued daily through value-at-risk, the banks can become technically insolvent rather quickly. Moreover, the very sharp fall of LTCM's capital increased the risk that lenders might seize its assets, even if these were insufficient to meet its obligations.

The salvage operation the Fed put together took a leaf out of J.P. Morgan's book. In 1907 the great financier had gathered fellow bankers at his office at 23 Wall Street to stem the stock market panic. There was, however, a difference. The 1907 market panic was public news, while as a result of the secrecy associated to hedge funds, as the news of LTCM's troubles spread,

- Most banks assumed that other hedge funds, too, held huge loss-making positions that might have to be unwound, and
- The market's nervousness was made worse by rumours that several investment banks, too, were on the verge of going bust.

In fact, some analysts pointed out that the September 1998 collapse in the dollar/yen exchange rate was probably due to forced liquidation of positions. This was done by both banks and hedge funds because they had borrowed in yen (where interest rates were rock bottom) and invested the proceeds in dollars. To avoid this rush, the consortium put together by the Fed gave itself three years to unwind the LTCM portfolio. The target was an orderly liquidation on the hypothesis that:

- Volatility would subside and global markets would recover sufficiently during the 3-year time frame
- While interest rates would move in the consortium's favour, allowing it to cut its losses and even make a profit.

Correctly, nobody hoped that it would be possible to change things appreciably in the short term, as dealers were sitting on large inventories of securities acquired from LTCM and they, too, liked to unload. That made it harder to sell many of the securities that LTCM held, particularly so at a time when financial institutions were shrinking their balance sheets and reducing risk capital.

- Less risk capital means fewer purchases of financial assets, and
- The result is that, for some time, highly leveraged assets are no longer in favour.

Also negative has been the fact that commercial and investment banks in the consortium that provided the salvage money were betting on the same hypotheses LTCM had done and went wrong – for instance, on the assumption volatility would subside and yields on junk bonds would converge with US Treasuries.

Only the best-managed institutions who make up their own mind and don't follow the crowd of speculators have a chance of avoiding LTCM's blunders.

Because of arrogance, lack of coordination, poor foresight, and absence of an enterprise risk management system, practically everything had gone wrong at the 'Rolls-Royce of hedge funds', starting with the way the fund was run.

The CEO and his partners were unable to appreciate that a nervous market will flee from risky investments into safe Treasuries. Yet, this happened during August 1998, a month and a half prior to LTCM's collapse. Neither did they show an understanding of the fact that, historically, risky securities plunge at once. When the blow-up approached, and risk management models flashed red, LTCM could not unwind its positions as quickly as its partners had assumed. With rising volatility, market liquidity dried up faster than LTCM's top brass had expected[12] – which is also a major management failure in foresight and in governance.

Had LTCM been pushed into bankruptcy and its net positions, first estimated at $116 billion, then at roughly $200 billion, and finally at $1.4 trillion, been liquidated, the markets would have been sucked into a maelstrom. Since the mis-calculation of interest rate trends had been one of the fund's undoings, a further rush to the safety of Treasuries would have made liquidating the LTCM positions all but impossible.

One of the lessons to be drawn from the LTCM debacle is that many people who handle money don't quite know how to calculate risk and return – or don't care to do so. Instead of sanctioning the pseudoscientists and their huge leverage of exposure, LTCM's chief executive and his associates seem to have prompted them to do more of the same.

As everybody in business should appreciate, 'doing more of the same' is the negation of *management oversight*. This is another lesson to be learned from the failure of Long-Term Capital Management. Prudence advises that the board should approve investment strategies, trading policies, portfolio objectives, and gearing initiatives which lead to diversification of risks. The board and CEO should also assure that all of these moves are consistent with the institution's:

- Financial condition
- Risk profile, and
- Risk tolerance.

It is the responsibility of the board to establish limits on aggregate trading, lever-aged loans, investment and exposure amounts, defining the types of permissible investments and their tolerances. The board and CEO should moreover assure there is an adequate system of internal controls with:

- Appropriate checks and balances, and
- Clear audit trails regarding business operations.

These bullets are two of the pillars on which an enterprise's risk management should rest. The Fed has not said so explicitly, but the board, CEO, and senior management should also understand the tools and methodology being used in betting, as well as the hypotheses being made and the risk(s) these might involve. It is good to be innovative in finance, but not everything new is sound – particularly *if* it is untested, or done lightly for novelty's sake; and *if* risk management is looked at as a bother rather than as a life-saver.

Notes

1 D.N. Chorafas, *After Basel II: Assuring Compliance and Smoothing the Rough Edges*, Lafferty/VRL Publishing, London, 2005.
2 Robert J. Schoenberg, *Geneen*, Norton, New York, 1985.
3 D.N. Chorafas, *Stress Testing: Risk Management Strategies for Extreme Events*, Euromoney, London, 2003.
4 D.N. Chorafas, *Implementing and Auditing the Internal Control System*, Macmillan, London, 2001.
5 D.N. Chorafas, *Modelling the Survival of Financial and Industrial Enterprises: Advantages, Challenges, and Problems with the Internal Rating-Based (IRB) Method*, Palgrave/Macmillan, London, 2002.
6 D.N. Chorafas, *Reliable Financial Reporting and Internal Control: A Global Implementation Guide*, John Wiley, New York, 2000.
7 D.N. Chorafas, *Economic Capital Allocation with Basel II: Cost and Benefit Analysis*, Butterworth-Heinemann, London and Boston, 2004.
8 *Insurance Economics*, No. 52, July 2005.
9 D.N. Chorafas, *After Basel II: Assuring Compliance and Smoothing the Rough Edges*, Lafferty/VRL Publishing, London, 2005.
10 D.N. Chorafas and Heinrich Steinmann, *Expert Systems in Banking*, Macmillan, London, 1991.
11 D.N. Chorafas, *Agent Technology Handbook*, McGraw-Hill, New York, 1998.
12 D.N. Chorafas, *Understanding Volatility and Liquidity in Financial Markets*, Euromoney Books, London, 1998.

The Role of the Audit Committee

1. Introduction

In many companies, the Board of Directors has several ongoing committees: Audit, Finance, Corporate Governance, Compensation, Technology, and more recently Risk Management, being among the most common. Because of malpractice and other events regarding audit-related weaknesses in corporate governance, many of them quite serious, the Audit and Finance committees became prominent and the range of their responsibilities expanded.

A recent document by the Basel Committee on Banking Supervision had this to say about the need that board directors pay personal attention to the entity's auditing activities: 'The Committee presumes that large, internationally active banks will have an *audit committee* ... responsible for providing oversight of internal and external auditors; approving their appointment, compensation and dismissal; reviewing and approving audit scope and frequency; receiving audit reports; and assuring that management is taking appropriate corrective actions in a timely manner to address:

- Control weaknesses
- Non-compliance with policies
- Laws and regulations, and
- Other problems identified by auditors.'[1]

In principle, both the Audit and Finance committees should consist of directors who have no financial or personal ties to the company. They should also meet standards established by the New York Stock Exchange for *independence* of opinion and of decisions. In addition, at least a couple of each committee's members should have accounting and/or financial management expertise.

To perform their functions in an able manner, members of the Audit Committee should meet with the company's management periodically during the year, to consider the adequacy of internal controls (see Chapter 16), assure that objectivity of financial reporting is always observed, and examine the outcome of studies by internal auditing. Such findings should be discussed with:

- The company's independent auditors, and
- Appropriate company financial and auditing personnel

An important mission of the Audit Committee is to elaborate with the company's management and independent auditors the processes used for certification of financial statements, particularly certification made by the company's chief executive officer and chief financial officer. As will be recalled, this is required by the Securities and Exchange Commission (SEC) and the Sarbanes–Oxley Act of 2002 (see Chapter 10) in connection to the company's filings with SEC.

Another vital function of the Audit Committee is that of recommending to the Board of Directors the appointment of independent auditors for the company, or a change in current appointment. This is typically done after reviewing the performance of the certified public accountants firm, and its independence from the company's management.

Nobody, however, said that Audit Committees cannot be manipulated, at least up to a point. When this happens, it reduces to nothing its role of external financial oversight. Martin Taylor, a British businessman who sits on five boards in five different countries, recalls one American Audit Committee that used to meet after the figures that it was supposed to scrutinize had already been released.[2]

Contrary to the mission performed by the Audit Committee, the role of the Finance Committee is focused on the budget, management of assets and liabilities, evaluation of cash flow, and verification of intrinsic value of the firm. All appropriations beyond a certain threshold, as well as the budgetary process as a whole (see Chapter 9), should be under the control of this committee. The same is true of the firm's financial policy.

The Corporate Governance Committee usually has several functions, including recommending to the Board of Directors nominees for election as senior executives and independent directors of the company; making recommendations to the board as to matters of corporate governance, including management control; evaluating policy issues, and recommending changes when and where necessary.

The Sarbanes–Oxley Act of 2002 requires companies to have procedures to receive, retain, and treat complaints made by third parties regarding accounting, internal controls, or auditing matters. Also to allow for the confidential and anonymous submission by employees of concerns regarding questionable accounting or auditing issues. Depending on the problems brought to light, this may involve both the Auditing and Corporate Governance Committees.

An integral part of the functions of the Compensation Committee is that of administering management incentive compensation plans; establishing the compensation of officers; and reviewing the compensation of directors. The Corporate Governance and Compensation Committees often jointly consider qualified candidates for directors suggested by shareholders.

A major risk to good governance is that the Compensation Committee can be packed. A survey by the *New York Times* found that in 420 out of a selection of 2000 large American public corporations, the board's Compensation Committee, which determines the CEO's pay, included relatives or people with ties either to the boss or to the company. This represents more than 20% of all sampled cases and therefore it is not an exception but a trend, and a matter that should deeply concern Audit Committees.

Basel defines the role of the Risk Management Committee as being that of providing oversight of activities by senior executives in managing credit, market, liquidity, operational, legal, compliance, reputational and other risks of the institution. According to the supervisors, this role should include receiving from senior management periodic information on:

- Risk exposures, and
- Risk control activities.

The objective of the Technology Committee is to assure that in terms of the technology it uses, and the investments which it makes, the company is ahead of the curve; or, at least, at state of the art with the best technology money can buy. Long years of experience in technology have convinced me that the Audit Committee should commission audits by independent consultants on the level of technology the company uses and its effectiveness. Slippages should not be allowed to happen, because pretty soon they develop into a falling behind in technology in a big way, with a severe effect on competitiveness.

2. An Audit Committee's charter

The list of companies stunning investors with painful revelations about accounting problems, and financial statement misrepresentations, grew significantly in the go-go 1990s. Usually, though not always, the blame for such shocks falls both on internal management and on the outside accounting firms. But increasingly, another party is being accused: the Board of Directors and its Audit Committee.

The Audit Committee signs off on all earnings statements and it is supposed to protect shareholders, acting as a check on management's corporate reporting methods, and asking tough questions about the quality of accounting procedures. Critics, however, say that many Audit Committees are woefully unprepared for what is an increasingly vital task in corporate life. Investors are starting to figure this out, and they become vocal. Some are filing lawsuits, not just against the management of companies that admit to accounting irregularities, but also against their Boards of Directors and members of their Audit Committees. This means that Audit Committee members who once operated with a sense of immunity could find themselves liable for not catching the accounting misdeeds of others – and could pay dearly for it.

While, as the Introduction has stated, the personal preparation of Audit Committee members to face the challenges embedded in accounting and financial statement irregularities, and other missions, is most important, just as vital is the status and charter of the Audit Committee itself. Being composed of board directors is not enough. The Audit Committee needs an explicit status which permits it to:

- Treat accounting irregularities as a whole
- Go to the roots of each identified problem, and
- Settle a solution to this problem upon permanent foundations.

No two companies have the same charter to characterize the authority, function, and responsibility of the Audit Committee. Therefore, in this section we will look, as a practical example, at two different companies and their policies in charting Audit Committee functions. Both are very well known corporations identified, for the purpose of this discussion, as Alpha and Beta.

In defining the role of its Audit Committee, company Alpha says that it is responsible for assisting the Board of Directors in fulfilling its responsibility for oversight of the quality and integrity of the accounting, auditing, and reporting practices of the company. Also in performing such other duties as directed by the board. The committee's role includes a particular focus on:

- Qualitative aspects of financial reporting to shareholders
- The company's processes to manage business and financial risk, and
- Compliance with significant applicable legal, ethical, and regulatory requirements.

Company Alpha outlines the Audit Committee's authority as being empowered to investigate any matter brought to its attention, with full power to retain outside counsel or other experts for this purpose. Correspondingly, the committee's specific responsibilities in carrying out its role are delineated in a regularly updated checklist focusing on:

- Authoritative guidance, and
- Evolving oversight practices.

The Audit Committee, company Alpha says, relies on the expertise and knowledge of management, the internal auditors, and the independent auditor in carrying out its duties. Management of the company is responsible for determining that the financial statements are complete, accurate, and in accordance with accounting principles required by the law of the land. The independent auditor is responsible for auditing the company's financial statements.

At Company Alpha, it is not the duty of the Audit Committee to plan or conduct audits. Neither is its duty to conduct investigations, or to assure compliance with laws and regulators or the company's internal policies, procedures, and controls. Its duty is to assure that audits pertaining to the above issues are done in a timely and dependable manner, with full transparency in terms of results.

According to Company Beta, the Audit Committee reviews the process of assessing the risk of fraudulent financial reporting, as well as the quarterly reporting and annual financial statements. In so doing, its mission is to ensure that the outside auditor performs timely reviews and results are discussed with at least the Audit Committee chairman before the annual financial statement is filed.

Company Beta bylaws require that Audit Committee members examine, with both internal auditors and the external auditor, what steps are planned for a review of the company's information technology procedures and controls, including inquiries as to the specific security programs to protect against computer fraud or misuse, from both within and outside the company. Other functions are those of:

- Maintaining a calendar of agenda items which reflects the Audit Committee responsibilities and processes specified in its charter, and
- Periodically reviewing that agenda, subsequently having all proposed revisions approved by the Board of Directors.

As can be attested by this brief comparison, the Audit Committee charter, and the specific missions being assigned to it, are quite different between Company Alpha to Company Beta, both being real entities. By contrast, both organizations have fairly similar guidelines in regard to Audit Committee membership and required form of communication.

The membership of the Audit Committee consists of at least three directors who are generally knowledgeable in financial and auditing matters. Each member is free of any relationship that, in the opinion of the board, would interfere with his or her individual exercise of independent judgment. The chairman is appointed by the full board.

In terms of communications and reporting, the Audit Committee is expected to maintain free and open communications with external public accountants, internal auditors, and the company's management. Such communication includes private executive sessions, at least annually, with each of these parties. The Audit Committee reports to the Board of Directors.

Apart from the duties outlined above, which can be found in several forms and wording, there exist other missions characterizing duties of the committee to be found in some companies, but not in others. Examples are making inquiries and taking actions to assist the Board of Directors in fulfilling its fiduciary responsibilities for financial reporting and internal controls; as well as obtaining from management explanations of significant variances in annual financial statements between years.

Audit Committees often inquire of the Chief Financial Officer and his or her assistants, internal and external auditors, and other parties, about significant risks or exposures, assessing the steps management has taken to minimize overall risk to the company. With these same parties, Audit Committee members review the audit scope, plan, and its execution, to assure:

- Completeness of coverage
- Reduction of redundant efforts, and
- Effective use of audit resources.

Audit Committee members inquire about the existence and substance of any significant accounting accruals, reserves, or estimates made by management that have a material impact on financial statements; then investigate if there were any significant financial reporting issues discovered during the accounting period and if so how they were resolved. They also meet privately with the external auditor to request its opinion on various matters, including the:

- Quality of financial and accounting personnel, and
- Aptitude of experience of internal audit staff.

A growing role of the Audit Committees is to discuss with management and the external auditor the substance of any significant issues raised by in-house and outside legal counsels concerning litigation, contingencies, claims or assessments.

Closely associated to this is their review of the adequacy of the company's internal controls.

For their part, external auditors are ultimately responsible to the Board of Directors through the Audit Committee – which selects, evaluates, and replaces them as appropriate; it also reviews annual audit plans and assesses the external auditor's performance against plan. The Audit Committee must:

- Receive annually from the external auditor a formal written statement on its independence, and
- Take the necessary steps to assure such independence as well as lack of conflict(s) of interest.

In June 2000, prior to his retirement as chairman of SEC, Arthur Levitt proposed strict limits on external auditors who also do consulting work for their clients. Levitt insisted that panels of independent directors should be their investors' first line of defence against financial fraud. By putting the burden on corporate Audit Committees he made his point that responsibility for accuracy of financial statements is indivisible – it is shared by everybody.

3. Auditing and the auditor connection

Auditing started as the systematic verification of books and accounts, including vouchers and other financial or legal records, of a physical or juridical person. The lion's share in this work was in accounting, but over the past 10 years, this function of verification has been extended to cover internal control (see Chapter 16), therefore organizational and operational issues. *Auditing* and *internal control* should not be confused even if, as Figure 17.1 shows, they tend to overlap in some of the notions and functions underpinning them.

Not only is auditing classically seen under the more confined perspective of books and accounts, casting upon itself the task of in-depth examination of accounts, in the most modern approach, this activity of thorough analysis also includes internal control. By contrast, as the reader will recall from the previous chapter, internal control's purpose is that of determining integrity and compliance of all activities, including matters connected to ethics limits, and risk management.

Within the perspective discussed in the preceding paragraphs, it is most important to appreciate that auditing is no general review and survey. Its mission is to

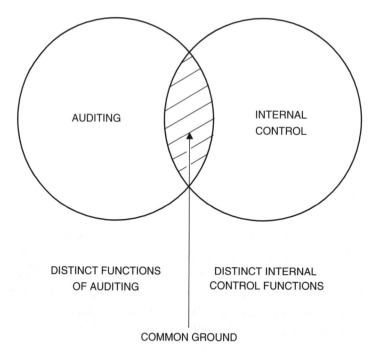

AUDITING

INTERNAL
CONTROL

DISTINCT FUNCTIONS
OF AUDITING

DISTINCT INTERNAL
CONTROL FUNCTIONS

COMMON GROUND

Figure 17.1   The concepts underpinning internal control and audit tend, up to a point, to overlap

perform a detailed analysis of every book, and of every business transaction in it. While some experts say that an audit is completely analytical, the fact remains that it consists of both:

- Analysis of accounts, and
- Interpretation of facts and figures.

Subsequent to the audit, the audited entity receives a report that contains opinion(s) and analytical figures, as well as information and reactions that cast light on the firm's accounts. These opinions may not be otherwise available, or they may not be duly appreciated at the level of the board, the chief executive officer, and his or her immediate assistants.

Put simply, the auditing process looks after presence or absence of what is 'normal' and 'expected', and its negation. Is anyone deliberately suppressing control data? Is anyone falsifying records? Are the company's financial reports dependable? Is there any disaster brewing? How much may this harm the firm?

- If the audit is *unqualified*, this means that experts involved in the process did not uncover something wrong.
- By contrast, if the audit is *qualified*, then the company's books and accounts aren't working like clockwork.

The qualification attached to the audit tells its reader what is wrong with the accounts and how bad the case may be. Once this has been stated, rigorous measures must be taken by senior management to redress the situation, redo the accounts, and punish those responsible. This is part of the process managed by the Audit Committee, whose importance has been detailed in section 2.

Precisely because auditing offers top management and the regulators the benefits of an independent review, its principles and conduct have to be beyond reproach. This is a matter of virtue. And it is also an issue of skills, since the domain in which auditing is exercised has expanded past accounting statements and financial operations into other complex ramifications of management practice, which itself has felt the impact of:

- Globalization
- Rapid product innovation
- Deregulation and reregulation, and
- The aftermath of a fast advancing technology.

Like all other professionals, auditors and their produce have to be regulated. Almost all accounting firms that audit US companies quoted in the exchanges have been subject to self-regulation by the American Institute of Certified Public Accountants (AICPA), the auditors' main professional body. AICPA has sensed that the debacle at Enron, Arthur Andersen (Enron's auditors), and other cases are likely to lead to questions about whether self-regulation is effective in:

- Upholding audit standards, and
- Preventing conflicts of interest.

Shortly after Enron's bankruptcy, the then Big Five (now Big Four) global audit firms, issued a highly unusual joint statement acknowledging that changes to the system were needed, but they also said self-regulation was 'right for investors, the profession and the financial markets'. American supervisors did not think the same way.

In the United States, the auditing profession features many more firms than the big certified public accountants (CPAs). AICPA has been monitoring the quality of audits by some 1300 firms through a programme of peer reviews every three years. It also inquires into cases in which lawsuits are filed alleging audit failure. In 1999 and 2000 peer reviews covered 441 firms and led AICPA to issue 67 instructions for action to improve deficiencies. Recommendations have included:

- Education programmes
- Continuous monitoring of firms' performance, and
- Employment of outside consultants to help in correcting outstanding auditing or procedural problems.

In the United States, this self-regulatory process is scrutinized from outside by the Public Oversight Board (POB), a five-member body set up in the late 1990s that theoretically is independent, but has been criticized as ineffective. Critics say that the POB, funded by the accounting firms, has been a weak supervisor and has hues of conflict of interest. Therefore, following the Arthur Andersen scam the government set up a new supervisory authority for accountants, under the authority of the Securities and Exchange Commission.

The first case the Public Interest Oversight Board (PIOB) – the new watchdog of the accounting and auditing profession – brought against CPAs came on 8 July 2005. This case, which has not yet been defined, concerns the Deloitte & Touche audit of Navistar accounts. (Navistar is a premier American agricultural equipment manufacturer.)

Between Enron and Navistar there have been many other cases involving the auditing connection. In December 2001, in the UK, the High Court approved an agreement for Coopers & Lybrand (now part of PriceWaterhouseCoopers) to pay £65 million (then $100 million) to KPMG, Baring's new liquidator, which represented creditors claiming a total of £200 million (then $300 million). Ernst & Young, Barings' liquidator until September 2000, had made a £1 billion ($1.42 billion) High Court claim against Coopers & Lybrand and Deloitte & Touche, the bank's auditors.

The High Court has also been hearing the remaining case against Deloitte, which audited Barings' Singapore subsidiary and, like Coopers, denied negligence. Deloitte and Coopers argued that the blame for failing to spot the fraudulent trading of Nick Leeson, a Singapore-based trader, lay with Barings' management, not with the auditor. In reality, it lay with both.

Part of the problem with CPAs when acting as external auditors is that they make more money from consulting and tax advising than from accounting and auditing – with the same client. It is a human tendency, fairly easy to explain, to weight one's interests in relation to one's income. How much each of these three functions represented as of December 2001 for the then Big Five, is shown in Table 17.1.

Because conflicts of interest have a nasty habit of growing as the business relationship between auditor and audited company gets stronger, some experts advise changing the auditor firm every few years, so that it does not have the time to grow roots at the client's site. Several companies have started doing so. An interesting case pointing to the wisdom of such a policy took place in Brazil.

In 1999, Comissao de Valores Mobiliarios (CVM), Brazil's securities commission, published a requirement that companies should change their auditors every three or four years. This ruling faced strong opposition in courts from the then Big Five accounting firms and its implementation was derailed. But there was a good reason for such a ruling, as has been revealed post mortem.

Brazil's capital markets are tiny compared with America's, but all capital markets face similar challenges, as José Luiz Osorio, Chairman Comissao de Valores Mobiliarios, stated in a letter to *Business Week*. Since the disasters from creative accounting have no frontiers, during the mid-1990s, two of the largest Brazilian banks required central bank intervention after serious accounting issues were uncovered. These had been going on for some time. On 14 May 1999, the CVM published Instruction 308, requiring that:

- Companies periodically change their auditors, and
- For any practical purpose, auditing be separated from consulting services.

The Brazilian accounting companies' union challenged CVM in the courts and, in a separate action, a major public accountant also challenged CVM in court for the same reasons. At the time Enron was still a disaster waiting to happen but,

Table 17.1 The conflict of interest in consulting vs. auditing: breakdown of gross fees as of December 2001

	Consulting (%)	Accounting and auditing (%)	Tax advising (%)
PwC	49	33	18
Deloitte & Touche	45	33	22
Ernst & Young	26	44	30
Arthur Andersen	22	46	32
KPMG	18	44	38

as we know today, that eventual debacle provided the best ever proof of the need for an arm's length relationship between CPAs.

The *creative accounting*, and therefore trickery, with Enron's financial statements is now a legend. As the statistics in Figure 17.2 show, income overstatements were not an accident but a policy executed year-after-year. Ironically, this policy of overstatements was rampant when things were going well. After that, financial reporting became more factual but it was too late to save the company and its stakeholders from the abyss.

4. The auditing of internal control

Internal control, its functions, and its importance to the organization have been discussed in Chapter 16. The message this section brings to the reader is that internal control has to be audited, and the more rigorous, factual, and documented this auditing is, the better for all stakeholders.

Webster's Dictionary defines *rigorous* as: Severe, exact, strict, scrupulous, accurate, allowing no abatement or mitigation. All these definitions apply to the auditing of internal control, and the way it should be executed. The mechanics to be adopted should facilitate the identification of failures in the analysis and communication of gaps in compliance to laws, regulations,

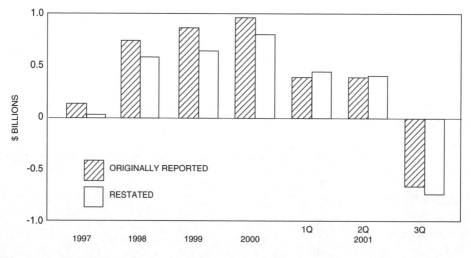

Figure 17.2   Working its way to bankruptcy, Enron made successive income overstatements

internal bylaws, as well as in connection to assumed risks from trading and non-trading activities.

Here is, as an example, how three different institutions look at the issue of internal control, and what is expected from it. At Bank Vontobel internal control focuses on limits (private and institutional); all types of derivatives trades; credit lines; risk policies (clients and correspondent banks); brokerage operations; and assets/liabilities management. A quantitative and qualitative risk analysis done by internal auditing involves 11 weighted queries:

- The highest weight has been given to internal control.
- Failures in the internal control system will alert senior management.

In the case of Bank Leu, the most important mission given to internal control is compliance. Bank Leu provided a good reason why internal control should be self-standing and should not be part of auditing. According to its policy, auditing is a supervisory meta-layer. To the contrary, internal control, risk management, treasury, lending, accounting, and other departments are concerned with day-to-day activities – which have to be regularly audited.

Lars O. Grönstedt, of Handelsbanken, suggested that at his institution credit risk and market risk are two distinct disciplines and, for practical reasons, the monitoring of these two risk classes is more efficient if they are kept in different organizations rather than integrated in the same one. However, Grönstedt added, internal control is over all business activities, providing a linkage between:

- The credit risk department, involved in setting market risk relevant limits, and
- Market risk parameters used in establishing counterparty limits.

A few of the technologically most advanced banks pressed the point that internal control can also be seen as a system supported through networks, computers and sophisticated software, which is at the service of all authorized managers and professionals in the bank. In this sense:

- Internal control is intelligence, which enables senior executives to track everything important that moves the wrong way in the organization, and
- The internal control system monitors exposure from credit risk, market risk, operational risk, settlement risk, legal risk and other risks relating to transactions, fraud, and to security issues.

Any interruption in the internal control process relating to the first bullet is a managerial failure; while internal control malfunctioning associated to the second bullet is a system failure. Both types of failure can be effectively audited, with the reasons behind them identified and brought into perspective. A similar statement can be made regarding internal control activities in areas such as:

- Safeguarding business assets
- Assisting in compliance, and
- Accounting reconciliation.

While auditing a company's books and its management control system, internal and external auditors are essentially producing something akin to military information, or more precisely *internal control intelligence*. Other domains where internal control activities offer themselves to auditing are:

- Promotion of personal accountability, and
- Measures taken for timely corrective action.

In other cases, however, the auditing of internal control is more complex because its goals include compliance to the company's policies and practices.

The pattern in Figure 17.3 presents a snapshot of focal areas entering into the internal control orbit. All of them should attract senior management's attention as they are, for decision-makers, what Socrates used to call his *demon* – this inner voice that whispers: 'Take care'.

Auditing aims to make internal control approaches more effective by identifying weak practices that require not only corrective action but also some form of sanction against people and departments supporting them. In the opinion of some experts, the Audit Committee is better positioned to supervise and monitor the internal control system than the internal auditors individually.

Practically all senior executives who participated in this research were of the opinion that internal control responsibilities start at board level and they affect the way people operate in every department of the institution. A well-tuned internal control system helps to assure that the information senior management receives is accurate. Expert opinions have converged on two facts:

- Internal controls are valid only as far as people working for the organization observe them, and
- Controls should be designed not only to prevent cases like Parmalat, WorldCom, Enron, Barings and Orange County, but also to underline the accountability of every person.

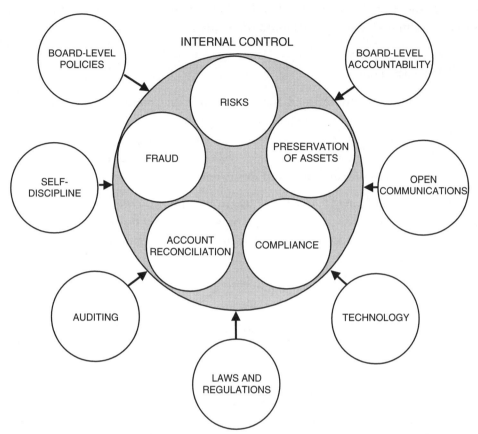

Figure 17.3   Focal areas of internal control and impact of internal and external key factors

'It is the responsibility of senior management to define the internal control structure,' said Claude Sivy, of the Bank for International Settlements. 'If internal control is going to work, management must be committed to it,' added Edward A. Ryan Jr of the Securities and Exchange Commission, in Boston. John B. Caouette, vice-chairman of MBIA Insurance Corp., concurred with this statement: 'Internal controls are only successful if embedded in a strict risk management culture.'

The auditing of internal controls can capitalize on the fact that one of the consistent themes of good management is the ability to know what happens in all corners of the organization. 'Internal control is a concept which reaches all levels of management and the activities pertinent to those levels,' said Jonathan E.C.

Grant, of the Auditing Practices Board in London, adding that 'To do the proper service to internal control we should not confuse:

- Monitoring, and
- The basic concept.'

Jonathan Grant also underlined the danger that line management might leave internal control duties to somebody else down the line of command. Therefore, he suggested that the definition must specifically emphasize *management's accountability* – as internal control is everybody's business and every employee, top to bottom, should care for it and for its deliverables.

Furthermore, as Figure 17.4 suggests, there is common core between the functions of internal control and other major organizational activities. Many financial industry executives who participated in this research underlined the need for

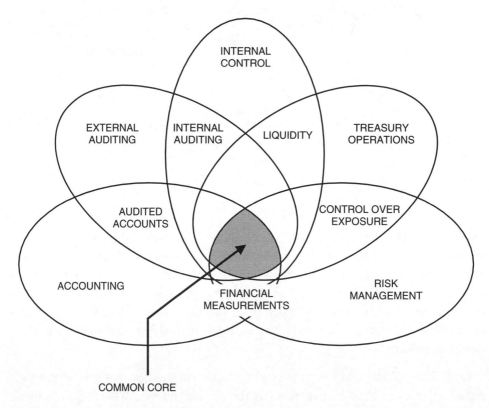

Figure 17.4 The functions of internal control, auditing, accounting, treasury and risk management overlap, but also have a common core

powerful tools to make internal control proactive. 'Most current tools are post-event,' said Clifford Griep, of Standard & Poor's in New York, 'but internal control must be proactive. It must deal with pre-transaction approval.'

In the opinion of David L. Robinson, of the Federal Reserve System, internal control must in principle be content-neutral, but a system designed to serve this purpose should be commensurate with the complexity of the business which it supports. This is as true of banking and finance as it is of any other industry. A content-neutral approach is a sound principle to follow in regard to organization and structure, particularly when it is enriched with measurable objectives which, in turn, make the auditing function feasible.

5. Auditing and risk management correlate

As we have seen in the Introduction, the board has several committees: Audit, Financial, Corporate Governance, Compensation, and Technology. Also, more recently, top-tier financial institutions have a Risk Management Committee at board level. This, however, is not yet a general practice even if it is beyond any doubt that risk management, and the unavoidable damage control associated with it, are two most critical functions. On both of them depends the very survival of the institution. Risk management should definitely be on the board's agenda.

One of the executives who participated in the research that led to this book made the suggestion: 'Why not give, at least in the interim till the appropriate Board authority on risk management is put in place, this responsibility to the Audit Committee?' Two reasons support the wisdom of doing so. The one is that, as we saw in sections 2 and 3, the functions of auditing are expanding well beyond the accounting books into areas where qualification is just as important as quantification – if not even more so. The auditing of internal control is an example.

The second reason is just as pragmatic. The Basel Committee suggests that in order to effectively control risk an independent review of the risk measurement system should be carried out regularly by the bank's internal auditing body. Basel adds that besides risk auditing, senior management must be actively involved in risk control and review the daily, or ad hoc reports produced by the independent risk control unit. More to the point:

- Risk management models must be closely integrated into both the day-to-day and longer-term management of the bank

- Board-level supervision of risk control methods, procedures, and results is a 'must', and
- The output of experimentation on exposure – including worst-case scenarios – should not only be reviewed by senior management, but also reflected in policies and limits set by the board.

Sound management practice would ensure that the bank's risk management organization (or organizations if credit, market, and operational risk control are not integrated), not only report(s) directly to senior management, but also is supervised by a committee that is given the authority to evaluate relationships between measures of:

- Corporate risk exposure
- Trading limits and lending, and
- Other variables keeping risk under lock and key.

The bank should also conduct regular backtesting, comparing the risk measures generated by models with actual results, including recognized but not yet realized profits and loss, in the way that IFRS stipulates it should be done. As cannot be repeated too often, new accounting rules, auditing, and risk control correlate one with another.

Well-managed banks have already taken steps in the direction of top management involvement, a process further promoted by supervisory authorities which note that a bank's primary objective should be to maintain its financial soundness and contribute to the stability of the financial system as a whole. The personal involvement of board members is necessary to make such a policy successful.

The likelihood is that committees established at middle management level will not be able to deliver, if for no other reason than because conflicts of interest handicap their work. Take Bank Gamma as a case study. In the late 1990s it instituted a *Risk Council* with four members: the director of treasury and trading, the chief credit officer, the assistant director of trading who also had backoffice functions, and the chief risk manager, reporting to the director of trading. This composition violated two cardinal rules at the same time:

- That traders and loans officers in exercise of such duties should never be entrusted with risk control, and
- The functions of the frontdesk and the backoffice should be separated by a thick wall, rather than being brought under the same authority.

As far as heavy trading losses go, the result has been a disaster. Post-mortem financial analysts, who looked into this case of conflicting duties, also said that Bank Gamma already had a first-class risk management organization, and the creation of another risk control function, under trading, diluted rather then strengthened the bank's central risk management system.

Compared to the functions of this rubber stamp 'risk council', the risk management responsibilities of the board should be a meta-layer using not only the bank's existing risk management organization and internal audit functions, but also independent advice from consultancies to form an independent opinion.

The results contained in reports submitted to the board on exposure should be the subject of both normal testing and stress testing (see Chapter 16), with metrics that help in providing perspective, like demodulating all derivatives contracts to establish credit equivalence.[3] This is tantamount to knowing what is the *capital at risk*. Every board member can understand the notion of capital at risk, and the torrent of red ink which may result from adverse conditions.

Equally important is that the board appreciates the notion of *confidence intervals*. People are usually trained to think that mean value is all that is needed to describe a distribution. This is not true. The mean is only a central tendency; around it exists a variance of values which has to be measured and brought into perspective.

Confidence intervals can be derived in a parametric context within a portfolio structure with distributed returns. They are usually set at a given level of significance which indicates to what extent events in this distribution are excluded from the risk being measured. An example is given in Figure 17.5, which maps spillover of yield volatility from the American debt securities market to the German market (courtesy of Deutsche Bundesbank):

- The thick line shows the mean value over seven years.
- The grey areas are the confidence intervals at 95% level of significance $(\alpha = 0.05)$.

Following the 1996 Market Risk Amendment, the regulators want to have a daily report on VAR at the 99% level of significance. The area corresponding to this level will be way outside the grey area in Figure 17.5. This, however, still leaves 1% of cases not accounted for; and there may be catastrophic spikes in this 1%.

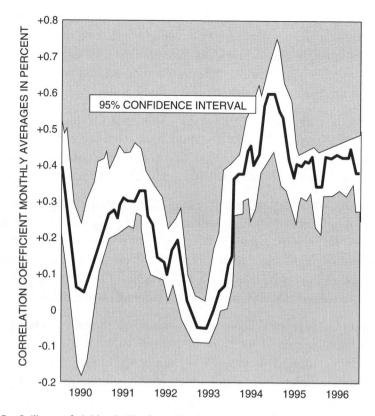

Figure 17.5   Spillover of yield volatility from the American debt securities market to the German market. (*Source:* Deutsche Bundesbank)

On the credit risk side, rating agencies want to see economic capital at the 99.97% level of significance for AA rating. This would mean only 0.03 of cases left outside. Still there may be outliers, but 0.03% is a great deal better than 1%, and 1% is better than 5%. The notion of a confidence interval is central to any appreciation of the amount of assumed risk.

Every step described in this section should be audited, like any other activity in the enterprise: from major organizational failures, like that of Bank Gamma; to double books kept to hide losses, as in the case of Barings; and miscalculation of capital at risk, because of forgetting about confidence intervals, or any other opportunities for 'creative solutions' which will eventually be paid for very dearly by the stakeholders.

6. The major responsibility of Audit Committee members is a steady watch

Auditing is an indispensable element of every management system, including of risk management and of internal control. The fact that auditors are responsible for assessing the soundness and adequacy of an entity's accounting, operating, and administrative functions as well as its day-to-day management controls, makes them and their work the cornerstone of good governance.

Audit reports must be clear, unambiguous, and well documented. They should be presented not only to the Audit Committee but to all members of the board, the CEO, and senior executives, identifying defects which must be remedied systematically and promptly. Follow-up audits should describe:

- Weaknesses which are not yet remedied, and
- Recommendations not yet implemented.

In the United States, the Federal Reserve instructs its examiners under its authority that they should review documents, taking into account the reporting process followed by the auditor. This permits them to subsequently evaluate in a firm manner the nature and efficiency of the tasks internal auditing has performed. The central bank's examiners also look into whether or not:

- Internal auditors have been given the authority necessary to carry out a dependable job, and
- If they have free access to any records needed for the proper conduct of their investigation.

These are issues the Audit Committee should always keep in mind. A sound way of looking at auditing is as a meta-layer (higher-up level) of day-to-day management control functions. As we have already seen, internal control is focused on daily ongoing activities, while auditing is responsible for the independent examination function, which must tell if financial reporting is reliable in all its aspects.

Because auditing procedures are an indispensable supplement in the ongoing evaluation provided by internal controls, it is important for the auditor to conduct his or her activities in a way permitting evaluation of:

- The way in which top management directives are being issued, and followed, and
- Whether compliance with designated laws, regulations, and internal bylaws is part of corporate culture.

Eventually this information will be part and parcel of the Audit Committee's watch. After World War II until about two decades ago, board members were practically immune from prosecution, and CEOs from firing. Stockholder activism, particularly from institutional investors, has changed that. Even if the company buys an insurance policy for legal protection for members of its board and its top brass, juries can award awfully big compensation and there is also the company's and the individual's reputation at stake. This is one more reason why all employees must be subject to internal control and auditing. Even if they have no financial responsibilities, they must be accountable for their actions.

As Chapter 16 brought to the reader's attention, a good system of internal control has significant impact on how the business is planned, conducted, and controlled. Moreover, everybody should contribute to internal control. The question is not whether each individual is honest, but rather whether situations exist that:

- Might permit an intentional error or bias to be concealed, or
- Make it possible for errors and biases to remain undetected, and hence unknown to top management.

Both points speak volumes about the internal and external directors' accountability. Authority is delegated, responsibility never. On the other hand, a person can really be accountable for something if he or she knows and understands the subject on which decisions are taken. Parkinson's Law says that, at board meetings, time spent to reach a decision is universally proportional to the importance this decision has for the company. Yet,

- The board will have many 'experts' on coffee brands, and discussions on which to choose for the cafeteria can take hours.
- But there are very few members who understand changes in the risk and return curve for the portfolio of derivatives, and the need to develop different risk estimates for different time brackets, instruments, and counterparties, and thus decisions concerning risk and return may be made on the fly.

As far as a credit institution's or other financial company's survival is concerned, decisions concerning risk are more than six orders of magnitude more important than the choice of a new brand of coffee.

On several occasions, the board's Audit Committee and Technology Committee will need to work together. A rigorous approach to auditing, risk management, and internal control would pay full attention to the information technology being used: from networks and databases, to datamining, models, and interactive reporting, through visualization (turning tables into graphs).

Not only must the channels of communication operate in real time and the modelling of all types of exposure be effectively done, but also market-related parameters have to be adjusted immediately to changing financial conditions and/or board decisions with an impact on the management of risk. Risk figures derived from *risk-based audits* must be continuously compared with actual market data, as well as trends indicating a change in direction.

The effectiveness of auditing, internal control, and risk management depends a great deal on understanding the business and the people, and this is one of the fundamental duties of the board. 'Problems arise when people at the top do not understand the professionals working for them, and therefore they can neither guide them nor control them,' suggested Brandon Davies, formerly treasurer of Barclays Bank. Institutions are very reliant on the expertise of a few people: the traders, financial analysts, and some other professionals, but:

- Quite often senior management makes no effort to comprehend how these people think and work, and
- Misunderstandings significantly diminish what can be done through management control, even if there is transparency in reporting.

Let me add this remark: 'The role of bank managers is not only to assure the proper functioning of their institution, but also to see to it that auditors obtain a consistent and coherent image of status and results,' said Alain Coune of the International Monetary Fund (IMF), adding that: 'This is true of the quantification side of internal control and of audit.' The qualification aspects, particularly those concerning internal controls, have not been till now tightly coupled to audit, but as we have seen this is changing.

*   *   *   *   *

Whether misrepresentations in financial accounting are due to omission or commission, they end by costing dear not only to the company but also its senior executives and members of the board. Mid-August 2005, the Securities and Exchange Commission (SEC) brought civil charges against Charles Conaway, former chief executive, and John McDonald, former chief financial officer, of Kmart. They were accused of trying to cover up a 'reckless' purchase of $850 million in inventory in

2001.[4] The pair are the most senior former directors at the retailer to face action in SEC's investigation into fraud stemming from Kmart's bankruptcy in 2002. And this is only one example. Increasingly, the corporate executives' and independent directors' everyday lives are measured against good governance principles. Therefore, I am often amazed by the bad judgment of top management people, including the chairman, president, and director of auditing when:

- Denunciations of malpractices are thrown in the wastepaper basket.
- Problems are covered up, to avoid disturbing the status quo, and
- Due investigations are not undertaken for fear that they will find the facts.

I have recently had such an experience which left me flabbergasted. The object of concern was malpractice to a client's disfavour at a major private banking institution.[5] The letter which I wrote to the bank's top management was factual and fully documented. The answer I received was neither based on facts, nor did it reflect the results of an investigation of malpractice. Yet, available evidence suggested a great deal of operational risk, as well as conflict of interest. Internal control it seemed had leave of absence.

In conclusion, a common mission of rigorous accounting, auditing, risk management, and internal control is to assure that those who have something to conceal receive no mercy. The value of all control activities lies in their ability to probe into the *secret places* of operations. Only on rare occasions should management control be outwitted in its examination, and one of the basic functions of the Audit Committee is to ensure that wrong-doers receive no mercy. The chairman and members of the Audit Committee should heed the advice of an Athenian senator in Shakespeare's *Timon of Athens*: 'Nothing emboldens sin so much as mercy'. But is anybody listening?

Notes

1   Basel Committee on Banking Supervision, 'Enhancing Corporate Governance for Banking Organizations' (Consultative Document), BIS, Basel, July 2005.
2   *The Economist*, 11 January 2003.
3   D.N. Chorafas, *Stress Testing. Risk Management Strategies for Extreme Events*, Euromoney, London, 2003.
4   *The Economist*, 27 August 2005.
5   D.N. Chorafas, *Wealth Management: Private Banking, Investment Decisions and Structured Financial Products*, Butterworth-Heinemann, London and Boston, 2005.

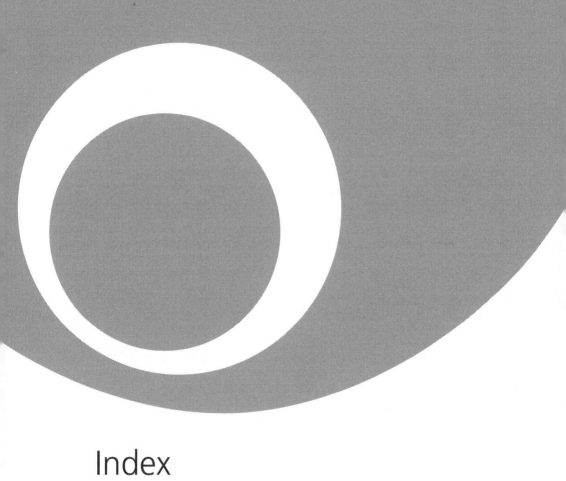

Index